CÉLINE MARCHAND

WOVEN CRYSTAL BEADED JEWELLERY

PHOTOGRAPHY: ÉLISE REBIFFÉ

SEARCH PRESS

CONTENTS

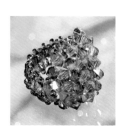

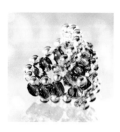

Larger rings

Rings made from connected circles

Raised rings

Materials and advice

Beads

The rings, tassels and beaded beads presented in this book are made from beads that are easy to find and are in a limited number of shapes and sizes. This means that you can easily use up any that are left over.

Bicones

These cut crystal beads will make your jewellery really sparkle. They come in different sizes and in a very wide range of transparent and opaque colours, as well as other types, e.g. satin-finished, iridescent or even metallic. The jewellery in this book is made using 3mm and 4mm bicones. To enable you to reproduce identical pieces or use other colours easily, the exact reference for the bicones is given at the start of each creation. Each piece can, of course, be made in different shades. Express your creativity by making up your own combinations. Test them out by putting some of each variety of beads into a neutral-coloured pot or in the palm of your hand.

Faceted beads

These are available in glass or crystal, and go perfectly with the bicones by enhancing them and counterbalancing their angular aspect, especially if you match the shades. Faceted beads come in various diameters. When making rings, tassels and beaded beads, you will need 3mm and 4mm faceted beads.

Round beads

These little round beads add a touch of sophistication to your jewellery. They are available in metal colours (silver, gilt, bronze, copper or lead) or as round crystal pearls. The pieces in this book only use 3mm round beads. Make sure you check their diameter so that your beadwork is regular.

Seed beads

These small, round beads come in different grades. The instructions for each piece state the size(s) to use. As long as you follow these instructions, your jewellery will be a success.

Seed beads

Small seed beads

Large seed beads

The most common seed beads measure approx. 2mm in diameter. You will find them in any bead shop. The best graded ones, suggested for embroidery, are usually sold in 5g boxes.

Small seed beads. Exclusively used for embroidery, they measure a little over 1mm in diameter and are sold in 2.5g boxes.

Large seed beads. The ones that are best for making the jewellery in this book have a diameter of 2.6mm. These are not to be confused with the even larger seed beads used in children's jewellery.

Other beads

8–12mm beads, in glass (round, cat's eye, faceted, etc.), in metal (round and spacer) or in stone, used for beaded beads and tassels, can be used for bracelets and necklaces too. Let the ideas in this book inspire you to intersperse your creations with beads that you already have, or those that you discover in specialist shops.

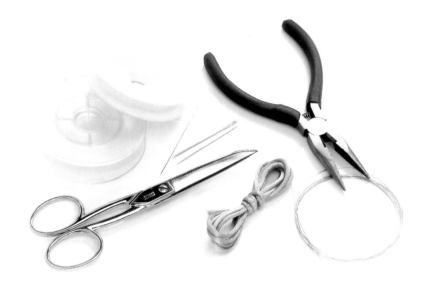

Threads and wires

Nylon thread

The majority of pieces are made using 0.25mm nylon thread. It is strong, yet fine, so it can be passed through the beads several times. For pieces that need more threading, 0.20mm thread should be used.

Elastic thread

This transparent, elasticated thread, usually 0.6mm in diameter, is ideal for threading bracelets.

Tiger tail

Made from twisted metallic strands coated in nylon, this thread enables you to attach beaded beads or hang tassels.

Satin cords

Available in a very wide range of colours, these cords enable you to create some stunning chokers.

Beading needles

You can buy these long, fine needles in bead shops and some haberdashers. They are indispensable for the amount of threading that is needed to make the pieces in this book. To make it easier to thread the needle, pinch the end of the nylon thread using a pair of flat-nose pliers or between your teeth.

Embroidery needles for seed beads are also recommended.

You can also buy needles without an eye that are slit in the middle. These needles are very useful for threading bracelet beads on to an elastic thread. However, they are not as easy to use, as their double point increases the risk of being pricked.

You can also find some very pliable needles, made from very fine folded and twisted metallic thread, which are handy for threading bracelets.

Jewellery findings

These are needed for finishing off and assembling certain items of jewellery.

Rings and clasps

Clasps are available in different designs and shades. Trigger clasps are easy to open and close.

Flat cord/leather crimps

These will give you a smart finish (see opposite page).

Crimp beads

These metallic beads act as a stop at the ends of the tassel fringes and are also used for fixing a clasp to tiger tail or nylon thread.

Other materials

All-purpose adhesive

A slow-acting adhesive is useful for reinforcing the finishing for bracelets and also for attaching flat cord/leather crimps.

Scissors and multi-function jewellery pliers

These are useful for finishing off your jewellery.

Following the instructions

To make them easier to understand, the illustrations in this book have been designed to distinguish between the two different ends of a piece of thread: one is coloured in red and the other in blue. The starting point is shown by an arrow.

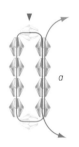

The beads already threaded in previous stages are shaded in grey. The new beads to be threaded are in colour; only the new threading is indicated.

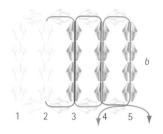

When the thread has to be taken back through beads threaded in a previous stage, these are outlined to make them clearer.

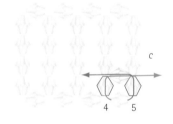

Getting ready

It is important to get everything ready first. Sort your beads by colour so that you can find them more easily. Make sure you are working in good light. Work on a tray, so that if a box of beads is knocked over, the beads will not go everywhere.

Abbreviations

To make the explanations easier, the names of the beads have been abbreviated. You will find the list of abbreviations at the start of each set of instructions.

Finishing off

Rings

The flat surface of the ring and the shank are made with two different threads. This makes it easy to undo the shank if the size needs to be adjusted. Two or three tight, simple knots are enough to secure the nylon thread. Pass the two strands of thread through the adjoining bead. Pull so that the knot enters the bead and then trim the surplus thread. To attach the shank, avoid passing back through the finishing-off bead for the flat surface. Finish by hiding the knot in a shank bead.

Bracelets

Thread the beads on to elastic thread using a slit needle or a pliable needle, preferably

starting with a bead with a large hole. Pass the thread back through all the beads to strengthen the threading, whilst regulating the tension of the thread. Knot two or three times. Trim the ends leaving a few millimetres of thread. Glue the knot and hide it in the hole of the first bead.

Attach a crimp bead

To attach a clasp to tiger tail or nylon thread. Thread the crimp bead and the clasp. Pass the thread in the opposite direction back through the crimp bead. Reduce the loop of thread and then pinch the crimp bead using jewellery pliers. Trim the excess thread.

To make a stop at the end of tassel fringes. After the last bead, thread on a crimp bead. Close up the beads, and pinch the crimp bead using jewellery pliers. Trim the excess thread.

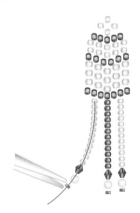

Attach a flat cord/leather crimp

Place the end of the cord in the crimp. Add a spot of adhesive, then fold down each side of the crimp, one after the other, using jewellery pliers.

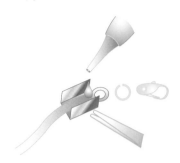

Link up a jump ring

To avoid deforming the jump ring, it is better to open it using one or two sets of jewellery pliers by pulling one side towards you and the other in the opposite direction. Close the jump ring in the same way.

Beaded discs

Whether you use bicones or round beads, the process is the same. Cut approx. 60cm (23½in) of thread. Thread a needle on to each end.

1 **Heart of the bead.** Thread three Ss and cross the threads through one LS (or one other S, see note) (a). Thread two Ss on to the left thread. Cross the threads through one S (b).

2 Thread two Ss on to the bottom thread, and cross the threads through one LS. Pass the left thread through the adjoining S previously threaded, then thread one S and cross the threads through one S. Thread two Ss on to the top thread and cross the threads through one LS. Pass the left thread through the adjoining S previously threaded, then thread one S and cross the threads through one S. Repeat this process until you have six ladders (c).

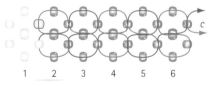

3 Close into a ring: thread one S on to the top thread and pass it through the top S at the other side of the beadwork. Cross the threads through one LS. Thread each thread down through the adjoining S and cross them in one S (d).

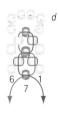

4 **Shaping the underneath.** To enable the bead to sit nicely, pass the longest thread back through the seven Ss at the bottom, until the thread passes again into the first bead (e).

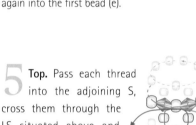

5 **Top.** Pass each thread into the adjoining S, cross them through the LS situated above and pull tight. Using the longest thread, pass it back through the central LSs, inserting one B3 or one R between each of them (f).

6 **Shaping the top side.** Pass each thread up through the adjoining S and cross them in the S situated above. Pass the longest thread back through the seven Ss at the top, until the threads cross through the S at the start. Pull tight (g).

7 **Finishing off.** Pass one of the threads back through the Ss so that it comes out next to the other one. Tie a knot, hide it in the Ss and trim the remaining threads (h).

Flat beaded bead

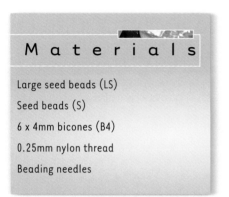

This beaded bead will bring more sparkle to bracelets, as it is a bit thicker than the discs described opposite. Cut approx. 60cm (23½in) of thread. Thread a needle on to each end.

1 **Heart of the bead.** Thread one S, two LSs and one S. Cross the threads through two LSs (a). Thread one S on to each thread and cross the threads through two LSs. Repeat this process until you have six ladders of two LSs. Finish by threading one S on each side (b).

2 Form a circle by crossing the threads through the two LSs in the first ladder (c). Pass the bottom thread through the bottom S spacer between the first and sixth ladders, through the sixth ladder, through the top S spacer and then through the LS at the top of the first ladder (d).

3 **Top.** Pass the top thread through the S spacer between the first and second ladders, then through the LS above the second ladder. Cross the threads through one B4 (e). Thread each thread down through the adjoining LS. Pass the left thread through the bottom S spacer between the first and second ladders and through the LS below the second ladder, so that it crosses with the other thread (f).

4 Pass the bottom thread through the next S spacer, then through the LS below the third ladder. Cross the threads through one B4 (g). Continue crossing in one B4 between the two LS ladders, all around the bead. Finish by crossing the threads through the top S spacer between the sixth and first ladders (h).

5 **Shaping.** To enable the bead to sit flat, pass the longest thread back through the top Ss, until the threads cross again through the S at the start (i). Do the same with the bottom Ss, by first passing each thread through the adjoining ladder of two LSs, then by crossing them through the bottom S spacer (j).

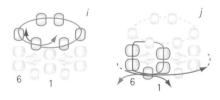

6 **Finishing off.** Pass the threads back up through the LSs to cross them through the B4 (k). Finish the top by inserting one S between each B4 (l). Pass the threads back again through the beads, so that they come out on either side of one of the bottom Ss. Tie a knot, hide it in some Ss and trim the remaining threads (m).

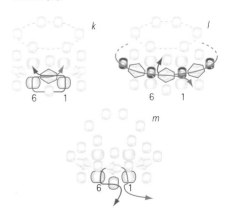

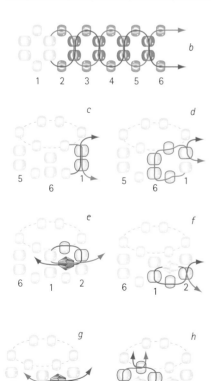

Cylindrical beaded beads

Materials

Seed beads (S)

Small seed beads (SS)

Large seed beads (LS) or 3mm round beads (R)

0.25mm nylon thread

Beading needles

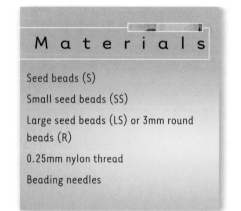

Small bead

Made with large seed beads, this piece forms a bead that is virtually round. By replacing the large seed beads with 3mm round beads, you will get a longer beaded bead. Cut approx. 60cm (23½ in) of thread. Thread a needle on to each end.

1 **LS ladders.** Thread one S, four LSs and one S and cross the threads through four LSs (a). Thread one S on to each thread and cross through four LSs, four times. Finish with one S on each thread (b). Close up into a circle by crossing the threads through the first ladder of LS (c).

2 **Weaving between the ladders.** Pass the top thread through the top S spacer between the first and second ladders, then into the first LS of the second ladder. Pass the bottom thread into the bottom S spacer between the first and second ladders, then into the four LSs of the second ladder (d). Pass the thread from the top into the next S spacer and the first LS of the third ladder. Cross the threads in one SS (e).

3 Pass each thread down into the next LS and cross the threads again in one SS (f). Repeat once. Pass the left thread into the next LS, then into the S spacer between the second and third ladders. Cross the threads through the LS at the bottom of the third ladder (g).

4 Continue in the same way, weaving one SS between the ladders at each level. Finish by crossing the threads through the top S spacer between the first and second ladders (h).

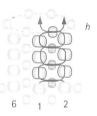

5 **Tightening the beaded bead.** Pass the longest thread through the six Ss until the threads cross through the one at the start and pull tight (i). Pass each thread down into the adjoining ladder and cross the threads through the S spacer at the bottom (j). Still using the longest thread, pull the bottom Ss tight (k).

6 **Finishing off.** Pass the threads back through the beads so that they come out again in front of one LS. Tie a knot, hide it in the LS and trim the remaining threads.

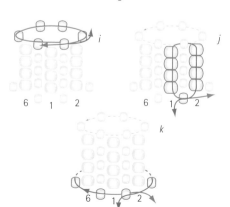

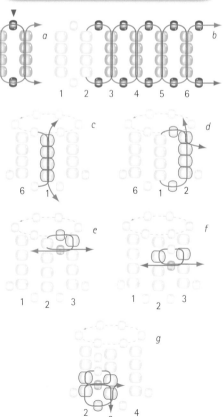

Small spacer bead

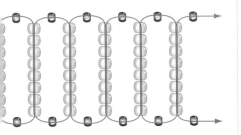

Long bead

Using approx. 80cm (31½ in) of thread, continue in the same way as for the small bead, making six ladders of eight LSs at the start. Feel free to play with the colours when weaving between the ladders.

M a t e r i a l s

Small seed beads (SS)

Seed beads (S)

0.25mm nylon thread

Beading needles

This bead is formed from three connected circles, the central circle being larger than the other two. For clarity, each circle is shown in a different colour. Cut approx. 40cm (15¾ in) of thread. Thread a needle on to each end.

1 **First circle.** Thread six SSs and cross the threads through the sixth (a).

2 **Second circle.** Cross the threads through one S (b). Thread on to one of the threads: one SS, one S, one SS, one S, one SS, one S, one SS, one S, one SS, one S, one SS. Cross this thread with the other thread through the S at the start (c).

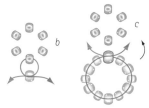

3 Using the longest thread, connect the two circles by passing the thread through the SS and the next S in the large circle. Pass from right to left through the corresponding SS in the small circle. Pass back through the S in the large circle. Repeat by connecting the next four Ss in the large circle to the four SSs in the small circle (d). Finish by crossing the threads through the S at the start (e).

4 **Third circle.** Cross the threads through one SS. Thread five SSs on to the longest thread, then pass the thread back through the first SS (f). Connect the SSs to the Ss in the large circle as before (g).

5 **Finishing off.** To strengthen the bead, pass the thread back through the beads in each circle, ensuring that the threads cross through the bead at the start at each level (h). Pass the threads back through some of the beads so that they come out together next to a bead in the central circle. Tie a knot, hide it in some of the beads in the central circle and trim the remaining threads.

13

Round beaded bead

Materials

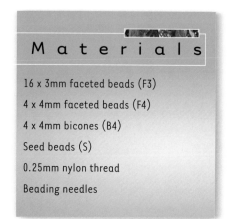

16 x 3mm faceted beads (F3)

4 x 4mm faceted beads (F4)

4 x 4mm bicones (B4)

Seed beads (S)

0.25mm nylon thread

Beading needles

First, make the bead ladders separated by seed beads to form the body of the beaded bead. Weave seed beads between the ladders to connect them with one another. Feel free to vary the colour of the seed beads. Cut approx. 60cm (23½ in) of thread. Thread a needle on to each end.

1 **Body of the bead.** Thread one F3, one B4 and one F3. Thread one S on to each side. Cross the threads through one F3, one F4 and one F3 (a). By alternating B4 and F4, create eight bead ladders separated by Ss (b). Close into a circle by crossing the threads through the first ladder (c).

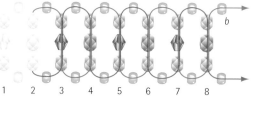

1 2 3 4 5 6 7 8

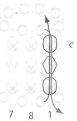

7   8   1

2 **Weaving.** Pass the top thread through the top S spacer between the first and second ladders, then through the first F3 of the second ladder. Pass the bottom thread through the bottom S spacer between the first and second ladders, then through all the beads in the second ladder (d). Pass the top thread through the next S spacer and the first F3 of the third ladder. Cross the threads through one S (e). Pass each thread down through the next bead, one F4 for one and one B4 for the other, then cross the threads through one S (f).

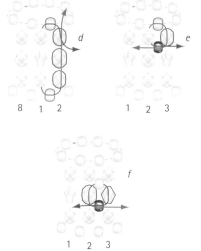

8   1   2   1   2   3

1   2   3

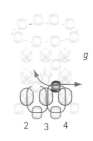

3 Pass the left thread through the next F3 and through the S spacer between the second and third ladders. Cross the threads through the F3 at the bottom of the third ladder. Pass the bottom thread through the S spacer between the third and fourth ladders and through the F3 at the bottom of the fourth ladder. Cross the threads through one S (g).

g

2   3   4

4 Continue crossing through one S at each level between all the ladders. Finish by crossing the threads through the top S spacer between the first and second ladders (h).

h

8   1   2

5 **Tightening the bead.** To form the shape of the bead, pass the longest thread through the eight Ss at the top until the threads cross through the S at the start, and pull tight (i). Pass each thread down through the adjoining ladder and cross them through the S spacer at the bottom (j). Pass the longest thread back through the Ss and pull tight (k).

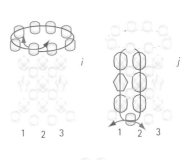

i

j

1   2   3   1   2   3

k

6 **Finishing off.** Pass the threads back through some of the beads, so that they come out in front of one F4 (l). Tie a knot, hide it in the F4 and trim the remaining threads.

l

Small tassel

Materials

8 x 3mm faceted beads (F3)

4 x 4mm faceted beads (F4)

4 x 4mm bicones (B4)

Seed beads (S)

1 large seed bead (LS), (optional, see variations)

For the fringes:

8 x 3mm round beads (R), 8 x 4mm faceted beads (F4), 8 crimp beads

0.25mm nylon thread

Beading needles

Jewellery pliers

Cut approx. 70cm (27½in) of thread. Thread a needle on to each end.

1 **Head of the tassel.** Thread one S, one F4, one F3 and one S (a). Cross the threads through one B4 and one F3. Always ensure that the F3s are aligned (b). Thread one S on to each thread, then cross the threads through one F3 and one F4 (c). Continue until you have eight ladders, alternating F4 and B4 (d). To finish, thread one S on to each thread. Close into a circle, by crossing the threads through the first ladder (e).

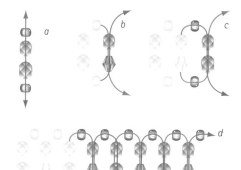

2 **Bottom of the head.** Pass the bottom thread back through all the bottom S spacers, inserting one new S between each. Pass the thread back through the first S (f).

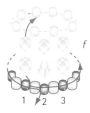

3 Pass the bottom thread through the second ladder and cross the threads through the top S spacer between the first and second ladders (g).

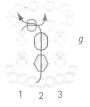

4 **Top of the head.** Pass the longest thread back through the Ss until the threads cross through the S at the start (h).

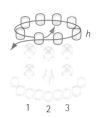

5 **Fringes.** Thread twenty Ss, one F4, one R and one crimp bead on to each thread. Pinch the crimp bead, pulling the work tight. Insert the fringes inside the head of the tassel and trim the threads (i).

i

6 Pass a new thread approx. 15cm (6in) long halfway along through the third S of the top of the head and make two fringes as before. Repeat this process twice in the fifth and seventh S (j).

j

7 **Cap.** Cut a new piece of thread approx. 30cm (11¾in) long. Pass it through one of the Ss without a fringe. Thread one S and pass the thread back through it at the start. Using the same thread, pass through the next two Ss, thread one S and pass the thread back through the last S. Repeat twice, then cross the threads through the S at the start (k).

k

8 **Attachment.** Still using the same thread, pass it back through the four upper Ss, then through the first S. Thread the other thread as far as the opposite S (l). Cross the threads through a new S, thread one S on to each thread, then cross the threads through one LS (m). Pass the threads back through some of the beads, tie a knot, hide it in the Ss and trim the remaining threads.

l   *m*

Variations

For added finesse, the fringes can be made with small seed beads and 3mm faceted beads.

The large seed bead at the top of the attachment can be replaced with a 4mm faceted bead or a traditional seed bead, depending on the jewellery that you want to make and the thickness of the thread that you are using.

Large tassel

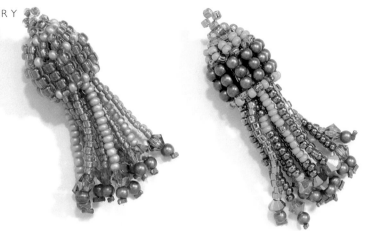

These instructions are for a tassel with a head made entirely from seed beads. For a different type of tassel, replace the LSs with 3mm round beads. Cut approx. 70cm (27½in) of thread. Thread a needle on to each end.

1 **Head of the tassel.** Thread one S, three LSs and one S and cross the threads through three LSs (a). Thread one S on to each thread and cross the threads again through three LSs. Repeat this process until you have ten ladders (b). Thread one S on to each thread and close the circle by crossing the threads through the first ladder (c).

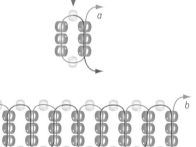

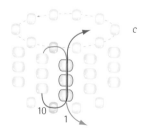

2 **Bottom of the head.** Pass the bottom thread back through all the bottom S spacers, inserting one new S between each of them. Pass the thread back through the first S (d).

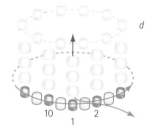

3 Pass the bottom thread through the second ladder and cross the threads through the spacer above between the first and second ladders (e).

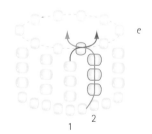

4 **Top of the head.** Thread three Ss on to the left thread. Cross the threads through two Ss. Pass the bottom thread through the next S spacer (f). Thread one S on to the top thread, then cross the threads through two Ss. Repeat all the way around. Finish by crossing the threads through the last top S spacer (g).

5 To tighten the head of the tassel, pass the longest thread back through the ten Ss at the top until the threads cross one another through the S at the start (h).

Variations

Feel free to use different coloured beads in the fringes and to use small seed beads to make them finer.

The seed bead at the top of the attachment can be replaced with a large seed bead or a 4mm faceted bead, depending on the jewellery that you want to make and the thickness of the thread that you are using.

f

g

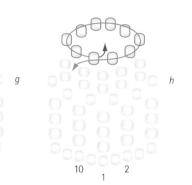

h

6 **Fringes.** Thread twenty-two Ss, one B4, one R and one crimp bead on to each thread. Pinch the crimp bead, pulling the work tight. Insert the fringes inside the head of the tassel and trim the threads (i). Pass a new thread approx. 15cm (6in) long halfway through the third S of the top of the head and make two fringes as before. Repeat this process three times in the fifth, seventh and ninth S (j).

7 **Cap.** Cut a new piece of thread approx. 30cm (11¾in) long and pass it through one of the Ss without a fringe. Thread one S and pass the thread back through the S at the start. Pass the same thread through the next two Ss, thread one S and pass it back through the last S. Repeat the process three times, then cross the threads through the S at the start (k).

8 **Attachment.** Still using the same thread, pass it back through the five upper Ss, then through the first S. Thread the other thread back as far as the third upper S (l). Cross the threads through a new S, thread one S on to each thread, then cross the threads through one S (m). Pass the threads back through some of the beads, tie a knot, hide it in the Ss and trim the remaining threads.

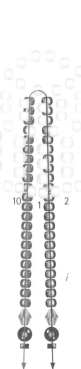

i

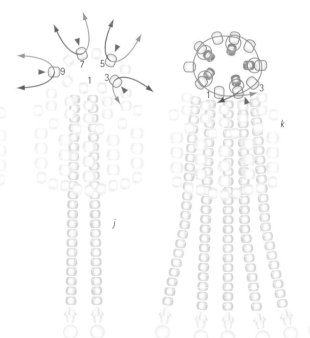

j

k

l

m

light pink   mirrored grey   mauve-grey

Materials

40 x 4mm bicones: 20 light pink and
20 mirrored grey

24 to 28 x 3mm faceted beads:
mauve-grey

Seed beads: iridescent mauve

0.25mm nylon thread

Beading needles

Marilyn ring

Flat surface of the ring

This ring is made in two stages: first five vertical
ladders of four bicones are made, then other
bicones are woven horizontally between the
ladders. Cut approx. 1m (39½ in) of thread.
Thread a needle on to each end.

1 **Vertical ladders of four bicones.** Thread
one pink B4, four grey B4s and one pink
B4. Cross the threads through four new grey
B4s (a). Thread one pink B4 on to each thread,
then cross them again through four grey B4s.
Repeat this process until there are five ladders
of four grey B4s. Finish by crossing the threads
through the pink B4 at the bottom (b).

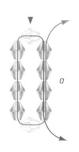

a

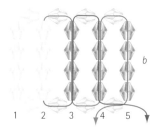

b

1   2   3   4   5

Abbreviations

B4: 4mm bicones

F3: 3mm faceted beads

S: seed beads

2 **Weaving between the ladders.** Pass each of the threads through the first B4 of the fourth and fifth ladders. Cross the threads through one pink B4 (c). Pass each of the threads through the next B4 for each ladder, then cross the threads through one pink B4. Repeat this process once. Pass the threads back through the B4s at the top to finish, crossing in the grey B4 at the top of the fourth ladder (d).

3 Pass the top thread through the pink B4 spacer between the fourth and third ladders, then through the first grey B4 of the third ladder. Cross the threads through one pink B4 (e). Continue passing back through the grey B4s of the ladders and cross in one pink B4 every time, in order to fill all the gaps in the flat surface (f).

4 **Around the flat surface of the ring.** Pass the right thread back through the outer B4s, inserting one S between the B4 spacers between the ladders (g). Pass the left thread back through the B4s in the corner, so that it joins up again with the other thread under the second ladder. Tie a knot. Hide it in the second B4 ladder and trim the remaining threads (h).

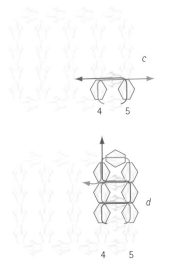
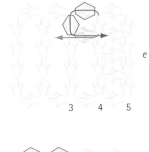
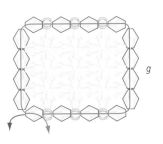
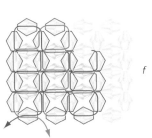
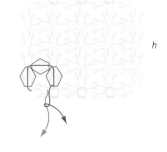

Shank

1 Cut approx. 50cm (19¾in) of thread. Thread a needle on to each end. Pass the thread halfway along through the two central B4s on the right side of the table (i).

2 Thread one S on to each thread, then cross them in two F3s. Repeat this process as often as required for the finger circumference. To finish, thread one S on to each thread.

Pass one of the threads from the other side of the table back through the two central B4s and the other thread through just one of the central B4s (j). Check for correct sizing.

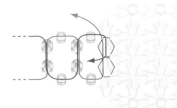

3 To strengthen the ring and make it round, pass the threads back through each bead in the opposite direction, crossing them in one new S on each side of the ladders of two F3s. Finish by crossing in the last outer S (k).

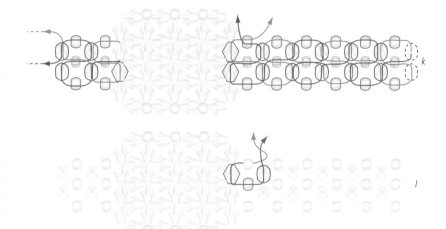

4 Pass the left thread back through the adjoining B4 of the flat surface of the ring, then through the next S and F3, so that it joins up with the second thread above the first ladder of two F3s. Tie a knot, hide it in the two F3s and trim the remaining threads (l).

Choker

mirrored grey

iridescent pink

mauve-grey

Materials

4 x 4mm bicones: mirrored grey

4 x 4mm faceted beads: iridescent pink

16 x 3mm faceted beads: mauve-grey

Seed beads: iridescent mauve and light pink

Beading needles

0.25mm nylon thread

Pink satin cord: 35 to 40cm (13½ to 15½in)

2 flat cord crimpers: silver

2 jump rings: silver

1 trigger clasp: silver

Jewellery pliers

A round beaded bead, mounted simply on a satin cord, will light up the décolletage of even the plainest of outfits.

Make the beaded bead by following the instructions on page 14 and use the photographs to help you with the colour pattern for the seed beads. Thread the beaded bead on to the cord, then attach the clasp, as shown on page 9.

Rainbow ring

light brown

orange

blue

iridescent light green

iridescent brown

Flat surface of the ring

Materials

32 x 4mm bicones: 8 light brown, 8 orange, 8 blue, 8 iridescent light green

14 to 18 faceted 4mm beads: iridescent brown

Seed beads: copper

0.25mm nylon thread

Beading needles

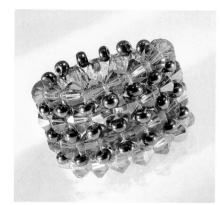

This ring is made in two stages: first, four horizontal ladders of eight bicones are made, between which seed beads are then woven. Cut approx. 1m (39½ in) of thread. Thread a needle on to each end.

a

1 **Horizontal ladders of eight bicones.** Thread one S, eight green B4s and one S. Cross the threads through eight orange B4s (a). Thread one S on to each thread, then cross the threads again in eight brown B4s. Repeat the process for the last colour (blue) (b).

b

4

3

2

1

Abbreviations

B4: 4mm bicones

F4: 4mm faceted beads

S: seed beads

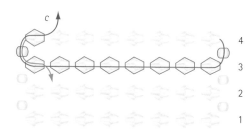

c

4

3

2

1

2 **Weaving between the ladders.** Pass the right thread (red) through the S spacer between the fourth and third ladders, through the eight B4s of the third ladder, through the left S spacer between the fourth and third ladders, then through the first B4 of the fourth ladder. Pass the other thread (blue) through the same S spacer, then through the first B4 of the third ladder (c).

3 Cross the threads through one S (d). Pass each of the threads through the second B4 of the third and fourth ladders, then cross the threads again in one S (e). Repeat the process as far as the outer edge of the third and fourth ladders (f). Pass the top thread (blue) through the S spacer between the third and fourth ladders and through the last B4 of the third ladder (g). Pass the other thread (red) through the S spacer between the third and second ladders, then through the first B4 of the second ladder (h).

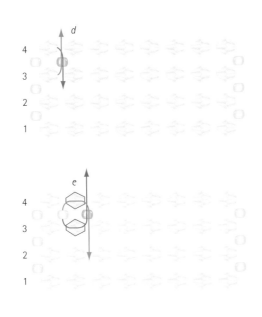

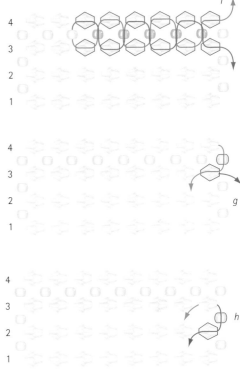

4 Cross the threads through one S (i). In the same way, weave Ss between the third and second ladders, then between the second and first ladders (j).

Pass the top thread (blue) back through the S spacer between the second and first ladders. Tie a knot, hide it in the corner B4 and trim the threads (k).

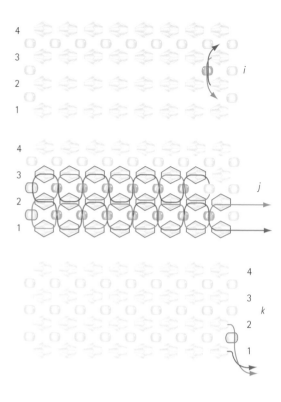

Shank

1 Cut approx. 50cm (19½ in) of thread. Thread a needle on to each end. Pass the thread halfway along through the S spacers between the ladders on the right side of the table of the ring, inserting one new S between each S (l).

2 Thread one S on to each thread and cross the threads through two F4s. Repeat this process as often as required for the finger circumference. To finish, thread one S on to each thread.

Cross the threads through the S spacers between the ladders of the other side of the table, whilst inserting one new S between each S (m). Check for correct sizing.

3 Pass the thread back through all the beads in the opposite direction to strengthen the shank. Tie a knot, pull it into the adjoining F4 and trim the remaining threads.

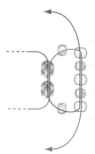

Pavé version

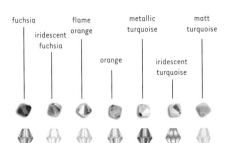

fuchsia
iridescent fuchsia
flame orange
orange
metallic turquoise
iridescent turquoise
matt turquoise

Materials

25 x 4mm bicones: 6 fuchsia,
4 iridescent fuchsia, 2 flame orange,
2 orange, 6 metallic turquoise,
1 iridescent turquoise and
4 matt turquoise

Seed beads: opaque turquoise and pink

Large seed beads: transparent blue

0.25mm nylon thread

Beading needles

Abbreviations

B4: 4mm bicones

S: seed beads

LS: large seed beads

Flat surface of the ring

This ring is made in the same way as the Rainbow ring. The only differences are the number of ladders, the number of beads per ladder, and the colour pattern. Cut approx. 1m (39½in) of thread. Thread a needle on to each end.

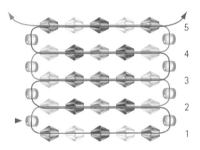

5
4
3
2
1

1 **Horizontal ladders of five bicones.** Thread one LS, five B4s (one fuchsia, one iridescent fuchsia, one metallic turquoise, one iridescent fuchsia, one fuchsia) and one LS. Cross the threads through five B4s (one matt turquoise, one metallic turquoise, one flame orange, one metallic turquoise and one matt turquoise). Thread one LS on to each thread. For the central ladder, cross the threads again in five B4s (one flame orange, one fuchsia, one iridescent turquoise, one fuchsia, one flame orange). Make the fourth and fifth ladders like the second and first ladders, by spacing with LSs.

2 **Weaving between the ladders.** Refer to the instructions and drawings given for the Rainbow ring, weaving pink Ss between the bicones according to the same principle, stages 2 to 4, pages 24 to 26. Tie off the threads.

Shank

1 Cut approx. 50cm (19½in) of thread. Thread a needle on to each end. Pass the thread halfway along through the LS spacers between the ladders on the right side of the flat surface of the ring, inserting three blue Ss between the LSs.

2 Thread one S on to each thread, then cross the threads through one LS, one S, one LS, one S, one LS, one S and one LS. Repeat this process as often as required for the finger circumference.

3 To finish, thread one S on to each thread. Cross the threads through the S spacers between the ladders on the other side of the flat surface of the ring, whilst inserting three new Ss between the LSs. Pass the thread back through all the beads in the opposite direction to strengthen the shank. Tie a knot, pull it into some of the shank beads and trim the remaining threads.

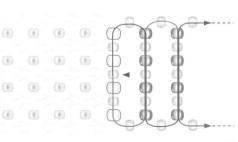

dark green   dark green

light green   silver

Crown ring

Flat surface of the ring

The flat surface of this ring is made in three stages: first, weave the central motif which is then edged, first at the top and then at the bottom. Cut approx. 1m (39½in) of thread. Thread a needle on to each end.

1 **Central motif.** Thread one R, two light green B4s and one R. Cross the threads through two dark green B4s (a). Thread one R on to each thread and cross the threads through two light green B4s. Thread one R on to each thread and cross through two dark green B4s. Continue, alternating the colours and spacing with Rs. At the seventh ladder, cross the threads through the top R (b).

2 Pass each thread through the first B4 of the seventh and sixth ladders. Cross the threads through one R. Pass each thread respectively through the next bicone in the same ladder. Pass the right thread through the R spacer, then through the adjoining B4 (c).

3 Pass the bottom thread through the R spacer between the sixth and fifth ladders, then through the adjoining B4 of the fifth ladder. Cross the threads through one R. Continue to weave Rs as far as the first ladder, following this principle. Finish by crossing the threads through the top R spacer, between the first and second ladder (d).

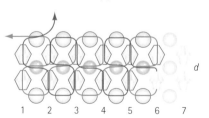

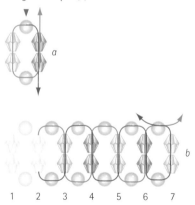

Abbreviations

B4: 4mm bicones

F4: 4mm faceted beads

R: round beads

S: seed beads

4 Upper edge. Thread one S and one R on to the left thread, then cross the threads through one S (e). Pass the bottom thread through the next R on the central motif. Thread one R on to the top thread. Cross the threads again in one S. Repeat this process until the end of the row (f).

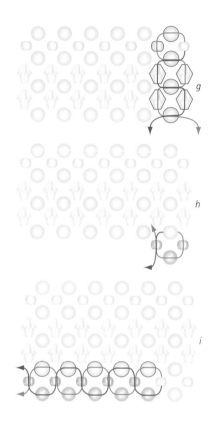

g

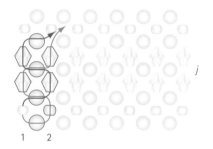

h

5 Lower edge. Pass the threads back through the beads on the outer edge of the flat part of the ring, so that they cross through the R spacer at the bottom on the right of the central motif (g). Thread one S and one R on to the right thread. Cross the threads through one S (h). Continue this edging as before (i).

6 Pass the threads back through the beads on the outer edge of the flat part of the ring, so that they come out on top of the second B4 ladder (j). Tie a knot, hide it in the B4s of the second ladder, then trim the remaining threads.

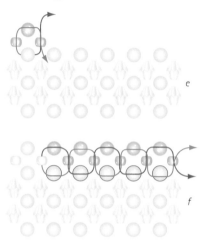

e

f

i

j

1   2

Shank

1 Cut approx. 40cm (15¾in) of thread. Thread a needle on to each end. Pass the thread halfway along through the B4s on the right side of the flat surface of the ring (k).

2 Thread one R on to each thread and cross the threads through one F4. Repeat this process as often as required for the finger circumference. To finish, thread one R on to each thread. Cross the threads through the B4s of the other side of the flat surface of the ring.

Check for correct sizing (l). Pass the thread back through all the beads in the opposite direction to strengthen the shank. Tie a knot, pull it into one F4 and trim the remaining threads.

k

l

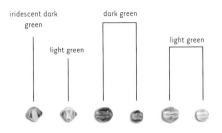

iridescent dark green

light green

dark green

light green

Matching bracelet

1 Make two round beaded beads following the instructions on page 14: the first with the light green B4s and F4s, the dark green F3s and the anthracite Ss, the second with the dark green B4s and F4s, the light green F3s and the diamante Ss.

2 Using a slit needle, thread the beaded beads and some round beads of varying diameters on to 40cm (15¾ in) of elastic thread, dividing them up and separating them with silver spacer beads. Pass the elastic thread back through all the beads to double the strength.

3 Tie the thread as explained on page 9, hiding the knot in the hole of a bead.

Materials

4mm bicones: 4 iridescent dark green, 4 light green

4mm faceted beads: 4 dark green, 4 light green

3mm faceted beads: 16 dark green, 16 light green

Seed beads: diamante and anthracite

An assortment of 8 to 12mm round beads and silver spacer beads

Slit needle

Beading needles

0.25mm nylon thread

0.6mm elastic thread

All-purpose adhesive

Abbreviations

B4: 4mm bicones

F4: 4mm faceted beads

F3: 3mm faceted beads

S: seed beads

black   silver

black

Woven ring

Flat surface of the ring

The flat surface of this ring is made in two stages: first, make the five vertical ladders of bicones and round beads, then connect these with two horizontal rows of round beads and small seed beads. Cut approx. 80cm (31½ in) of thread. Thread a needle on to each end.

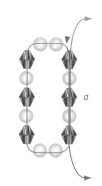

1 **Vertical ladders.** Thread two Rs, one B4, one R, one B4, one R, one B4 and another two Rs. Cross the threads through one B4, one R, one B4, one R and one B4 (a). Thread two Rs on to each thread, then cross the threads again in one B4, one R, one B4, one R and one B4. Repeat this process twice until you have five ladders in total (b).

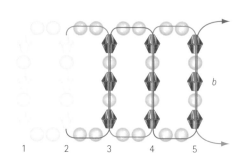

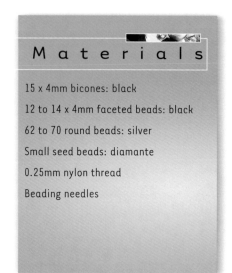

Abbreviations

B4: 4mm bicones

F4: 4mm faceted beads

R: round beads

SS: small seed beads

2 To make the first horizontal row, work the threads in the following way: pass the bottom thread (blue) through the two R spacers between the fifth and fourth ladders, through the fourth ladder, through the two R spacers at the top between the fourth and fifth ladders, then through the first B4 and first R of the fifth ladder. Pass the other thread in the opposite direction so that it crosses with the first thread in the same R (c).

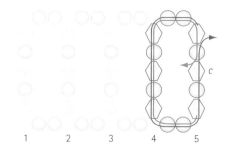

3 **First horizontal row.** Thread one SS on to each thread. Cross the threads through one R. Thread one SS on to each thread and cross the threads through the first R of the fourth ladder (d). Repeat by threading one SS on to each thread, cross the threads through one R, thread one SS on to each thread, then cross the threads through the first R of the next ladder. Repeat twice more (e).

4 Work the threads to make the second horizontal row: pass the red thread through the B4 of the top of the first ladder, through the two R spacers between the first and second ladders, through the second ladder, through the two R spacers at the bottom between the second and first ladder, then through the first B4 and the first R of first ladder. Pass the blue thread through the central B4 and the next R of the first ladder (f).

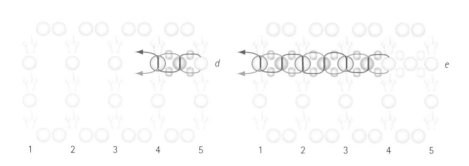

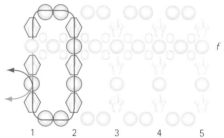

5 **Second horizontal row.** Weave some SSs and some Rs as far as the fifth ladder, as for the first row (g).

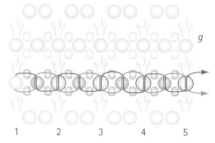

6 Pass the threads back through the beads of the fifth and fourth ladders so that they meet under the fourth ladder (h). Tie a knot, hide it in the first B4 of the fourth ladder, then trim the remaining threads.

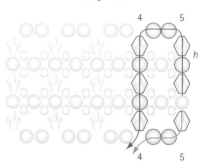

Shank

1 Cut approx. 40cm (15¾in) of thread. Thread a needle on to each end. Pass the thread halfway along through the beads in the fifth ladder. Thread two Rs on to each thread and cross the threads through three F4s. Thread two Rs on to each thread and cross the threads through two F4s. Thread two Rs on to each thread and cross the threads through one F4. Repeat this process one or more times according to the finger circumference. Finish the shank symmetrically by finishing off with two Rs on each thread. Cross the threads through the first ladder of the other side of the flat surface of the ring (i).

2 Pass the threads back through all the beads in the opposite direction as far as the fifth ladder of the flat surface to strengthen the shank (j). Pass each thread through all the Rs of the shank, then through the spacers between the ladders of the flat surface. Bring the threads out together above the first ladder of the three F4s of the shank (k). Tie a knot, hide it in the F4s and trim the remaining threads.

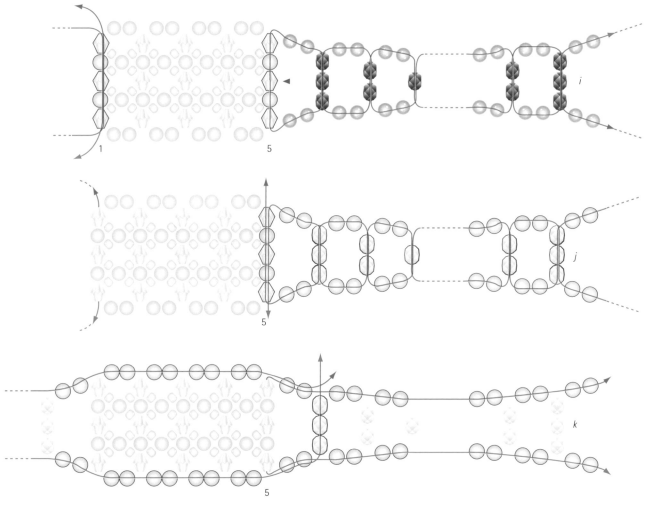

Small hanging tassel

silver

silver grey

black

silver

Materials

4 x 4mm bicones: silver

12 x 4mm faceted beads: 4 black,
8 silver grey

8 x 3mm faceted beads: black

8 x 3mm round beads: silver

Seed beads: black

Small seed beads: diamante

12 silver crimp beads

0.25mm nylon thread

Beading needles

Fine tiger tail

1 trigger clasp and 1 jump ring: silver

Jewellery pliers

Using the photographs as a guide to the colour
pattern, make a small beaded tassel as shown
on page 16. Cut approx. 50cm (19¾ in) of tiger
tail, thread the tassel on to the middle, then
attach the clasp and the jump ring, adjusting
the tiger tail to the desired length, as shown on
page 9.

Pareo ring

Flat surface of the ring

orange

bronze

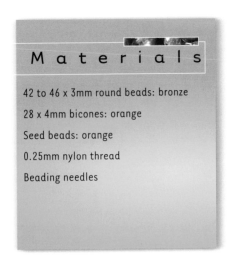

The flat surface of this ring is made in three stages: first weave the bicones and the bronze round beads at the top, then the central motif of round beads and finally the bicones and round beads at the bottom. Cut approx. 1m (39½in) of thread. Thread a needle on to each end.

1 Upper edge. Make seven ladders of two B4s using R spacers, as follows: thread one R, two B4s and one R. Cross the threads through two B4s (a). Thread one R on to each thread and cross the threads through two B4s. Repeat this process three times. For the seventh ladder, thread one R, two B4s and one R on to the top thread and pass the bottom thread through the last R (b).

2 Pass the right thread through the first B4 of the seventh ladder, then the left thread through the first B4 of the sixth ladder. Cross the threads through one B (c). Pass the right thread through the second B4 of the seventh ladder and the spacer bead at the top between the seventh and sixth ladders, then through the adjoining B4 on the sixth ladder. Cross the left thread in this same bead (d).

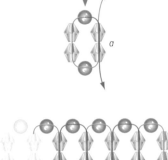

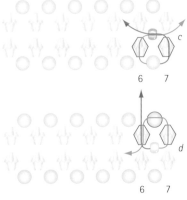

Abbreviations

B4: 4mm bicones

R: round beads

S: seed beads

3 Pass the top thread through the next R spacer and through the first B4 of the fifth ladder. Cross the threads through one S. Ensure that the Ss are threaded on the same side as the first one: they are more obvious at this point, which is actually the back of the flat surface of the ring. Continue like this by weaving one S between each ladder until the end of the row. To finish, cross the threads through the R at the bottom (e).

4 **Central motif.** Thread one S and one R on to the left thread. Cross the threads through one S (f). Pass the top thread through the R spacer on the row of bicone ladders. Thread one R on to the bottom thread, then cross the threads through one S. Repeat this process until the end of the row and finish by crossing the threads through the R at the bottom (g).

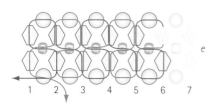

5 **Lower edge.** Make seven new ladders of two B4s in the following way: thread two B4s and one R on to the right thread, then cross the threads through two B4s (h). Pass the top thread through the next R spacer in the previous row, thread one R on to the bottom thread, then cross the threads through two B4s. Repeat this process three times. For the seventh ladder, pass the top thread through the next R spacer in the previous row, thread two B4s, then cross the threads through one R (i).

6 Weave Ss between the B4 ladders as for the upper edge and on the same side. Finish by joining the threads at the level of the second ladder of two B4s (j). Tie a knot, hide it in the B4s in the second ladder, then trim the remaining threads.

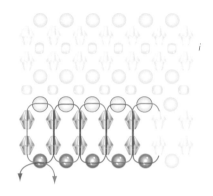

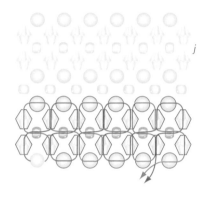

Shank

1 Cut approx. 40cm (15¾in) of thread. Thread a needle on to each end. Turn over the flat surface of the ring so that the side where the seed beads are more obvious is underneath. Pass the thread halfway along through the central S on the right side of the flat surface, then on each side through one R, one B4, one S and one B4, as indicated in the diagram (k).

2 Thread one R on to each thread and cross the threads through one S. Repeat this process as often as required for the finger circumference. Finish by threading one R on to each thread. Attach the shank to the other side of the flat surface, passing the threads through the beads opposite those at the start (l).

3 Pass the threads back through all the beads in the opposite direction to strengthen the shank, finishing off by passing one of the threads through the central S on the right of the flat surface. Tie a knot, hide it in one R and trim the remaining threads.

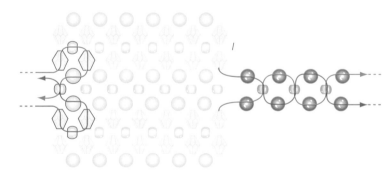

topaz   gilt   bronze

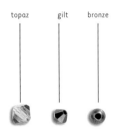

Matching bracelet

Materials

6 x 4mm bicones: topaz

7 x 3mm bicones: gilt

7 x 3mm round beads: bronze

Seed beads: orange, bronze and brown

Large seed beads: orange

Small seed beads: orange and brown

0.25mm nylon thread

Beading needles

Slit needle

An assortment of 10 to 12mm round beads and small bronze spacer beads

0.6mm elastic thread

All-purpose adhesive

1 Following the instructions on pages 10, 11 and 13, make a flat beaded bead with orange LSs and Ss, bronze Ss and topaz B4s, a disc with brown Ss and gilt B3s, a disc with brown Ss and brown Rs, as well as three small spacer beads (two brown and one orange).

2 Using a slit needle, thread the round beads on to 40cm (15¾in) of elastic thread, spacing them evenly and separating them with the beads that you have made or with small, bronze spacer beads. Pass the thread back through all the beads to double the strength.

3 Knot the thread as shown on page 9, hiding the knot in the hole of a bead.

Abbreviations

B4: 4mm bicones

B3: 3mm bicones

R: round beads

S: seed beads

SS: small seed beads

LS: large seed beads

smoky turquoise   gilt

Materials

23 x 4mm bicones: 7 smoky turquoise and 16 gilt

Large seed beads: sea green

Seed beads: sea green, gilt and dark red

0.25mm nylon thread

Beading needles

Abbreviations

B4: 4mm bicones

S: seed beads

LS: large seed beads

Iroquoian ring

Flat surface of the ring

This is made in three stages. First, make the vertical ladders of bicones, then weave other bicones between the ladders. Finish by adding seed beads to form the top and the edging. Cut approx. 80cm (31½ in) of thread. Thread a needle on to each end.

1 **Vertical ladders.** Thread one LS, two gilt B4s, then one LS. Cross the threads through two gilt B4s (a). Thread one LS on to each side and cross the threads again in two gilt B4s. Repeat this process another five times until you have eight ladders of two B4s (b).

2 **Weaving between the ladders.** Pass the top thread through the top LS spacer between the eighth and seventh ladders, then through the first B4 of the seventh ladder. Pass the bottom thread through the bottom LS spacer between the eighth and seventh ladders, through the B4s of the seventh ladder, through the top LS spacer between the seventh and eighth ladders, then through the first B4 of the eighth ladder (c).

3 Cross the threads through one turquoise B4 (d). Pass each thread respectively through the next B4 of the seventh and eighth ladders (e). Pass the right thread through the bottom LS spacer between the seventh and eighth ladders, then through the adjoining B4 of the seventh ladder (f). Pass the bottom thread through the LS spacer between the sixth and seventh ladders, then through the first B4 of the sixth ladder (g).

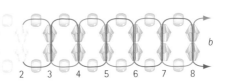

a

1   2   3   4   5   6   7   8   *b*

c

7   8

d

7   8

e

7   8

f

7   8

g

6   7   8

4 Cross the threads through one turquoise B4 (h). Continue like this, weaving the turquoise B4s between all the ladders. Finish by crossing in the bottom B4 of the first ladder (i).

5 **Top and around the flat surface of the ring.** Pass the top thread through all the central B4s, inserting one red S between each (j). Turning clockwise, pass the same thread through all the beads around the flat surface, inserting one gilt S between each spacer LS. Go back halfway to meet the other thread (k). Tie a knot, hide it in the LSs and the adjoining Ss. Trim the remaining threads.

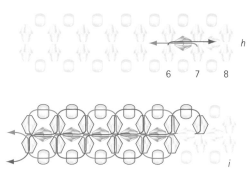

Shank

1 Cut approx. 50cm (19¾in) of thread. Thread a needle on to each end. Pass the thread halfway along through the B4s on the right of the flat surface. Thread one sea green S on to each thread, then cross the threads through two LSs. Repeat this process as often as required for the finger circumference. Finish by threading one S on to each thread. Pass the top thread through the two B4s on the left of the flat surface, and the bottom thread through the B4 at the bottom (l). Check for correct sizing.

2 To strengthen the shank and to make it round, weave the threads by passing them back through all the LSs and Ss already threaded and crossing them in one gilt S between each ladder of two LSs. Finish by joining the threads above the LSs on the right of the flat surface (m and n). Tie a knot, hide it in the LSs and trim the remaining threads.

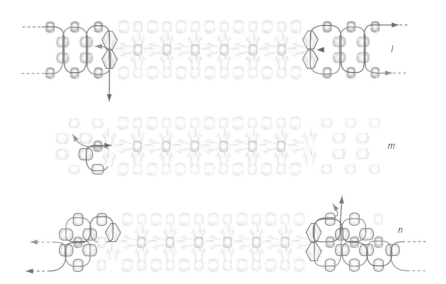

Scarf-necklace

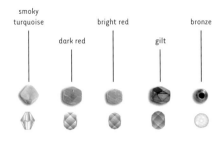

smoky turquoise
dark red
bright red
gilt
bronze

Materials

8 x 4mm bicones: smoky turquoise

27 x 4mm faceted beads: 25 dark red and 2 gilt

16 x 3mm faceted beads: bright red

16 x 3mm round beads: bronze

Seed beads: gilt, red and turquoise blue

Small seed beads: bronze

Large seed beads: sea green, red and gilt

16 crimp beads: copper

0.25mm nylon thread

Beading needles

Jewellery pliers

Abbreviations

B4: 4mm bicones

F4: 4mm faceted beads

F3: 3mm faceted beads

R: round beads

S: seed beads

SS: small seed beads

LS: large seed beads

Whether worn doubled around, tied simply or in a more sophisticated way, this necklace is very versatile.

1 Tassels. Using the photographs to help with the colour pattern, make two identical small tassels, as shown on page 16. For the fringes, use some Ss or SSs, or a mixture of both.

2 Necklace. Cut approx. 2.30m (90½ in) of thread. Thread a needle on to each end. Pass the thread halfway along through the S at the top of the first tassel. Thread one gilt S on to each thread. Thread one gilt S, one gilt F4 and one gilt S, one red F4 and three gilt LSs on to the two threads at the same time. Then thread LSs for just over 1m (39½ in) in no particular pattern.

3 Finish by threading one gilt LS and one sea green LS, one gilt F4, one gilt LS and one gilt S. Thread one gilt S on to each thread and cross the threads through the S at the top of the second tassel. Pass the threads back through in the opposite direction as far as the F4. Tie a knot, hide it in the F4 and trim the remaining threads.

purple   violet

Materials

27 x 4mm bicones: purple

10 to 12 x 4mm faceted beads: violet

Large seed beads: violet

Seed beads: purple and light blue

0.25mm nylon thread

Beading needles

Baïona ring

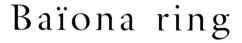

Flat surface of the ring

This ring is made in three stages: first, make seven vertical ladders of bicones, spacing a horizontal bicone between the outer ladders. Add other bicones between the central ladders to create the volume. Finish the weaving by passing back through the horizontal bicones to add the seed beads and four new bicones. Cut approx. 1m (39½ in) of thread. Thread a needle on to each end.

1 **Bicone ladders.** Thread one B4, one LS and one B4. Cross the threads through one B4 (a). Thread one B4 and one LS on to the left thread, then cross the threads again in one B4 (b). Pass the top thread through the B4 just above: the two first B4 ladders are finished (c).

2 Thread one LS on to each thread and cross the threads through three B4s. Repeat this process twice (d).

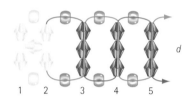

3 Thread one LS on to each thread and cross the threads through two B4s (e). Thread one LS, two B4s, then one LS on to the top thread and pass the thread through the first B4 of the sixth ladder. Pass the bottom thread through the right LS spacer and through the first B4 of the seventh ladder. Cross the threads through one B4 (f).

 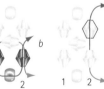

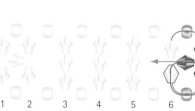

Abbreviations

B4: 4mm bicones

F4: 4mm faceted beads

S: seed beads

LS: large seed beads

4 Pass the right thread through the B4 at the top of the 7th ladder, then through the LS spacer between the 6th and 7th ladders. Cross the threads through the 1st B4 of the 6th ladder (g). Pass the bottom thread through the bottom B4 of the 6th ladder. Pass each thread through the top and bottom LS spacers between the 5th and 6th ladders. Cross the threads through the 5th ladder (h).

5 **Central volume.** Pass the bottom thread through the bottom LS spacer between the 4th and 5th ladders, through the 4th ladder, then the top LS spacer, then the 1st B4 of the 5th ladder. Pass the top thread through the top LS spacer between the 4th and 5th ladders and through the 1st B4 of the 4th ladder. Cross the threads through one B4 (i). Pass each thread down through the next B4, then cross again through one B4 (j).

6 Pass the right thread through the B4 at the bottom of the 5th ladder, then through the LS spacer between the 4th and 5th ladders. Cross the threads through the B4 at the bottom of the 4th ladder (k). Pass the bottom thread through the LS spacer between the 3rd and 4th ladders, then through the 1st B4 of the 3rd ladder. Cross the threads through one B4 (l). Pass each thread up through the next B4. Cross the threads again in one B4.

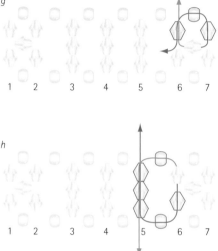

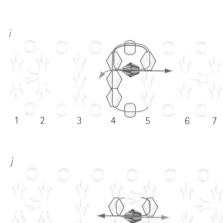

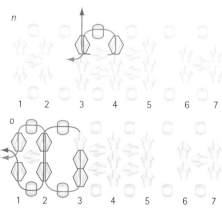

7 Pass the right thread through the B4 at the top of the 4th ladder, then through the LS spacer between the 3rd and 4th ladders. Cross the threads through the B4 at the top of the 3rd ladder (n). Pass the threads back through the B4s of the first three ladders and through the LS spacers, so they come between the two B4s of the 1st ladder (o).

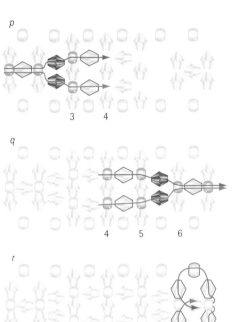

p

3 4

q

4 5 6

r

6 7

8 **Finishing off the weaving.** Use the blue Ss. Thread one S on to the two threads at the same time. Pass the two threads through the B4 spacer between the two first ladders. Thread one S on to the two threads at the same time. Thread one B4 and one S on to each thread. Pass each thread through the B4 spacers between the third and fourth ladders (p). Thread one S on to each thread, then finish the weaving on the opposite side (q).

9 Pass each thread respectively through one B4 of the seventh ladder, through the top or bottom LS spacer between the sixth and seventh ladders and through one B4 of the sixth ladder. Tie a knot, hide it in the B4 spacer between the sixth and seventh ladders and trim the remaining threads (r).

Shank

1 Cut approx. 40cm (15¾ in) of thread. Thread a needle on to each end. Pass the thread halfway along through the two B4s on the right of the flat surface of the ring. Thread one LS on to each thread, then cross the threads through one F4. Repeat this process as often as required for the finger circumference. Finish by threading one LS on to each thread. Cross the threads through the two B4s on the left side of the table (s). Check for correct sizing.

2 To strengthen the shank, pass the threads back through all the beads in the opposite direction until they cross through the two B4s at the start (t).

3 To make neat edges, pass the threads back through the LSs of the shank, then those of the flat surface, using purple Ss as spacers. Finish by passing each thread back through one LS, one S and one LS at the start of the shank. Pass one of the threads through the second F4 of the shank. Tie a knot, hide it in the F4 and trim the remaining threads (u).

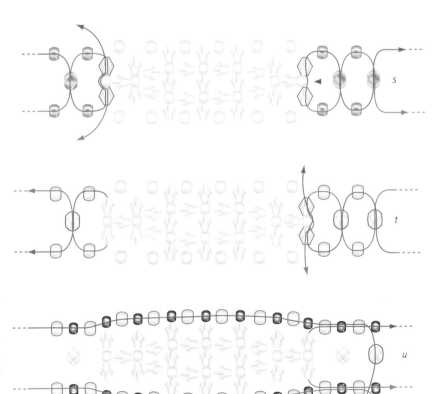

s

t

u

dark purple

Choker

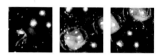

Materials

24 x 3mm round crystal pearls:
dark purple

Seed beads: light blue and black

Beading needles

0.25mm nylon thread

Light blue satin cord: 35 to 40cm
(13¾ to 15¾in)

2 flat cord crimpers: silver

1 trigger clasp and 2 jump rings: silver

Jewellery pliers

Make this elegant bead following the instructions for the small, cylindrical bead on page 12. Simply replace the large seed beads with 3mm round crystal pearls.

Thread the bead on to the cord, then attach the clasp as shown on page 9.

light brown   light beige

beige

Champagne ring (wide)

Materials

46 x 4mm bicones: 12 light brown,
6 beige, 28 light beige

Large seed beads: beige

Seed beads: beige

0.20mm nylon thread

Beading needles

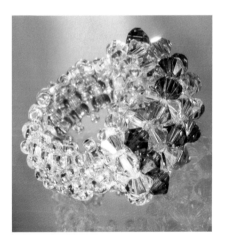

Abbreviations

B4: 4mm bicones

S: seed beads

LS: large seed beads

F4: 4mm faceted beads

Plateau

This ring is made in two stages. First, make the seven vertical ladders of four bicones separated by a large seed bead, then weave other bicones horizontally. The closeness of the vertical ladders creates the volume. Cut approx. 1m (39½ in) of thread. Thread a needle on to each end.

1 **Vertical ladders of four bicones.** Thread one LS, four light beige B4s and one LS. Cross the threads through four light beige B4s (a). Thread one LS on to each thread and cross again through four light beige B4s. Repeat this process until you have made seven ladders (b).

2 **Weaving between the ladders.** Pass the bottom thread through the bottom LS spacer between the sixth and seventh ladders, through the B4s of the sixth ladder, through the top LS spacer between the sixth and seventh ladders, then through the first B4 of the seventh ladder. Pass the top thread through the top LS spacer then through the first B4 of the sixth ladder. Cross the threads through one light brown B4 (c).

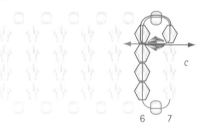

3 Pass each thread respectively through the next B4 and cross them again in one light brown B4. Repeat this process once. Pass the right thread through the B4 below the seventh ladder, then through the LS spacer. Cross the threads through the B4 below the sixth ladder (d).

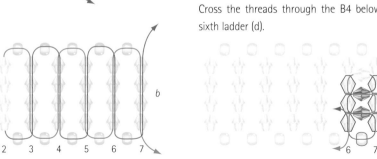

4 Pass the bottom thread through the LS spacer between the fifth and sixth ladders, then through the first B4 of the fifth ladder. Cross the threads through one beige B4 (e). Keep weaving B4s in the correct colour pattern. Finish by crossing the threads through the top LS spacer between the first and second ladders (f).

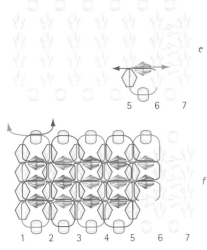

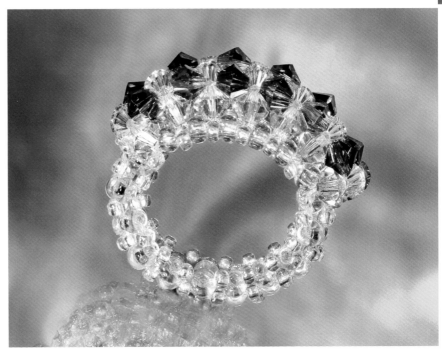

5 **Around the flat surface of the ring.** Pass the right thread through all the beads around the flat surface, inserting one S between each LS. Finish by passing the thread back through the LS at the start (g). Pass the left thread through the B4s in the upper left corner of the flat surface, so that the threads meet above the second ladder (h). Tie a knot, hide it in some Ss and LSs around the edge and trim the remaining threads.

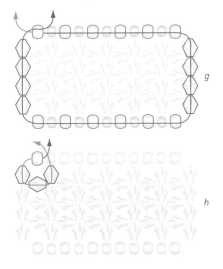

Shank

1 Cut approx. 70cm (27½in) of thread. Thread a needle on to each end. Pass the thread halfway along through the B4s on the right of the flat surface. Thread one S on to each thread, then cross the threads through four LSs. Repeat this process as often as required for the finger circumference. Finish by threading one S on to each thread and cross the threads through the four B4s on the left of the flat surface (i). Check for correct sizing.

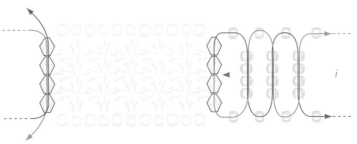

2 Pass the top thread through the top S spacer in front of the B4s, then through the last LS ladder made. Pass the other thread through the bottom S spacer, then through the first LS of the ladder. Cross the threads through one S (j).

Back of the ring

49

3 Weave Ss between all the ladders using the weaving technique for the bicones on the flat surface of the ring. Finish by bringing the threads back out opposite the first LS ladder (k). Tie a knot, hide it in the LS ladder and trim the remaining threads.

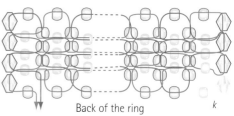

Back of the ring   k

Narrow version

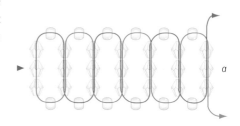

Flat surface of the ring

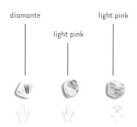

diamante   light pink

light pink

Materials

33 x 4mm bicones: 21 diamante and 12 light pink

8 to 11 x 4mm faceted beads: light pink

Large seed beads: transparent AB

Seed beads: transparent AB

0.20mm nylon thread

Beading needles

The flat surface of this ring is made according to the same principle as the wide ring, but with a different number of beads. However, unlike the first example, the edges of the flat surface are finished at the same time as the shank. Cut approx. 80cm (31½in) of thread. Thread a needle on to each end.

1 Vertical ladders of three bicones. Make seven ladders of three diamante B4s, separated by LSs (a).

a

2 **Weaving between the ladders.** Refer to stages 2 to 4 on the previous pages to weave the light pink B4s (b) and (c). Pass the threads back through as in the drawing (d). Tie a knot, hide it in the light pink B4 and trim the remaining threads.

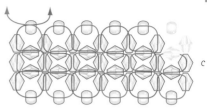

c

b

d

Shank

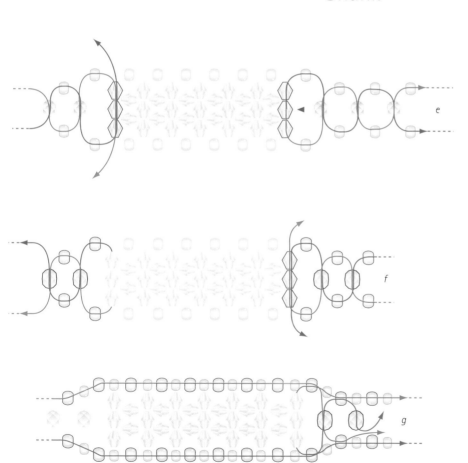

e

f

g

1 Cut approx. 50cm (19¾ in) of thread. Thread a needle on to each end. Pass the thread halfway along through the three B4s on the right of the flat surface. Thread one LS on to each thread, then cross the threads through one F4. Repeat this process as often as required for the finger circumference. Finish by threading one LS on to each thread and cross the threads through the three B4s on the left of the flat surface (e). Check for correct sizing.

2 To strengthen the shank, pass the threads back through all the beads in the opposite direction until they cross through the three B4s at the start (f).

3 To make neat edges, pass the threads back through the LSs of the shank, then those of the flat surface of the ring, spacing using Ss. Finish by passing each thread back through the first LS of the shank, cross through the first F4, pass back through the next LS. Pass one of the threads through the second F4 of the shank (g). Tie a knot, hide it in the F4 and trim the remaining threads.

brown

light brown

amber

burgundy

brown

lead

Basque ring

Flat surface of the ring

Materials

14 x 4mm bicones: 10 amber, 4 brown

3 x 3mm bicones: 2 burgundy and
1 light brown

27 to 33 x 4mm faceted beads: brown

3mm round beads: lead

Seed beads: brown and light orange

0.25mm nylon thread

Beading needles

Abbreviations

B4: 4mm bicones

B3: 3mm bicones

F4: 4mm faceted beads

R: 3mm round beads

S: seed beads

This ring is made in two stages: first, make the column of three flowers, then weave the beads on the right side in three rows, followed by those on the left. Cut approx. 1m (39½ in) of thread. Thread a needle on to each end.

1 **Flowers.** Thread two Rs, one F4 and two Rs. Cross the threads through one F4 (a). Thread one amber B4 on to each thread. Cross the threads through one burgundy B3. Thread one amber B4 on to each thread and cross the threads through the F4 opposite (b).

2 Thread two Rs on to each thread and cross through one F4 (c). Cover this base as before with four brown B4s and one light brown B3 (d).

3 Pass each thread back through the two Rs on the sides and cross the threads through the bottom F4 (e). Thread the beads for the base. Make the third flower like the first (f).

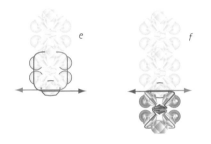

4 **Right side of the table.** Use the brown Ss to weave the top. Pass the threads back through the beads of the base of the flower and cross them in the right two Rs (g). Thread one S on to each thread and cross the threads through the two Rs, three times (h).

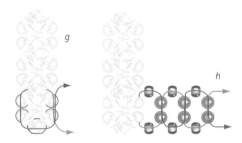

Basque

5 Pass the threads back through the beads to cross them through the top S spacer (i). Thread two Rs and one S on to the right thread and cross the threads through the two Rs (j). Thread one S on to the top thread, pass the other thread through the S spacer in the previous row and cross the threads through one amber B4 (k). Pass the bottom thread through the S spacer in the previous row then through the two Rs of the central flower. Cross the threads through one S (l).

6 Pass the left thread through the two Rs of the top flower, then thread one S. Cross the threads through two Rs (m). Thread one S on to the top thread. Pass the bottom thread through the S spacer in the previous row and cross the threads through two Rs, twice (n).

7 Pass each thread through the S spacers on either side of the last row, inserting one S between the Ss already threaded. Then pass through the F4s of the first flower and cross the threads through the left two Rs (o).

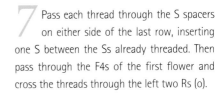

8 **Left side of the flat surface.** Proceed as for the right side (p).

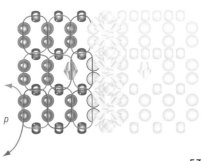

53

9 **Finishing off.** Pass each thread through the S spacers in each row, inserting one S between the Ss already threaded. Tie a knot, hide it in the F4 and trim the remaining threads (q).

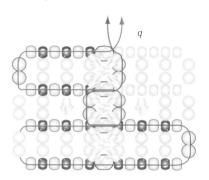

Shank

1 Cut approx. 60cm (23½in) of thread. Thread a needle on to each end. Pass the thread halfway along through the two Rs at the top, on the right of the flat surface of the ring (r).

2 Use some orange Ss to weave the shank. Thread one S and one F4 on to the top thread and cross the threads through one S (s). Pass the left thread through the next two Rs,

thread one F4 on to the right thread and cross the threads through one S (t). Pass the left thread through the next two Rs, thread one S and cross the threads through one F4 (u).

3 Continue weaving Ss and F4s on as many columns as needed for the finger circumference. To attach the shank, pass back through the Rs on the other side of the flat surface of the ring (v). To strengthen the shank, pass the threads back through all the beads in the opposite direction. Tie a knot, hide it in one F4 and trim the remaining threads.

Triple bracelet with tassel

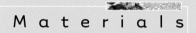

eddish brown

topaz

light brown

amethyst

bronze

lead

Materials

An assortment of 10 x 4mm bicones, for example: 2 reddish brown, 3 amethyst, 2 light brown, 3 topaz

3mm round beads: lead and bronze

Large seed beads: light orange

Seed beads: light orange, bright orange, brown and copper

8 x 8 to 12mm matching faceted beads

12 spacer beads: copper

10 crimp beads: bronze

A 0.5cm diameter jump ring: bronze

0.25mm nylon thread

Beading needles

Slit needle

Jewellery pliers

0.6mm elastic thread

All-purpose adhesive

1 **Tassel.** Using the photograph for the colour pattern, make a tassel from seed beads, as shown on page 18.

2 **Attaching to the bracelet.** Using a pair of pliers, place the jump ring in the top of the tassel. Cut 60cm (23½ in) of elastic thread.

3 Thread the faceted beads, spacer beads, round beads and the tassel to form the first circle. Cross through one large faceted bead. Check for correct sizing (a). Make the second circle by passing back through the faceted beads and the spacer beads, and doubling the round bead sections (b). Form the third circle in the same way until the threads meet (c). Tie a triple knot, glue it and hide it in the large faceted bead.

a

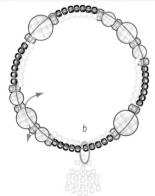

b

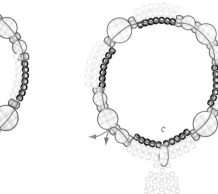

c

Venice ring

ruby
red
orange
turquoise
metallic black
silver

This ring is the perfect accessory for a smart outfit. It is made of five interconnected circles. Cut approx. 1m (39½in) of thread. Thread a needle on to each end.

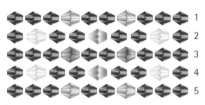

1
2
3
4
5

Colour pattern for the top of the ring

Materials

12 x 4mm bicones: 2 ruby, 4 red, 4 orange, 2 turquoise

36 x 3mm bicones: metallic black

15 x 3mm round beads: silver

Seed beads: black

Small seed beads: diamante

0.25mm nylon thread

Beading needles

1 First circle. Thread three B3s, one red B4, two B3s, one red B4 and three B3s (a). Thread on to each side one S, one R and eight Ss (depending on finger circumference). Centre the beads in the middle of the thread. Cross the threads through one R (b). Check for correct sizing.

2 Second circle. Thread one SS on to each thread. Cross the threads through one R (c). Thread eight Ss, one R and one S on to the right thread, the top bicones, one S, one R and eight Ss and pass the thread through the R at the start (d).

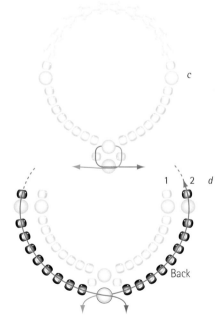

Abbreviations

B4: 4mm bicones

B3: 3mm bicones

R: round beads

S: seed beads

SS: small seed beads

3 **Centre circle.** Thread one SS on to each thread. Cross the threads through one R. Thread eight Ss, one R and one S, the top bicones, one S, one R and eight Ss on to the longest thread. Pass the thread through the R at the start (e).

4 **Fourth and fifth circles.** Before each of the last two circles, thread one SS on to each thread, then cross the threads through one R, as before. Using the longest thread each time, make the fourth circle like the second and the fifth like the first (f) and (g).

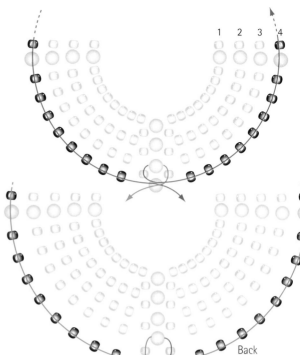

Back

5 **Connect the circles.** Pass the right thread through the eight Ss and through the next R. Pass the left thread through all the other beads of the circle until the threads cross through the same R. Thread one SS on to each thread, then cross the threads through the R of the next row. Continue until the fifth circle, pulling the threads tight at each crossing (h).

6 Pass the left thread through the eight Ss, through the central R, then through the eight other Ss and the next R. Pass the right thread through the other beads, until the threads cross through the same R. Connect the five circles to one another again as before (i).

7 **Finishing off.** Pass the right thread (blue) through all the beads of the fifth circle until it comes out next to the other thread. Tie a knot, hide it in some Bs and trim the remaining threads (j).

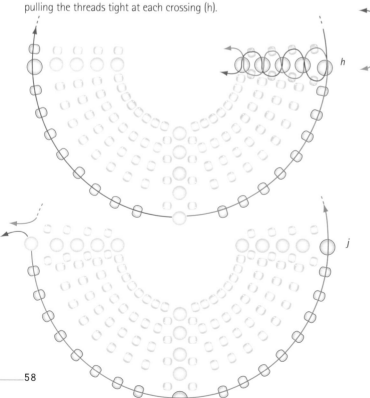

Tassel bracelet

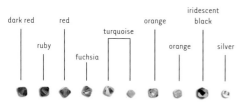

dark red   red   orange   iridescent
                                    black
     ruby   turquoise
           fuchsia   orange   silver

Materials

20 x 4mm bicones: 6 dark red for the flat bead, 4 turquoise for the round bead, 10 for the tassel (3 turquoise, 3 orange, 2 red, 1 ruby and 1 fuschia)

14 x 3mm bicones: turquoise

4 x 4mm faceted beads: iridescent black

16 x 3mm faceted beads: orange

3mm round beads: silver

Seed beads: black, pink and silver

Large seed beads: red

An assortment of 8 to 10mm black faceted beads and silver round and spacer beads

0.25mm nylon thread

0.6mm elastic thread

Beading needles

Slit needle

10 crimp beads

Jewellery pliers

All-purpose adhesive

Follow the instructions on pages 10, 11, 14 and 18 to make the discs (two with bicones and one with round beads), the round beaded bead, the flat beaded bead and the tassel. Refer to the photographs for the colour pattern.

Using a slit needle, thread the different beads made and the black and silver beads on to 40cm (15¾ in) of elastic thread, beginning with the round beaded bead. Pass the thread back through all the beads to double the strength. Tie the thread as shown on page 9.

Melody ring with two flowers

metallic
black

metallic
transparent

light grey

dark grey

iridescent
transparent

silver

Materials

8 x 4mm bicones: 4 metallic black and
4 metallic transparent

24 to 30 x 3mm faceted beads: 8 to 10
light grey, 8 to 10 dark grey, 8 to 10
iridescent transparent

33 to 39 x 3mm round beads: silver

Seed beads: black, diamante
and hematite

Small seed beads: diamante

0.25mm nylon thread

Beading needles

Abbreviations

B4: 4mm bicones

F3: 3mm faceted beads

R: round beads

S: seed beads

SS: small seed beads

This ring, a timeless classic, is made in two stages: first, make the column of two flowers, then the shank, connected to one another at the back as you go along. Cut approx. 1m (39½ in) of thread. Thread a needle on to each end.

1 **Central flowers.** To make the base of the first flower, thread two Rs and one SS on to each side and cross the threads through one R. Thread one SS on to each thread and cross the threads through two Rs (a). Thread one metallic transparent B4 on to each thread. Cross the threads through one diamante S. Thread another metallic transparent B4 on to each thread. Cross the threads through the two opposite Rs (b).

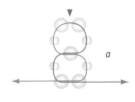

a

b

2 Thread one SS on to each thread, cross the threads in one R, thread one SS on to each thread and cross in two Rs (c). Cover this base with some metallic black B4s as before (d). Pass the threads back through the beads of the base of the first flower. Cross them in the two bottom Rs (e).

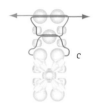

c

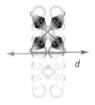

d

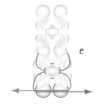

e

3 **Rings.** Thread one hematite S and eight dark grey F3s on to the right thread. Adjust the number of F3s according to the finger circumference.

Thread the same length of black Ss on to the left thread (f). Cross the threads through one R (g). Check the size of this first ring.

4 Thread one SS on to each thread and cross the threads again in one R. Make a second ring, on the longest thread, the same diameter as the first, passing the thread, in front, through the central R of the base of the first flower. Refer to the photograph for the colour pattern. To close the ring, pass the thread through the R at the start (h).

f

Front

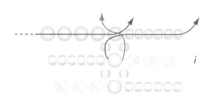

g

Back

h

5 To make the third ring, thread one SS on to each thread and cross in one R. Pass the longest thread in front through the two Rs between the two flowers. Finish by passing the thread back through the R at the start (i). Repeat the process to make the fourth and fifth rings.

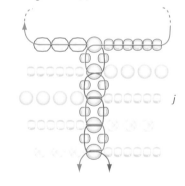

i

6 **Finishing off.** Pass the longest thread back through all the beads in the last ring, finishing off in the R at the start. Pass the threads back through the SSs and cross them in the Rs up to the first ring (j). Pass the longest thread back through all the beads of the first ring, until it comes out next to the other thread. Tie a knot, hide it in the F3s and trim the remaining threads (k).

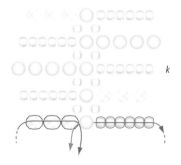

j

k

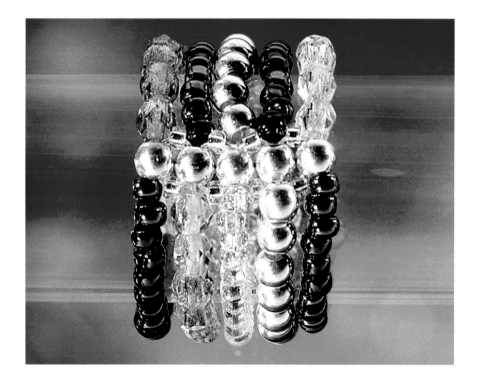

Three-flower version

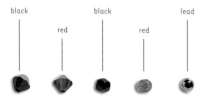

black   black   lead
      red   red

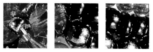

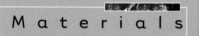

Materials

12 x 4mm bicones: 8 black and 4 red

24 to 30 x 3mm faceted beads: 16 to 20 black, 8 to 10 red

51 to 59 x 3mm round beads: lead

Seed beads: black, light red, dark red and grey

Small seed beads: red

0.25mm nylon thread

Beading needles

This version is made along the same lines as the Melody ring with two flowers: just add a flower to the central column before making the rings. To reduce the height of the ring at the back, cross in seed beads rather than in round beads.

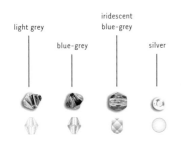

light grey

blue-grey

iridescent
blue-grey

silver

Storm ring

Flat surface of the ring

Materials

32 x 4mm bicones: 16 light grey and
16 blue-grey

7 to 9 x 4mm faceted beads: iridescent
blue-grey

30 to 34 x 3mm round beads: silver

Seed beads: diamante

0.25mm nylon thread

Beading needles

This is made of two ribs of bicones, covered with round beads, separated by a weave of seed beads. These three parts are made one after the other. Cut approx. 1m (39½ in) of thread. Thread a needle on to each end.

1 **First rib.** Thread one S, one light grey B4, one blue-grey B4 and one S. Cross the threads in two B4s placing the colours in the same order (a). Thread one S on to each thread and cross the threads in two B4s as before. Repeat this process until you have made eight ladders of two B4s. Finish by crossing the threads in the bottom S (b).

a

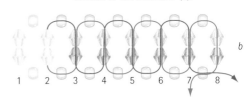

1   2   3   4   5   6   7   8

b

Abbreviations

B4: 4mm bicones

F4: 4mm faceted beads

R: round beads

S: seed beads

2 Pass the right thread through the first B4 of the eighth ladder, then the left thread through the first B4 of the seventh ladder. Cross the threads in one R (c). Pass the right thread through the next B4 and through the S spacer between the seventh and eighth ladders, then cross the threads in the B4 above the seventh ladder (d).

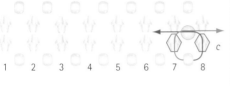

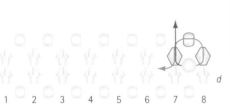

3 Pass the top thread through the next S spacer and through the first B4 of the next ladder. Cross the threads in one R. Continue weaving one R between each ladder (e), then pass the threads back through the beads until they cross in the bottom S (f).

4 **Central part.** Thread two Ss on to the left thread. Cross the threads in one S. Pass the top thread through the next S, previously used as a spacer. Thread one S on to the bottom thread. Cross the threads in one new S. Repeat this process until the end of the row and finish by crossing the threads in the bottom S (g).

5 **Second rib.** Thread one blue-grey B4, one light grey B4 and one S on to the right thread. Cross the threads in two B4s, keeping to the colour order. Pass the top thread through the S spacer in the previous row. Thread one S on to the bottom thread. Cross the threads in two B4s. Line up eight ladders. Finish by crossing the threads in the bottom S (h).

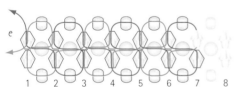

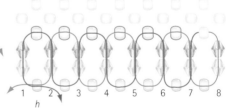

6 Weave Rs between the ladders, as for the first rib. Finish by crossing the threads through the B4 below the last ladder (i).

7 **Finishing off.** Pass the bottom thread through the adjoining S and the top thread through the R, then through the bottom B4 of the second ladder. Tie a knot, hide it in the B4s of the second ladder and trim the remaining threads (j).

Shank

1 Cut approx. 40cm (15¾in) of thread. Thread a needle on to each end. Pass the thread halfway along through the two B4s and the central S on the right side of the flat surface of the ring. Thread one R on to each thread. Cross the threads through one F4. Repeat this process as often as required for the finger circumference. Thread one R on to each thread and cross the threads through the two B4s and the central S of the other side of the flat surface (k).

2 To strengthen the shank, pass the threads back through all the beads in the opposite direction. Tie a knot, hide it in one F4 and trim the remaining threads.

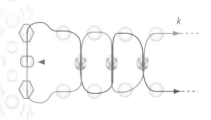

Matching bracelet with small tassel

metallic transparent
blue-grey
white opalescent
light grey
blue-grey
iridescent transparent
white opalescent
silver

Materials

16 x 4mm bicones: 8 metallic transparent, 4 blue-grey and 4 white opalescent

17 x 4mm faceted beads: 4 light grey, 4 blue-grey, 5 iridescent transparent and 4 white opalescent

64 x 3mm faceted beads: 16 blue-grey, 16 light grey and 32 iridescent transparent

3mm round beads: silver

Seed beads: transparent, diamante, white opalescent and blue

Small seed beads: diamante

An assortment of 8 to 12mm faceted beads and an assortment of silver spacer beads

8 crimp beads: silver

0.25mm nylon thread

0.6mm elastic thread

Beading needles

Slit needle

Jewellery pliers

All-purpose adhesive

Make a small bead tassel as shown on page 16, with 3mm faceted beads and 4mm iridescent transparent beads and metallic transparent bicones. At the top of the tassel, replace the large seed bead with a 4mm faceted bead. Use small seed beads and 3mm faceted beads for the fringes.

Make three round beaded beads as shown on page 14, using the photograph as a guideline for the colours. Using a slit needle, thread the various beads made and the other beads on to 40cm (15¾ in) of elastic thread, starting with a round beaded bead. Pass the thread back through all the beads to double the strength. Knot the thread as shown on page 9.

Subway ring

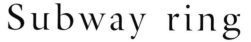

Flat surface of the ring

red

iridescent pink

brown

iridescent brown

The flat surface of the ring has three rows made one after the other. In a second stage, seed beads, inserted between the rows on the reverse of the work, make the bicones stand out as if they are standing on a track! Cut approx. 1m (39½in) of thread. Thread a needle on to each end.

1 **First row.** Thread one bronze S, two red Ss and one bronze S. Cross the threads through one red B4. Thread one bronze S and two red Ss on to the left thread. Cross the threads through one bronze S (a). Thread two red Ss and one bronze S on to the bottom thread. Cross the threads through one red B4. Pass the left thread through the adjoining bronze S already threaded and thread two red Ss. Cross the threads through one bronze S (b).

3 **Second row.** Pass the threads back through the beads so that they cross through the two bottom red Ss (d). Thread one bronze S on to each thread. Cross the threads through one brown B4. Thread one bronze S and two pink Ss on to the right thread. Cross the threads through one bronze S (e). Thread two pink Ss and one bronze S on to the bottom thread. Cross the threads through one brown B4. Pass the right thread through the adjoining bronze S already threaded, then through the two red Ss of the first row. Cross the threads through one bronze S (f).

2 Continue the first row until the seven red B4s align. Finish by crossing the threads through the bottom bronze S (c).

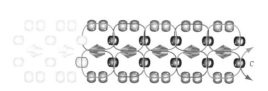

Abbreviations

B4: 4mm bicones

F4: 4mm faceted beads

S: seed beads

4 Pass the top thread through the next two red Ss and thread one bronze S. Cross the threads through one brown B4. Pass the right thread through the adjoining bronze S and thread two pink Ss. Cross the threads through one bronze S (g).

5 Continue until the seven brown B4s align. Finish the row by crossing the threads through the bronze S on the left at the bottom (h). Pass the threads back through the beads so that they cross through the two pink Ss at the bottom (i).

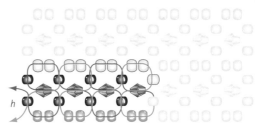

6 **Third row.** Proceed as for the first two rows. Finish by crossing the threads through the bronze S at the bottom (j). Pass the threads back through the beads so that they cross through the two pink Ss at the bottom (k).

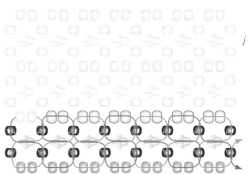

7 **Weaving seed beads.** Thread one bronze S on to the left thread, pass through the next two pink Ss, and repeat this process until the end of the row. On each side, insert one pink S between the two bronze Ss. Turn the work over and thread one of the threads through the pink Ss between the third and second rows, inserting one bronze S between each group of two Ss. Next, pass the other thread in the opposite direction (l).

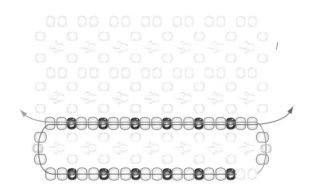

8 On each side, insert one bronze S between the two central bronze S. Turn the work over again and proceed between the second and first rows as before. On each side, insert one red S between the two bronze Ss. Pass each thread as far as the middle of the work inserting bronze Ss between the red Ss. Tie a knot, hide it in the Ss and trim the remaining threads (m).

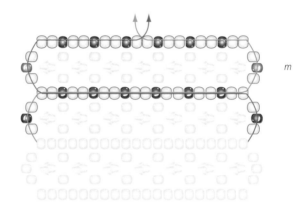

Shank

1 Cut approx. 60cm (23½ in) of thread. Thread a needle on to each end. Pass the thread through the red S on the right side of the flat surface of the ring, and thread two bronze Ss. Pass the thread through the bronze S in the middle of the side of the flat surface, and thread two bronze Ss. Pass the thread through the pink S on the side of the flat surface.

Adjust the lengths of the threads so that they are the same. Thread one bronze S on to each thread, and cross the threads through two F4s. Repeat this process as often as required for the finger circumference. Finish by threading one bronze S on to each thread. Join the shank by inserting Ss as on the right (n).

2 To strengthen the shank, pass the threads back through all the F4s and Ss in the opposite direction. Tie a knot, hide it in one F4 and trim the remaining threads.

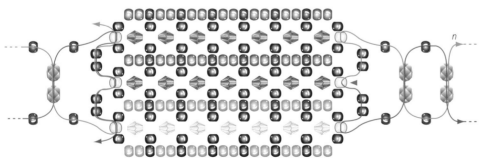

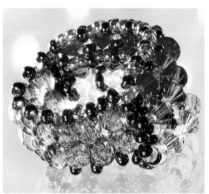

Matching bracelet with flat beads

red

iridescent pink

brown

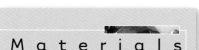

Materials

18 x 4mm bicones: 6 red, 6 iridescent pink and 6 brown

Seed beads: pink and red

Large seed beads: pink and bronze

12 x 10mm iridescent brown faceted beads and 15 copper spacer beads: adjust the number of beads for the size of wrist

0.25mm nylon thread

0.6mm elastic thread

Beading needles

Slit needle

All-purpose adhesive

Make three flat beaded beads as shown on page 11, referring to the photographs for the colour pattern.

Using a slit needle, thread the beads made, the faceted beads and the spacers on to 40cm (15¾ in) of elastic thread, creating a regular pattern. Pass the thread back through all the beads to double the strength. Knot the thread as shown on page 9.

blue

silver

Indigo ring

Flat surface of the ring

Materials

20 x 4mm bicones: blue

60 to 66 x 3mm round beads: silver

Seed beads: blue

Small seed beads: diamante

0.25mm nylon thread

Beading needles

The flat surface of the ring is made of horizontal ladders with seed beads woven in between. The alternating pattern of bicones and round beads creates a raised appearance. Cut approx. 1m (39½in) of thread. Thread a needle on to each end.

1 First rib. Thread ten Rs on to the middle of the thread, then one S on to either side. Cross the threads through ten B4s (a). Pass the left thread through the S spacer, through the ten Rs, then through the next S and through the first B4. Pass the other thread through the S, then through the first R (b).

3 Pass the right thread through the next nine B4s. Thread one S and ten Rs on to the other thread. Cross the threads through one S, then pass the bottom thread through the first R and the top thread through the first B4 (e). Weave Ss between the B4s and Rs as before. Finish by passing the top thread back through the S spacer, then cross the threads through the last R (f).

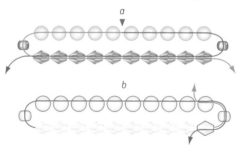

a

b

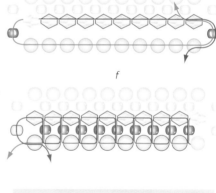

e

f

2 Cross the threads through one S. Pass the top thread through the next R and the bottom thread through the next B4, then cross the threads again in one S (c). Repeat until the end of the row. Finish by passing the top thread back through the S spacer, then crossing the threads through the last B4 (d).

c

d

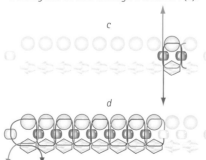

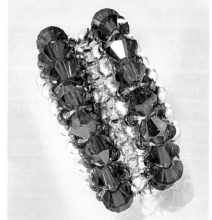

Abbreviations

B4: 4mm bicones

R: round beads

S: seed beads

SS: small seed beads

4 **Groove.** Pass the right thread through the next nine Rs. Thread one S and ten Rs on to the left thread. Cross the threads through one S, then pass each back through the first R of each ladder (g). Weave SSs between the two ladders of R as before. Finish by passing the top thread back through the S spacer, then cross the threads through the last R (h).

5 **Second rib.** Make a new ladder of ten B4s as before, then weave blue Ss (i) and (j). Make a new ladder of Rs, then weave blue Ss again (k) and (l).

g

j

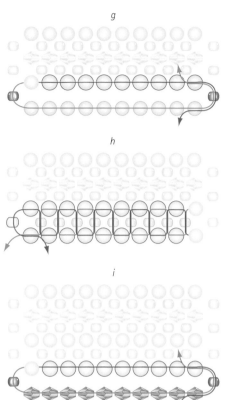

h

k

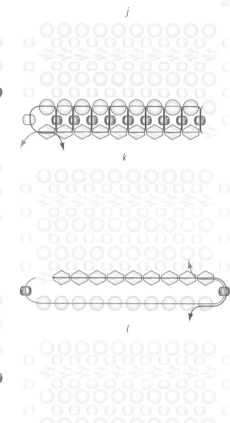

i

l

6 **Finishing off.** Pass each thread through the nearest S, cross through the adjoining B4, pass each thread through the next S, then the right thread through the adjoining R. Tie a knot, hide it in the R and trim the remaining threads (m).

m

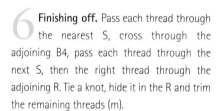

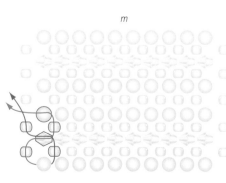

Shank

1 Cut approx. 50cm (19¾in) of thread. Thread a needle on to each end. Pass the thread halfway along through the three central Ss on the right side of the flat surface of the ring. Thread one blue S on to each thread. Cross the threads through two Rs. Repeat this process as often as required for the finger circumference. Finish by threading one blue S on to each thread, then cross the threads through the three central Ss of the other side of the flat surface (n). Check for correct sizing.

2 To strengthen the shank and to make it round, pass the threads back through in the opposite direction weaving one SS between the R ladders (o). Finish by passing one of the threads through the last ladder, through the S spacer and through the three Ss of the flat surface. Tie a knot, hide it in the adjoining R and trim the remaining threads.

n

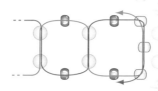

o

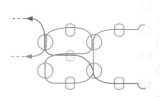
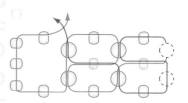

Bracelet with small tassel and round beaded bead

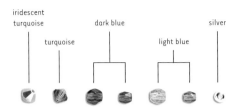

iridescent turquoise

turquoise

dark blue

light blue

silver

Materials

8 x 4mm bicones: 4 iridescent turquoise and 4 turquoise

10 x 4mm faceted beads: 6 dark blue and 4 light blue

32 x 3mm faceted beads: 20 dark blue and 12 light blue

8 x 3mm round beads: silver

Seed beads: dark blue and light blue

1 large seed bead: dark blue

An assortment of beads: 10 to 14mm faceted beads or cat's eye beads; oblong beads (chalcedony used here) and silver spacer beads

8 crimp beads: silver

0.25mm nylon thread

0.6mm elastic thread

Beading needles

Slit needle

Jewellery pliers

All-purpose adhesive

Make the tassel as shown on page 16. For the top, use iridescent turquoise bicones, 4mm dark blue faceted beads and 3mm light blue faceted beads. To add more shades to this magnificent blue monochrome piece, mix the colours of the 3mm faceted beads of the fringes (four light blue and four dark blue).

Refer to the instructions on page 14 for the round beaded bead.

Using a slit needle, thread the beads and the tassel on to 40cm (15¾ in) of elastic thread, starting with the round beaded bead. Pass the thread back through all the beads to double the strength. Knot the thread as shown on page 9.

Revolution ring

Plateau

violet   dark purple

mauve

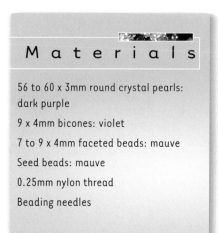

Materials

56 to 60 x 3mm round crystal pearls:
dark purple

9 x 4mm bicones: violet

7 to 9 x 4mm faceted beads: mauve

Seed beads: mauve

0.25mm nylon thread

Beading needles

This is made in three stages: first, make round
bead ladders, weaving seed beads between
them, then the central crown and finally more
ladders of round beads. Cut approx. 1m (39½ in)
of thread. Thread a needle on to each end.

1 Ladders of round beads at the top of
the flat surface of the ring. Thread one
S, two Rs and one S. Cross the threads through
two Rs (a). Thread one S on to each thread and
cross the threads through two Rs. Repeat this
process until you have made ten ladders (b).

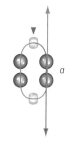

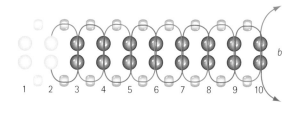

Abbreviations

B4: 4mm bicones

F4: 4mm faceted beads

R: round beads

S: seed beads

Weaving. Pass the top thread through the top S spacer between the 9th and 10th ladders, then through the 9th R ladder. Cross the threads through the bottom S spacer between the 9th and 10th ladders (c). Pass each thread through the adjoining R. Cross the threads through one S. Pass each thread through the next R (d).

Pass the right thread through the top S spacer between the 9th and 10th ladders, then between the first R of the 9th ladder (e). Pass the top thread through the top S spacer between the 8th and 9th ladders, then through the first R of the 8th ladder. Cross the threads through one S. Pass each thread through the adjoining R (f). Pass the right thread through the next S spacer and the adjoining R of the 8th ladder (g).

Continue weaving one S in the middle between each ladder until the end of the row. Finish by crossing the threads through the top S spacer between the 1st and 2nd ladders (h). Pass the threads back through the beads so that they cross through the bottom S spacer between these same ladders (i).

Central crown. Thread one S on to each thread. Cross the threads through one B4. Thread two Ss on to the left thread. Cross the threads through one other S (j). Thread two Ss on to the bottom thread and cross the threads again in one B4. Pass the left thread through the adjoining S, then through the S spacer of the previous row. Cross the threads through one other S (k).

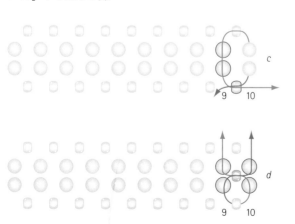

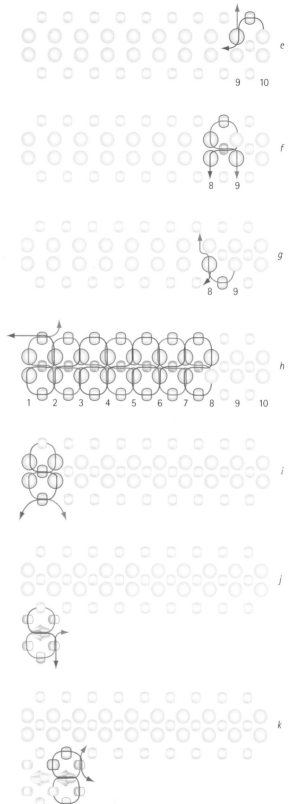

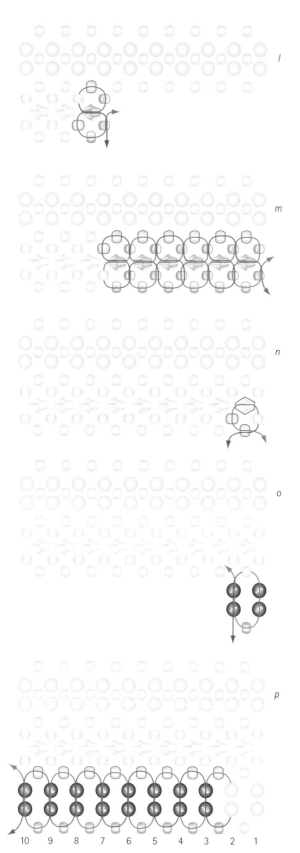

l

m

n

o

p

10 9 8 7 6 5 4 3 2 1

6 Pass the top thread through the next S spacer in the previous row and thread one S. Cross the threads through one B4. Pass the left thread through the adjoining S and thread one S. Cross the threads through one S (l). Continue until the end of the row to line up nine B4s (m). Pass the thread back through the beads so they cross through the bottom S spacer (n).

7 **Ladders of round beads at the bottom of the flat surface of the ring.** Thread two Rs and one S on to the right thread. Cross the threads through two Rs (o). Pass the top thread through the next S spacer in the previous row. Thread one S on to the bottom thread and cross the threads through two Rs. Repeat until you have ten ladders of two Rs.

8 **Weaving.** Pass the top thread through the S spacer of the previous row, then through the two Rs of the ninth ladder. Cross the threads through the S spacer at the bottom (q). Weave one S in the middle between each ladder as for the top of the flat surface (r). Tie a knot, hide it in the second ladder and trim the remaining threads.

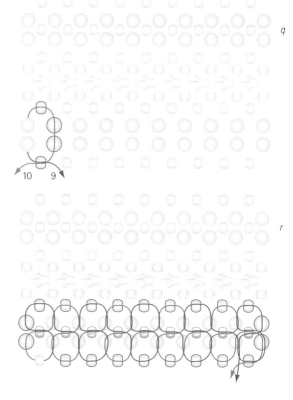

q

10   9

r

Shank

1. Cut approx. 60cm (23½in) of thread. Thread a needle on to each end. Pass the thread halfway along through the central Ss and the two Rs on either side, on the right side of the flat surface of the ring. Thread one R on to each thread and cross the threads in one F4 as often as required for the finger circumference. Thread one R on to each thread and cross the threads through the opposite beads on the other side of the flat surface (s). Check for correct sizing.

2. To strengthen the shank, pass the threads back through all the beads in the opposite direction. Tie a knot, hide it in one F4 and trim the remaining threads.

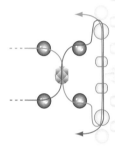
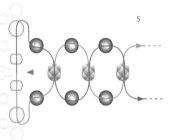

Bracelet with cylindrical beaded beads

Materials

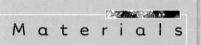

Large seed beads: mauve and iridescent mauve

Seed beads: mauve and violet

Small seed beads: metallic violet

An assortment of 8 to 12mm faceted beads or cat's eye beads and silver spacer beads

0.25mm nylon thread

0.6mm elastic thread

Beading needles

Slit needle

All-purpose adhesive

Make beaded beads as shown on page 12. Vary the number as you wish.

Using a slit needle, thread the beads of the bracelet on to 40cm (15¾ in) of elastic thread, preferably starting with a beaded bead. Pass the thread back through all the beads to double the strength. Knot the thread as shown on page 9.

Scottish SECONDARY MATHEMATICS

R1

Tom Sanaghan

Jim Pennel

Carol Munro

Carole Ford

John Dalton

James Cairns

heinemann.co.uk

✓ Free online support
✓ Useful weblinks
✓ 24 hour online ordering

01865 888058

Heinemann

Inspiring generations

Heinemann is an imprint of Pearson Education Limited,
a company incorporated in England and Wales, having
its registered office at 80 Strand, London, WC2R 0RL.
Registered company number: 872828

Heinemann is a registered trademark of Pearson Education Limited

© Tom Sanaghan, Jim Pennel, Carol Munro, Carole Ford, John Dalton,
James Cairns, 2004

First published 2004

ARP impression 98

British Library Cataloguing in Publication Data is available
from the British Library on request.

ISBN: 978 0 435040 11 6

Illustrations by Gustavo Mazali
Cover design by mcc design ltd.
Printed and bound by Ashford Colour Press Ltd
Cover photo: © StockScotland

Acknowledgements

The authors and publishers would like to thank the following for permission to
use photographs:

P8: Pearson Index/Corbis; P9: PA; P40: John Walmsley; P66: Rex Features; P71: Pearson
Index/Photodisc; P84: Pearson Index/Photodisc; P97: Cumulus/Giraudon; The National
Gallery of Scotland/Bridgeman Art Library; P98: Getty Images UK/Digital Divison; Corbis;
P107: Rijksmuseum Van Gogh, Amsterdam zen 128682; P110: Alamy; P111: Pearson
Index/Photodisc; P113: Pearson Index /Photodisc; P145: Stilldigital; P151: Pearson
Index/Corbis; P154: Pearson Index/Photodisc; P155: ePicScotland; P157: Pearson
Index/Photodisc; P158: Pearson Index/Photodisc; P167: Corbis/Arnos Design; P169:
David Oakley/Arnos Design; P170: Pearson Index/Photodisc; P171: Pearson
Index/Photodisc; P175: Alamy; P183: Empics; P185: Britain on View; P206: Pearson
Index/Photodisc

Map of Penicuik Estate reproduced by permission of the Edinburgh Southern
Orienteering Club.

Contents

How to use this book

Every chapter is divided into sections.
Each section begins with a list of key points:

1.1 Rounding

Our numbers were developed from the Arabic system giving the digits 0–9.

An exercise follows:

Exercise 1.1

1 Round the following numbers to the nearest: (**i**) ten   (**ii**) hundred   (**iii**) thousand
   (**a**) 6172   (**b**) 18 776   (**c**) 5217

At the end of the chapter is a review exercise and a summary of all the key points.

Special instructions are shown by these symbols:

 Use a calculator to answer these questions.

1 Whole numbers and decimals

In this chapter you will learn to round numbers and practise working with numbers.

1.1 Rounding numbers

When using large numbers it is often useful to round them to give an approximation.

Example

Round 2462 to the nearest:

(a) ten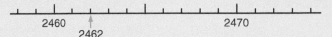

2462 is closer to 2460 than 2470

2462 rounded to the nearest ten is **2460**

(b) hundred

2462 is closer to 2500 than 2400

2462 rounded to the nearest hundred is **2500**

Exercise 1.1

1 Round the following numbers to the nearest
  (**i**) ten   (**ii**) hundred   (**iii**) thousand:
  (**a**) 6172   (**b**) 18 776   (**c**) 5217   (**d**) 126 250   (**e**) 5208
  (**f**) 37 509   (**g**) 8399   (**h**) 7257   (**i**) 129 790   (**j**) 999

2 Use the information in the table to round
  (**a**) the land areas to the nearest
      (**i**) ten
      (**ii**) hundred
  (**b**) the populations to the nearest
      (**i**) hundred
      (**ii**) thousand
      (**iii**) ten thousand.

Authority	Population	Land Area (km²)
Aberdeen City	212 125	182
Argyll & Bute	91 306	7023
Dundee City	145 663	55
Edinburgh	451 710	263
Fife	349 429	1340
Glasgow	611 440	175
Highland	208 600	25 728
Midlothian	80 941	349
Moray	2237	2237
Perth & Kinross	134 949	5395

3 The table shows the number of cars produced in 2001.
  Round each number to the nearest
  (**a**) 10 000   (**b**) 100 000   (**c**) million.

Country	Cars produced
Japan	8 117 563
Germany	5 299 700
USA	4 879 119
Spain	2 211 172
UK	1 492 138
Brazil	1 481 975

1.2 Further rounding

Numbers which include decimals can be rounded using a similar method.

Example   Round 42·625 to   (**a**) the nearest whole number
                                     (**b**) one decimal place
                                     (**c**) two decimal places.

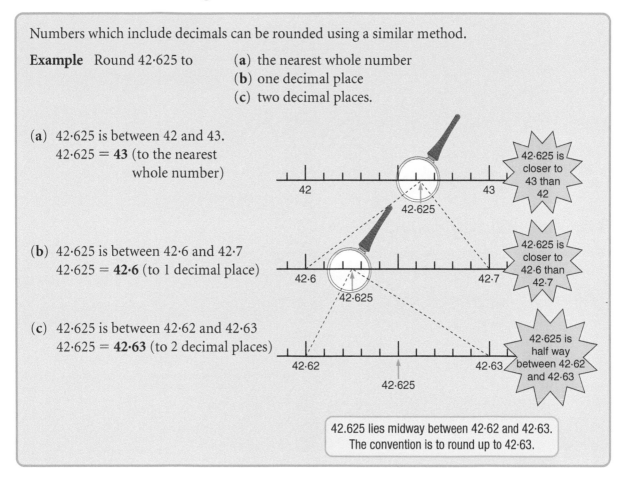

(**a**)   42·625 is between 42 and 43.
      42·625 = **43** (to the nearest
                   whole number)

> 42·625 is closer to 43 than 42

(**b**)   42·625 is between 42·6 and 42·7
      42·625 = **42·6** (to 1 decimal place)

> 42·625 is closer to 42·6 than 42·7

(**c**)   42·625 is between 42·62 and 42·63
      42·625 = **42·63** (to 2 decimal places)

> 42·625 is half way between 42·62 and 42·63

> 42.625 lies midway between 42·62 and 42·63.
> The convention is to round up to 42·63.

Exercise 1.2

1   Round the following to
    (**i**)   the nearest whole number   (**ii**)   one decimal place   (**iii**)   two decimal places:

    (**a**) 65·374   (**b**) 18·726   (**c**) 20·749   (**d**) 139·692   (**e**) 18·052   (**f**) 234·919

    (**g**) 674·599   (**h**) 239·501   (**i**) 12·155   (**j**) 18·999   (**k**) 36·207   (**l**) 18·925

2   The table shows the annual consumption per person of fizzy drinks in four countries.
    Round each figure to the nearest whole litre.

Country	Consumption (litres)
USA	214·8
Bahrain	128·2
Luxembourg	119·6
UK	85·1

3   Five classes took a survey to find the average amount spent on sweets per week.
    Round each amount to the nearest penny.

Class	Amount (p)
3S1	53·476
3S2	48·533
4S1	56·059
4S2	31·178
5S	40·983

4 The table shows the fastest
Grand Prix speeds in 2001.
Round each speed to

(**a**) 1 decimal place

(**b**) 2 decimal places.

Grand Prix	Speed (km/h)
Italy	239·103
Germany	235·351
Belgium	221·050
Austria	209·977
San Marino	202·062

5 Round to the required number of decimal places:

(**a**) 17·5376 (to 3 d.p.)   (**b**) 12·89967 (to 4 d.p.)   (**c**) 467·281231 (to 3 d.p.)

(**d**) 9·1117 (to 3 d.p.)   (**e**) 5·0029 (to 3 d.p.)   (**f**) 23·20299 (to 4 d.p.)

1.3 Working with whole numbers

Rounding helps to estimate the answers to calculations.

Example

Furry Friends cattery uses 78 grammes of food per cat per day.

(**a**) If they have 2 cats staying for 4 days how much food will they use?

(**b**) They have a 2500 gramme bag of food. How much will be left after 4 days?

Answer

(**a**)   78 × 8   (**b**)   2500 − 624

  Estimate   80 × 8 = 640 g   Estimate   2500 − 600 = 1900 g

  Calculate 78 × 8 = 624 g   Calculate 2500 − 624 = 1876 g

Exercise 1.3

For each question:
- Estimate the answer by rounding each number appropriately.
- Find the exact answer.
- Check that both answers are about the same.

1 Donna bought her house for £56 595 in 2001 and sold it in 2003 for £62 482.
How much profit did she make?

2 At the 2002 Christmas shoebox appeal 2358 boxes had to be checked. This job was
shared evenly among three people. How many boxes did they each have to check?

3 Stephanie is buying some new furniture. She buys a chest of drawers for £799,
a bookcase for £689 and four chairs at £87 each. If she has gift vouchers for £25
and £38, how much extra will she have to pay?

4 For safety reasons parcel trolleys at Quickie Couriers should not hold more than
200 kilogrammes. Robert has two parcels weighing 38 kilogrammes, five weighing
15 kilogrammes and three weighing 19 kilogrammes. Can these parcels be loaded
safely onto a trolley? Give a reason for your answer.

5 For the opening of the Commonwealth Games, 2048 dancers were split into eight groups. How many were in each group?

6 The Wilson family shop each week at Intersave where they get 3 bonus points for every £1 spent. On four visits they spend £88, £179, £93 and £96.

   (**a**) How much did they spend in total?

   (**b**) How many bonus points did they collect?

7 The number of votes for each party in a local election were 20 446, 10 866, 7994 and 5743.

   (**a**) How many people voted?

   (**b**) What was the difference between the highest and lowest number of votes?

1.4 Multiplying by multiples of 10

> **Remember**
> To multiply a number by 10, move every digit one place to the left.
> To multiply a number by 100, move every digit two places to the left.

You can use this to multiply by multiples of 10 and 100.

Example

Calculate

   (**a**) 43×200
       $= 43 \times 2 \times 100$
       $= 86 \times 100$
       $= \mathbf{8600}$

   (**b**) $12{\cdot}7 \times 50$
       $= 12{\cdot}7 \times 5 \times 10$
       $= 63{\cdot}5 \times 10$
       $= \mathbf{635}$

   (**c**) $6{\cdot}7 \times 800$
       $= 6{\cdot}7 \times 8 \times 100$
       $= 53{\cdot}6 \times 100$
       $= \mathbf{5360}$

> To multiply by 200, multiply by 2 then by 100

> To multiply by 50, multiply by 5 then by 10

> To multiply by 800, multiply by 8 then by 100

Exercise 1.4

1 Calculate:

   (**a**) 823×100
   (**b**) 450×100
   (**c**) $2{\cdot}6 \times 1000$

   (**d**) $1{\cdot}75 \times 10$
   (**e**) $2{\cdot}05 \times 100$
   (**f**) $21{\cdot}0341 \times 1000$

2 Calculate:

   (**a**) 14×30
   (**b**) 27×80
   (**c**) 182×400

   (**d**) $2{\cdot}17 \times 20$
   (**e**) $3{\cdot}9 \times 400$
   (**f**) $18{\cdot}2 \times 50$

   (**g**) 50×60
   (**h**) $8{\cdot}7 \times 5000$
   (**i**) $203{\cdot}84 \times 600$

   (**j**) 234×300
   (**k**) 1050×600
   (**l**) $2{\cdot}07 \times 90$

   (**m**) $1005{\cdot}7 \times 30$
   (**n**) 200×700
   (**o**) $2006{\cdot}1 \times 4000$

3 When Elvis was cashing up at the end of the day he counted the bank notes in the till. He had eight £50 notes, thirty-seven £20 notes, fifty-eight £10 notes and twenty-seven £5 notes. How much did he have in total?

4 A sherbet straw costs 12 pence. What would a box of 60 sherbet straws cost?

5 If £1 = €0.667, convert each of the following to euros:

 (**a**) £10 (**b**) £40 (**c**) £100 (**d**) £500

6 Unleaded petrol costs 74.9 pence per litre at the Quickstop petrol station. Find the cost, in pounds, of

 (**a**) 20 litres (**b**) 30 litres (**c**) 50 litres.

7 A basket of strawberries holds 1·15 kilogrammes. Calculate the weight of

 (**a**) 20 baskets (**b**) 600 baskets (**c**) 3000 baskets.

8 Mr Reynolds buys a new car. He pays a deposit of £650 then pays 36 instalments of £200. How much did he pay in total?

9 Orla is arranging book launches around the United Kingdom and has been given a budget of £7000 to spend. She is planning 24 launches and estimates that each launch will cost £300. Has she been given enough money? Explain your answer.

1.5 Dividing by multiples of 10

> **Remember**
> To divide a number by 10, move every digit one place to the right.
> To divide a number by 100, move every digit two places to the right.

Example

(**a**) $540 \div 30$
 $540 \div 3 = 180$
 $180 \div 10 = 18$
so **$540 \div 30 = 18$**

> To divide by 30,
> divide by 3
> then by 10

(**b**) $25 \div 500$
 $25 \div 5 = 5$
 $5 \div 100 = 0·05$
so **$25 \div 500 = 0·05$**

> To divide by 500,
> divide by 5
> then by 100

(**c**) $0·27 \div 600$
 $0·27 \div 6 = 0·045$
 $0·045 \div 100 = 0·000\,45$
so **$0·27 \div 600 = 0·000\,45$**

$$\begin{array}{r} 0·045 \\ \hline 6)\overline{0·270} \end{array}$$

> To divide by 600,
> divide by 6
> then by 100

Exercise 1.5

1 Calculate:

 (**a**) $40 \div 10$ (**b**) $1·6 \div 10$ (**c**) $108·4 \div 100$

 (**d**) $20\,800 \div 1000$ (**e**) $176 \div 1000$ (**f**) $7 \div 100$

2 Calculate:

(**a**) $460 \div 20$

(**b**) $\dfrac{960}{30}$

(**c**) $320 \div 40$

(**d**) $1610 \div 70$

(**e**) $850 \div 50$

(**f**) $\dfrac{72}{60}$

(**g**) $1 \cdot 08 \div 90$

(**h**) $4920 \div 60$

(**i**) $\dfrac{6000}{400}$

(**j**) $0 \cdot 012 \div 600$

(**k**) $\dfrac{144}{30}$

(**l**) $\dfrac{240}{4000}$

(**m**) $\dfrac{19\,200}{6000}$

(**n**) $34 \cdot 2 \div 3000$

3 The ten staff at the Heron restaurant share their tips equally. Calculate one person's share of the tips for the following days.

Friday £37.60   Saturday £56.00   Sunday £78.20

4 Robert received £167.20 from 40 sales. What was the average amount of each sale?

5 Gina's Gifts was open 6 days per week for 50 weeks. It made a profit of £57 342.

(**a**) Calculate the average profit per working day.

(**b**) Lisa worked in the shop every day it was open and earned £33.74 per day. How much did she earn in a year?

6 Mr Bell bought thirty 4500 gramme packets of rice. If he uses 900 grammes each day, how long will the rice last?

7 Emma has 5 boxes each containing 240 envelopes. She uses 60 envelopes every month to send invoices to customers. How many months will these envelopes last?

8 A car travels 20 miles per litre of fuel. How many litres would be needed to travel 450 miles?

1.6 Multiplying by two digit numbers

Example 1   A thermometer takes a reading of the air temperature 36 times an hour. How many measurements will it take in twenty four hours?

$$
\begin{array}{r}
36 \\
\times 24 \\
\hline
144 \\
720 \\
\hline
864
\end{array}
$$

$4 \times 36 = 144$

$20 \times 36 = 720$

It will take **864** measurements.

Example 2   Mr Garfield buys 52 litres of fuel at 62.7 pence per litre. How much does this cost him?

$$
\begin{array}{r}
62 \cdot 7 \\
\times 52 \\
\hline
1254 \\
31350 \\
\hline
3260 \cdot 4 \text{ pence}
\end{array}
$$

2×627

50×627

The cost is **£32.60.**

Exercise 1.6

1 Dr Elton's car travels 15 kilometres per litre of fuel. If the tank holds 46 litres, how far will it travel on a full tank?

2 Mr Rigg travels from Aberdeen to Edinburgh and back every week, a round trip of 232 miles. If he works for 46 weeks each year, how many miles will he travel in a year?

3 Twelve pupils go on a school trip which costs £145 each. If the total cost of the trip is £1644, how much will each pupil be refunded?

4 (**a**) How much would it cost to buy 7 litres of each type of fuel?

(**b**) How much would it cost to buy 23 litres of each type of fuel?

5 Louise needs 4·2 metres of wood to build one section of fence. How much wood does she need to build 35 sections?

```
Unleaded
72.9p

Diesel
65.9p

Lead replacement
77.9p
```

6 Calculate the total cost of these bills.

(**a**)
```
35 m lace @  £0.48 per metre
12 m white satin @ £3.50 per metre
26 m brocade @ £22.49 per metre
7 zips @ £1.49 each
1 packet of pins @ £0.60
                              Total
```

(**b**)
```
24 fixed price lunches @ £10.50 each
32 bottles of water @ £2.95 each
27 bottles of wine @ £8.99
18 coffees  @ £2.20 each
                              Total
```

7 Mr Antony spends £16 buying 3 crates of juice each containing 25 cans. If he sells each can for 48 pence, how much profit does he make?

8 Rachel is paid £5.62 per hour. What is her pay for a 35 hour week?

9 A crate of ginger biscuits holds 24 boxes. Each box holds 50 packets of biscuits. Each packet holds 12 biscuits. How many biscuits are in a crate?

10 What is the (**a**) largest and (**b**) smallest number you can make using the digits 1, 3, 7 and 8 and the multiplication symbol? Justify your answer.

11 Find three consecutive numbers whose product is 6840.

12 There is an old rhyme:
As I was going to St Ives I met a man with seven wives.
Each wife had seven sacks, each sack had seven cats,
each cat had seven kits.
How many were going to St Ives?

1.7 Using a calculator

Example 1

A meal for 27 people came to £421.20. If the bill was to be shared equally, how much would each person pay?

Enter $\boxed{4}\boxed{2}\boxed{1}\boxed{\cdot}\boxed{2}\boxed{0}\boxed{÷}\boxed{2}\boxed{7}\boxed{=}\boxed{15.6}$

Each person would pay **£15.60**

> Remember pounds and pence need 2 decimal places.

Example 2

Joanna buys candles costing 65 pence each.

(a) If she has £30 how many candles could she buy?

(b) How much change does she receive?

> Make sure all units are the same.

(a) Enter $\boxed{3}\boxed{0}\boxed{÷}\boxed{0}\boxed{\cdot}\boxed{6}\boxed{5}\boxed{=}\boxed{46.15384615}$

Joanna could buy **46 candles**.

> Interpret answer

(b) Enter $\boxed{4}\boxed{6}\boxed{×}\boxed{0}\boxed{\cdot}\boxed{6}\boxed{5}\boxed{=}\boxed{29.9}$

$\boxed{3}\boxed{0}\boxed{-}\boxed{2}\boxed{9}\boxed{\cdot}\boxed{9}\boxed{=}\boxed{0.1}$

Joanna receives **10 pence** change.

Exercise 1.7

Remember to estimate your answers before you calculate.

1 Ateka's phone bill showed a 40 minute phone call costing £1.327.
How much did it cost per minute? Give your answer to the nearest penny.

2 Calculate the total bill:

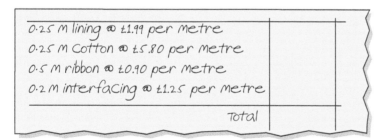

0.25 m lining @ £1.99 per metre
0.25 m cotton @ £5.80 per metre
0.5 m ribbon @ £0.90 per metre
0.2 m interfacing @ £1.25 per metre

Total

3 If £1 = €0.637, convert the following to euros giving your answer to the nearest cent:

(a) £15   (b) £35   (c) £76   (d) £54.50

4 Banchory Young Enterprise group have decided to sell T-shirts. They buy 70 plain T-shirts at £2.50 each and it costs £1.25 per T-shirt for printing. They spent £20 on advertising. If they charge £4.25 per T-shirt, how many will they have to sell before they make a profit?

5 (**a**) Calculate the cost of one gramme of cornflakes for each box.

(**b**) Which box is the best value for money? Explain your answer.

Cornflakes
500g
98p

Cornflakes
750g
£1.25

Cornflakes
1000g
£1.58

6 (**a**) Calculate the cost of one toilet roll in each pack.

(**b**) Which pack is the best value for money? Explain your answer.

Toilet rolls
4 rolls
£1.72

Toilet rolls
9 rolls
£3.69

Toilet rolls
12 rolls
£4.89

7 (**a**) Mr Abril put 20·27 litres of unleaded petrol in his car. How much did this cost him? Give your answer to the nearest penny.

(**b**) Mr Smith spent £25 on unleaded and Mr Reeves spent £25 on diesel. How many litres, to 2 decimal places, did they each buy?

Price per litre

Unleaded
76.9p

Diesel
62.9p

Lead replacement
79.9p

8 On the way home from practice the Queensferry Ski Group stopped at a chip shop. Thirteen suppers cost £24.55. How many people had chicken and how many had fish?

Fish supper £1.85
Chicken supper £1.95

1.8 Order of operations

Examples

(**i**) $3 + 7 \times 2$
$= 3 + 14$
$= \mathbf{17}$

(**ii**) $(3 + 7) \times 2$
$= 10 \times 2$
$= \mathbf{20}$

(**iii**) $31 - 27 \div 3$
$= 31 - 9$
$= \mathbf{22}$

(**iv**) $3 \times (12 - 5) + 4$
$= 3 \times 7 + 4$
$= 21 + 4$
$= \mathbf{25}$

'6 + 3 x 7 = 63'

'In mathematics, the order in which you carry out a calculation is important. The order is shown here.'

'No, I think the answer is 27.'

6 + 3 x 7

B brackets
O of
D divide
M multiply
A add
S subtract

Exercise 1.8

1 Calculate:

(**a**) $16 - 3 \times 5$

(**b**) $4 \times 27 \div 9$

(**c**) $45 + 12 \times 4$

(**d**) $220 \div 11 + 7$

(**e**) $430 + 2 \times 0$

(**f**) $28 - 51 \div 3$

2 Calculate:

(**a**) $48 \div (3 + 5)$ (**b**) $(5 + 4) \times 14$ (**c**) $(40 + 30) \div 5$

(**d**) $(27 + 21) \div 3$ (**e**) $(22 + 33) \div 11$ (**f**) $(342 - 62) \div 10$

(**g**) $600 + 3 \times 8$ (**h**) $5 \times 6 \div 2$ (**i**) $(40 \div 20) \times 3$

3 Calculate:

(**a**) $3 + 6 \times 2 + 5$ (**b**) $(4 + 3) \times 5 - 2$ (**c**) $15 - 6 \div 2 \times 4$

(**d**) $15 - 16 \div (3 + 1)$ (**e**) $3 + 6 \times 2 + 10$ (**f**) $29 - 27 \div 3 - 1$

4 Calculate:

(**a**) $(14 + 6) \times (26 - 9)$ (**b**) $(58 - 18) \times (27 + 13)$

(**c**) $(32 - 8) \div (30 - 24)$ (**d**) $(76 + 24) \div (13 + 7)$

5 Insert brackets to make the following calculations correct.

(**a**) $5 + 4 \times 8 = 37$ (**b**) $5 + 4 \times 8 = 72$ (**c**) $6 + 15 \div 3 = 11$

(**d**) $6 + 15 \div 3 = 7$ (**e**) $5 + 4 + 3 \times 7 = 54$ (**f**) $16 + 3 \times 2 + 5 = 37$

(**g**) $24 \div 4 + 2 \times 7 = 28$ (**h**) $240 \div 5 + 7 - 4 \times 3 = 8$

6 Ryan has these seven cards. He has to arrange some or all of the cards to make as many different numbers as possible. List the numbers he can make.

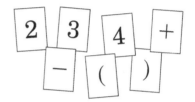

1.9 Mental calculations

Method 1	Method 2	Method 3
£5.99 × 7	15 − 16 + 12	25 × 7 × 8
£6 × 7 = £42	= 15 + 12 + − 16	= 25 × 8 × 7
Subtract 6 × 1p	= 27 − 16	= 200 × 7
So, £5.99 × 7 = **£41.94**	= **11**	= **1400**

Re-arrange the numbers to make the problem simpler.

Exercise 1.9

Double CDs	**£12.99**	Single CDs	**£9.99**
Second hand CDs	**£4.99**	Discount CDs	**£6.99**
Cassettes	**£6.99**	DVDs	**£17.99**

1 What is the total cost of

(**a**) a DVD and a single CD (**b**) 8 cassettes (**c**) 9 single CDs

(**d**) 2 DVDs and 3 single CDs (**e**) 3 double CDs and 4 discount CDs?

2 Calculate:

(**a**) $30 - 16 + 28$ (**b**) $150 - 72 + 18$ (**c**) $109 - 72 + 63$

(**d**) $25 - 3 + 7 - 21$ (**e**) $12 - 9 + 21 - 3$ (**f**) $72 - 6 + 12 - 9$

(**g**) $54 - 18 - 23 + 17$ (**h**) $38 - 12 + 15 - 27$ (**i**) $43 - 17 + 24 - 11$

3 Calculate:

(a) $4 \times 3 \times 25$ (b) $2 \times 4 \times 75$ (c) $5 \times 18 \times 2$ (d) $6 \times 3 \times 5$

(e) $7 \times 5 \times 4$ (f) $25 \times 3 \times 8$ (g) $15 \times 7 \times 4$ (h) $12 \times 3 \times 5$

(i) $8 \times 4 \times 5$ (j) $36 \times 2 \times 5$ (k) $8 \times 6 \times 25$ (l) $15 \times 5 \times 4$

4 Calculate:

(a) $22 + 4 \times 5$ (b) $73 \times 100 - 250$ (c) $1000 - 50 \times 20$ (d) $67 + 16 \times 3$

(e) $108 - 72 \div 9$ (f) $75 - 66 \div 3$ (g) $(27 + 42) \times 100$ (h) $(125 - 45) \div 5$

(i) $6 \times (17 + 23)$ (j) $240 \div (23 - 17)$ (k) $250 \times (3 + 7)$ (l) $(6 + 1) \times (5 - 1)$

Review exercise 1

1 Round the following numbers to the nearest
(i) hundred   (ii) thousand   (iii) ten thousand:

(a) 2 472 654   (b) 8 774 203   (c) 3 999 290   (d) 4 798 294

2 Round the following numbers to
(i) the nearest whole number   (ii) 1 decimal place   (iii) 2 decimal places:

(a) 1·4873   (b) 4·746   (c) 10·0725   (d) 0·0479   (e) 60·09733   (f) 99·995

3 Jenna uses 2·7 metres of material to make a bridesmaid's dress. How much will she need to make 8 dresses?

4 Mr Crick has £263.42 in his account. His weekly wage of £547.60 is paid in to the bank and he pays a bill for £176.33. How much money will be in his account after this?

5 The times for the 100 metre men's freestyle swimming competition are shown on the table.

(a) List the times in order from fastest to slowest.

(b) What was the difference in time between the fastest and slowest competitors?

Country	Time (seconds)
Netherlands	47·84
USA	48·77
UK	48·09
France	47·96
Spain	48·50
Italy	48·06

6 Mrs Brown uses these ingredients to make 3 cakes. How much of each ingredient was used for one cake?

1·65 kg flour
1·26 kg sugar
6 eggs
1·68 kg butter

7 Mr and Mrs Green bought 5 identical tyres for £240. How much did one tyre cost?

8 A group of 8 friends have a meal which costs £185.36. They decide to share the bill equally. Find the cost per person.

9 Calculate:

(a) 37×200 (b) 14×80 (c) 2.7×30 (d) 0.12×5000 (e) 116×40 (f) 12.2×600

10 Calculate:

(a) $27 \div 300$ (b) $68 \div 2000$ (c) $126 \div 70$ (d) $0.56 \div 70$ (e) $32.1 \div 30$ (f) $23.2 \div 800$

11 Calculate:

(**a**) $450 - 6 \times 9$ (**b**) $17 + 5 \times 26$ (**c**) $13 - 48 \div 8$

(**d**) $4 \times (23 + 19)$ (**e**) $16 \times (27 - 18)$ (**f**) $(27 + 22) \div 7$

12 A lift carries a maximum of 1000 kilogrammes.
Andrew has 28 boxes each weighing 16 kilogrammes.
Will the lift be able to carry all the boxes? Justify your answer.

13 Alfred buys 27 litres of petrol at 72·9 pence per litre. How much did this cost? Give your answer to the nearest penny.

14 If 1 euro = 8·52 Hong Kong dollars, convert 250 euros into Hong Kong dollars.

15 (**a**) Calculate the cost of one gramme of flour for each packet.

(**b**) Which packet is the best value for money? Explain your answer.

Flour
250g
98p

Flour
500g
£1.25

Flour
1000g
£1.58

Summary

Rounding numbers

64·739 is 65 to the nearest whole number
      is 64·7 to one decimal place
      is 64·74 to two decimal places

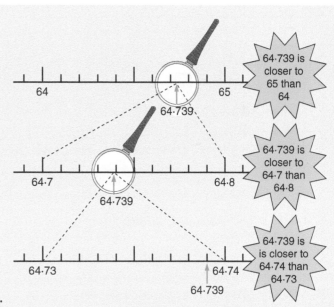

64·739 is closer to 65 than 64

64·739 is closer to 64·7 than 64·8

64·739 is is closer to 64·74 than 64·73

Multiplying by multiples of 10

To multiply a number by 10, move every digit one place to the left.
To multiply a number by 100, move every digit two places to the left.
To multiply by 20, multiply by 2 then by 10.
To multiply by 300, multiply by 3 then by 100.

Division by multiples of 10

To divide a number by 10, move every digit one place to the right.
To divide a number by 100, move every digit two places to the right.
To divide by 20, divide by 2 then by 10.
To divide by 300, divide by 3 then by 100.

Order of operations

B Brackets   **O** of   **D** divide   **M** multiply   **A** add   **S** subtract

2 Sequences, multiples and factors

In this chapter you will learn about sequences of numbers and extend your knowledge of multiples and factors.

2.1 Sequences

A **sequence** is a list of numbers that are in a particular order.
The numbers in a sequence are called **terms**.
Each term is connected to the next using the same rule.

$$1, 3, 5, 7, 9, 11, 13, 15, \ldots$$

The 4th term is 7.   The 9th term will be 17.

Example

Sequence	Rule
0, 5, 10, 15, 20, 25, ...	add 5 to find the next term
2, 6, 18, 54, 162, 486, ...	multiply by 3 to find the next term

Exercise 2.1

1 For the sequence   2, 4, 6, 8, 10, 12, 14, 16, ... find

(**a**) the 3rd term   (**b**) the 6th term   (**c**) the 9th term

2 Copy these sequences, filling in the missing numbers.

(**a**) 4, 7, 10, 13, __ , __ , __ , 25, ...

(**b**) 5, 12, 19, 26, __ , __ , __ , 54, ...

(**c**) 38, 34, 30, 26, __ , __ , __ , 10, ...

(**d**) 85, 73, 61, 49, __ , __ , __ , 1, ...

(**e**) 1, 3, 9, 27, __ , __ , __ , 2187, ...

(**f**) 64, 32, 16, 8, __ , __ , __ , $\frac{1}{2}$, ...

3 For each sequence in question 2 write the rule which gives the next term.

4 Write the first **six** terms in each sequence.

	First term	Rule		First term	Rule
(**a**)	3	add 5	(**i**)	0	add 10
(**b**)	8	add 9	(**j**)	0.1	add 0.5
(**c**)	50	subtract 6	(**k**)	99	subtract 9
(**d**)	92	subtract 11	(**l**)	7000	subtract 500
(**e**)	2	multiply by 2	(**m**)	5	multiply by 1
(**f**)	729	divide by 3	(**n**)	208	divide by 2
(**g**)	1	multiply by 10	(**o**)	96	multiply by $\frac{1}{2}$
(**h**)	42	subtract 5	(**p**)	0	add $\frac{1}{4}$

5 For each sequence find:
   (**i**) the 1st term   (**ii**) the 6th term   (**iii**) the 7th term

   (**a**) 5, 11, 17, 23, …   (**b**) 56, 51, 46, 41, …   (**c**) 3, 6, 12, 24, …

   (**d**) 10 000, 1 000, 100, 10, …   (**e**) 1, 3, 6, 10, 15, …   (**f**) 2, 3, 5, 9, 17, …

6 Find the next three numbers in each of these special sequences.
   (**a**) Triangular numbers

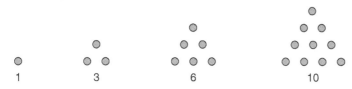

   (**b**) Rectangular numbers

   (**c**) Square numbers

7 The following are called Fibonacci sequences.
   (**i**) 2, 3, 5, 8, 13, 21, …   (**ii**) 1, 5, 6, 11, 17, 28, …
   (**iii**) 10, 12, 22, 34, 56, …   (**iv**) 20, 22, 42, 64, …

   (**a**) Copy each sequence and write the next two terms.

   (**b**) Explain the rule for finding the next term in all Fibonacci sequences.

8 Here is the start of Pascal's triangle.

   Copy the triangle and complete the next three lines.

9 Billy Smart is given £0.25 pocket money in July. This is doubled each month for the rest of the year. How much money should Billy receive in December?

2.2 Multiples and factors

The **multiples** of 8 are 8, 16, 24, 32, 40, 48, …
The multiples of 6 are 6, 12, 18, 24, 30, …
The lowest number common to both lists is 24.
24 is the **lowest common multiple** of 8 and 6.

The **factors** of 45 are 1, 3, 5, 9, 15, 45
The factors of 30 are 1, 2, 3, 5, 6, 10, 15, 30
The biggest number common to both lists is 15.
15 is the **highest common factor** of 45 and 30.

> Use factor pairs to find all factors:
> 16 = 1 × 16
>   = 2 × 8
>   = 4 × 4
> Factors of 16 are 1, 2, 4, 8, 16

Exercise 2.2

1 Write down all the multiples of 4 between 30 and 70.

2 Write down all the multiples of 7 between 50 and 100.

3 (**a**) Which of these numbers are multiples of 6?
2, 16, 28, 18, 52, 48, 70, 86, 108

(**b**) Which of these numbers are multiples of 9?
19, 81, 32, 36, 54, 87, 117, 134, 162

4 Write:

(**a**) a multiple of 6 which is between 32 and 39

(**b**) the three smallest multiples of 5 which are even

(**c**) the smallest multiple of 8 which is over 50

(**d**) the smallest number which is a multiple of 3 and 5

(**e**) the smallest number which is a multiple of 8 and 9

(**f**) the smallest number which is a multiple of 4 and 7

(**g**) an odd multiple of 4.

5 Find the lowest common multiple of

(**a**) 2 and 5   (**b**) 4 and 9   (**c**) 2 and 6   (**d**) 2, 3 and 5   (**e**) 3, 7 and 8.

6 The Olympic Games take place every 4 years. The Halbridge charity
cycle race takes place every 5 years. Both events take place in the year 2000.
What is the next year they will both take place?

7 At Gorton's factory the tablet mixture is stirred every two minutes, a
sample is taken every three minutes and a batch of tablet is made
every five minutes. If all three things happen together at 11 am, when
is the next time they will happen together?

8 At the side of a road there is a lamp post every 7 metres, a
fence post every 2 metres and a speed sign every 15 metres.
Jane sees all three objects at the same place. How far will she
have to walk before she sees all three objects together again?

9 12, 15, 60, 40, 3, 8, 1, 9

   Which of the above numbers are factors of

   (**a**) 60   (**b**) 45   (**c**) both 60 and 45?

10 Write all the factors of

   (**a**) 12   (**b**) 48   (**c**) 100

   (**d**) 5   (**e**) 27   (**f**) 56.

11 (**a**) Write all the common factors of

   (**i**) 20 and 28   (**ii**) 45 and 36
   (**iii**) 18 and 42   (**iv**) 15 and 75.

   (**b**) Find the highest common factor of

   (**i**) 20 and 28   (**ii**) 45 and 36
   (**iii**) 18 and 42   (**iv**) 15 and 75.

12 Find the highest common factor of

   (**a**) 7 and 35   (**b**) 16 and 56   (**c**) 36 and 72   (**d**) 24 and 56.

13 What is the smallest number which has eight factors?

14 (**a**) What is the smallest number which has three factors?

   (**b**) Find another three numbers which have an odd number of factors.

   (**c**) Do you notice anything about the answers to part (**a**) and (**b**)?
        Explain your answer.

15 How many factors has   (**a**) 100   (**b**) 360?

16 Find all the possible whole number dimensions for a rectangle with an area of

   (**a**) 120 cm^2 (**b**) 400 cm^2 (**c**) 620 cm^2.

2.3 Prime numbers

Exercise 2.3

1 On 1 cm squared paper draw a square 10 cm by 10 cm
   and number the boxes from 1 to 100 as indicated.

   Use a coloured pencil and shade in the following sets of
   numbers in your sieve:

   (**a**) the number 1

   (**b**) the multiples of 2 but not 2 itself

   (**c**) the multiples of 3 but not 3 itself

   (**d**) the multiples of 5 but not 5 itself

   (**e**) the multiples of 7 but not 7 itself.

The Sieve of Eratosthenes

1	2	3	4	5	6	7	8	9	10
11	12	13	14						
21	22								

2 List the numbers which are left in your sieve.

These numbers are called **prime numbers**.
A prime number has exactly two factors.

2.4 Prime factors

A **prime factor** is a factor which is also a prime number.

Example 1

Find the prime factors of 30.

$$30 = 5 \times 6$$
$$= 5 \times 2 \times 3$$

The prime factors of 30 are **2, 3** and **5**.

Example 2

Find the prime factors of 48.

$$48 = 6 \times 8$$
$$= 2 \times 3 \times 2 \times 4$$
$$= 2 \times 3 \times 2 \times 2 \times 2$$

The prime factors of 48 are **2** and **3**.

Exercise 2.4

1 (**a**) Copy and complete:

$$60 = 6 \times 10 \qquad 60 = 5 \times 12 \qquad\qquad 60 = 4 \times \blacksquare$$
$$= 2 \times 3 \times 2 \times \blacksquare \qquad = 5 \times \blacksquare \times \blacksquare \qquad = 2 \times \blacksquare \times \blacksquare \times \blacksquare$$
$$= 5 \times \blacksquare \times \blacksquare \times \blacksquare$$

(**b**) List the prime factors of 60.

2 Find the prime factors of each of these numbers.

(**a**) 45   (**b**) 72   (**c**) 81   (**d**) 84   (**e**) 78   (**f**) 64

(**g**) 125   (**h**) 126   (**i**) 420   (**j**) 230   (**k**) 273   (**l**) 1080

2.5 Squares and cubes

1, 4, 9, 16, 25, … are called square numbers.
To square a number, multiply it by itself.
$3^2 = 3 \times 3 = 9$ 3^2 is read as 'three squared'.

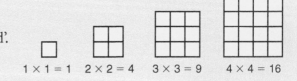

$1 \times 1 = 1$ $2 \times 2 = 4$ $3 \times 3 = 9$ $4 \times 4 = 16$

Exercise 2.5

1 Find:

(**a**) 5^2 (**b**) 8^2 (**c**) 6^2 (**d**) 1^2 (**e**) 7^2

(**f**) 12^2 (**g**) 0^2 (**h**) 11^2 (**i**) 100^2 (**j**) 15^2

2 Match the following numbers to their squares.

169	196	25	81	400	10 000

20^2	13^2	9^2	5^2	100^2	14^2

3 Which of these numbers are square?

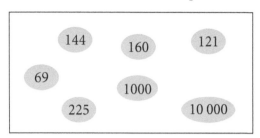

144   160   121

69   1000

225   10 000

4 Make two square numbers using all the digits 6, 5, 2.

5 Find all the square numbers between 400 and 500 inclusive.

6 Use the diagram below to copy and complete this list of cubic numbers up to 10^3.

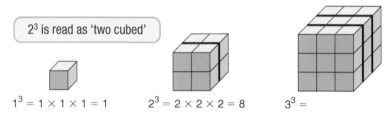

2^3 is read as 'two cubed'

$1^3 = 1 \times 1 \times 1 = 1$ $2^3 = 2 \times 2 \times 2 = 8$ $3^3 =$

7 Match the following numbers to their cubes:

125	8000	1	64	1000	27
20^3	4^3	10^3	3^3	5^3	1^3

8 Find:
  (**a**) 2^2 (**b**) 6^2 (**c**) 13^2 (**d**) 6^3 (**e**) 1^3
  (**f**) 2^3 (**g**) 10^3 (**h**) 30^2 (**i**) 600^2 (**j**) 4^3

9 You can build up a pattern using square tiles.

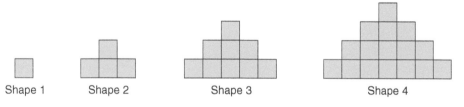

Shape 1   Shape 2   Shape 3   Shape 4

  (**a**) Draw the next two shapes in the pattern.
  (**b**) Count the number of tiles in each shape and put your results in a table.

Shape number	1	2	3	4
Tiles				

  (**c**) How many tiles would be in
      (**i**) shape 5   (**ii**) shape 9   (**iii**) shape 15?
  (**d**) Without drawing, explain how to find the number of tiles when you know the number of the shape.

10 This pattern is built up using square tiles.

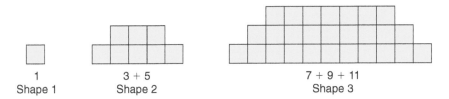

1	3 + 5
Shape 1	Shape 2

7 + 9 + 11
Shape 3

(**a**) Draw the next two shapes in the pattern.

(**b**) Count the number of tiles in each shape and put your results in a table.

Shape number	1	2	3	4
Tiles				

(**c**) How many tiles would be in
(**i**) shape 5   (**ii**) shape 7   (**iii**) shape 10?

(**d**) Without drawing, explain how to find the number of tiles when you know the number of the shape.

2.6 Number puzzles

Exercise 2.6

1 Find the missing numbers in these calculations.

(**a**)
$$\begin{array}{r} 3\;\blacksquare \\ \times\;\;7 \\ \hline \blacksquare 5\,9 \end{array}$$

(**b**)
$$\begin{array}{r} 3\,4\,\blacksquare \\ +\;\blacksquare 2\,5 \\ \hline 5\,\blacksquare 1 \end{array}$$

(**c**)
$$\begin{array}{r} \blacksquare 5\,\blacksquare \\ \times\;\;\;\;7 \\ \hline 2\,\blacksquare\,\blacksquare 1 \end{array}$$

(**d**)
$$\begin{array}{r} \blacksquare 5\,8\,\blacksquare \\ -\;\,1\,9\,\blacksquare 9 \\ \hline 3\,\blacksquare 7\,7 \end{array}$$

2 The total of every row, column and diagonal is equal on a magic square. Copy and complete these magic squares.

(**a**)
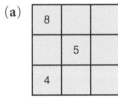

Total = 15

(**b**)
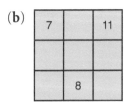

Total = 30

(**c**)
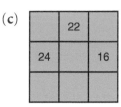

Total = 60

3 Farmer Bell is picking apples. He finds that the number of apples could be divided by 2, 3, 4, 5, 6 and 7. What is the minimum number of apples he picked?

4 Cassie finds a page of three pence stamps and a page of eight pence stamps. She can use them to create different postage values, for example

$$14p = 3p + 3p + 8p$$

What values of stamps could she **not** make?

5 Use the listed numbers to complete each diagram so that the total of each side is the same.

(**a**) 5, 6, 7, 8, 9, 10

(**b**) 0, 1, 2, 3, 4, 5, 7, 9

(**c**) 9, 11, 12, 15, 17, 18, 19, 20

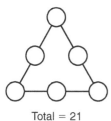

Total = 21

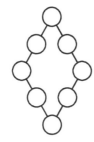

Total = 13

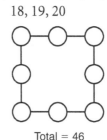

Total = 46

6 This magic square has had two pairs of numbers swapped. Can you correct it?

6	13	8
11	12	5
10	7	9

7 Use the clues below to find the numbers.

(**a**) This number, greater than one, is a square and cubic number.

(**b**) Doubling this number will give the same answer as squaring.

(**c**) This number is the smallest palindromic square number.

(**d**) This number is a three digit odd square number whose digit sum is nine and whose last digit is larger than the first.

> Something which reads the same backwards as forwards is called **palindromic**. For example 686.

8 Find four consecutive numbers whose sum is 130.

Review exercise 2

1 Write (**i**) the next two numbers in each sequence and
     (**ii**) a rule to find the next number.

(**a**) 3, 10, 17, 24, …

(**b**) 100, 89, 78, 67, …

(**c**) 1, 4, 16, 64, …

(**d**) 729, 243, 81, 27, …

2 Write the first six terms in each sequence.

	First term	Rule
(**a**)	17	add 9
(**b**)	99	subtract 9
(**c**)	23	multiply by 1
(**d**)	3125	divide by 5

3 For each sequence write the 3rd, 5th and 7th terms.

(**a**) 2, 4, 8, 16, …

(**b**) 1, 4, 5, 9, …

4 Copy this list of numbers.
Put a circle round the prime numbers and a square round the square numbers.

2, 4, 6, 7, 10, 11, 12, 13, 16, 19, 20, 24, 27, 29

5 (a) Which of these numbers are multiples of
  (i) 4   (ii) 9?
 (b) Which of these numbers are factors of
  (i) 32   (ii) 48?

2	4	8	9
12	16	24	27
32	45	48	63

6 Find the lowest common multiple of
  (a) 6 and 9   (b) 2, 4 and 10   (c) 2, 5 and 7.

7 Find the highest common factor of
  (a) 12 and 18   (b) 27 and 36   (c) 24 and 60.

8 Find:
  (a) the smallest even multiple of 7
  (b) the smallest multiple of 9 which is between 110 and 120
  (c) a number which is a multiple of 6 and 5.

9 Find the lowest common multiple of
  (a) 5 and 7   (b) 3 and 8   (c) 4 and 6   (d) 8 and 10.

10 Find:
  (a) 5^2 (b) 8^2 (c) 10^2 (d) 11^2 (e) 15^2
  (f) 3^3 (g) 1^3 (h) 2^3 (i) 10^3 (j) 50^2.

Summary

Sequence

A **sequence** is a list of numbers which are in a particular order.

Sequence	Rule
3, 8, 13, 18, 23, …	add 5 to find the next number

Multiples and factors

Multiples of 6 are 6, 12, 18, 24, 30, 36, …
Multiples of 8 are 8, 16, 24, 32, 40, 48, …
The lowest common multiple of 6 and 8 is 24.

The factors of 30 are 1, 30, 2, 15, 3, 10, 5, 6
The factors of 54 are 1, 54, 2, 27, 3, 18, 6, 9
The highest common factor of 30 and 54 is 6.

Prime numbers and factors

A prime number has exactly two factors.
A prime factor is a factor which is also a prime number.

Square and cubic numbers

$8^2 = 8 \times 8 = 64$
64 is called a square number.
The square numbers are 1, 4, 9, 16, 25, 36, 49, …

$2^3 = 2 \times 2 \times 2 = 8$
8 is called a cubic number.
The cubic numbers are 1, 8, 27, 64, 125, …

3 Symmetry

In this chapter you will learn about axes of symmetry, bilateral and rotational symmetry.

3.1 Axes of symmetry

The dotted line cuts this shape in half so that one half will fold exactly onto the other.

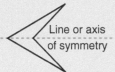

Line or axis of symmetry

This is called a **line of symmetry**.
or **axis of symmetry**.

Some shapes have more than one line of symmetry.

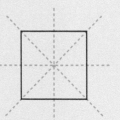

Exercise 3.1

1 List any shapes that you can see in the room which have a line or lines of symmetry.

2 How many axes of symmetry could be drawn on each shape?

   (a)   **(b)**   **(c)**  **(d)**  **(e)**   **(f)**

3 Which of the following pictures have an axis of symmetry?

   (a)   **(b)**   **(c)**  **(d)**  **(e)**

   (f)   **(g)** 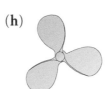 **(h)**   **(i)**   **(j)**

4 How many axes of symmetry could you draw on each shape below?

   (a)  **(b)**   **(c)**   **(d)**   **(e)**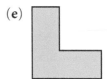

   (f)   **(g)**   **(h)** 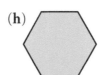 **(i)**   **(j)**

5 Draw these shapes and all possible axes of symmetry.

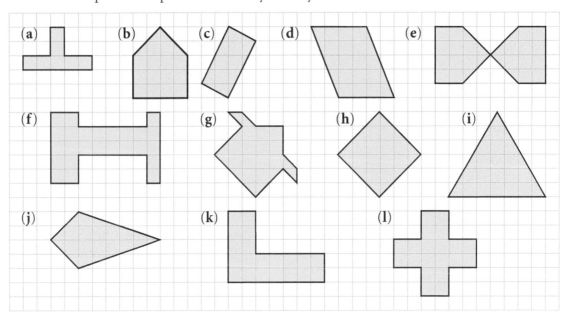

3.2 Reflection

If you place a mirror on an axis of symmetry you can see the full shape.

This is called **reflection**.

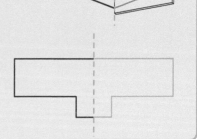

You can use **reflection** to find the missing half of a shape.

The completed shape is said to have **bilateral symmetry** about the dotted line.

Exercise 3.2

1 Sketch and complete the following shapes using reflection.

   (**a**)   (**b**)   (**c**)   (**d**)

2 Copy and complete the following shapes using reflection.

   (**a**)   (**b**)   (**c**)

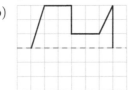 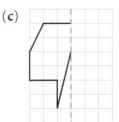

3 Complete the shapes so that they have bilateral symmetry about the axis.

(a)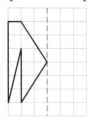

(b)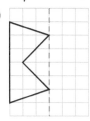

(c)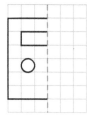

(d)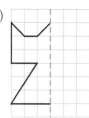

(e)

(f)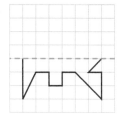

(g)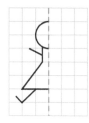

(h)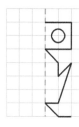

(i)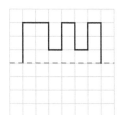

(j)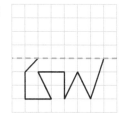

(k)

(l)

3.3 Images

The reflection of a point or a shape is called its **image**.

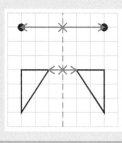

The point and its image are the same distance from the line of symmetry.

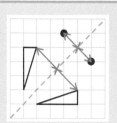

Exercise 3.3

Copy and complete the diagrams showing all images under reflection.

1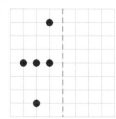

2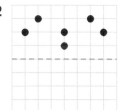

3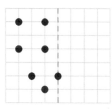

4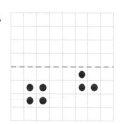

5

6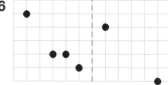

7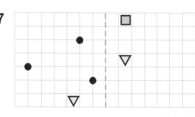

8

9

10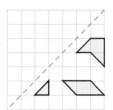

11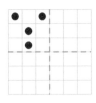

12

13

14

3.4 Image notation

The image of a point A under reflection in a line of symmetry is denoted by A′.

Example The image of PQR is P′Q′R′.

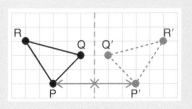

Exercise 3.4

1 Copy and complete each diagram to show all images under reflection in the axes.

(a)

(b)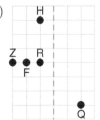

(c)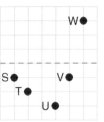

(d)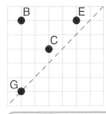

G and G′ are the same point

2 Copy and complete to show the images under reflection.

(a)

(b)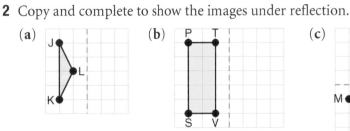

(c)

(d)

(e)

(f)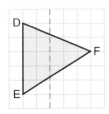

(g)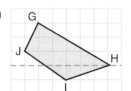

(h)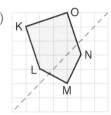

3.5 Rotational symmetry

A shape which can be rotated about its central point to fit its own outline has **rotational symmetry**.

A rectangle, given a half turn about its centre, fits its own outline.

This is called **half-turn symmetry**.
A rectangle has **rotational symmetry of order** 2.

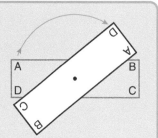

 This shape fits its own outline in 8 different positions.

It has rotational symmetry of order 8.

Exercise 3.5

1 Which of the following shapes have half-turn symmetry?

(**a**)    (**b**)   (**c**)   (**d**)   (**e**)

(**f**)   (**g**)   (**h**)

(**i**)   (**j**)   (**k**)

(**l**)   (**m**)   (**n**)   (**o**)

2 For each shape in question 1 with rotational symmetry, state the order.

3 (**a**) Write the capital letters of the alphabet which have half-turn symmetry.
 (**b**) Write the order of symmetry below each letter.

4 (**a**) What do you think is meant by 'quarter-turn symmetry'?
 (**b**) Draw some shapes with quarter-turn symmetry.

3.6 Rotating shapes

A shape may be rotated about a fixed point.

Example   Rotate each shape 180° about the fixed point.

(a) 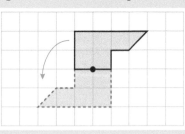   (b)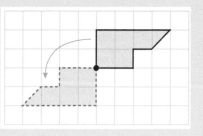

Exercise 3.6

You may use tracing paper for this exercise.
Copy and complete each diagram. Rotate each shape 180° about the fixed point.

1   2   3   4

5   6   7   8

9   10 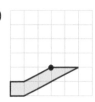   11 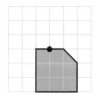   12

13 Rotate each shape 90°, 180° and 270° about the fixed point.

(a)   (b)   (c)   (d)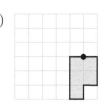

Review exercise 3

1 Which of the following shapes have at least one line of symmetry?

(a)    (b)    (c) 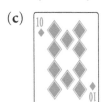   (d)

2 How many axes of symmetry could be drawn on each object?

(a)   (b)   (c)    (d)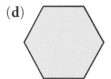

3 Copy these shapes and draw all axes of symmetry.

(a)   (b)   (c) 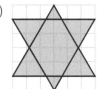   (d)

4 Copy the diagram and draw the image of each shape under reflection in the line of symmetry.

(a)   (b) 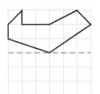   (c)    (d)

5 State the order of rotational symmetry for each of the following.

(a)   (b)   (c)   (d)

6 Copy each diagram and draw the image.

(a)   (b) 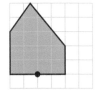   (c)   (d)

Rotate 180° about the fixed point.   Rotate 180° about the fixed point.   Rotate 180° about the fixed point.   Rotate 90°, 180° and 270° about the fixed point.

Summary

Axes of symmetry

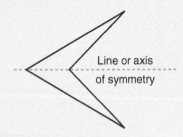

Line or axis of symmetry

Some shapes have more than one line of symmetry.

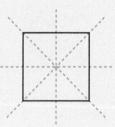

Reflection

Reflection may be used to complete the missing half of a symmetrical shape.

These shapes are said to have **bilateral symmetry**.

The reflection of a point or a shape is called its **image**.

P′, Q′ and R′ are the images of P, Q, R.

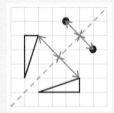 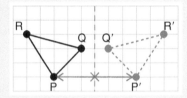

Rotational symmetry

A shape which can be rotated about its central point to fit its own outline has **rotational symmetry**.

A rectangle, given a half-turn about its centre, fits its own outline.

This is called **half-turn symmetry**.

A rectangle has rotational symmetry of order 2.

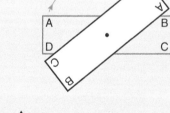

A shape with quarter-turn symmetry has rotational symmetry of order 4.

Order 4   **Order 3**   **Order 6**

Rotation

A shape may be rotated about a fixed point.

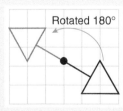

Rotated 180°

4 Fractions

In this chapter you will extend your knowledge of fractions to include equivalent fractions, fractions of quantities, decimal equivalence and the four operations.

4.1 Equivalent fractions

Multiplying the numerator and denominator of a fraction by the same number gives an **equivalent fraction**.

> The **numerator** is on the **top** and the **denominator** is on the **bottom**.

$$\frac{7}{8} \xlongequal{\times 3} \frac{21}{24}$$ (×3)

$$\frac{2}{5} \xlongequal{\times 5} \frac{10}{25}$$ (×5)

$\frac{7}{8}$ and $\frac{21}{24}$ are equivalent fractions.

$\frac{7}{8} = \frac{21}{24}$

$\frac{2}{5}$ and $\frac{10}{25}$ are equivalent fractions.

$\frac{2}{5} = \frac{10}{25}$

Exercise 4.1

1 Copy and complete by filling in the missing numbers.

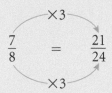

(a) ×3
$$\frac{1}{3} = \frac{3}{9}$$ ×☐

(b) ×5
$$\frac{3}{5} = \frac{15}{25}$$ ×☐

(c) ×☐
$$\frac{3}{8} = \frac{30}{80}$$ ×10

(d) ×☐
$$\frac{5}{8} = \frac{30}{48}$$ ×☐

(e) ×☐
$$\frac{4}{9} = \frac{36}{81}$$ ×☐

(f) ×☐
$$\frac{9}{10} = \frac{54}{60}$$ ×☐

2 Copy and complete:

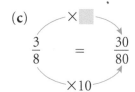

(a) $\dfrac{5}{8} = \dfrac{\square}{16}$

(b) $\dfrac{3}{10} = \dfrac{\square}{30}$

(c) $\dfrac{9}{10} = \dfrac{36}{\square}$

(d) $\dfrac{1}{4} = \dfrac{7}{\square}$

(e) $\dfrac{5}{9} = \dfrac{45}{\square}$

(f) $\dfrac{6}{11} = \dfrac{\square}{55}$

(g) $\dfrac{2}{3} = \dfrac{6}{\square} = \dfrac{\square}{45}$

(h) $\dfrac{3}{4} = \dfrac{\square}{16} = \dfrac{24}{\square}$

3 Taking one from each list, find pairs of equivalent fractions.

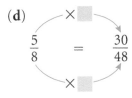

List A $\frac{1}{6}, \frac{3}{7}, \frac{5}{9}, \frac{7}{8}, \frac{12}{18}, \frac{45}{50}, \frac{6}{15}, \frac{15}{20}$ List B $\frac{9}{10}, \frac{2}{12}, \frac{3}{4}, \frac{12}{28}, \frac{2}{5}, \frac{14}{16}, \frac{2}{3}, \frac{20}{36}$

4 (a) Write these fractions as twelfths and list them from smallest to largest: $\frac{3}{4}, \frac{5}{12}, \frac{2}{3}, \frac{5}{6}$.

(b) Which is greater, $\frac{2}{3}$ or $\frac{3}{4}$?   (c) What fraction is midway between $\frac{1}{4}$ and $\frac{1}{3}$?

4.2 Simplest form

To simplify a fraction **divide** numerator and denominator by the same number.

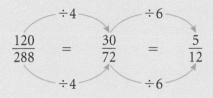

$$\frac{35}{56} = \frac{5}{8}$$

To express a fraction in **simplest form** divide more than once if necessary.

Example

Express $\frac{120}{288}$ in simplest form.

$$\frac{120}{288} = \frac{30}{72} = \frac{5}{12}$$

Exercise 4.2

1 Simplify these fractions where possible.

(a) $\frac{5}{10}$ (b) $\frac{7}{14}$ (c) $\frac{3}{9}$ (d) $\frac{5}{18}$ (e) $\frac{11}{33}$ (f) $\frac{3}{30}$ (g) $\frac{5}{25}$

(h) $\frac{7}{49}$ (i) $\frac{15}{20}$ (j) $\frac{9}{12}$ (k) $\frac{14}{49}$ (l) $\frac{3}{39}$ (m) $\frac{9}{56}$ (n) $\frac{17}{51}$

2 Express these fractions in simplest form. (Some may already be in simplest form.)

(a) $\frac{16}{72}$ (b) $\frac{20}{60}$ (c) $\frac{70}{120}$ (d) $\frac{21}{70}$ (e) $\frac{40}{48}$ (f) $\frac{48}{84}$ (g) $\frac{12}{29}$ (h) $\frac{24}{108}$

(i) $\frac{32}{112}$ (j) $\frac{350}{560}$ (k) $\frac{60}{160}$ (l) $\frac{31}{72}$ (m) $\frac{63}{72}$ (n) $\frac{24}{96}$ (o) $\frac{52}{78}$ (p) $\frac{37}{74}$

(q) $\frac{30}{105}$ (r) $\frac{24}{72}$ (s) $\frac{36}{96}$ (t) $\frac{54}{90}$ (u) $\frac{25}{625}$ (v) $\frac{47}{81}$ (w) $\frac{144}{168}$ (x) $\frac{108}{120}$

3 In a bag of 80 marbles, 20 are red.
In simplest form, what fraction is red?

4 There are 18 girls in a class of 30 pupils.

(a) What fraction are girls?

(b) What fraction are boys?

5 There are 270 pupils in first year.

(a) If 45 travel by train, what fraction is this?

(b) What fraction do not travel by train?

4.3 Simple adding and subtracting

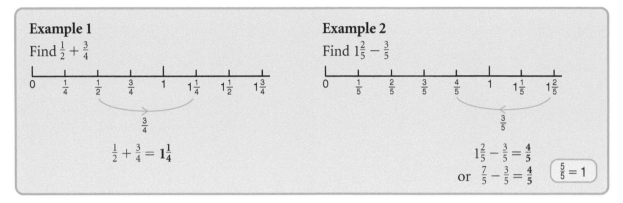

Example 1

Find $\frac{1}{2} + \frac{3}{4}$

$$\frac{1}{2} + \frac{3}{4} = 1\frac{1}{4}$$

Example 2

Find $1\frac{2}{5} - \frac{3}{5}$

$$1\frac{2}{5} - \frac{3}{5} = \frac{4}{5}$$

or $\frac{7}{5} - \frac{3}{5} = \frac{4}{5}$ $\boxed{\frac{5}{5} = 1}$

Exercise 4.3

1 Find:

(a) $\frac{1}{4} + \frac{1}{4}$ (b) $\frac{1}{2} - \frac{1}{4}$ (c) $\frac{1}{4} + \frac{1}{2}$ (d) $\frac{3}{4} - \frac{1}{4}$ (e) $1 - \frac{1}{2}$ (f) $1 - \frac{1}{4}$

(g) $\frac{1}{4} + \frac{3}{4}$ (h) $1 - \frac{3}{4}$ (i) $\frac{3}{4} + \frac{3}{4}$ (j) $1\frac{1}{4} - \frac{1}{2}$ (k) $1\frac{1}{2} - \frac{3}{4}$ (l) $\frac{1}{2} + \frac{3}{4}$

(m) $\frac{1}{5} + \frac{3}{5}$ (n) $\frac{6}{7} - \frac{4}{7}$ (o) $\frac{1}{3} + \frac{2}{3}$ (p) $\frac{7}{9} - \frac{5}{9}$ (q) $\frac{5}{6} + \frac{5}{6}$ (r) $1\frac{3}{8} + \frac{7}{8}$

2 (a) What weight is left if $\frac{1}{2}$ kg of cheese is cut from a $\frac{3}{4}$ kg piece?

(b) What is the total weight of two pieces of butter each $\frac{3}{5}$ kg?

(c) Three bottles of lemonade contain $\frac{2}{3}$ litre, $1\frac{1}{3}$ litres and $2\frac{2}{3}$ litres.
Find the total volume of lemonade.

(d) A plank is $2\frac{5}{7}$ metres. What length is left if $\frac{6}{7}$ metres is cut off?

(e) What volume of lemonade is left in a $1\frac{1}{4}$ litre bottle after $\frac{3}{4}$ litre has been used?

(f) A piece of ribbon is $2\frac{1}{4}$ metres long. Two pieces are cut from it.
One is $\frac{1}{2}$ m and the other is $\frac{3}{4}$ m. What length of ribbon is left?

(g) Jim cycles to a friend's house $8\frac{8}{9}$ miles away. After $2\frac{4}{9}$ miles he stops to speak to Bill and
after a further $\frac{5}{9}$ mile he calls at the shop. How far does Jim still have to cycle?

4.4 Adding and subtracting – changing one denominator

Fractions may only be added or subtracted when they have the same denominator.
Use equivalent fractions to make denominators the same.

Example 1

$\frac{3}{10} + \frac{4}{5}$ $\boxed{\frac{4}{5} = \frac{8}{10}}$

$= \frac{3}{10} + \frac{8}{10}$

$= \frac{11}{10}$

$= 1\frac{1}{10}$

Example 2

$\frac{3}{4} - \frac{7}{12}$ $\boxed{\frac{3}{4} = \frac{9}{12}}$

$= \frac{9}{12} - \frac{7}{12}$

$= \frac{2}{12}$

$= \frac{1}{6}$

Exercise 4.4

1 Find:

(a) $\frac{1}{4} + \frac{3}{8}$ (b) $\frac{1}{2} - \frac{1}{8}$ (c) $\frac{5}{8} + \frac{1}{4}$ (d) $\frac{3}{4} - \frac{3}{8}$ (e) $\frac{5}{8} + \frac{1}{2}$ (f) $\frac{1}{4} + \frac{7}{8}$

(g) $\frac{1}{3} - \frac{1}{6}$ (h) $\frac{2}{9} + \frac{1}{3}$ (i) $\frac{2}{3} - \frac{1}{6}$ (j) $\frac{5}{12} + \frac{2}{3}$ (k) $\frac{2}{3} + \frac{8}{9}$ (l) $\frac{7}{15} - \frac{1}{3}$

(m) $\frac{3}{5} + \frac{1}{10}$ (n) $\frac{7}{10} - \frac{1}{2}$ (o) $\frac{4}{5} + \frac{3}{10}$ (p) $\frac{1}{2} - \frac{5}{10}$ (q) $\frac{4}{5} + \frac{9}{10}$ (r) $\frac{3}{10} - \frac{1}{5}$

(s) $\frac{3}{4} + \frac{1}{12}$ (t) $\frac{5}{12} + \frac{1}{6}$ (u) $\frac{7}{12} - \frac{1}{2}$ (v) $\frac{3}{4} - \frac{7}{12}$ (w) $\frac{3}{8} + \frac{3}{16}$ (x) $\frac{11}{18} - \frac{1}{3}$

2 A bag of Jello Babes weighs $\frac{1}{4}$ kg and a bag of Dolly Jems weighs $\frac{5}{16}$ kg.
What is the total weight of sweets?

3 A carton of orange juice holds $\frac{3}{4}$ litre and Jim drinks $\frac{5}{12}$ litre from the carton.
What volume of juice is left?

4 Craig runs $\frac{3}{4}$ of a mile on Monday, $\frac{5}{6}$ of a mile on Tuesday and $\frac{11}{12}$ of a mile on Wednesday.
How far did he run altogether in the three days?

4.5 Adding and subtracting – changing both denominators

When one denominator is not a multiple of the other, **both** denominators must be changed.
Choose the **lowest common multiple** for the common denominator and use equivalent fractions.

Example 1

$\frac{1}{2} + \frac{1}{3}$

$= \frac{3}{6} + \frac{2}{6}$

$= \frac{5}{6}$

Example 2

$\frac{2}{3} - \frac{1}{5}$

$= \frac{10}{15} - \frac{3}{15}$

$= \frac{7}{15}$

Example 3

$\frac{3}{4} + \frac{5}{6}$

$= \frac{9}{12} + \frac{10}{12}$

$= \frac{19}{12}$

$= 1\frac{7}{12}$

Example 4

$\frac{3}{8} - \frac{1}{6} - \frac{1}{12}$

$= \frac{9}{24} - \frac{4}{24} - \frac{2}{24}$

$= \frac{3}{24}$

$= \frac{1}{8}$

$1\frac{7}{12}$ is a mixed number

Exercise 4.5

1 Find:

(a) $\frac{1}{2} + \frac{2}{3}$ (b) $\frac{1}{3} - \frac{1}{4}$ (c) $\frac{3}{4} - \frac{2}{3}$ (d) $\frac{1}{3} + \frac{3}{8}$

(e) $\frac{1}{8} + \frac{2}{3}$ (f) $\frac{2}{3} - \frac{3}{8}$ (g) $\frac{1}{2} - \frac{2}{5}$ (h) $\frac{1}{4} + \frac{1}{5}$

(i) $\frac{3}{4} - \frac{3}{5}$ (j) $\frac{1}{3} + \frac{4}{5}$ (k) $\frac{2}{3} + \frac{2}{5}$ (l) $\frac{4}{5} - \frac{3}{4}$

(m) $\frac{1}{7} + \frac{1}{3}$ (n) $\frac{5}{8} - \frac{1}{5}$ (o) $\frac{1}{6} + \frac{2}{5}$ (p) $\frac{5}{7} - \frac{1}{6}$

(q) $\frac{3}{8} + \frac{2}{7}$ (r) $\frac{6}{7} - \frac{4}{5}$ (s) $\frac{1}{4} + \frac{5}{6}$ (t) $\frac{3}{4} - \frac{1}{6}$

(u) $\frac{7}{8} - \frac{5}{6}$ (v) $\frac{1}{10} + \frac{3}{4}$ (w) $\frac{5}{6} - \frac{7}{10}$ (x) $\frac{5}{8} + \frac{3}{20}$

2 Calculate:

(a) $\frac{1}{2} + \frac{1}{3} + \frac{1}{4}$ (b) $\frac{1}{2} - \frac{1}{5} + \frac{1}{10}$ (c) $\frac{2}{3} + \frac{1}{6} + \frac{3}{4}$ (d) $\frac{3}{4} + \frac{1}{3} - \frac{1}{2}$

(e) $\frac{1}{6} + \frac{3}{4} - \frac{2}{3}$ (f) $\frac{1}{3} + \frac{2}{5} + \frac{1}{2}$ (g) $\frac{3}{8} + \frac{1}{2} + \frac{3}{4}$ (h) $\frac{5}{8} - \frac{1}{4} - \frac{1}{3}$

(i) $\frac{5}{18} + \frac{2}{3} - \frac{5}{6}$ (j) $\frac{2}{5} + \frac{3}{4} + \frac{3}{10}$ (k) $\frac{1}{2} - \frac{2}{7} - \frac{1}{14}$ (l) $\frac{1}{2} + \frac{1}{5} + \frac{1}{7}$

3 Laura bought a $\frac{1}{2}$ kg bag of Dolly Mixtures. She ate $\frac{1}{3}$ kg herself and gave the rest to Millie. How much did she give to Millie?

4 Last night Jim spent $\frac{3}{8}$ of an hour on French homework and $\frac{5}{6}$ of an hour on his maths. If he started his homework at 5 o'clock, was he finished in time to watch The Simpsons, which started at 6 o'clock? Explain your answer.

5 In a relay race Bob ran $\frac{3}{4}$ of a kilometre, Bill ran $\frac{2}{3}$ km and Ben ran $\frac{5}{6}$ km. What was the total length of the race?

6 A bottle of Iron Brew holds $\frac{7}{8}$ of a litre. Is there enough to give $\frac{1}{4}$ litre to Joe, $\frac{1}{3}$ litre to John and leave $\frac{1}{2}$ litre for later?

7 James opened a $\frac{3}{4}$ litre bottle of wine. John drank $\frac{1}{3}$ litre and Carole drank $\frac{1}{5}$ litre. How much did James have left for himself?

4.6 Calculating a fraction of a quantity

> To calculate a fraction of a quantity divide by the denominator then multiply by the numerator.
>
> To find $\frac{1}{5}$ divide by 5   To find $\frac{3}{4}$ find $\frac{1}{4}$ then multiply by 3
>
> **Example 1**
> Calculate $\frac{1}{3}$ of £75
>
> $\frac{1}{3}$ of £75 = £75 ÷ 3
> $\qquad = £25$
>
> **Example 2**
> There are 960 pupils at Alnwath Academy.
> $\frac{2}{3}$ of the pupils walk to school. How many is this?
> $\frac{1}{3}$ of 960 = 320
> So $\frac{2}{3}$ of 960 = 2 × 320
> $\qquad = 640$
> **640** pupils walk to school.
>
> $\dfrac{2}{3} \times \dfrac{960^{320}}{1} = \dfrac{640}{1}$
> $\qquad\qquad = 640$

Exercise 4.6

1 Calculate:

  (**a**) $\frac{1}{3}$ of 42 g   (**b**) $\frac{1}{7}$ of 84 m   (**c**) $\frac{1}{6}$ of 96 tonnes

  (**d**) $\frac{1}{8}$ of 96 litres   (**e**) $\frac{1}{9}$ of 63 pence   (**f**) $\frac{1}{2}$ of 156 km

  (**g**) $\frac{1}{7}$ of 98 litres   (**h**) $\frac{1}{3}$ of 108 g   (**i**) $\frac{1}{7}$ of 1463 g

2 Find:

  (**a**) $\frac{5}{8}$ of 200 m   (**b**) $\frac{2}{3}$ of £45   (**c**) $\frac{3}{5}$ of 95 km

  (**d**) $\frac{3}{8}$ of 128 g   (**e**) $\frac{9}{10}$ of 90 mm   (**f**) $\frac{4}{9}$ of £198

  (**g**) $\frac{7}{8}$ of 192 cm   (**h**) $\frac{6}{7}$ of £147   (**i**) $\frac{8}{9}$ of 270 kg

  (**j**) $\frac{3}{7}$ of 1470 g   (**k**) $\frac{3}{10}$ of 2 km (in metres)   (**l**) $\frac{3}{4}$ of 3 kg (in grammes)

  (**m**) $\frac{4}{5}$ of 1 litre (in ml)   (**n**) $\frac{4}{9}$ of 1·8 km (in metres)   (**o**) $\frac{9}{10}$ of 5 tonnes (in kg)

  (**p**) $\frac{5}{12}$ of 3·6 cm (in mm)   (**q**) $\frac{3}{5}$ of 2 hours (in minutes)   (**r**) $\frac{6}{7}$ of 5 weeks (in days)

  (**s**) $\frac{5}{6}$ of 2 days (in hours)   (**t**) $\frac{1}{6}$ of a leap year (in days)   (**u**) $\frac{3}{8}$ of £7.20

3 There are 720 pupils at Alnwath Academy. Calculate the number of pupils if:

(**a**) $\frac{1}{2}$ are boys   (**b**) $\frac{1}{3}$ have fair hair

(**c**) $\frac{1}{4}$ wear glasses   (**d**) $\frac{1}{5}$ are in first year

(**e**) $\frac{1}{8}$ own a computer   (**f**) $\frac{1}{10}$ cycle to school.

4 The Mathematics Department at Alnwath spent £4200 on books and equipment. Calculate the amount spent on each item.

(**a**) $\frac{1}{4}$ on jotters   (**b**) $\frac{1}{5}$ on calculators

(**c**) $\frac{1}{7}$ on photocopying   (**d**) $\frac{1}{8}$ on stationery items

(**e**) $\frac{1}{10}$ on other equipment   (**f**) $\frac{1}{20}$ on a projector

5 There are 720 pupils at Alnwath Academy.
Find the number of pupils in each group if:

(**a**) $\frac{2}{3}$ have lunch in school   (**b**) $\frac{3}{4}$ wear school uniform

(**c**) $\frac{5}{6}$ say they enjoy school   (**d**) $\frac{2}{5}$ expect to go to university or college

(**e**) $\frac{5}{8}$ attend after-school clubs   (**f**) $\frac{9}{10}$ complete their homework.

6 A bag contains 960 coloured beads, $\frac{3}{8}$ are red, $\frac{1}{6}$ are blue and $\frac{3}{10}$ are yellow. Calculate the number of

(**a**) red beads

(**b**) blue beads

(**c**) yellow beads.

7 One complete revolution is 360°. Calculate the sizes of angles which are

(**a**) $\frac{3}{5}$ of a revolution   (**b**) $\frac{5}{6}$ of a revolution

(**c**) $\frac{5}{8}$ of a revolution   (**d**) $\frac{4}{9}$ of a revolution

(**e**) $\frac{7}{10}$ of a revolution   (**f**) $\frac{11}{12}$ of a revolution.

4.7 Multiplying a fraction by a whole number

Example 1

A bottle of shampoo holds $\frac{2}{5}$ litre.
Calculate the total volume of 8 bottles
of shampoo.

Total volume $= 8 \times \frac{2}{5}$

$= \frac{8}{1} \times \frac{2}{5}$

$= \frac{16}{5} = 3\frac{1}{5}$ **litres**

Example 2

Calculate $\frac{3}{4} \times 34$.

$\frac{3}{4} \times \frac{34}{1}^{17} = \frac{51}{2}$

$= 25\frac{1}{2}$

Exercise 4.7

1 Calculate:

(**a**) $5 \times \frac{1}{6}$ (**b**) $7 \times \frac{1}{7}$ (**c**) $5 \times \frac{1}{8}$ (**d**) $9 \times \frac{1}{9}$

(**e**) $4 \times \frac{1}{10}$ (**f**) $10 \times \frac{1}{2}$ (**g**) $8 \times \frac{1}{5}$ (**h**) $11 \times \frac{1}{4}$

(**i**) $3 \times \frac{2}{3}$ kg   (**j**) $8 \times \frac{3}{4}$ km   (**k**) $3 \times \frac{3}{10}$ cm   (**l**) $5 \times \frac{2}{9}$ litres

(**m**) $4 \times \frac{5}{7}$ m   (**n**) $3 \times \frac{7}{8}$ miles   (**o**) $7 \times \frac{5}{6}$ kg   (**p**) $9 \times \frac{3}{8}$ m

2 Calculate the weight of

(**a**) six $\frac{1}{2}$ kg bags of rice   (**b**) eleven $\frac{1}{4}$ kg bags of flour

(**c**) eight $\frac{1}{3}$ kg bags of sugar   (**d**) fourteen $\frac{1}{5}$ kg packets of curry powder

(**e**) thirty $\frac{1}{9}$ kg packets of nutmeg   (**f**) nineteen $\frac{1}{10}$ kg packets of parmesan.

3 Calculate the volume of

(**a**) sixteen $\frac{2}{3}$ litre bottles of lemonade   (**b**) eighteen $\frac{3}{5}$ litre cups of water

(**c**) twelve $\frac{7}{8}$ litre glasses of cola   (**d**) thirty $\frac{4}{9}$ litre glasses of wine.

4 (**a**) A bottle of wine holds $\frac{7}{10}$ of a litre. What is the volume of 8 bottles?

(**b**) A packet of fish fingers weighs $\frac{4}{5}$ of a kilogram. What is the weight of 7 packets?

(**c**) A can of Iron Bru holds $\frac{2}{7}$ of a litre. What is the volume of 9 cans?

(**d**) The width of a desk top is $\frac{7}{8}$ of a metre.
What is the total width of 6 desks placed side by side?

(**e**) John trains in the gym for $\frac{3}{4}$ of an hour each day. How long is this each week?

5 Calculate:

(**a**) $48 \times \frac{5}{6}$ (**b**) $63 \times \frac{2}{7}$ (**c**) $64 \times \frac{5}{8}$ (**d**) $48 \times \frac{3}{4}$

(**e**) $125 \times \frac{4}{5}$ (**f**) $354 \times \frac{2}{3}$ (**g**) $\frac{5}{7} \times 49$ (**h**) $\frac{5}{9} \times 72$

(**i**) $\frac{3}{10} \times 90$ (**j**) $\frac{5}{12} \times 84$ (**k**) $\frac{7}{11} \times 110$ (**l**) $\frac{7}{8} \times 104$

(**m**) $\frac{5}{8} \times 20$ (**n**) $27 \times \frac{5}{6}$ (**o**) $\frac{7}{9} \times 33$ (**p**) $\frac{3}{5} \times 16$

(**q**) $93 \times \frac{2}{9}$ (**r**) $40 \times \frac{5}{12}$ (**s**) $\frac{11}{12} \times 27$ (**t**) $25 \times \frac{7}{15}$

4.8 Multiplying fractions

Example 1

Zoe is given a half pizza but only eats a third of it.
What fraction of the pizza did she eat?

Fraction eaten $= \frac{1}{3}$ of $\frac{1}{2} = \frac{1}{3} \times \frac{1}{2} = \frac{1}{6}$ of the pizza

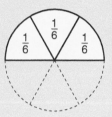

Example 2

Calculate $\frac{3}{4} \times \frac{2}{5}$

$\frac{3}{4} \times \frac{2}{5} = \frac{6}{20}$

$\qquad = \frac{3}{10}$

Example 3

Calculate $\frac{5}{8} \times \frac{4}{5} \times \frac{6}{7}$

$\frac{5}{8} \times \frac{4}{5} \times \frac{6}{7} = \frac{120}{280}$ or $\frac{5}{8} \times \frac{4}{5} \times \frac{6^{3}}{7} = \frac{3}{7}$

$\qquad = \frac{12}{28}$

$\qquad = \frac{3}{8}$

Exercise 4.8

1 Multiply these fractions giving your answers in simplest form.

  (**a**) $\frac{1}{3} \times \frac{1}{5}$ (**b**) $\frac{1}{6} \times \frac{1}{7}$ (**c**) $\frac{1}{4} \times \frac{2}{3}$ (**d**) $\frac{1}{2} \times \frac{7}{8}$

  (**e**) $\frac{3}{4} \times \frac{5}{8}$ (**f**) $\frac{2}{5} \times \frac{5}{7}$ (**g**) $\frac{1}{4} \times \frac{1}{4}$ (**h**) $\frac{2}{3} \times \frac{7}{10}$

  (**i**) $\frac{3}{10} \times \frac{7}{10}$ (**j**) $\frac{5}{9} \times \frac{2}{5}$ (**k**) $\frac{3}{4} \times \frac{4}{7}$ (**l**) $\frac{5}{8} \times \frac{2}{9}$

  (**m**) $\frac{9}{10} \times \frac{5}{8}$ (**n**) $\frac{5}{7} \times \frac{7}{10}$ (**o**) $\frac{8}{9} \times \frac{3}{4}$ (**p**) $\frac{3}{7} \times \frac{2}{9}$

  (**q**) $\frac{7}{8} \times \frac{7}{8}$ (**r**) $\frac{5}{6} \times \frac{8}{9}$ (**s**) $\frac{7}{12} \times \frac{3}{14}$ (**t**) $\frac{3}{8} \times \frac{24}{27}$

2 Calculate:

  (**a**) $\frac{1}{2} \times \frac{2}{3} \times \frac{3}{4}$ (**b**) $\frac{3}{8} \times \frac{1}{3} \times \frac{7}{8}$ (**c**) $\frac{1}{4} \times \frac{2}{3} \times \frac{6}{7}$ (**d**) $\frac{1}{2} \times \frac{1}{8} \times \frac{8}{9}$

  (**e**) $\frac{4}{5} \times \frac{3}{4} \times \frac{5}{7}$ (**f**) $\frac{5}{16} \times \frac{8}{9} \times \frac{2}{3}$ (**g**) $\frac{5}{6} \times \frac{3}{10} \times \frac{4}{5}$ (**h**) $\frac{7}{12} \times \frac{4}{5} \times \frac{3}{7}$

3 (**a**) A fifth of the pupils in 1C wear glasses and a third of those have
fair hair. What fraction of the class have fair hair and wear glasses?

  (**b**) Billy spends a third of the day asleep. He spends $\frac{1}{8}$ of his time
when awake playing on his computer. What fraction of his day
does Billy spend playing on the computer?

  (**c**) In his will a man leaves half his estate to his wife and the rest is
shared equally among his five sons.
What fraction of his estate does each son inherit?

  (**d**) A farmer uses half of a field for grazing his cows. The remaining
area has equal areas for potatoes, turnips, corn and barley.
What fraction of the field is used to grow turnips?

4.9 Dividing with fractions

Example

Each carton holds $\frac{1}{4}$ litre of liquid. How many $\frac{1}{4}$ litres are in
(a) a 1 litre bottle   (b) a $2\frac{1}{4}$ litre bottle?

(a) $1\,\ell = \frac{4}{4}\,\ell$ so a 1 litre bottle fills 4 cartons. $\boxed{1 \div \frac{1}{4} = 4}$

(b) $2\frac{1}{4}\,\ell = \frac{9}{4}\,\ell$ so a $2\frac{1}{4}$ litre bottle fills 9 cartons. $\boxed{2\frac{1}{4} \div \frac{1}{4} = 9}$

Exercise 4.9

1 How many $\frac{1}{2}$ litres are there in:

   (a) 1 litre   (b) 2 litres   (c) 3 litres   (d) 5 litres   (e) $1\frac{1}{2}$ litres?

2 How many $\frac{1}{3}$ litres are there in:

   (a) 1 litre   (b) 2 litres   (c) 3 litres   (d) $1\frac{1}{3}$ litres   (e) $5\frac{2}{3}$ litres?

3 How many pieces would there be if:

   (a) 2 pizzas are divided into thirds

   (b) 3 apples are divided into fifths

   (c) 5 cakes are divided into eighths

   (d) $1\frac{1}{4}$ pies are divided into quarters

   (e) $3\frac{2}{7}$ loaves are divided into sevenths

   (f) $2\frac{5}{6}$ tarts are divided into sixths?

4 In Fazzini's café Alasdair sells ice cream in tubs like this.

   (a) How many $\frac{1}{2}$ litre tubs can he fill from
       a 3 litre container?

   (b) How many $\frac{1}{3}$ litre tubs can he fill from
       a $4\frac{2}{3}$ litre container?

   (c) How many $\frac{1}{5}$ litre tubs can he fill from
       a $7\frac{4}{5}$ litre container?

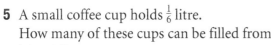

5 A small coffee cup holds $\frac{1}{6}$ litre.
   How many of these cups can be filled from
   (a) a 2 litre pot

   (b) a $1\frac{1}{2}$ litre pot?

6 A tray of fudge had been divided into equal pieces.
   After $\frac{3}{4}$ of the fudge was eaten 6 pieces were left.

   (a) What fraction of the original amount of fudge was left on the tray?

   (b) How many pieces had the tray of fudge been divided into?

   (c) What fraction of the whole tray was each piece of fudge?

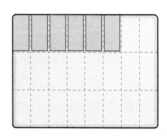

4.10 Dividing by a fraction

A chef divides 3 pizzas into quarters.
This gives 12 slices.
So $3 \div \frac{1}{4} = 12$
$3 \times \frac{4}{1} = \frac{12}{1} = 12$
To divide by a fraction multiply by the **reciprocal**.

> The reciprocal is the fraction turned upside down.

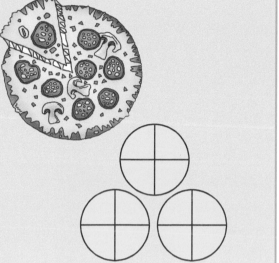

Example

Calculate $9 \div \frac{3}{8}$

$9 \div \frac{3}{8}$

$= 9 \times \frac{8}{3} = \frac{72}{3}$

$\qquad = \mathbf{24}$

Exercise 4.10

1 Calculate:

(**a**) $9 \div \frac{1}{3}$ (**b**) $15 \div \frac{1}{4}$ (**c**) $12 \div \frac{1}{10}$ (**d**) $39 \div \frac{1}{2}$

(**e**) $102 \div \frac{1}{5}$ (**f**) $9 \div \frac{1}{9}$ (**g**) $10 \div \frac{1}{8}$ (**h**) $2 \div \frac{2}{3}$

(**i**) $12 \div \frac{3}{4}$ (**j**) $8 \div \frac{2}{5}$ (**k**) $15 \div \frac{3}{7}$ (**l**) $35 \div \frac{5}{6}$

(**m**) $18 \div \frac{2}{9}$ (**n**) $50 \div \frac{2}{3}$ (**o**) $270 \div \frac{9}{10}$ (**p**) $25 \div \frac{5}{8}$

(**q**) $42 \div \frac{6}{7}$ (**r**) $49 \div \frac{7}{10}$ (**s**) $56 \div \frac{8}{9}$ (**t**) $60 \div \frac{5}{12}$

2 (**a**) A 4 metre length of ribbon is cut into $\frac{1}{10}$ metre pieces.
How many pieces are produced?

(**b**) A social worker holds client interviews for 4 hours. The time is
divided equally with each interview lasting $\frac{1}{4}$ of an hour.
How many interviews does he hold?

(**c**) A 3 kg tub of peanuts is divided into $\frac{1}{8}$ kg bags.
How many bags does this give?

(**d**) A 25 litre container of juice is divided into $\frac{1}{5}$ litre cartons.
How many cartons are produced?

(**e**) In a factory 35 metre lengths of metal rod are divided into $\frac{7}{8}$ metre pieces.
How many pieces can be made from each length?

(**f**) A 45 acre area of land has to be divided into $\frac{5}{6}$ of an acre plots.
How many plots are created?

(**g**) A 9 tonne load of top soil is divided into $\frac{3}{25}$ tonne plant containers.
How many containers can be filled?

Review exercise 4

1 Copy and complete:

(a) $\frac{7}{8} = \frac{\blacksquare}{16}$ 　　 (b) $\frac{8}{9} = \frac{64}{\blacksquare}$ 　　 (c) $\frac{7}{12} = \frac{\blacksquare}{36}$ 　　 (d) $\frac{3}{25} = \frac{12}{\blacksquare}$

(e) $\frac{3}{5} = \frac{\blacksquare}{10} = \frac{\blacksquare}{15}$ 　　 (f) $\frac{2}{7} = \frac{6}{\blacksquare} = \frac{10}{\blacksquare}$ 　　 (g) $\frac{5}{9} = \frac{\blacksquare}{18} = \frac{25}{\blacksquare}$

2 Write these fractions as twenty fourths and then list them in order from smallest to largest.

$\frac{1}{4}, \frac{3}{8}, \frac{1}{6}, \frac{1}{3}, \frac{5}{12}, \frac{1}{2}, \frac{7}{24}$

3 Express these fractions in simplest form.

(a) $\frac{7}{21}$ 　　 (b) $\frac{10}{45}$ 　　 (c) $\frac{3}{57}$ 　　 (d) $\frac{180}{300}$ 　　 (e) $\frac{72}{96}$

4 Find:

(a) $\frac{5}{8} + \frac{7}{8}$ 　　 (b) $1\frac{1}{2} - \frac{3}{4}$ 　　 (c) $\frac{3}{8} + \frac{3}{4}$ 　　 (d) $\frac{7}{12} + \frac{1}{4}$ 　　 (e) $\frac{4}{5} - \frac{4}{15}$

5 A plank is $3\frac{1}{4}$ metres long. Two lengths are cut from it. One is $\frac{3}{4}$ m and the other is $1\frac{1}{2}$ m. What length is left?

6 Each morning Jill spends $\frac{1}{4}$ hour washing and dressing, $\frac{3}{8}$ hour eating breakfast and $\frac{1}{2}$ an hour completing homework. How long is this altogether?

7 Find:

(a) $\frac{1}{4} + \frac{3}{10}$ 　　 (b) $\frac{5}{6} - \frac{3}{5}$ 　　 (c) $\frac{5}{8} + \frac{1}{6} - \frac{3}{4}$ 　　 (d) $\frac{2}{3} + \frac{1}{5} - \frac{7}{10}$

8 There were two bottles of milk in the fridge holding $\frac{11}{12}$ of a litre and $\frac{3}{4}$ of a litre. If Bill drank $\frac{1}{3}$ litre at tea how much was left?

9 Calculate:

(a) $\frac{1}{9}$ of 468 km 　　 (b) $\frac{7}{8}$ of 72 g 　　 (c) $\frac{9}{10}$ of 1500 m 　　 (d) $\frac{5}{12}$ of 360°

10 There were 720 people in an audience. $\frac{4}{9}$ of them were women and $\frac{1}{6}$ were children.

(a) What fraction of the audience were men?　　 (b) How many men were in the audience?

11 Calculate:

(a) $63 \times \frac{5}{9}$ 　　 (b) $\frac{7}{8} \times 56$ 　　 (c) $\frac{11}{12} \times 96$ 　　 (d) $\frac{3}{4} \times 18$ 　　 (e) $35 \times \frac{6}{15}$

12 Every day during the month of April, John spent $\frac{5}{6}$ of an hour revising for a maths exam. How many hours was this altogether?

13 Multiply these fractions giving your answers in simplest form.

(a) $\frac{7}{8} \times \frac{5}{14}$ 　　 (b) $\frac{4}{9} \times \frac{7}{9}$ 　　 (c) $\frac{1}{6} \times \frac{4}{5} \times \frac{3}{7}$ 　　 (d) $\frac{3}{10} \times \frac{3}{8} \times \frac{9}{11}$

14 Mr Bright is a maths teacher and spends $\frac{4}{5}$ of his week in school teaching his classes. If a quarter of his teaching time is spent with his first year class what fraction of the week does he spend teaching first year?

15 How many pieces would there be if $4\frac{3}{10}$ melons were divided into tenths?

16 Calculate:

(a) $8 \div \frac{1}{7}$ 　　 (b) $24 \div \frac{2}{3}$ 　　 (c) $720 \div \frac{8}{9}$

17 Ron packed 28 kg of apples into $\frac{7}{12}$ kg bags. How many bags did he have?

Summary

Equivalent fractions – multiply numerator and denominator by the same number

$$\frac{3}{4} = \frac{9}{12} = \frac{45}{60}$$

(×3 and ×5 applied to numerator and denominator)

$\frac{3}{4}, \frac{9}{12}$ and $\frac{45}{60}$ are equivalent fractions.

Simplest form – divide numerator and denominator by the same number

$$\frac{24}{84} = \frac{6}{21} = \frac{2}{7}$$

(÷4 and ÷3 applied to numerator and denominator)

$\frac{24}{84} = \frac{2}{7}$ in simplest form.

Adding and subtracting

Choose the **lowest common multiple** for the common denominator.

$$\frac{1}{2} + \frac{2}{3} - \frac{3}{4}$$
$$= \frac{6}{12} + \frac{8}{12} - \frac{9}{12} = \frac{5}{12}$$

Calculating a fraction of a quantity

To find $\frac{5}{8}$ of £24 first find $\frac{1}{8}$ then multiply by 5

$\frac{1}{8}$ of £24 = £3

$\frac{5}{8}$ of £24 = £3 × 5 = £15 $\qquad$ or $\qquad$ $\frac{5}{8}$ of 24 $= \frac{5}{8} \times \frac{24^{3}}{1} = 15$

Multiplying a fraction by a whole number

$$9 \times \frac{3}{4} = \frac{27}{4}$$
$$= \frac{24}{4} + \frac{3}{4} = 6\frac{3}{4}$$

Multiplying fractions

$$\frac{7}{8} \times \frac{2}{3} \times \frac{9}{14} = \frac{126}{336} \qquad \text{or} \qquad \frac{7^{1}}{8} \times \frac{2^{1}}{3_{1}} \times \frac{9^{3}}{14_{2_{1}}} = \frac{3}{8}$$
$$= \frac{21}{56} = \frac{3}{8}$$

Dividing by a fraction – multiply by the reciprocal

$$45 \div \frac{9}{10}$$
$$= 45 \times \frac{10}{9} = \frac{450}{9} = 50$$

5 Angles

In this chapter you will learn to work with related angles.

5.1 Review of angles

An angle is formed where two **arms** meet at a **vertex**.

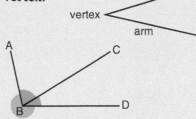

Naming angles

The red angle is called ∠ABC or ∠CBA.
The blue angle is called ∠CBD or ∠DBC.
The green angle is called ∠ABD or ∠DBA.

Types of angles

- An angle between 0° and 90° is called an **acute angle**.
- One **right angle** is 90°.
- Any two lines which form a right angle are said to be **perpendicular**.
- An angle between 90° and 180° is called an **obtuse angle**.
- Two right angles fitted together make a **straight angle** which is 180°.
- An angle between 180° and 360° is called a **reflex angle**.
- Four right angles fitted together make a **complete turn** which is 360°.

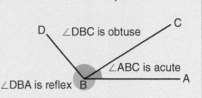

Exercise 5.1

1 Name and state the type of each angle in the following diagrams.

(**a**) 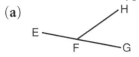　　　(**b**) 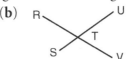　　　(**c**)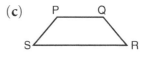

2 (**a**) How many right angles are there at vertex B in this cube?

(**b**) Name these angles.

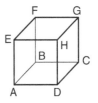

3 In each of the following diagrams, what type of angle is the named angle?

(**a**) ∠ABC　　　(**b**) ∠RTV　　　(**c**) ∠POR　　　(**d**) ∠XYZ

　　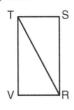　　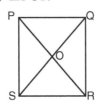　　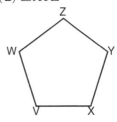

5.2 Drawing angles

Draw ∠ABC = 42°

Step 1 Draw line AB 6 cm long.

A ——————————— B

Step 2 Place the centre of the
protractor on B with the base
line on AB as shown.

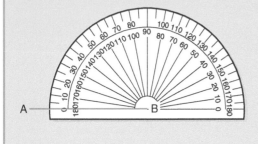

Step 3 Find the zero which is on the line AB,
count up the number of degrees and
put a dot at 42°.

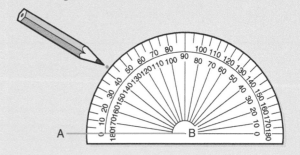

Step 4 Draw a line from B through the dot and
mark C. Label your angle as shown.

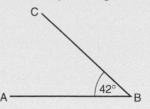

Exercise 5.2

You need a protractor and a ruler for this exercise.

1 Draw accurately the following angles:

(**a**) ∠XYZ = 65°   (**b**) ∠DEF = 12°   (**c**) ∠GHI = 165°   (**d**) ∠JKL = 92°

(**e**) ∠MNO = 115°   (**f**) ∠PQR = 87°   (**g**) ∠STU = 123°   (**h**) ∠VWX = 136°

(**i**) ∠SFA = 23°   (**j**) ∠DAT = 157°   (**k**) ∠ANG = 38°   (**l**) ∠KOP = 168°

2 (**a**) Make an accurate drawing of each of the following triangles.

(**b**) Measure the remaining angle in each case.

(**i**)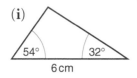

(**ii**)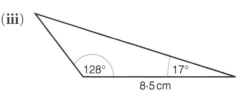

(**iii**)

3 The diagram shows a star, not drawn to scale.
OA, OC, OE, OG and OI are all 10 centimetres in length.
OB, OD, OF, OH and OJ are all 6 centimetres in length.
All angles at the centre are 36°.
Make an accurate copy of the star.

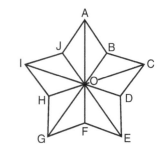

5.3 Calculating angles

Example Calculate the size of the missing angle in each diagram.

(a)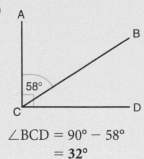

$\angle BCD = 90° - 58°$
$= \mathbf{32°}$

(b)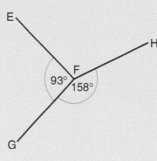

$\angle EFG + \angle GFH = 93° + 158°$
$= 251°$
$\angle EFH = 360° - 251°$
$= \mathbf{109°}$

Exercise 5.3

1 Calculate the size of the shaded angles in each diagram.

(a)   (b)   (c)   (d)

(e)   (f)   (g)   (h)(i)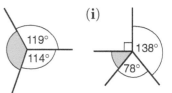

2 Through how many degrees would the minute hand of a clock move in:
(a) 15 minutes (b) 30 minutes (c) 1 hour
(d) 5 minutes (e) 1 minute (f) 42 minutes?

3 (a) Write down two times when the hands of a clock form a right angle.
(b) Do the hands of a clock form a right angle at 09 30? Explain your answer.
(c) Write down a time when the hands of a clock form a straight angle.
(d) Do the hands of a clock form a straight angle at 12 30? Explain you answer.

4 (a) Calculate $\angle ACB$ when $\angle BCD$ is (i) 35° (ii) 68° (iii) 17°.
(b) If $\angle BCD$ increases by 15°, what happens to $\angle ACB$?
(c) If $\angle BCD$ decreases by 20°, what happens to $\angle ACB$?
(d) If $\angle BCD = x°$ write an expression for the value of $\angle ACB$.

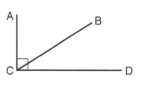

5 (**a**) Calculate ∠PQR when ∠PQS is
(**i**) 142°   (**ii**) 127°   (**iii**) 107°.

(**b**) If ∠PQS increases by 15°, what happens to ∠PQR?

(**c**) If ∠PQS decreases by 20°, what happens to ∠PQR?

(**d**) If ∠PQS = $x°$ write an expression for the value of ∠PQR.

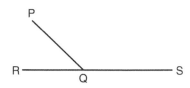

5.4 Related angles

In the diagram ∠ABD is a right angle.
∠ABC + ∠CBD = 90°.
∠ABC and ∠CBD are **complementary angles**.
∠ABC is the **complement** of ∠CBD.

In the diagram ∠XYZ is a straight angle.
∠XYW + ∠WYZ = 180°.
∠XYW and ∠WYZ are **supplementary angles**.
∠XYW is the **supplement** of ∠WYZ.

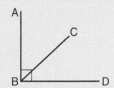

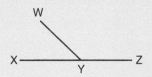

Example

Find the complement of 20°.

The complement is 90° − 20° = **70°**

Example

Find the supplement of 25°.

The supplement is 180° − 25° = **155°**

Exercise 5.4

1 Calculate the complement of:

(**a**) 20°   (**b**) 40°   (**c**) 89°

(**d**) 71°   (**e**) 18°   (**f**) 3°

2 Calculate the supplement of:

(**a**) 120°   (**b**) 145°   (**c**) 179°

(**d**) 73°   (**e**) 12°   (**f**) 9°

3 For each diagram
(**i**) name a pair of complementary angles and
(**ii**) calculate the size of each complementary angle.

(**a**)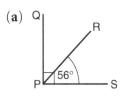

(**b**)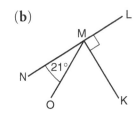

(**c**)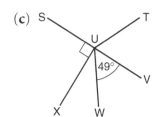

4 In the following diagrams:
  (**i**) name a pair of supplementary angles and
  (**ii**) calculate the size of each supplement.

  (**a**)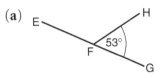

  (**b**)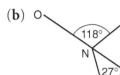

  (**c**)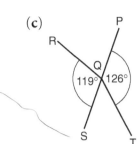

5 Find the value of *x* in each of the following diagrams.

  (**a**)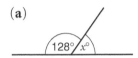

  (**b**)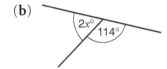

  (**c**)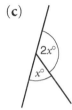

  (**d**)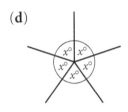

  (**e**)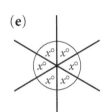

  (**f**)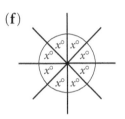

  (**g**)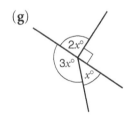

  (**h**)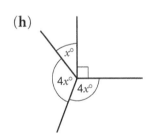

  (**i**)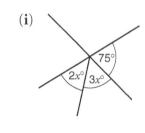

6 (**a**) Look at Diagram 1.
      Which angles are supplementary to $\angle PQT$?
   (**b**) Calculate the size of each supplement if $\angle PQT = 67°$.
   (**c**) Calculate the size of $\angle SQR$.

Diagram 1

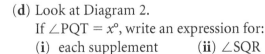

   (**d**) Look at Diagram 2.
      If $\angle PQT = x°$, write an expression for:
      (**i**) each supplement   (**ii**) $\angle SQR$
   (**e**) Which pairs of angles are equal?

Diagram 2

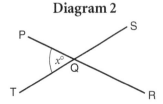

5.5 Vertically opposite angles

a and b are supplementary   so $a + b = 180°$
a and d are also supplementary   so $a + d = 180°$
Hence $a + b = a + d$
         $b = d$

b and d are called **vertically opposite** angles and are equal.
a and c are also vertically opposite and are also equal.

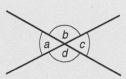

The word vertically comes from vertex.

Vertically opposite angles are equal.

Example

Find the size of each angle.
$\angle VYW$ is vertically opposite $\angle XYZ$.
Hence $\angle VYW = \mathbf{105°}$
$\angle ZYW$ and $\angle XYZ$ are supplementary.
Hence $\angle ZYW = 180° - 105° = \mathbf{75°}$
$\angle XYV$ is vertically opposite $\angle ZYW$.
Hence $\angle XYV = \mathbf{75°}$

Exercise 5.5

1 You need a protractor and a ruler.

   (**a**) Make an accurate copy of the sketch opposite. Line AD
      bisects line EC. Both AD and EC are 12 centimetres long.

   (**b**) Confirm, by measuring, that $\angle ABC = \angle EBD$.

   (**c**) Confirm, by measuring, that $\angle ABE = \angle CBD$.

   (**d**) Draw another pair of intersecting lines and repeat parts
      (**a**), (**b**) and (**c**).

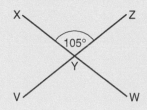

2 Calculate the size of each coloured angle, a to u.

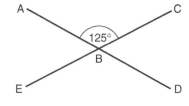

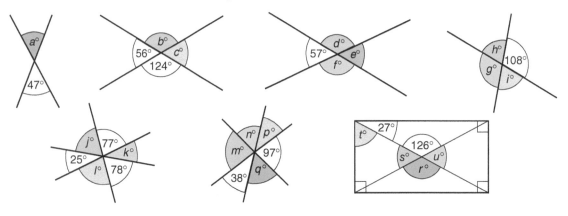

3 Find the value of x in each of the following diagrams.

(a)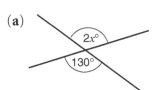

(b)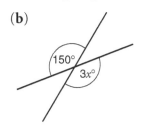

(c)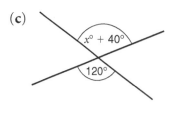

(d)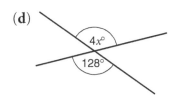

(e)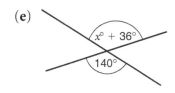

(f)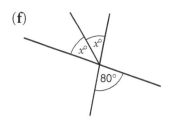

(g)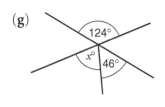

(h)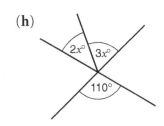

(i)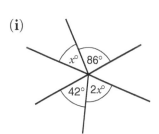

4 Trace this hexagon into your jotter.

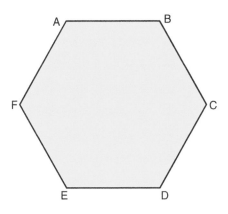

(a) Join A to C, A to D and D to F.

(b) How many triangles have you formed?

(c) Measure all the angles in each triangle and copy and complete this table.

Triangles	Angles	Sum of angles
ABC	30, 120, 30	

(d) What do you notice about the sum of the angles in each triangle?

5.6 Angles in a triangle

When the angles of triangle ABC are fitted together
they form a straight angle.
The angles fit together to make 180°.
$a° + b° + c° = 180°$

The sum of the angles of a triangle is 180°.

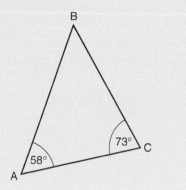

Example

Find the size of $\angle ABC$.

$\angle BAC + \angle ACB = 58° + 73° = 131°$
$\qquad \angle ABC = 180° - 131°$
$\qquad \angle ABC = \mathbf{49°}$

Exercise 5.6

1 Calculate the size of each coloured angle, a to j.

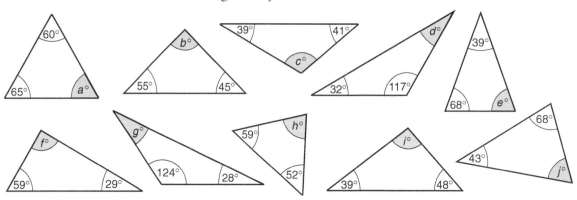

2 Calculate the value of x in each triangle.

(a)

(b)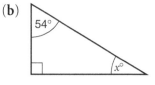

(c)

(d)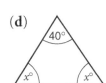

(e)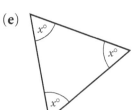

(f)

(g)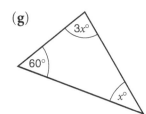

3 Copy each diagram and calculate all missing angles.

(a)
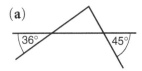

(b)
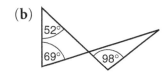

(c)
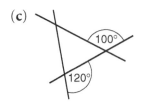

(d)
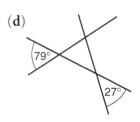

(e)
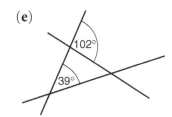

(f)
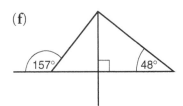

(g)
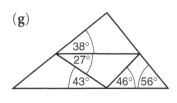

4 Calculate the size of x, y and z in the following regular shapes.
All triangles in each diagram are congruent.

(a)
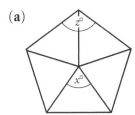

(b)
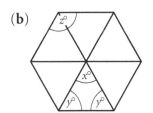

(c)
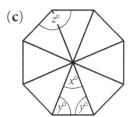

(d)
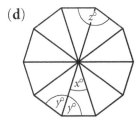

(e)
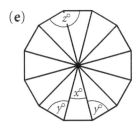

5.7 Corresponding angles

This diagram shows a tessellation of congruent parallelograms.
A tracing of the red parallelogram can be slid to cover the
blue parallelogram.
This shows that angle a is equal to angle e.

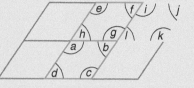

$$a = e$$

Angles in the same position in each parallelogram are equal and
are called **corresponding angles**.
Corresponding angles are formed when any pair of parallel lines
are crossed. $\angle ABC$ and $\angle BDE$ are corresponding angles.

This line is called a **transversal**.

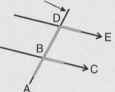

Corresponding angles are equal.

$$\angle ABC = \angle BDE$$

Each time a transversal crosses a pair of parallel
lines, four pairs of corresponding angles are formed.

Exercise 5.7

1 You need tracing paper.

   (**a**) Trace the red parallelogram above and mark in angles e, f, g and h.

   (**b**) Slide your tracing to cover over the yellow parallelogram.

   (**c**) Check that $e = i$.

   (**d**) List 3 other pairs of corresponding angles.

2 Copy each of the following diagrams and, without measuring, find
the values of angles a to n.

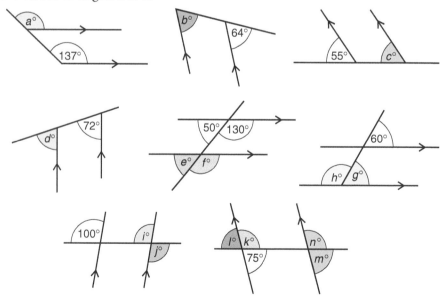

3 The diagram shows part of a banister in which all the supports are vertical. Sketch the diagram and mark in corresponding angles.

4 ABCD is a trapezium. AB is parallel to DC.
Copy the diagram and fill in the sizes of all missing angles.
Explain each answer.

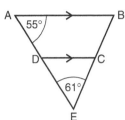

5 PQRS is a parallelogram. Copy the diagram.
  (**a**) Find the sizes of all of the missing angles. Explain each answer.
  (**b**) What can be said about opposite angles in parallelogram PQRS?

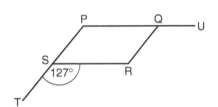

6 Calculate each angle in this parallelogram.

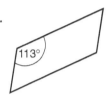

7 (**i**) Calculate the value of x in each of the following diagrams.
　(**ii**) Copy each diagram and fill in the sizes of all angles.

(**a**)　　　　　(**b**)　　　　　(**c**)

(**d**)　　　　　(**e**)　　　　　(**f**)

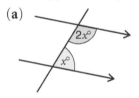
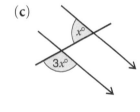
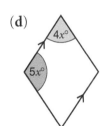
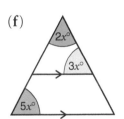

8 The diagram shows beams supporting a roof. Beams CD and EF are parallel. The pitch of the roof will not meet building regulations if angle EGF is less than 85°.
  (**a**) Does this roof meet the regulations? Explain your answer.
  (**b**) If ∠BDC is fixed at 110°, what is the minimum size that ∠DCA can be made so that the regulations are still met?

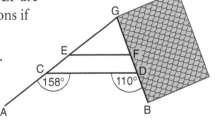

5.8 Alternate angles

The diagram shows a tessellation of congruent parallelograms.

A tracing of the red parallelogram can be rotated 180° about the marked point to fit over the blue parallelogram.

This shows that angle d is equal to angle f.

$$d = f$$

d and f are called **alternate angles**.

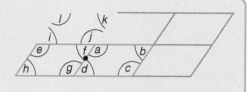

Alternate angles are formed when any pair of parallel lines are crossed by a transversal.

$\angle$EDC and $\angle$DCG are alternate angles.

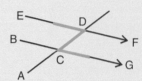

Alternate angles are equal.

$$\angle EDC = \angle DCG$$

Each time a transversal crosses a pair of parallel lines, two pairs of alternate angles are formed.

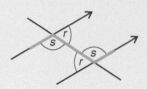

Exercise 5.8

1 You need tracing paper.

  (**a**) Trace the blue parallelogram above and mark in angles e, f, g and h.

  (**b**) Rotate your tracing to cover over the yellow parallelogram.

  (**c**) Check that $e = j$.

  (**d**) List another pair of alternate angles.

2 Copy each of the following diagrams and, without measuring, find the values of angles m to z.

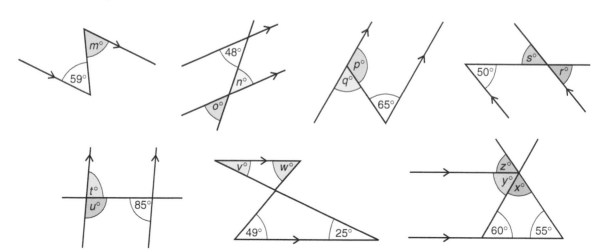

3 The diagram shows a banister in which all the supports are vertical.
Sketch the diagram and mark in pairs of alternate angles.

4 The diagram shows the frame of a deckchair. AB is parallel to CD.
Sketch the diagram and find the sizes of the missing angles.

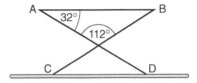

5 The diagram shows part of the frame of a bicycle. WX is
parallel to YZ and YX is parallel to WU.
Find the sizes of the missing angles in the frame.

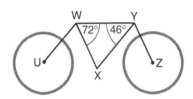

5.9 Interior and exterior angles of a polygon

The red angle shows an **interior** angle of the pentagon.
The blue angle shows an **exterior** angle of the pentagon.

This diagram shows a regular pentagon constructed from 5 congruent isosceles triangles.
The angle at the centre, $x = 360 \div 5$

$$= 72$$

$2y = 180 - 72$ Angles in a triangle add to give 180°

$$2y = 108$$

$$y = 54$$

Hence $z = 108$ Note $z = 2y$

All interior angles of a pentagon are 108°.
All exterior angles of a pentagon are $180° - 108° = 72°$

Exercise 5.9

1 Copy and complete the following to find the interior and exterior
angles of a regular hexagon.
The angle at the centre, $x = 360 \div$ ___

$$= \underline{\hspace{1cm}}$$

$2y = 180 -$ ___ (angles in a triangle add to give 180°)

$$2y = \underline{\hspace{1cm}}$$

$$y = \underline{\hspace{1cm}}$$

Hence $z = \underline{\hspace{1cm}}$

All interior angles of a hexagon are ___°.
All exterior angles of a hexagon are $180° -$ ___° $=$ ___°

2 Find the interior and exterior angles of each of the following polygons.

(a)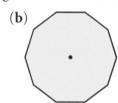

(b)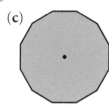

(c)

3 (a) Copy and complete this table.

Polygon	Square	pentagon	hexagon	octagon	dodecagon
No. of sides	4	5			12
Angle at centre	90°	72°			
Interior angle	90°	108°			
Exterior angle	90°	72°			

  (b) What do you notice about the angle at the centre and the exterior angle?

  (c) Find the exterior angles for a nonagon (9 sides).

  (d) What do you notice about the exterior and interior angles?

  (e) Find the interior angles for a nonagon (9 sides).

  (f) Find the exterior and interior angles for a 36 sided polygon.

  (g) Write a rule for finding the interior angle of any polygon.

Review exercise 5

1 **(i)** Make an accurate drawing of each of the following triangles.
   (ii) Measure the remaining angle in each case.

  (a)

  (b)

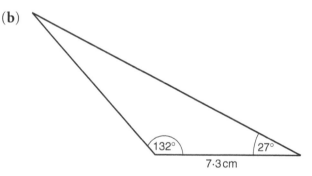

2 From the following diagrams
   (i) name a pair of complementary angles
   (ii) name a pair of supplementary angles
   (iii) calculate the size of each complement or supplement.

  (a)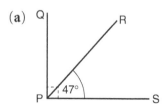

  (b)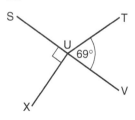

3 Find the value of *x* in each of the following diagrams.

(a)

(b)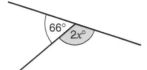

(c)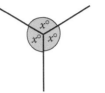

(d)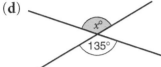

(e)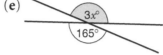

(f)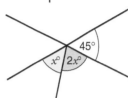

(g)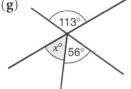

(h)

(i)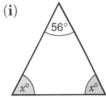

(j)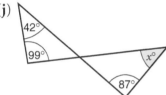

(k)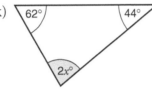

(l)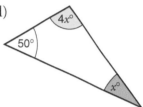

4 Calculate the size of *x* in each of the following, giving a reason for your answer.

(a)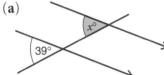

(b)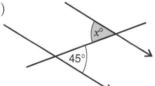

(c)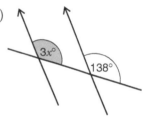

(d)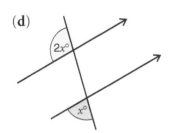

(e)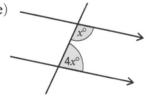

5 (i) Calculate the value of *x* in each of the following diagrams.
(ii) Copy each diagram and fill in the sizes of all angles.

(a)

(b)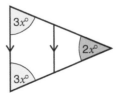

6 Calculate the exterior and interior angles of a decagon.

Summary

An angle is formed where two **arms** meet at a **vertex**.

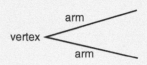

Naming angles

The red angle is called ∠ABC or ∠CBA.
The blue angle is called ∠CBD or ∠DBC.
The green angle is called ∠ABD or ∠DBA.

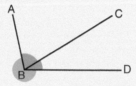

Types of angles

- An angle between 0° and 90° is called an **acute angle**.
- One **right angle** is 90°.
- Any two lines which form a right angle are said to be **perpendicular**.
- An angle between 90° and 180° is called an **obtuse angle**.
- Two right angles fitted together make a **straight angle** which is 180°.
- An angle between 180° and 360° is called a **reflex angle**.
- Four right angles fitted together make a **complete turn** which is 360°.

Angle facts

- Complementary angles add to give 90°.

- Supplementary angles add to give 180°.

- The sum of the angles of a triangle is 180°.

- Vertically opposite angles are equal.

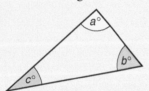

- Corresponding angles are equal.
  ∠ACG = ∠CDF

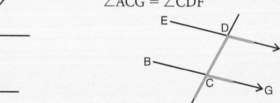

- Alternate angles are equal.
  ∠EDC = ∠DCG

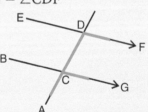

- Angles in a polygon

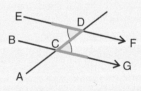

Exterior angle

Interior angle

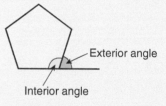

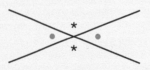

6 Negative numbers

In this chapter you will learn about negative numbers.

6.1 Below zero

Numbers below zero are used in many situations. One of the most common is temperature. These numbers are called negative numbers. They belong to a set of numbers called **integers**.

The set of integers = $\{\dots -3, -2, -1, 0, 1, 2, 3, \dots\}$

Exercise 6.1

1 Write down the temperatures shown on these thermometers.

(a) (b) (c) (d) (e)

2 Write down the temperature which is:
  (**a**) 7 degrees lower than 5 °C   (**b**) 6 degrees lower than 4 °C
  (**c**) 5 degrees higher than −8 °C   (**d**) 9 degrees higher than −3 °C
  (**e**) 12 degrees higher than −5 °C   (**f**) 15 degrees lower than 8 °C
  (**g**) 6 degrees higher than −13 °C   (**h**) 9 degrees lower than −5 °C

3 What is the difference in temperature between each pair of thermometers?

(a) (b) (c) (d)

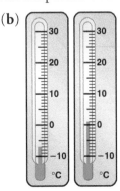 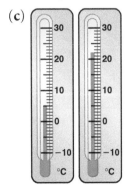 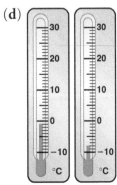

4 The temperature in Oban at 8 p.m. was 4 °C. At midnight the temperature had fallen by 7 °C. What was the temperature at midnight?

5 The average temperature in Moscow in January is -10 °C. The average temperature in Sydney is 23 °C. What is the difference in temperature?

6 Find the difference in temperature between:
  (**a**) London 2 °C and Washington -5 °C   (**b**) Thurso -6 °C and Dubai 18 °C
  (**c**) Oslo -3 °C and Edinburgh 4 °C   (**d**) Adelaide 24 °C and Glasgow -1 °C.

6.2 Adding and subtracting positive integers

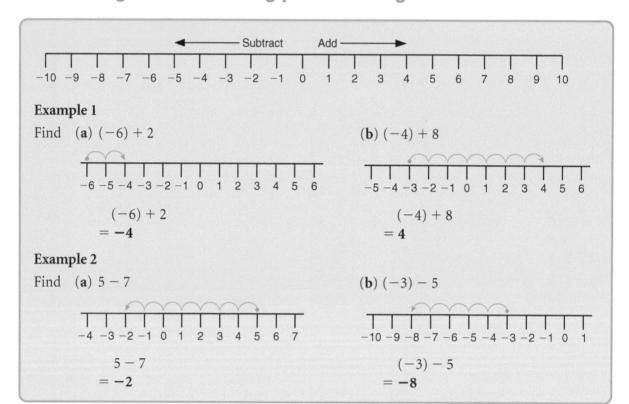

Exercise 6.2

1 Calculate:
  (**a**) $7 + 2$ (**b**) $(-7) + 2$ (**c**) $(-7) + 10$ (**d**) $(-3) + 5$ (**e**) $(-1) + 6$
  (**f**) $(-6) + 15$ (**g**) $(-20) + 30$ (**h**) $(-10) + 7$ (**i**) $(-32) + 15$ (**j**) $(-23) + 100$

2 Calculate:
  (**a**) $5 - 3$ (**b**) $(-7) - 9$ (**c**) $7 - 10$ (**d**) $(-3) - 5$ (**e**) $(-1) - 6$
  (**f**) $6 - 15$ (**g**) $20 - 30$ (**h**) $(-10) - 7$ (**i**) $(-32) - 15$ (**j**) $23 - 100$

3 Calculate:
  (**a**) $(-5) + 12$ (**b**) $4 - 5$ (**c**) $(-3) - 5$ (**d**) $(-9) + 6$ (**e**) $(-1) + 8$
  (**f**) $(-10) - 5$ (**g**) $12 - 30$ (**h**) $(-16) + 40$ (**i**) $19 - 32$ (**j**) $(-14) + 53$

6.3 Using negative numbers

Example

Which year is (**a**) 200 years after 830 BC   (**b**) 1500 years before 1100 AD?

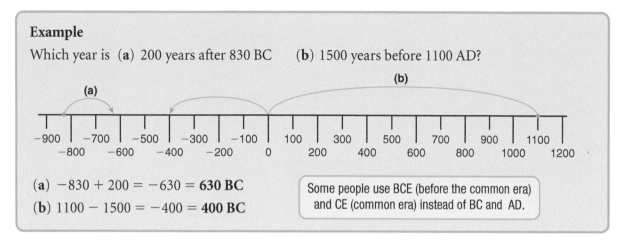

(**a**) $-830 + 200 = -630 =$ **630 BC**

(**b**) $1100 - 1500 = -400 =$ **400 BC**

> Some people use BCE (before the common era) and CE (common era) instead of BC and AD.

Exercise 6.3

1 Which year is
  (**a**) 32 years after 10 BC   (**b**) 270 years before 180 AD
  (**c**) 700 years after 2000 BC   (**d**) 2420 years before 1990 AD?

2 Archaeologists on a dig in 2002 found a bowl made in 400 BC.
   How old was the bowl?

3 Lucy's bank account is £65 overdrawn.
   If she pays in £150 how much will she have in her account?

4 In 2003 Filbert's Folders had sales of £26 000 and costs of £29 000.
   Did they make a profit or loss and by how much?

5 Jane's video timer showed 00 : 30 : 00. When she had rewound the
   video by 1 hour it showed $-00 : 30 : 00$. On another occasion the
   timer showed 1 : 30 : 00. If she then rewound the video by 4 hours
   what would the timer have shown?

6 Put the following numbers in order starting with the lowest:
  (**a**) $-10, 13, 0, -9, 1, 7, -6, 5$
  (**b**) $12, 15, -6, -2, -5, -10, 13$
  (**c**) $1, -6, 10, 0, -2, -0·5, 6, -8, -12, 7$
  (**d**) $-0·3, -0·5, 0·7, 0·6, -0·7, -0·9, 0·8, -1, -0·1, 0·2$
  (**e**) $-2, 1·8, 0·3, -0·6, -2·1, -0·4, 1·5, -1·3, 0·1$

7 (**a**) Put these cities in order of temperature starting with the lowest:

Brisbane	25 °C	Budapest	$-1·6$ °C	Casablanca	12·4 °C
Edinburgh	2·9 °C	London	3·9 °C	Los Angeles	13·4 °C
Madras	24·6 °C	Montreal	$-9·7$ °C	Moscow	$-10·3$ °C
Singapore	26.2 °C	Stockholm	$-3·5$ °C	Ulan Bator	$-19·4$ °C

  (**b**) Which two cities have the biggest temperature difference?
  (**c**) What is the biggest temperature difference?

6.4 Adding negative integers

Addition of whole numbers is **commutative**.
This means that we can add them in any order. $5 + 3 = 3 + 5$
Addition of integers is also commutative.

$5 + (-7)$ also $5 - 7 = -2$ $7 + (-3)$ also $7 - 3 = 4$
$= (-7) + 5$ $= (-3) + 7$
$= -2$ $= 4$

Adding a negative number is the same as subtracting the positive number.

Example 1   **(a)** $3 + (-5)$ **(b)** $(-4) + (-6)$
                              $= 3 - 5$ $= (-4) - 6$
                              $= -2$ $= -10$

Example 2
The number of points scored in each round of a quiz by the Wellington Whizzkids was
$10, 12, -5, 7, -3$. What was their total score?

$10 + 12 + (-5) + 7 + (-3)$ First put the negative
$= 10 + 12 + 7 + (-5) + (-3)$ numbers together.
$= 10 + 12 + 7 - 5 - 3$
$= 21$

Exercise 6.4

1 Copy and complete:

(a) $7 + (-6)$ **(b)** $12 + (-5)$ **(c)** $3 + (-8)$ **(d)** $7 + (-20)$
$= 7 - \blacksquare$ $= 12\ \blacksquare\ \blacksquare$ $= 3\ \blacksquare\ \blacksquare$ $= \blacksquare\ \blacksquare\ \blacksquare$
$= 1$ $= \blacksquare$ $= \blacksquare$ $= \blacksquare$

2 Calculate:

(a) $7 + (-3)$ **(b)** $2 + (-9)$ **(c)** $8 + (-14)$ **(d)** $7 + (-12)$
(e) $(-5) + (-13)$ **(f)** $3 + (-3)$ **(g)** $(-1) + (-8)$ **(h)** $4 + (-20)$
(i) $9 + (-35)$ **(j)** $(-32) + (-4)$ **(k)** $12 + (-50)$ **(l)** $(-19) + (-19)$

3 Calculate:

(a) $15 - 27$ **(b)** $6 + (-4)$ **(c)** $10 + (-3)$ **(d)** $(-16) - 22$
(e) $(-7) + 40$ **(f)** $(-38) - 7$ **(g)** $(-3) + (-12)$ **(h)** $(-16) + (-7)$
(i) $14 + (-33)$ **(j)** $(-8) + 32$ **(k)** $39 - 48$ **(l)** $(-12) + (-29)$

4 In a dance competition scores were given for technique and artistic
impression. Calculate the total scores of the following couples.

Couple	Technique	Artistic impression
Tom and Val	−3	8
Mandy and Alan	7	−5
Ron and Eileen	−6	10
Fred and Ginger	−6	1

5 Copy and complete the following:

(a)

+	−4	−2	0	2
−5		−7		
−3			−3	
−1				
1	−3			

(b)

+	−10	−6	−5	21
−23			−28	
−18				
−7	−17			
4				25

6 Copy and complete:

(a) $2 + 6 + (−7)$
   $= 2 + 6 − \blacksquare$
   $= \blacksquare$

(b) $6 + (−4) + 8$
   $= 6 + 8 + (−4)$
   $= 6 + 8 − \blacksquare$
   $= \blacksquare$

(c) $7 + (−7) + (−5)$
   $= 7 − \blacksquare \; \blacksquare \; \blacksquare$
   $= \blacksquare$

7 Calculate:

(a) $(−6) + 5 + 8$

(b) $5 + 9 + (−3)$

(c) $12 + (−30) − 5$

(d) $4 + (−27) + (−4)$

(e) $48 + (−32) − 18$

(f) $(−22) + (−67) − 12$

(g) $(−34) + (−50) + 11$

(h) $(−19) + 46 + (−8)$

(i) $12 + 56 + (−27) − 11$

(j) $(−12) + 56 + 12 + (−56)$

(k) $34 + (−20) + (−5) + 9$

(l) $175 + (−70) + (−20)$

8 Copy and complete:

(a) $6 + \blacksquare = 4$

(b) $24 + \blacksquare = 20$

(c) $63 + \blacksquare = 52$

(d) $(−50) + \blacksquare = −43$

(e) $(−19) + \blacksquare = −34$

(f) $(−64) + \blacksquare = 0$

9 When playing a computer game Michael scored the following points for each round:

   400   −200   1400   −800   −600

What was his total score?

10 Use the listed numbers to complete these triangles so that the total of each side is the same.

(a) −4, −2, 0, 2, 3, 5

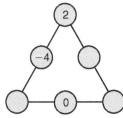

Total = 3

(b) 1, −2, −3, −5, −4, 3

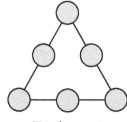

Total = −6

(c) −1, −2, −3, −4, −5, −6

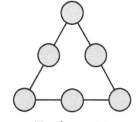

Total = −10

11 The temperatures in Fort William during one week are shown in the table.

Day	Mon	Tues	Wed	Thurs	Fri	Sat	Sun
Temperature	−1	6	7	6	1	−1	−4

Calculate the average temperature for the week.

6.5 Subtracting negative integers

The difference between 7 and 3 is $7 - 3 = 4$.

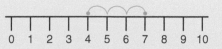

The difference between 7 and −3 is $7 - (-3) = 10$
and $7 + 3 = 10$.
Hence $7 - (-3) = 7 + 3$.

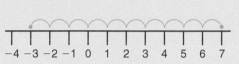

Subtracting a negative number is the same as adding the positive number.

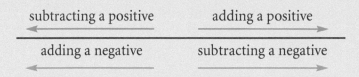

Examples

$7 - (-5)$
$= 7 + 5$
$= 12$

$(-5) - (-7)$
$= (-5) + 7$
$= 2$

$(-8) - (-3)$
$= (-8) + 3$
$= -5$

Exercise 6.5

1 Write the difference between:

(**a**) 8 and 2   (**b**) 3 and (-5) (**c**) 5 and (-7) (**d**) (-3) and (-6)

(**e**) 10 and (-7) (**f**) (-5) and (-9) (**g**) 8 and (-7) (**h**) (-2) and (-8)

2 Copy and complete:

(**a**) $6 - (-2)$
$= 6 \; \blacksquare \; 2$
$= \blacksquare$

(**b**) $(-2) - (-9)$
$= (-2) \; \blacksquare \blacksquare$
$= \blacksquare$

(**c**) $(-7) - (-3)$
$= (-7) \; \blacksquare \blacksquare$
$= \blacksquare$

(**d**) $5 - (-2)$
$= 5 \; \blacksquare \blacksquare$
$= \blacksquare$

3 Calculate:

(**a**) $5 - (-1)$ (**b**) $3 - (-6)$ (**c**) $(-2) - (-5)$ (**d**) $(-9) - (-7)$

(**e**) $(-9) - (-10)$ (**f**) $(-8) - (-4)$ (**g**) $5 - (-3)$ (**h**) $(-7) - (-1)$

(**i**) $5 - (-8)$ (**j**) $3 - (-5)$ (**k**) $(-7) - (-2)$ (**l**) $(-2) - (-7)$

(**m**) $(-5) - (-5)$ (**n**) $(-2) - (-8)$ (**o**) $8 - (-2)$ (**p**) $16 - (-1)$

4 Calculate:

(**a**) $8 + (-2)$ (**b**) $2 - (-9)$ (**c**) $2 - (-6)$ (**d**) $5 + (-7)$

(**e**) $5 - (-1)$ (**f**) $(-10) - (-3)$ (**g**) $9 + (-3)$ (**h**) $(-12) - (-2)$

(**i**) $9 - (-7)$ (**j**) $(-5) + (-5)$ (**k**) $(-7) + (-9)$ (**l**) $(-7) - (-8)$

(**m**) $(-3) + (-3)$ (**n**) $(-1) - (-7)$ (**o**) $0 + (-4)$ (**p**) $(-6) - (-6)$

5 Copy and complete:

(**a**) $4 + (-6) + 3$ (**b**) $9 - (-5) - 8$ (**c**) $(-2) - 5 + 7$

$= 4 + 3 + (\ \ )$ $= 9 - 8 - (\ \ )$ $= 7 + (\ \ ) - \ $

$= 4 + 3 \ \square \ \square$ $= 9 - 8 + \ \square$ $= 7 - 2 - \ \square$

$= \ \square$ $= \ \square$ $= \ \square$

6 Calculate:

(**a**) $5 + 6 - 9$ (**b**) $(-4) + 1 - 7$ (**c**) $3 - 2 - 4$

(**d**) $(-3) + 8 + 7$ (**e**) $5 - 7 + (-4)$ (**f**) $8 + (-2) + (-5)$

(**g**) $(-4) + (-6) + 8$ (**h**) $(-3) - (-2) + 4$ (**i**) $7 - (-1) - 8$

(**j**) $5 - (-3) - 4$ (**k**) $3 - (-7) + 3$ (**l**) $8 - (-2) + (-9)$

(**m**) $(-2) - (-7) + 3$ (**n**) $(-5) - (-2) + 3$ (**o**) $2 - (-5) + (-9)$

7 Find the missing number:

(**a**) $\square + 6 = -2$ (**b**) $\square + 10 = 3$ (**c**) $\square - 7 = -5$

8 Write down the next two numbers in each sequence.

(**a**) $2, -2, -6, -10, \ldots$ (**b**) $-30, -22, -14, \ldots$

(**c**) $-200, -193, -186, -179, \ldots$ (**d**) $50, 36, 22, 8, \ldots$

9 Meena and Callum are playing a game. They have two piles of cards both of which contain a mixture of positive and negative numbers. The pink cards are to be added and the green cards are to be subtracted. They each choose four cards and the person with the highest total wins.
For example, if Meena chooses pink 7, -4, 1 and green -6 then her total is

$7 + (-4) + 1 - (-6)$
$= 7 - 4 + 1 + 6$
$= 10$

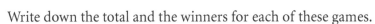

Write down the total and the winners for each of these games.

Game 1

	Pink	Green
Meena	5, −9	−1, −6
Callum	4, −10, 7	−9

Game 2

	Pink	Green
Meena	7, 5	6, −2
Callum	9, −6	5, −4

10 Calculate:

(**a**) $(-1) + (-1) + (-1)$

(**b**) $(-4) + (-4) + (-4) + (-4)$

(**c**) $(-5) + (-5) + (-5) + (-5) + (-5)$

(**d**) $(-3) + (-3) + (-3) + (-3) + (-3)$

(**e**) $(-2) + (-2) + (-2)$

(**f**) $(-3) + (-3) + (-3) + (-3) + (-3) + (-3)$

11 Can you find an easier way to complete the calculations in question 10?

6.6 Greater than or less than

$<$ means 'is less than' $>$ means 'is greater than'

$3 < 7$ means '3 is less than 7' $10 > 6$ means '10 is greater than 6'

These symbols show an **inequality**

Exercise 6.6

1 State whether each of the following inequalities is true or false.

(**a**) $5 < 8$ (**b**) $4 > 2$ (**c**) $7 < 0$ (**d**) $-2 < 1$ (**e**) $3 < -3$

(**f**) $-6 > 0$ (**g**) $-1 < -2$ (**h**) $-5 < -3$ (**i**) $-7 > -5$ (**j**) $0 < -5$

2 Copy each pair of numbers and write $<$ or $>$ between them.

(**a**) $4 \quad 6$ (**b**) $10 \quad 17$ (**c**) $2 \quad 13$ (**d**) $2 \quad 7$

(**e**) $0 \quad 5$ (**f**) $100 \quad 200$ (**g**) $50 \quad 10$ (**h**) $13 \quad 7$

3 Copy each pair of numbers and write $<$ or $>$ between them.

(**a**) $-1 \quad 5$ (**b**) $7 \quad -7$ (**c**) $3 \quad -2$ (**d**) $0 \quad -4$

(**e**) $-4 \quad -2$ (**f**) $-1 \quad -5$ (**g**) $-7 \quad -9$ (**h**) $-20 \quad -12$

Review exercise 6

1 Which year is:

(**a**) 1260 years before 1008 AD   (**b**) 70 years after 2000 BC?

2 Put these numbers in order, starting with the lowest:

$1\cdot8, 1\cdot1, -0\cdot9, -0\cdot8, 0\cdot4, -1\cdot5, -1, 0\cdot7, -0\cdot7, -0\cdot1$

3 Calculate:

(**a**) $17 - 25$ (**b**) $(-14) + 8$ (**c**) $(-27) + 32$ (**d**) $(-5) - 28$

(**e**) $150 - 307$ (**f**) $(-7) - 35$ (**g**) $(-52) - 16$ (**h**) $(-40) - 56$

4 In 2002 the lowest recorded temperature in Montana was $-30\,°C$. The highest was $39\,°C$. What was the range in temperature?

5 Write down the temperature that is

(**a**) 7 degrees lower than $5\,°C$ (**b**) 12 degrees lower than $12\,°C$

(**c**) 10 degrees higher than $-3\,°C$ (**d**) 7 degrees lower than $-4\,°C$.

6 Ten contestants' scores in a quiz were

$-5, 20, -12, -1, 12, 16, -10, 15, 15, 10$

Calculate the average score.

7 Calculate:

(**a**) $(-4) + (-6)$ (**b**) $7 + (-10)$ (**c**) $4 - (-3)$

(**d**) $15 + (-7)$ (**e**) $(-7) + (-112)$ (**f**) $607 - (-89)$

(**g**) $37 + (-15)$ (**h**) $324 - (-133)$ (**i**) $(-17) + (-12)$

(**j**) $(-30) + (-3)$ (**k**) $(-132) - (-60)$ (**l**) $(-87) + (-87)$

8 State whether each of the following inequalities is true or false.

(**a**) $3 > -6$ (**b**) $-1 < 0$ (**c**) $-2 > -3$ (**d**) $-7 < -5$

9 Copy each pair of numbers and write $<$ or $>$ between them.

(**a**) $3\ \ \ 7$ (**b**) $-2\ \ \ 6$ (**c**) $-11\ \ \ -12$ (**d**) $-4\ \ \ -1$

Summary

Integers

The set of integers $= \{\ldots, -3, -2, -1, 0, 1, 2, 3, \ldots\}$
Use a number line to help calculate with integers.

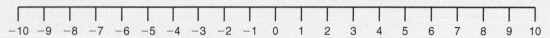

Adding and subtracting

- When adding a positive integer move right along the number line.
  $(-6) + 2 = -4$

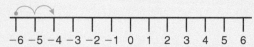

- When subtracting a positive integer, move left along the number line.
  $4 - 7 = -3$

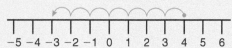

- When adding a negative integer, move left along the number line.
  $6 + (-2) = 6 - 2 = 4$

- When subtracting a negative integer, move right along the number line.
  $-3 - (-5) = 3 + 5 = 8$

Adding a negative number is the same as subtracting the positive number.

$$6 + (-2) = 6 - 2 = 4$$

Subtracting a negative number is the same as adding the positive number.

$$3 - (-5) = 3 + 5 = 8$$

Inequalities

$3 < 7$ means '3 is less than 7' $10 > 6$ means '10 is greater than 6'
These symbols show an inequality.

7 Coordinates

In this chapter you will extend your knowledge of coordinates, including reflection in a line.

7.1 Reading coordinates

On a coordinate diagram the horizontal line is called the **x-axis** and the vertical line is called the **y-axis**.

The point where the x-axis and y-axis meet is called the **origin, O.**

The position of a point may be described by its **coordinates**.

From the origin, the point A is 5 lines along then 2 lines up.

This is written as **A**(5, 2)
(5, 2) are the coordinates of A.

The coordinates of B are (1, 4)

The **x**-coordinate of B is 1
The **y**-coordinate of B is 4

The origin has coordinates (0, 0)

This is called a **Cartesian** diagram.

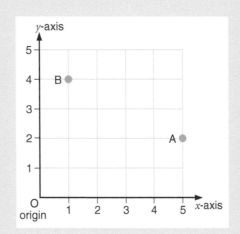

Exercise 7.1

1 (a) Write the coordinates of A, B, C, D, E, F, G and H.

(b) Write the x-coordinate of
   (i) D   (ii) G   (iii) F
   (iv) H   (v) C

(c) Write the y-coordinate of
   (i) A   (ii) H   (iii) G
   (iv) F   (v) C

(d) Which two points have the same x-coordinate?

(e) Which two points have the same y-coordinate?

(f) Which point has the same x and y-coordinate?

(g) The point K has the same x-coordinate as G and the same y-coordinate as D. Write the coordinates of K.

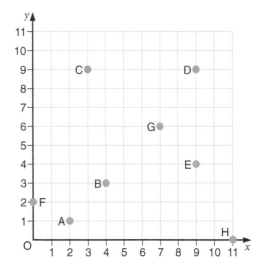

2 (**a**) Write the coordinates of A, B and C.

(**b**) Write the coordinates of D so that ABCD is a rectangle.

(**c**) Point E is exactly halfway between points B and C.
Write the coordinates of E.

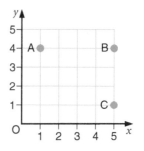

3 The points shown are two vertices of a square. Write the coordinates of the other two vertices.

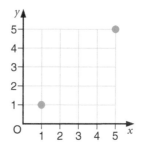

7.2 Plotting coordinates

Marking a point on a Cartesian diagram is called **plotting** a point.

When drawing a coordinate diagram, use the largest coordinate to decide the length of each axis.

To plot A(**8**, 1) and B(2, **9**)

(**i**) draw the x-axis from zero to **8**.

(**ii**) draw the y-axis from zero to **9**.

To plot (4, 6) count along 4 lines from the origin then up 6 lines. Mark the point.

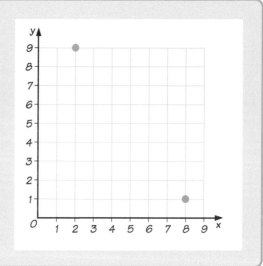

Exercise 7.2

1 (**a**) Draw an x-axis from 0 to 12.
Draw a y-axis from 0 to 10.

(**b**) Plot these points on your diagram:
A(3, 1)   B(1, 5)   C(7, 0)   D(0, 3)

2 (**a**) Draw another Cartesian diagram with the same axes as for question 1.

(**b**) Plot the points :
E(4, 6)   F(1, 8)   G(5, 0)   H(7, 6)   I(0, 8)   J(11, 9)   K(4, 2)

3 Look at the coordinates for each set of points to decide the length of each axis.
Draw a coordinate diagram for each set, plot the points and join them in order.
Name the object.

(**a**) $(0, 0), (10, 0), (10, 11), (5, 16), (0, 11)$ STOP $(4, 0), (4, 3), (6, 3), (6, 0)$ STOP

(**b**) $(3, 0), (9, 6), (11, 4), (11, 10), (5, 10), (7, 8), (1, 2), (3, 0)$ STOP

(**c**) $(1, 5), (4, 5)$ $(7, 5)$ STOP $(4, 5), (4, 0)$ STOP $(9, 5), (15, 5), (15, 1)$, STOP $(9, 1), (9, 5)$ STOP
$(17, 5), (20, 3), (23, 5)$ STOP $(20, 3), (20, 0)$ STOP

(**d**) $(3, 2), (1, 5), (12, 5), (10, 2), (3, 2)$ STOP $(8, 5), (8, 13), (3, 7), (8, 7)$ STOP

(**e**) $(4, 2), (4, 5), (1, 5), (4, 8), (2, 8), (4, 10), (3, 10), (5, 12), (7, 10), (6, 10), (8, 8),$
$(6, 8), (9, 5), (6, 5), (6, 2), (4, 2)$ STOP

For each question below, draw a new coordinate diagram.

4 Plot the points, join them in order and name each shape.

(**a**) A$(1, 0)$, B$(5, 0)$, C$(5, 3)$, D$(1, 3)$.   (**b**) K$(3, 3)$, L$(5, 3)$, M$(5, 7)$ and N$(3, 7)$

5 (**a**) A$(1, 0)$, B$(5, 0)$ and C$(5, 2)$.   (**b**) Plot the point D so that ABCD is a rectangle.

(**c**) Write the coordinates of E, where the diagonals of the rectangle meet.

6 (**a**) Plot the points A$(2, 1)$ and B$(5, 1)$.

(**b**) If ABCD is a square, plot the points C and D and write their coordinates.

(**c**) Write the coordinates of E, where the diagonals cross.

7 (**a**) Plot the points J$(2, 0)$ and L$(7, 3)$.

(**b**) Plot K which has the same y-coordinate as J and the same x-coordinate as L.

(**c**) Plot M which has the same y-coordinate as L and the same x-coordinate as J.

8 Draw a line joining the points P$(6, 3)$ and R$(1, 5)$.
If PR is a diagonal of rectangle PQRS, plot and write the coordinates of Q and S.

9 Plot the points J$(1, 2)$, K$(5, 2)$ and L$(8, 4)$.
If JKLM is a parallelogram, plot M and write its coordinates.

7.3 Reading coordinates in four quadrants

The axes may be extended to include negative numbers.

This gives a diagram with four **quadrants**.

Points may be plotted in all four quadrants.

Example   A has coordinates $(5, 1)$
B has coordinates $(2, -2)$
C has coordinates $(-2, 4)$
D has coordinates $(-4, -3)$
E has coordinates $(0, -5)$

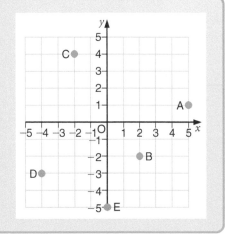

Exercise 7.3

For questions 1 to 3 write the coordinates of each point.

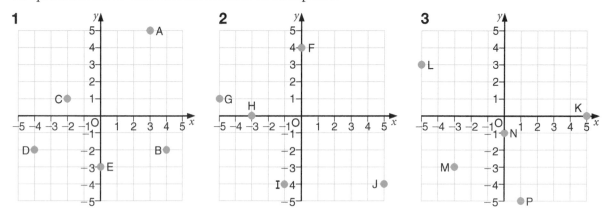

4 For the questions above, write:

(**a**) all the points that have the same *y*-coordinate,

(**a**) all the points that have the same *x*-coordinate

(**c**) the point that has the same *x*- and *y*-coordinate.

5 Look at the map of Sun Island.

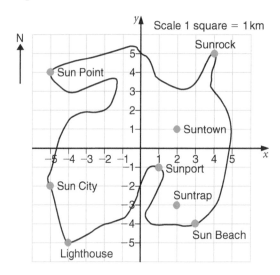

(**a**) Write the coordinates of each feature and place on Sun Island.

(**b**) What has
   (**i**) an *x*-coordinate of −4
   (**ii**) a *y*-coordinate of −3
   (**iii**) a *y*-coordinate of −4?

(**c**) Bob is in Sun Beach.
   He travels 3 km north then 2 km west.
   Where is Bob now?

(**d**) Max is at the lighthouse.
   He travels 5 km north then 7 km east, then 4 km south.
   Where is Max now?

7.4 Plotting coordinates in four quadrants

To plot A(−4, −2) from the origin, count **along** 4 lines to the left, then **down** 2 lines.

To plot B(−3, 4) from the origin, count **along** 3 lines to the left and 4 lines **up**.

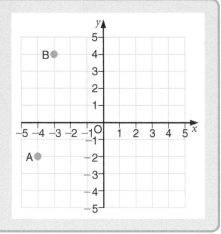

Exercise 7.4

1 Copy the diagram above and plot each point.
C(−2, 1), D(−5, 3), E(1, −3), F(4, −1), G(−2, 0) and H(0, −5).

2 (**a**) Draw a coordinate diagram with *x*-axis and *y*-axis numbered from −10 to 10.

   (**b**) Plot the points J(5, −1), K(−9, −5), L(1, 3), M(7, −3), N(−7, 0)
                    P(1, −1), Q(−3, −1), R(0, −8), S(−1, 5), T(−5, −10)
                    U(10, −10), V(−3, 3) and W(1, −5)

   (**c**) Which four points form the vertices of a square starting with L?

   (**d**) Which four points form the vertices of another square?

3 For each question below:
  ● draw a coordinate diagram
  ● plot each point
  ● join the points in order.

   (**a**) (0, 7), (−5, −5), (5, −5), (−5, 6), (0, −9), (0, 7)

   (**b**) (0, 2), (2, 4), (4, 4), (6, 3), (5, 0), (4, −2), (2, −4), (0, −5), (−2, −4),
      (−4, −2), (−5, 0), (−6, 3), (−4, 4), (−2, 4), (0, 2) STOP

   (**c**) (1, 1), (5, 2), (−1, 2), (−5, 1), (−5, −5), (1, −5), (5, −4), (−1, -4),
      (−5, −5), STOP (−1, 2), (−1, −4) STOP (5, 2), (5, −4) STOP
      (−5, 1), (1, 1), (1, −5) STOP

4 Each set of points forms the vertices of a square.
Plot the points and find the coordinates of the missing vertices.

   (**a**) ABCD where A(−3, −2), B(1, −2) and C(1, 2).

   (**b**) EFGH where EF is a side, E(4, −1) and F(0, −1).

   (**c**) IJKL where JK is a side, J(0, −3) and K(4, 0).

   (**d**) PQRS where PR is a diagonal, P(−3, −4) and R(1, 0).

   (**e**) STUV where TV is a diagonal, T(−3, −2) and V(3, 2).

5 Draw the diagonals of each square in question 4 and write the coordinates of M, the intersection of the diagonals.

6 Rhombus JKLM has vertices J(3, 2), K(−1, −4) and L(−5, 2).
Find the coordinates of: (**a**) M
(**b**) the intersection of the diagonals at N.

7 Parallelogram QRST has vertices Q(1, 0), R(−1, 0) and S(−3, −8).
Find the coordinates of: (**a**) T
(**b**) the intersection of the diagonals at U.

8 The line joining A(0, −7) and C(6, −3) is a diagonal of a square.
Find the coordinates of the other two vertices B and D.

9 The line joining P(3, 3) and Q(−3, 1) is a side of square PQRS.
(**a**) Find the coordinates of R and S if both points have negative *y*-coordinates.
(**b**) Find the coordinates of the intersection of the diagonals.

7.5 Reflection using coordinates

The images of the points A(4, 2) and B(−2, −4) under reflection in the *x*-axis are A′(4, −2) and B′(−2, 4).

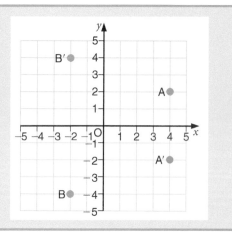

Exercise 7.5

1 (**a**) Write the coordinates of each point and its image under a reflection in the *x*-axis.
(**b**) What do you notice about the coordinates of these points and their images?
(**c**) What do you notice about F and its image?

2 Repeat question 1(**a**) and (**b**) under a reflection in the *y*-axis.

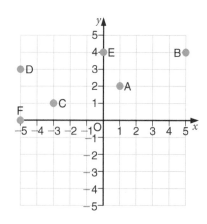

3 Write the coordinates of the image of each point under a reflection in the *x*-axis.

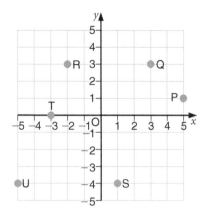

For each question below, draw a new coordinate diagram.

4 (**a**) Draw the triangle with vertices J(4, 2), K(1, 2) and L(3, 5).
 (**b**) Draw the images of the vertices under a reflection in the *x*-axis.
 (**c**) Draw the images of J, K and L under a reflection in the *y*-axis.

5 (**a**) Draw the triangle with vertices U(2, 0), V(5, 3) and W(3, 4).
 (**b**) Plot U′, V′ and W′ under a reflection in the y-axis, and draw triangle U′V′W′.

6 (**a**) Draw a dotted line joining A(−5, −5) and B(5, 5).
 (**b**) Plot the points C(2, 3), D(−5, 0), E(−4, −3), F(−3, 2) and G(4, 1).
 (**c**) Write the coordinates of C′, D′, E′, F′ and G′ under a reflection in the line AB.

7 (**a**) Draw the triangle with vertices P(1, 3), Q(−3, 0) and R(−2, −3).
 (**b**) Reflect triangle PQR in the line AB as in question 6.
 (**c**) Write the coordinates of P′, Q′ and R′.

Review exercise 7

1 (**a**) Write the coordinates of each point.
 (**b**) Which points have the same *x*-coordinate?
 (**c**) Which points have the same *y*-coordinate?
 (**d**) Which four points form the vertices of a rectangle?
 (**e**) Write the coordinates of W, the intersection of the diagonals of the rectangle.
 (**f**) Write the coordinates of V, the midpoint of SP.

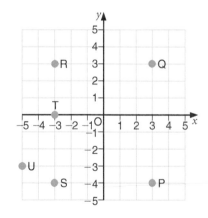

2 (**a**) Draw a Cartesian diagram with *x*- and *y*-axes numbered from −10 to 10.
 (**b**) Plot the points A(1, 5), B(3, −1), C(−5, −2), D(−5, 1), E(7, −2), F(0, −5) and G(−3, −3).
 (**c**) B, F, G and H are the vertices of a parallelogram. Find the coordinates of H.
 (**d**) Find the coordinates of J, the intersection of the diagonals of the parallelogram.

3 The centre of square ABCD has coordinates $(0, -2)$.
If A is the point $(3, 0)$, find the coordinates of the other vertices.

4 Find the coordinates of the images of $J(-2, 3)$, $K(-3, -4)$, $L(-5, 0)$, $M(-6, -6)$, $N(57, 29)$ and the origin under reflection in the

(**a**) y-axis   (**b**) x-axis.

5 (**a**) Draw a dotted line joining $G(-4, -4)$ and $H(4, 4)$.

(**b**) Plot the points $J(3, 2)$, $K(-2, 0)$, $L(-4, -2)$, $M(-2, 3)$ and $N(6, -1)$.

(**c**) Write the coordinates of J', K', L', M' and N' under a reflection in the line GH.

6 (**a**) Draw a dotted line joining $S(-4, 2)$ and $T(4, -6)$.

(**b**) Draw a triangle with vertices $A(1, 3)$, $B(-3, 0)$ and $C(-2, -3)$.

(**c**) Write the coordinates of A', B' and C' under a reflection in the line ST.

Summary

Cartesian coordinates in four quadrants

$J(1, 2)$
$K(-5, 4)$
$L(-4, -3)$
$M(3, -4)$
$N(0, -5)$

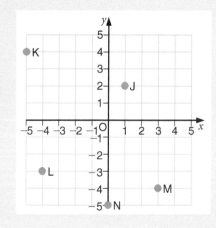

Reflection in a line

Points may be reflected in a line.

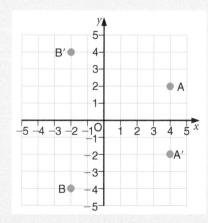

8 Measurement

In this chapter you will extend your knowledge of calculations using different units of measurement, particularly metric units.

8.1 Length

A variety of different units have been used in the past. Some imperial units are still in common use today. You may, for example give your height in feet and inches or you may give it in metres. You may give a distance in miles or in kilometres.

My height is 5'3" or 1 metre 60 centimetres.

In Europe most people use the metric system.

Remember

1000 millimetres (mm)	= 1 metre (m)	10 millimetres (mm)	= 1 centimetre (cm)
1000 metres (m)	= 1 kilometre (km)	100 centimetres (cm)	= 1 metre (m)

It is useful to estimate measurements using common objects as a guide before measuring accurately.
The length of the Forth Bridge is about 1 kilometre.
The height of most doors is about 2 metres.
The thickness of a fingernail is about 1 millimetre.

Accuracy is essential in many situations. It is also useful to be able to convert between different units.

The length of this page is 26 centimetres 3 millimetres or 26·3 centimetres or 263 millimetres

$$26 \text{ cm } 3 \text{ mm} = 26 \cdot 3 \text{ cm} = 263 \text{ mm}$$

A length of 9 centimetres can be written as 0·09 metres   9 cm = 0·09 m
A length of 17 millimetres can be written as 0·017 metres   17 mm = 0·017 m

Exercise 8.1

1 Measure the width of this page and write it in three different ways.

2 Write each of the following in centimetres.
   (**a**) 4 cm 2 mm   (**b**) 18 cm 9 mm   (**c**) 6 mm   (**d**) 85 mm   (**e**) 159 mm
   (**f**) 5 m   (**g**) 8·45 m   (**h**) 47·5 m   (**i**) 875 mm   (**j**) 5 m 659 mm

3 Write each of the following in millimetres.
   (**a**) 5·8 cm   (**b**) 87·3 cm   (**c**) 0·7 cm   (**d**) 4 cm 3 mm   (**e**) 8 km
   (**f**) 5 m   (**g**) 8·45 m   (**h**) 47·5 m   (**i**) 47 km   (**j**) 4 m 7 cm

4 Write each of the following in metres.
   (**a**) 4 m 19 cm   (**b**) 90 m 45 cm   (**c**) 8 m 4 cm
   (**d**) 10 m 899 mm   (**e**) 8 m 43 mm   (**f**) 4 m 2 mm

Work with a partner for questions **5** and **6**.

5 You need a tape measure or metre stick for this question. Measure each of the following expressing the answer in
   (**i**) metres and centimetres   (**ii**) metres   (**iii**) centimetres.

Make an estimate before you measure accurately.
   (**a**) your height   (**b**) your partner's height
   (**c**) the width of the classroom (**d**) the height of the door
   (**e**) the length of the corridor (**f**) the length of 10 paces

6 Measure 20 metres.
   (**a**) Count the number of paces which you take to walk 20 metres.
   (**b**) How many paces would you take to walk
      (**i**) 100 metres   (**ii**) 1 kilometres?

7 Write each of the following in kilometres.
   (**a**) 8000 m   (**b**) 625 m   (**c**) 86 m   (**d**) 4 m   (**e**) 58 971 m

8 Round each of the following measurements to the nearest centimetre.
   (**a**) 8·9 cm   (**b**) 4·3 cm   (**c**) 6 m 15 mm
   (**d**) 8·009 m   (**e**) 1·6 cm   (**f**) 85 mm

9 Round each of the following measurements to the nearest metre.
   (**a**) 4·2 m   (**b**) 96·8 m   (**c**) 5·5268 km
   (**d**) 855 cm   (**e**) 6953 mm   (**f**) 99 km 999 mm

8.2 Calculating length

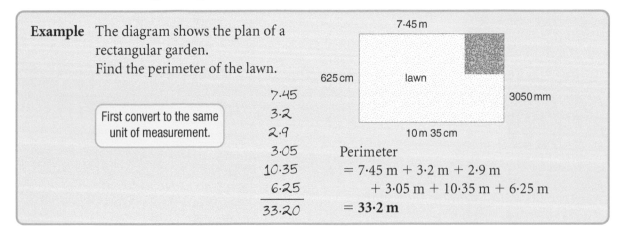

Example   The diagram shows the plan of a rectangular garden.
Find the perimeter of the lawn.

First convert to the same unit of measurement.

```
 7·45
 3·2
 2·9
 3·05
10·35
 6·25
─────
33·20
```

Perimeter
= 7·45 m + 3·2 m + 2·9 m
    + 3·05 m + 10·35 m + 6·25 m
= **33·2 m**

7·45 m
625 cm   lawn
3050 mm
10 m 35 cm

Exercise 8.2

1 Find the perimeter of each shape.

(**a**)
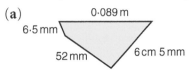
0·089 m
6·5 mm
52 mm
6 cm 5 mm

(**b**)
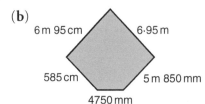
6 m 95 cm   6·95 m
585 cm   5 m 850 mm
4750 mm

(**c**)
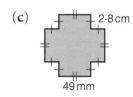
2·8 cm
49 mm

2 Find the perimeter of each lawn.

(**a**)
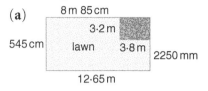

(**b**)
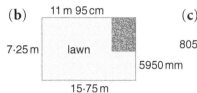

(**c**)

3 Find a quicker method to calculate the perimeters in question 2. Show your method.

4 Find the perimeter of each shape.

(**a**)
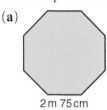

(**b**)
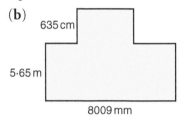

(**c**)
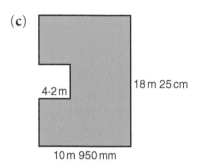

5 The perimeter of each rectangle is given. Find the length of the side marked x in each case.

(**a**) perimeter
= 8 m 24 cm
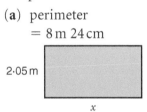

(**b**) perimeter
= 12 cm 6 mm
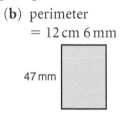

(**c**) perimeter
= 9·8 m
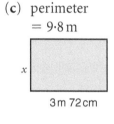

(**d**) perimeter
= 35·6 cm
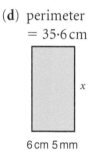

6 Daniel is planning to pave a patio with square slabs of side
50 centimetres. The diagram shows a plan of the rectangular area to
be paved.

(**a**) How many slabs are required altogether?

(**b**) What would be the total cost if one slab costs £2.75?

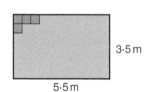

7 Penny would like to put down decking in her garden. The area is
shown in the diagram.
The decking comes in planks 3000 millimetres long by
150 millimetres wide.
Each plank can be cut to fit.

(**a**) How many planks are required altogether?

(**b**) The decking comes in packs of 5 planks each costing £10.99.
What would it cost to deck this area?

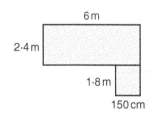

8 A queue of traffic on the road to the Erskine Bridge stretches for 3·595 kilometres.
The average length of a vehicle is 3·5 metres.
How many vehicles are there in the queue if there is a space of
50 centimetres between each vehicle?

8.3 Weight

Remember: 1000 milligrammes (mg) = 1 gramme (g)
1000 gramme (g) = 1 kilogramme (kg)
1000 kilogramme (g) = 1 tonne

Estimating weights using common objects as a guide is a useful start before measuring accurately.
For example, the weight of an A4 sheet of paper is 1 gramme.
The weight of a can of cola is 250 grammes.
The weight of a baby is 3.5 kilogrammes.
The average weight of a first year girl is 40 kilogrammes.

Measuring weight

The weight of John's car is 1.5 tonnes
or 1500 kilogrammes
or 1 500 000 grammes
or 1 500 000 000 milligrammes

Exercise 8.3

1 You need a set of bathroom scales.

(**a**) Estimate your weight in kilogrammes.

(**b**) Find your weight accurately using the scales.

2 Using the metric units listed estimate the weight of each of the following items.

tonnes   kilogrammes   grammes   milligrammes

(**a**) a double decker bus   (**b**) a football   (**c**) a pen

(**d**) a feather   (**e**) your teacher   (**f**) bicycle.

3 Write each of the following in grammes.

(**a**) 8 g 500 mg   (**b**) 6 g 42 mg   (**c**) 587 mg

(**d**) 1 mg   (**e**) 34·002 kg   (**f**) 6·8 tonnes

4 Write each of the following in milligrammes.

(**a**) 3·2 g   (**b**) 6·794 g   (**c**) 42·64 g

(**d**) 0·32 g   (**e**) 1 kg   (**f**) 1 tonne

5 Write each of the following in kilogrammes.

(**a**) 8 kg 625 g   (**b**) 14 kg 25 g   (**c**) 8250 g

(**d**) 540 g   (**e**) 25 mg   (**f**) 3·1 tonnes

6 Write each of the following in tonnes.

(**a**) 8625 kg   (**b**) 500 mg   (**c**) 25 g

(**d**) 1 kg   (**e**) 5 g 250 mg   (**f**) 90 kg

8.4 Calculating weight

Example   A box contains 20 cans of cola each weighing 250 grammes.
What is the total weight in kilogrammes of the contents of the box?

Weight of 1 can   = 250 grammes = 0·25 kg
Total weight   = 0·25 kg × 20
                   = **5 kg**

Exercise 8.4

1 Find the total weight in kilogrammes of each group of pupils.

(a) 72 kg 500g   68kg 200g   79kg 250g   66kg 850g

(b) 75kg 450g   68kg 250g   58kg 250g   64kg 600g   73kg 750g

2 Work in a group of four. You need a set of bathroom scales.
   (**a**) Measure and record the weight of each member of the group to the
      nearest kilogramme.
   (**b**) Calculate the average weight of the group.

3 The total weight of 6 vehicles is 14 tonnes 700 kilogrammes.
   Find the average weight of 1 vehicle.

4 The average weight of a group of ten boys is 72 kilogrammes 890 grammes.
   When one boy leaves the group the average of the nine becomes 72·5 kilogrammes.
   Find the weight of the boy who left the group.

5 A bridge has been designed so that it can carry the weight of 300 vehicles
   at any time. The average weight of a vehicle is taken as 1 tonne 850 kilogrammes.
   If the bridge is built to support a total weight of 550 tonnes, is it safe to have
   this number of vehicles on the bridge at one time?

6 A builders merchant makes a concrete mix using 3 tonnes 625 kilogrammes
   of cement and 6 tonnes 125 kilogrammes of sand.
   (**a**) Find the total weight of the mix.
   (**b**) The mix has to be packaged in bags each weighing 50 kilogrammes.
      How many bags can be produced?
   (**c**) Cement costs the builder £100 per tonne while sand costs £50 per tonne.
      How much profit does the merchant make if he sells the bags of mix at £10.25 each?

7 A builder's lorry can carry a maximum
   of 3 tonnes. He would like to load the
   items shown onto the lorry. Can this be
   safely done? Explain your reasons clearly.

> Scaffolding
> 15 poles @ 58 kg each
> Planks   0.425 tonnes
> Mixes   0.350 tonnes
> Sand bags 6 × 250 kg
> Cement   3 × 250 kg

8.5 Capacity

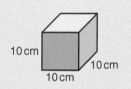

Remember:

 1 cubic centimetre (cm³)   = 1 millilitre (ml)
 1000 cubic centimetres (cm³) = 1000 millilitres (ml) = 1 litre (ℓ)
 1 cubic metre (m³)   = 1000 litres (ℓ)

Estimating capacity using common objects as a guide is a useful start before measuring accurately.

> 1 litre of water weighs exactly 1 kilogramme

For example, a teaspoon contains about 5 millilitres,
  a bottle of squash contains 1 litre,
  a 25 metre long school swimming pool contains about 500 cubic metres.

Example A car petrol tank can hold 64 litres 500 millilitres of petrol when full. How much petrol will be left in the car after it travels 250 miles if it uses 140 millilitres per mile?
 Volume used = 250 × 140 ml = 35 000 ml = 35 ℓ
 Volume left = 64·5 ℓ − 35 ℓ = **29·5 ℓ**

Exercise 8.5

1 Write each of the following in litres.
  (**a**) 6 ℓ 500 ml (**b**) 5 ℓ 42 ml (**c**) 655 ml
  (**d**) 3657 ml (**e**) 12 689 cm³ (**f**) 5·2 m³

2 Write each of the following in cubic metres.
  (**a**) 5785 ℓ (**b**) 25·3 ℓ (**c**) 5050 ml
  (**d**) 120 673 ℓ (**e**) 0·01 ℓ (**f**) 250 cm³

3 Write each of the following in millilitres.
  (**a**) 5·6 ℓ (**b**) 8·165 ℓ (**c**) 0·235 ℓ
  (**d**) 0·0655 m³ (**e**) 8 m³ 25 ℓ (**f**) 6 ℓ 125 cm³

4 Write each of the following in cubic centimetres.
  (**a**) 4 ℓ 500 ml (**b**) 7 ℓ 325 ml (**c**) 0·125 ℓ
  (**d**) 5 ℓ 5 ml (**e**) 25 ml (**f**) 0·5 ml

5 (**a**) How many centimetres are there in a metre?
  (**b**) Calculate the number of cubic centimetres in a cubic metre.
  (**c**) Hence justify the number of litres in a cubic metre.

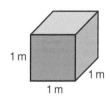

6 Aimee is having a party for her six friends. She thinks that each friend will drink three 250 millilitre glasses of juice and plans to buy 2 litre bottles.
  (**a**) What is the total capacity of juice required?
  (**b**) How many bottles will she need?
  (**c**) If each bottle costs £1.75, how much will Aimee have to spend on juice?

7 A bottle of mineral water contains 330 millilitres. Each bottle has a diameter of 5 centimetres.

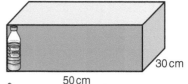

30 cm

50 cm

(**a**) How many bottles will fit into a box with a base measuring 30 centimetres by 50 centimetres?

(**b**) What is the total volume of mineral water contained in the box?

(**c**) John requires to drink 0·5 litres three times a day as part of a training programme. He claims that the box of mineral water will last him a fortnight. Is his claim true? Explain your answer clearly.

8 A swimming pool contains 2500 cubic metres of water when full.

(**a**) If the pool is filled at a rate of 4000 litres per minute, how long will it take to fill the pool?

(**b**) How many cubic metres of water does the pool contain after 5 hours?

9 The Juicee Soft Drinks Company uses bottles with a capacity of 500 millilitres, 0·75 litre, 1·5 litre and 2 litres. The following table shows the number of each type of bottle which the company produces each week.

Size	Number	Selling price per bottle
500 ml	12 000	56 p
0.75 ℓ	6000	£0.84
1.5 ℓ	3000	£1.65
2 ℓ	2500	£2.30

(**a**) What is the total volume of soft drinks bottled each week?

(**b**) The soft drink costs £0.50 per litre, including bottling, to produce. How much profit would the company make if it sold its entire weekly production?

(**c**) Which size of bottle is the best value for money? Explain your answer.

10 The petrol tank of Fiona's car can hold 37 litres 950 millilitres when full.

(**a**) If the car uses 110 millilitres per mile, how much petrol will be left in the car after it travels 300 miles?

(**b**) How many more miles can she drive the car before it runs out of petrol?

Review exercise 8

1 Find the length of the perimeter of each shape.

(**a**)
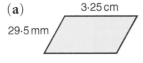
3·25 cm
29·5 mm

(**b**)
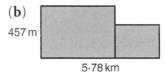
457 m
5·78 km

(**c**)
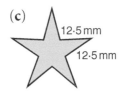
12·5 mm
12·5 mm

2 The perimeter of a farmer's rectangular field is 1·26 kilometres. If the length of one side is 168 metres, find the breadth.

3 A joiner requires to cut a plank of wood 2·4 metres in length into equal pieces each 25 centimetres long.

(**a**) How many pieces can be cut?

(**b**) What length is left over?

4 The table gives the weight of coins in use in 2003. Calculate the total weight of the bags of coins shown in the diagram in kilogrammes.

Coin	Weight (mg)
1 pence	3600
2 pence	7100
5 pence	18 000
10 pence	24 500
20 pence	5000
£1	9500
£2	1200

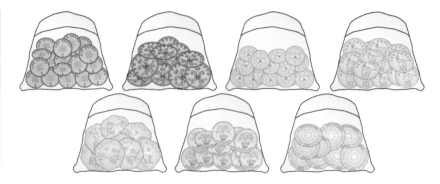

5 On a morning in June, there was a queue of cars stretching for 1 kilometres 600 metres on the bridge over the River Dubh.

   (**a**) Assuming that the average car is 2·5 metres long and that there is a gap of 50 centimetres between each car, how many cars are there in the queue?

   (**b**) The bridge is old and engineers have estimated that it can safely carry a load of 12 000 tonnes. Assuming that the average weight of a car is 2250 kilogrammes, is the bridge safe with this load? Explain your answer.

6 Bottles of mineral water are packed into a rectangular box 30 centimetres by 0·9 metres. Each bottle is 60 millimetres in diameter and has a capacity of 290 millilitres.

   (**a**) How many bottles can fit into the box?

   (**b**) What is the total volume of water contained in 1 box?

   (**c**) The company van can be packed with 250 boxes. What weight of water is carried if 1 litre of water weighs 1 kilogramme?

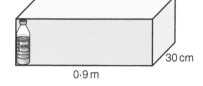

7 Lochan High School swimming pool measures 25 metres by 10 metres by 2 metres deep.

   (**a**) What is the capacity of the pool in
     (**i**) cubic metres   (**ii**) litres?

   (**b**) Find the total weight of the water in tonnes.

8 In a normal week, the school cafeteria vending machine dispenses 150 bottles of orange, 255 bottles of mineral water, 550 bottles of cola.

   (**a**) Calculate the total volume of drinks dispensed by the machine in a normal week.

   (**b**) In a normal week, the cafeteria spends £250 each week on restocking the machine. How much profit does it make selling drinks in a normal week?

Orange	275 ml	40p
Water	330 ml	50p
Cola	425 ml	75p

Summary

Length

1000 millimetres (mm) = 1 metre (m)   10 millimetres (mm) = 1 centimetre (cm)
1000 metres (m)   = 1 kilometre (km)   100 centimetres (cm) = 1 metre (m)

Weight

1000 milligrammes (mg) = 1 gramme (g)
1000 grammes (g)   = 1 kilogramme (kg)
1000 kilogrammes (kg)   = 1 tonne

Capacity

1 cubic centimetre (cm^3)   = 1 millilitre (ml)
1000 cubic centimetres (cm^3) = 1000 millilitres (ml) = 1 litre (ℓ)
1 cubic metre (m^3)   = 1000 litres (ℓ)

9 Scale drawing

In this chapter you will learn to use angles and scales to model situations.

Scales are used by many people including map makers, surveyors, architects and builders. Scales are found on plans and maps to allow us to extract accurate information.

9.1 Finding true measurements

Example

This fish is drawn to scale.
Find the true length of the fish.

Scale 1 cm to 6 cm

Scale drawing (cm)	True length (cm)
1	6
4·8	6 × 4·8 = 28·8

The true length of the fish is **28·8 centimetres**.

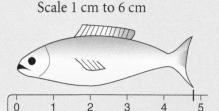

Exercise 9.1

You need a ruler for this exercise.

1 Find the true length of each fish.

(**a**) Scale 1 cm to 5 cm   (**b**) Scale 1 cm to 8 cm   (**c**) Scale 1 cm to 6 cm

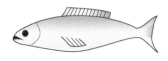   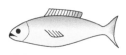   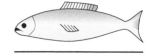

2 Find the true length of each item of furniture.

(**a**) Scale 1 cm to 40 cm   (**b**) Scale 1 cm to 80 cm

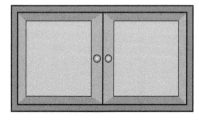   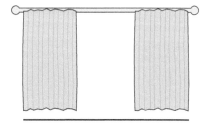

(**c**) Scale 1 cm to 25 cm

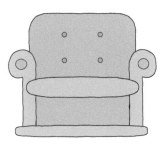

(**d**) 1 cm to 50 cm

3 Calculate the true dimensions of these rooms using the plans.
Give your answers in metres.

(**a**) Scale 1 cm to 50 cm

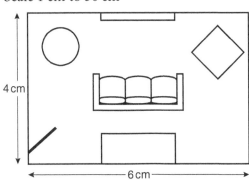

(**b**) Scale 1 cm to 150 cm

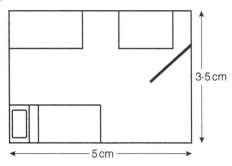

4 The map shows the position of headquarters and 7 scout tents.
Find the distance in metres between headquarters and each tent.

Scale 1 cm to 2 m

• A

B •

F
•

C •

H.Q.
•

• G

D •

•
E

5 Jonathan measures the length of a Hawker Hurricane aeroplane in his
textbook and finds it is 15 centimetres long. If the scale of the drawing
is 1 centimetre to 40 centimetres, what is the real length of the plane
in metres?

6 Arthur and Tariq are planning to build a kit car. They are also having a new garage built for the car. They have a scale drawing of their car and a scale drawing of the garage. Will the car fit into the garage?

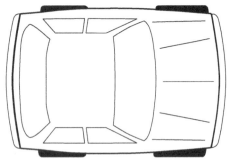

Scale 1 cm : 50 cm

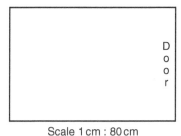

Scale 1 cm : 80 cm

9.2 Representative fractions

The scale on a map can be written as a **representative fraction**.
Instead of writing 1 centimetre represents 25 000 centimetres, we can write it as 1 : 25 000.
This means 1 centimetre would represent 25 000 centimetres or 1 metre would represent 25 000 metres.

Example

The scale on a map is 1 : 50 000. Alex measures his journey as 12·4 centimetres on the map. How far is his actual journey in kilometres?

Map distance	True distance
1	50 000
12·4	50 000 × 12·4
	= 620 000 centimetres
	= 6200 metres
	= 6·2 kilometres

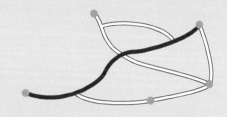

The actual journey is **6·2** kilometres.

Exercise 9.2

1 Convert to metres:

(**a**) 4985 cm   (**b**) 193 cm   (**c**) 20 000 cm   (**d**) 45 000 000 mm

(**e**) 32 000 mm   (**f**) 190·05 km   (**g**) 36·8 km   (**h**) 9073·9 km

2 Convert to kilometres:

(**a**) 4500 m   (**b**) 9700 m   (**c**) 345 000 cm

(**d**) 5000 cm   (**e**) 82 000 000 cm   (**f**) 456 000 000 mm

3 Mhairi is planning a walk using a map with a representative fraction of 1 : 35 000. The route measures 20 centimetres on the map. Give the real distance of the journey in

(**a**) centimetres   (**b**) kilometres.

4 For a map with scale 1 : 50 000 find the true distance for each measurement. Give your answer in kilometres.

(**a**) 2 cm   (**b**) 12 cm   (**c**) 4 cm   (**d**) 7·5 cm

5 For a map with scale 1 : 25 000 find the true distance for each measurement. Give your answer in kilometres.

(**a**) 8 cm   (**b**) 10 cm   (**c**) 6 cm   (**d**) 11 cm

6 Copy the table below and use the map to help you complete it.

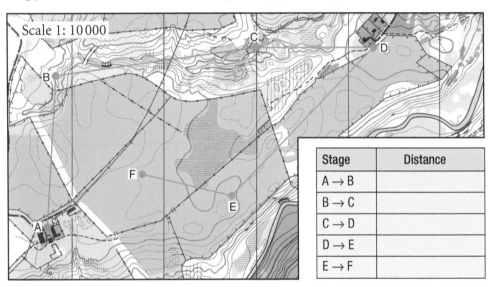

Stage	Distance
A → B	
B → C	
C → D	
D → E	
E → F	

7 The McLeod family have been given a plan of the new kitchen which has been designed for their house. The scale on the plan is 1 : 20.

(**a**) When they measure the sink unit on the plan it is 5·2 centimetres. What is the real length of the unit?

(**b**) Mrs McLeod asked for a work bench in the centre of the kitchen which had an area of at least 3 square metres. When she measured it on the plan it was 9 centimetres long and 7·5 centimetres wide. Does this meet her requirements? Explain your answer fully.

8 Laura is planning to walk from Ford to Millhouse using a map with representative fraction 1 : 50 000. The map distance is 18 centimetres.

(**a**) Calculate the real distance in kilometres.

(**b**) If she estimates her walking speed to be 4 kilometres per hour, how long will it take her to complete the journey?

9 Hans is flying from London to St Petersburg. His world map has representative fraction 1 : 43 000 000. On the map London and St Petersburg are 7·5 centimetres apart. How far would this be in real life?

10 The scale on the box of a model car was 1 : 36. The length of the toy car was 10 centimetres. What would the length of the real car be?

11 Mr Lewis was given a model train set. The models were made to a scale of 1 : 45. If the engine was 15 centimetres long, how long should it be in real life?

9.3 Making plans

This is a plan of Julie's bedroom.
Scale 1 : 40

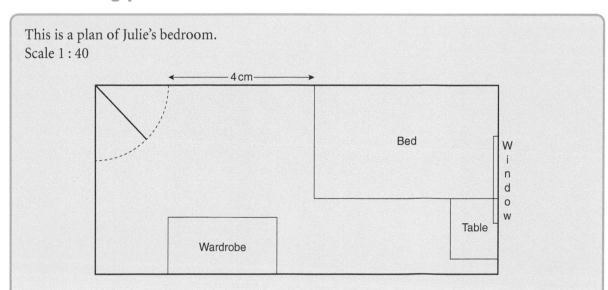

Julie wants to have a bookcase against the wall between the door and the bed. She sees one which is 140 cm wide. Will this fit in the space?

True width	Plan width
40	1
140	140 ÷ 40 = 3·5 cm

On the plan the space measures 4 centimetres so the bookcase will fit as it only measures 3·5 centimetres.

Exercise 9.3

You will need squared paper and scissors for this exercise.

1 (**a**) Measure the width of the window on the plan.

(**b**) Julie buys a blind which is 80 centimetres wide. Will this fit her window?

2 Julie's aunt has a chair which is 60 centimetres wide and 60 centimetres long. Will this fit into the corner of her room next to the wardrobe?

3 Angela has made a sketch of the front elevation of a table she wants to copy.

(**a**) Calculate the dimensions for the plan using a scale of 1 : 8.

(**b**) Make an accurate scale drawing of this elevation of the table.

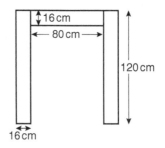

Front elevation

4 Miss Whitehead is furnishing a tutorial room at her school.

The room is 6 metres by 8 metres.

She has a teacher's desk, a computer desk, 2 bookcases, 1 cupboard and 10 pupil desks to go into the room.

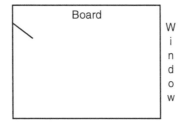

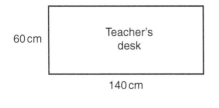

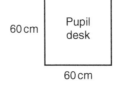

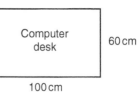

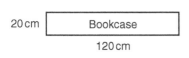

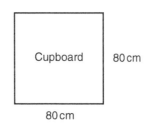

(**a**) Using a scale of 1 : 40 make a scale drawing of
   (**i**) the room in your jotter
   (**ii**) the furniture on squared paper.

(**b**) Cut out the plans of the furniture and show how you could arrange them in the room.

5 Victor is buying a carpet and makes a scale drawing of his living room floor. The room is 5 metres long and 4 metres wide. What will the dimensions of the room be on the drawing if he uses a scale of

(**a**) 1 : 50   (**b**) 1 : 20   (**c**) 1 : 1000?

6 Alex is redecorating her kitchen, which is 6 metres long and 3·5 metres wide. She makes a plan of the kitchen to scale.

 (**a**) What will the dimensions of the kitchen be on the drawing if she uses a scale of

  (**i**) 1 : 10

  (**ii**) 1 : 25

  (**iii**) 1 : 50?

 (**b**) Alex only has A4 paper. Which would be the most sensible scale to use?

7 Charlie Diamond is redesigning a neighbour's garden. She wants to make the largest possible scale drawing of the garden to plan the layout. The garden is a rectangle 12 metres long and 9·5 metres wide. If her A4 paper is 29·7 centimetres long and 21 centimetres wide, which scale should she choose?

 A 1 : 100   **B** 1 : 50   **C** 1 : 25

8 Scale 1:500 000

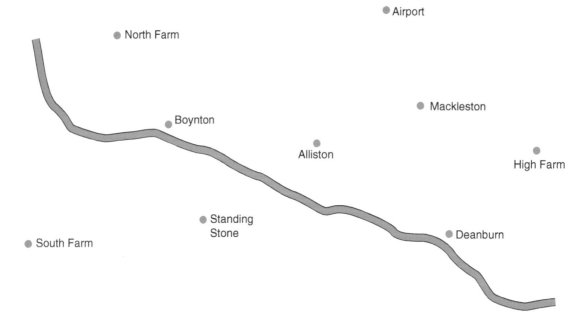

Use the above map to answer these questions.

 (**a**) There is a straight path along the river from Boynton to Deanburn. How long is this path?

 (**b**) There is a large hotel in the village 20 kilometres from the airport. Which village is this?

 (**c**) Which two villages are exactly 15 kilometres apart?

 (**d**) Which farmhouses are within a 30 kilometres radius of the standing stone?

9.4 Calculating the scale

Julia has a souvenir brochure from an art gallery.
It includes photographs of the paintings and their true heights.

Find the scale and calculate the true width of the painting.

Measure the height of the photo. This is 5 cm.

Scale	
Photo	Painting
5	90
1	90 ÷ 5 = 18

This scale is **1 : 18.**

Width	
Photo	Painting
1	18
3·5	18 × 3·5 = 63

The true width is **63** centimetres.

True height 90 cm

Exercise 9.4

1 For each photograph, calculate the scale used and the true width of the paintings.

(**a**)

True height 42 cm

(**b**)

True height 125 cm

2 Angela has ordered a new bookcase. She has a scale drawing of the design. The actual height of the bookcase is 140 centimetres; the height on the drawing is 10 centimetres.

(**a**) What scale has been used in the diagram?

(**b**) The width on the plan is 8 centimetres. What is the real width?

3 Vicky is a model maker for an architects company. She has to build a model of a new skyscraper which is 240 metres high. Her model is 40 centimetres high. What is the scale of the model?

Units should be the same.

4 Calculate the missing dimension for each picture.

True height 96 cm

True width 50 cm

5 A new extension is being built at Balgornie School.
Mrs Robertson knows that her room will be 7·5 metres
wide.

   (**a**) What scale has been used on the plan?

   (**b**) Calculate the length of the room.

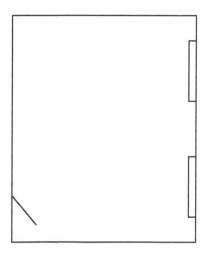

6 Adam was given a scale model of a Euro 90 aeroplane. His brother
could not remember the scale which had been written on the box.
Adam measured the length of the model and found that it was
29 centimetres. He looked on the internet and found that the actual
length of the plane was 14·5 metres. What was the scale of the model?

7 While on holiday in Paris, Billy bought a model of the Eiffel Tower. In
his guide book he read that the tower is 300 metres high and
125 metres wide at the base. He measures his model and finds that its
height is 12 centimetres and it is 5 centimetres wide at the base. Is the
model made to scale? Explain your answer.

9.5 Constructing triangles

Draw each triangle accurately.

Method 1: two sides and one angle	**Method 2:** one side and two angles	**Method 3:** three sides
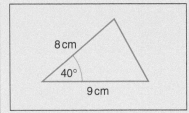	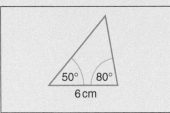	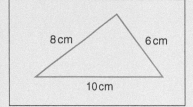
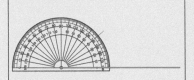 Draw a line 9 cm long.	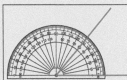 Draw a line 6 cm long.	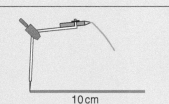 Draw a line 10 cm long.
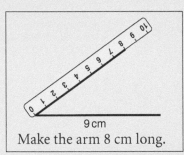 Draw an angle of 40° at the end of the 9 cm line.	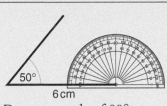 Draw an angle of 50° at one end of the line and extend the arm.	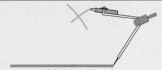 Set the compasses at 8 cm. Draw an arc as shown
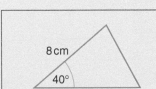 Make the arm 8 cm long.	 Draw an angle of 80° at the other end.	Set the compasses at 6 cm. Draw a second arc to cut the first one.
Join the ends of the arms to form the triangle.	Draw the final arm of the triangle.	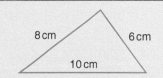 Join the point where the arcs meet to the ends of the 10 cm line.

Exercise 9.5

You need a ruler, protractor and a pair of compasses for this exercise.

1 (**a**) Using method 1 draw these triangles accurately and measure all the missing sides and angles.

(**b**) For each triangle check that the angles add up to 180°.

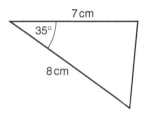 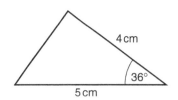 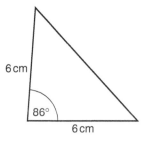

2 (**a**) Using method 2 draw these triangles accurately and measure all the missing sides and angles.

(**b**) For each triangle check that all the angles add up to 180°.

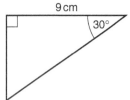 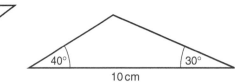 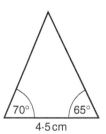

3 (**a**) Using method 3 draw these triangles accurately and measure all the missing angles.

(**b**) For each triangle check that all the angles add up to 180°.

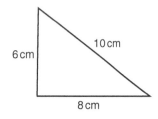 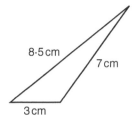 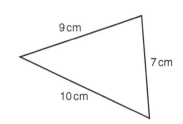

4 Construct each of the following triangles ABC where

(**a**) AB = 6 cm, ∠CAB = 40°, ∠CBA = 82°.

(**b**) AB = 10 cm, BC = 9 cm, ∠CBA = 50°.

(**c**) AB = 8 cm, AC = 7 cm, BC = 5 cm.

5 The Phoenix garden is to have triangular raised flower beds. Make scale drawings of each of these flower beds using the scale 1 centimetre to 1 metre.

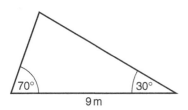

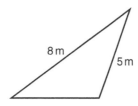

6 Construct **two** triangles ABC where AB = 8 centimetres, BC = 6·3 centimetres and ∠BAC = 36°.

9.6 Angles of elevation and depression

You can find heights and distances by making a scale drawing.

angle of elevation is the angle measured upwards from the horizontal.

angle of depression is the angle measured downwards from the horizontal.

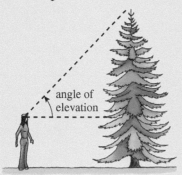

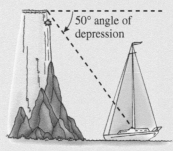

Example

Use a scale of 1 cm represents 10 m to make a scale drawing to find the height of the Glasgow Science Centre Tower.

Scale drawing

Actual drawing

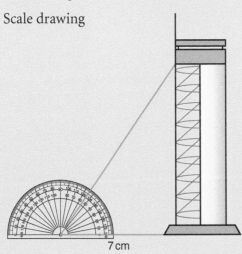

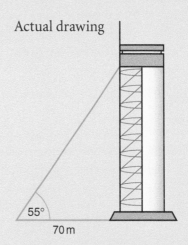

Scale drawing (cm)	True length
1	10
10	100

The true height of the tower is **100 m.**

Exercise 9.6

1 Make a scale drawing to find the height of each building.

(**a**) Scale 1 : 500   (**b**) Scale 1 cm = 40 m   (**c**) Scale 1 : 2000

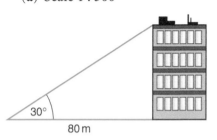 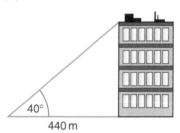 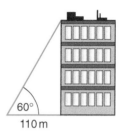

2 A surveyor is hired to investigate a church steeple which seems to be sinking. According to the plans the steeple should be 33 metres high. Make a scale drawing using the scale 1 : 500 to find out how high the steeple is at present.

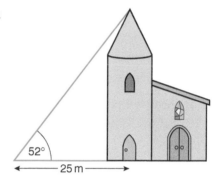

3 (**a**) Calculate the angle marked *x* in the diagram.

(**b**) Use a scale drawing with a scale of 1 : 1000 to find the distance of the boat from the cliff.

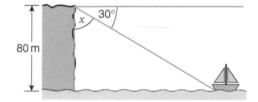

4 Charlie is a coastguard based at Landsea Point lighthouse. He wants to find out the height of the lighthouse. The angle of elevation of the sun is 40°. The shadow of the lighthouse is 30 metres long.

(**a**) Use a scale of 1 : 500 to make a scale drawing.

(**b**) What is the height of the lighthouse?

5 Charlie sees a windsurfer in difficulty. The angle of depression is 25°. The cliff is 70 metres high. Choose a suitable scale and make a scale drawing. How far is the windsurfer from the foot of the cliff?

6 Use a scale drawing to find the distance between boat A and boat B.

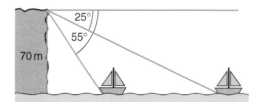

9.7 Bearings

Every direction on the **compass rose** can also be given as a **bearing**.

Bearings are
- measured from north
- measured clockwise
- given as 3 figures.

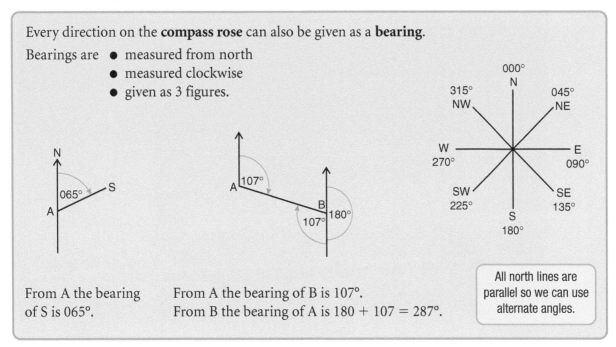

From A the bearing of S is 065°.

From A the bearing of B is 107°.
From B the bearing of A is 180 + 107 = 287°.

All north lines are parallel so we can use alternate angles.

Exercise 9.7

1 What is the size of the smaller angle between

(**a**) east and south west

(**b**) north east and north west?

2 If you were facing south, in which direction would you be facing if you turned:

(**a**) 135° clockwise   (**b**) 225° clockwise   (**c**) 45° anticlockwise?

3 (**a**) Sketch a diagram to show that from C the bearing of D is 053°.

(**b**) From D calculate the bearing of C.

4 (**a**) Sketch a diagram to show that from T the bearing of S is 145°.

(**b**) From S calculate the bearing of T.

5 (**a**) Sketch a diagram to show that from G the bearing of H is 220°.

(**b**) From H calculate the bearing of G.

6 (**a**) Sketch a diagram to show that from J the bearing of K is 305°.

(**b**) From K calculate the bearing of J.

7 You will need a protractor for this question.
Copy and complete the table.

Stage	Bearing
Start → marker 1	
marker 1 → marker 2	
marker 2 → marker 3	
marker 3 → marker 4	
marker 4 → marker 5	
marker 5 → Start	

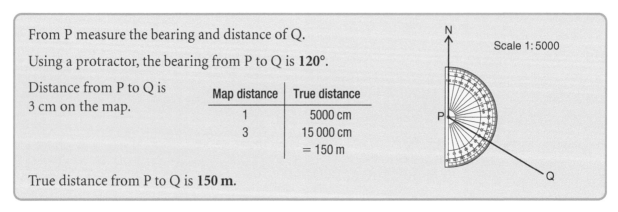

9.8 Bearings and journeys

From P measure the bearing and distance of Q.

Using a protractor, the bearing from P to Q is **120°**.

Distance from P to Q is
3 cm on the map.

Map distance	True distance
1	5000 cm
3	15 000 cm
	= 150 m

True distance from P to Q is **150 m**.

Scale 1 : 5000

Exercise 9.8

1 From Aberdeen measure the bearing and distance of
H.M.S. Glasgow.

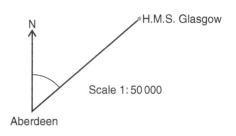

Scale 1 : 50 000

2 From each coastguard station measure the bearing and direction of the rescue boat.

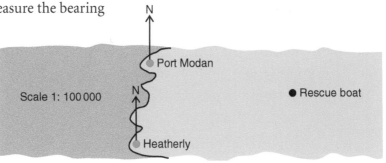

3 Copy and complete the table below.

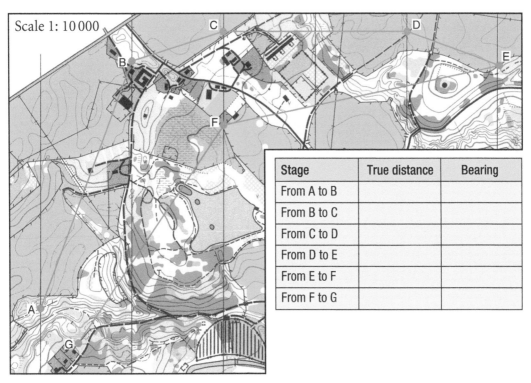

Stage	True distance	Bearing
From A to B		
From B to C		
From C to D		
From D to E		
From E to F		
From F to G		

4 On the map below, the red line shows the course sailed by a ship through a dangerous channel. Find the distance and bearing of

(**a**) L from K　　　(**b**) M from L　　　(**c**) N from M.

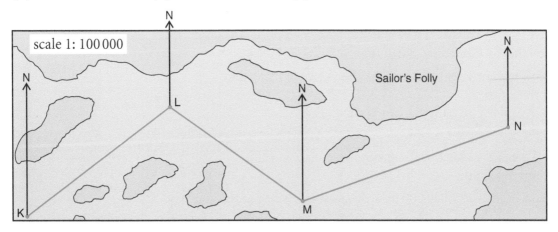

5 This map shows the position of three lighthouses. Without measuring, use the angles marked to find the bearing of

(**a**) Morin from Taye   (**b**) Legg from Taye

(**c**) Legg from Morin   (**d**) Taye from Legg

(**e**) Taye from Morin   (**f**) Morin from Legg.

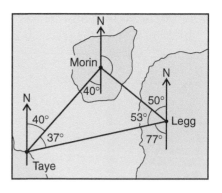

9.9 Drawing diagrams

A ship leaves port A and travels 60 kilometres east to B; then 40 kilometres south east to C.

(**a**) Use a scale of 1 centimetre to 10 kilometres to make a scale drawing of this journey.

(**b**) Find the shortest distance back to port.

Step 1
Make a sketch

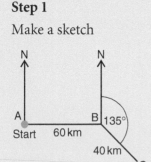

Step 2
Calculate map distances

True distance	Map distance
10	1
60	6
40	4

Step 3
Make scale drawing

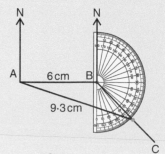

Using the scale drawing, the shortest distance back to port is 9·3 × 10 = **93 km.**

Exercise 9.9

1 A path is to be constructed over a moor from Hannells End to Mavery Pit. The path is to be built in a north easterly direction and is 4 kilometres long. Use a scale of 1 centimetre to 1 kilometre to make a scale drawing of the path.

2 A plane flies 60 kilometres north then 90 kilometres east.

(**a**) Use a scale of 1 centimetre to 10 kilometres to make a scale drawing of the journey.

(**b**) Calculate the shortest distance back home.

3 From Aberdeen a ship travels 30 kilometres east and then 50 kilometres south.

(**a**) Use a scale of 1 : 1 000 000 to make a scale drawing of this journey.

(**b**) Calculate the shortest distance back to Aberdeen.

4 Use the scale 1 centimetre to 1 kilometre to make scale drawings of
   the following journeys and find the distance AC.

(a)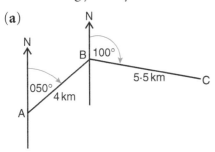

(b)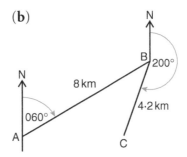

5 A group of ramblers walk 7 kilometres north east from Aviemore
   then 2 kilometres west.

   (a) Use a suitable scale to make a scale drawing of this journey.

   (b) Calculate the shortest distance back to Aviemore.

Review exercise 9

1 Use the given scales to calculate the true lengths of these objects.

   (a) scale 1 cm to 50 cm   (b) scale 1 cm to 20 cm

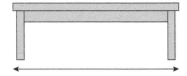

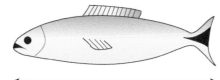

2 On a map with representative fraction 1 : 25 000 Daljit measured his
   walk was 23 centimetres. Calculate the real distance in kilometres.

3 Fred Brown is having an extension built which is to be three metres high.
   If his plan uses a scale of 1 : 10, how high will the extension be on the plan?

4 A model of the boat 'Sarky Annie' is 34 centimetres long. The real
   length is 17 metres. Calculate the scale of the model as a
   representative fraction.

5 Calculate the true width of this painting
   if the true height is 65 centimetres.

6 Construct the following triangles.

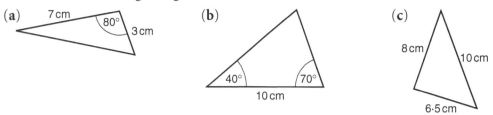

(a) 7 cm 80° 3 cm

(b) 40° 70° 10 cm

(c) 8 cm 10 cm 6·5 cm

7 Use a scale drawing to find the height of the bridge above ground.

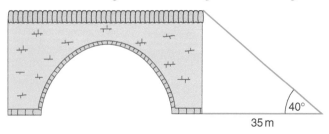

40° 35 m

8 Copy and complete the table using this map.

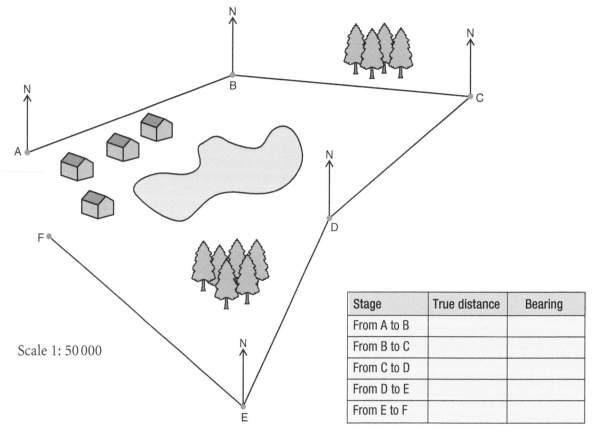

Scale 1: 50 000

Stage	True distance	Bearing
From A to B		
From B to C		
From C to D		
From D to E		
From E to F		

9 The Ocean Adventurer leaves port and sails 250 kilometres north east then 125 kilometres east. How far away from port is the ship now?

Summary

Using scales

A scale can be written as a representative fraction.
1 cm represents 25 000 cm is equivalent to 1 : 25 000.

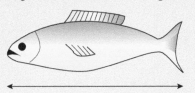

Scale drawing (cm)	True length (cm)
1	6
4·8	6 × 4·8 = 28.8

Scale 1 cm to 6 cm
The true length of the fish is **28·8 centimetres**.

Calculating scales

The length of a tunnel is 240 centimetres.
On the engineer's plan the length is 6 centimetres.
The scale is **1 : 40**.

Plan length	True length
6	240
6 ÷ 6	240 ÷ 6
1	40

Angles of elevation and depression

The angle measured upwards from the horizontal is the angle of elevation.

The angle measured downwards from the horizontal is the angle of depression.

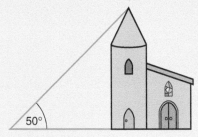

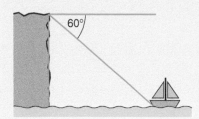

Bearings

Bearings are
- measured from north
- measured clockwise
- given as 3 figures.

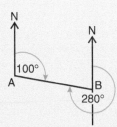

The bearing of B from A is 100°. The bearing of A from B is 280°.

Scale drawing

When constructing a scale drawing:
Step 1 Make a sketch.
Step 2 Calculate distances.
Step 3 Make a scale drawing.

10 Algebra 1

In this chapter you will learn how to simplify and evaluate expressions.

10.1 Simplifying expressions

An **expression** uses letters for numbers.
There are x pencils in each box.
Total number $= x + x + x = 3x$
This is called **simplifying**.

Examples

$a + a + a + a$ can be written as **4a**

$2g + 2g + 2g + 2g = 8g$

$2x + 4x = 6x$

$4a + 3a - 2a = 5a$

$4t + 2t + t = 7t$

4a means
$4 \times a$

t is the same as 1t

Exercise 10.1

1 Copy and complete to simplify the expressions:

(a) $x + x =$

(b) $m + m + m =$

(c) $a + a + a =$

(d) $t + t + t + t =$

(e) $b + b + b + b + b + b =$

(f) $g + g + g + g + g + g + g =$

(g) $k + k + k + k + k =$

(h) $h + h + h + h + h + h + h + h =$

2 Simplify each expression:

(a) $3a + 3a$

(b) $3b + 3b + 3b$

(c) $8c + 8c + 8c$

(d) $4m + 4m + 4m$

(e) $2e + 2e + 2e + 2e + 2e + 2e$

(f) $5f + 5f + 5f + 5f + 5f + 5f + 5f + 5f$

(g) $4t + 3t - 2t$

(h) $4e + 5e + 2e - 4e$

(i) $3a + 6a + 7a - a$

(j) $12v + 13v + 2v$

(k) $b + 15b + 17b$

(l) $52f + 30f - 43f$

(m) $12p + 13p - 2p$

(n) $2r + 3r + 24r$

(o) $21x + 13x - 17x$

(p) $17h + 13h + h$

(q) $111k - 12k + 60k$

(r) $150u - 100u + 20u$

(s) $17k - k + 50k$

(t) $121p - p - 96p$

3 Simplify:

(a) $16b + 12b - 17b$

(b) $15t + 12t - 25t$

(c) $31h - 12h - 17h$

(d) $34k - 19k - 13k$

(e) $107g - 51g - 39g$

(f) $71p - 56p - 12p - p$

(g) $301d - 276d - 16d$

(h) $215w + 130w - 344w$

(i) $91x - 17x + 3x - 40x$

10.2 Collecting like terms

Each part of an expression is called a **term**.
$$5x + 3y \quad \text{has two terms}$$
$$7a + 3b + 2c + d \quad \text{has four terms.}$$

Unlike terms may represent different
numbers so cannot be simplified.

To simplify an expression, collect like terms:
$$2b + c + b = 3b + c$$
$$9e + 3t - 4e = 5e + 3t$$
$$5p + 3u - 2p - u = 3p + 2u$$
$$2p + 6 + 3p - 4p - 1 = p + 5$$

Exercise 10.2

1 Copy and complete to simplify these expressions.

(a) $2e + y + 3e =$

(b) $5a + 2b + 3a =$

(c) $4t + 6y + 2t =$

(d) $7g + 4f + 3g =$

(e) $3n + 4v + 5n + 2v + 3n =$

(f) $4b + 5g + 3b + 4g + 3g =$

(g) $3y + 5w + 2y + 7w =$

(h) $12k + 4s + s + s + 8k =$

2 Copy and complete to simplify these expressions.

(a) $6b - 2b + 4a =$

(b) $9a + 6a + b - 10a =$

(c) $5p - 2a + 4p =$

(d) $9e - 8f + e =$

(e) $14y - 9y + 3 =$

(f) $31x + 2a - 17x =$

(g) $122w - 48w + 10 =$

(h) $252z + 67a - 200z =$

(i) $4a + 6b - 3a =$

(j) $2e + 4e - 5f =$

(k) $15f + 7 - 13f =$

(l) $5 + 3a - 2a + 4 =$

(m) $62w + 21 - 57w =$

(n) $121k + 39t - 60k =$

(o) $16u + 36u - 51p =$

3 Simplify:

(a) $3a + 2b + 4 + 4a + 2b + 3$

(b) $5r + 3u + 2s + 2u + 5r + 4s$

(c) $2p + 4r + 5q + 3q + 7r + 9p$

(d) $2e + 5i + 4 + 4i + 6e + i + 3$

(e) $5u + 7d + e + 3u + d + 5e$

(f) $v + a + v + 3v + 8 + 4a + 4v$

(g) $3a + 3b + 2c + 3a + 2b + 4c$

(h) $5t + 2s + 2 + 2s + 5t + 4$

(i) $5p + r + 2q + 3q + 4r + 5p$

(j) $7e + i + 3a + 4i + 4e + 9i$

(k) $5k + 5t + 2y + 5k + 5t + 8y + t$

(l) $10p + 2p + 8i + 4g + 3i + p + 8g$

(m) $2f + b + 7v + 14f + 11b + 6f$

(n) $25p + 34 + u + 2p + 31 + 17u + 5$

4 Simplify:

(a) $3f + 3v - 2f$

(b) $4d + 3 - 2d$

(c) $7e + 6g - 3e$

(d) $31p + 22k - 27p$

(e) $21h + 9z - 6h$

(f) $16t + 7 - 9t$

(g) $5a + 4b - 2a - 2b$

(h) $5f + 7 - 3f - 4$

(i) $6y + 3h - 4y - 2h$

(j) $15t + 12q - 10t - 12q$

(k) $14r + 11s - 9r$

(l) $12w - 6w + 3a - 2a - 6w$

(m) $9 + 8y - 6 - 7y + 2y$

(n) $12h + 3b - 8h - 3b - 4h$

10.3 Evaluating expressions

A letter or **variable** in an expression may be replaced by a number.

Example 1

Evaluate $5a - b$ when $a = 3$ and $b = 4$,

$$5a - b$$
$$= 5 \times 3 - 4$$
$$= 15 - 4$$
$$= 11$$

Example 2

Substitute $k = 2$, $t = 4$ and $v = 3$ into

(a) $ktv + 6$

$$= 2 \times 4 \times 3 + 6$$
$$= 24 + 6$$
$$= 30$$

(b) $\dfrac{vt}{k}$

$$= \dfrac{3 \times 4}{2}$$
$$= \dfrac{12}{2}$$
$$= 6$$

vt means $v \times t$

Replacing a letter by a number is called **substitution**.

Exercise 10.3

1 Copy and complete to evaluate the following expressions when $a = 3$, $b = 2$ and $c = 1$:

(**a**) $a + b + c$

$= 3 + \ldots + \ldots$

$= \ldots$

(**b**) $3a + 6b - c$

$= \ldots + \ldots - \ldots$

$= \ldots$

(**c**) $5b - 3c + a$

$=$

$=$

2 Given $p = 3$, $k = 5$ and $h = 2$, evaluate:

(**a**) $p + k + h$
(**b**) $2p + 3k - h$
(**c**) $5p + 2k - 10h + 3$
(**d**) $p + k - 4h$
(**e**) $11p - 5k - 3h$
(**f**) $kp + hk + 5$
(**g**) $2hk + 3hp$
(**h**) $5hp - 2kp$
(**i**) $2h + 3hk - hkp + 1$
(**j**) $5p + 6k + 7h$
(**k**) $5k + 2p - 9h$
(**l**) $hkp - 29$

3 Given $w = 2$, $x = 3$, $y = 4$ and $z = 5$, evaluate:

(**a**) $5w + 3x + 2y + z$
(**b**) $6z - 5y + 3w$
(**c**) zy
(**d**) $wx + zy$
(**e**) $wxy - 4z$
(**f**) $3wy + 2wz$
(**g**) $5yz - 10wx$
(**h**) $3wx + 3wy - wyz$
(**i**) $z + 2wx$
(**j**) $\dfrac{wyz}{2} - 4z$
(**k**) $\dfrac{wxyz}{2} - 5z$
(**l**) $\dfrac{wxz}{3} - \dfrac{yz}{4}$

4 Substitute, $r = 2$, $s = 5$, $t = 7$ and $u = 10$ into the following expressions and evaluate them:

(**a**) $rs + ut$
(**b**) $rst - 7u$
(**c**) $rstu - 60u$
(**d**) $\dfrac{ru}{s}$
(**e**) $\dfrac{rst}{u}$
(**f**) $rs + st + tu - rsu$
(**g**) $\dfrac{st}{u}$
(**h**) $\dfrac{tu}{2st}$
(**i**) $ru + su + tu - rtu$

5 Substitute each letter by its numerical position in the alphabet:

e.g. $a = 1$, $b = 2$, $c = 3$, $d = 4$, $e = 5$, $\ldots$ $x = 24$, $y = 25$, $z = 26$.

(**a**) $abc + def$
(**b**) $jk - gh$
(**c**) $jw - 10t$
(**d**) $aze + bay$
(**e**) $dog - cat$
(**f**) bob
(**g**) joy
(**h**) $james$
(**i**) Your own name!

10.4 Evaluating formulae

Substitution may be used to evaluate formulae.

Example 1

A rectangle has length 5 cm
and breadth 4 cm.
Find the area of the rectangle
$l = 4, b = 5$

$A = lb$

$= 5 \times 4$

$= 20 \text{ cm}^2$

Example 2

Substitute $C = 20$ into the formula, $F = \dfrac{9C}{5} + 32$

$F = \dfrac{9C}{5} + 32$

$= \dfrac{9 \times 20}{5} + 32$

$= \dfrac{180}{5} + 32$

$= 36 + 32$

$= 68$

Exercise 10.4

1 Evaluate each formula:

   (a) $A = lb$ $l = 7, b = 5$ **(b)** $V = IR$ $I = 12, R = 3$

   (c) $P = a - c$ $a = 3, c = 2\cdot45$ **(d)** $S = \dfrac{D}{T}$ $D = 28, T = 7$

   (e) $P = 2a + 2b$ $a = 5, b = 3$ **(f)** $K = 3T - 7$ $T = 3\cdot5$

   (g) $D = \dfrac{m}{v}$ $m = 180, v = 6$ **(h)** $V = lbh$ $l = 3, b = 4, h = 5$

   (i) $F = \dfrac{9C}{5} + 32$ $C = 25$ **(j)** $A = \frac{1}{2}bh$ $b = 12, h = 8$

   (k) $P = xyz$ $x = 4, y = 5, z = 6$ **(l)** $V = \dfrac{2t}{3k}$ $t = 12, k = 6$

2 **(a)** To calculate the force (F) of an object with mass (m) and
       acceleration (a) we use the formula

         $F = ma$

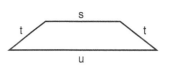

       Find the force on a satellite that has mass 300 kg and acceleration 20 m/s².

   (b) The perimeter of this shape is given by the formula

        $P = 2t + s + u$

       Find the perimeter when $u = 7, s = 5$ and $t = 3$

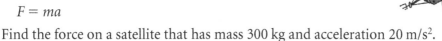

   (c) The volume of a cuboid is found using

        $V = lbh$

       Find the volume of the cuboid with length 5 cm, breadth 2 cm
       and height 7 cm.

   (d) Miles (M) may be converted to kilometres (K) using the formula:

        $K = \dfrac{8M}{5}$

       Convert these to kilometres:

       (i) 20 miles   **(ii)** 65 miles   **(iii)** 131 miles.

(e) The cooking time (T) in minutes for a chicken may be calculated
using the formula

$T = 20w + 30.$

where w is the weight (kg) of the chicken.
Find the cooking time for a 3 kilogramme chicken.

(f) Gary the car salesman earns a basic wage (W) of £8000.
He also earns commission of 10% of the value (V) of all cars he sells.
He works out his total pay (P) with the formula

$P = W + 0 \cdot 1V$

Last year Gary sold £90 000 worth of cars.
What was his total pay?

Review exercise 10

1 Copy and complete to simplify these expressions.

(a) $a + a + a =$ (b) $g + g + g + g =$ (c) $z + z + z + z + z + z + z =$

(d) $2y + 3y =$ (e) $5k + 4k =$ (f) $4b + 3b + 5b =$

(g) $8t + 3t + t =$ (h) $3d + d + 3d =$ (i) $8e + 4e + 2e + e =$

2 Simplify:

(a) $4a + 3a + 2b$ (b) $3w + 2x + 5w$ (c) $4p + 2m + 3p$

(d) $2x + 4q + 2x + 6q$ (e) $3w + 2z + w + z$ (f) $2a + 3k + 4a + 5k + a$

(g) $11h - 9h$ (h) $23j - 11j$ (i) $12b - 12b$

(j) $5b + 3a - 3b$ (k) $6y + 2x - 5y$ (l) $7s + 2r - 7s$

(m) $4e + 5t - 2e - 3t$ (n) $2w + 3z - w - z$ (o) $9a + 3e - 8a - 3e$

3 Substitute $p = 4, q = 3, r = 2, s = 1$ and $t = 0$ into the following
expressions and evaluate them:

(a) $p + q + t$ (b) $3t + 5q - 2p$ (c) $3p - 4q + r - 2s$

(d) $3p + q$ (e) $2p + 4q - 20t$ (f) $pq - rs$

(g) $5t + 4s + 2p + q$ (h) $pqr - rst$ (i) $pqrst$

4 Substitute $a = 2, b = 3, c = 4$ and $d = 6$, to evaluate the following
expressions:

(a) $\dfrac{bc}{a}$ (b) $\dfrac{ad}{b}$ (c) $\dfrac{abd}{c}$ (d) $\dfrac{c}{a} + \dfrac{d}{b}$

5 Evaluate each formula:

(a) $A = \frac{1}{2}bh$, where $b = 8$ and $h = 6$

(b) $F = \dfrac{9C}{5} + 32$ when $C = 15$

Summary

Simplifying expressions

Expressions may be simplified by collecting like **terms**.

$$a + a + a = 3a$$
$$6x + 2x = 8x$$
$$7b - b = 6b$$
$$3a + 4b + 2a = 5a + 4b$$
$$5e + 2u - e + 3 = 4e + 2u + 3$$
$$7a + 5b - a - 4b = 6a + b$$

> b is the same as $1b$

Evaluation

To evaluate an expression or formula, **substitute** the number for each **variable**.

For the formula $v = u + at$ find the value of v when $u = 2$, $t = 3$ and $a = 4$.

$$v = u + at$$
$$v = 2 + 4 \times 3$$
$$= 2 + 12$$
$$= 14$$

11 Percentages

In this chapter you will revise and extend your knowledge of percentages.

11.1 Percentages, fractions and decimals

83% can be written as $\frac{83}{100}$ or $0 \cdot 83$

83%, $\frac{83}{100}$ and $0 \cdot 83$ are **equivalent**.

Exercise 11.1

1 Write each percentage as a fraction and as a decimal.

   (**a**) 53%   (**b**) 81%   (**c**) 17%   (**d**) 21%   (**e**) 87%   (**f**) 57%   (**g**) 3%

2 Write each fraction as a percentage and as a decimal.

   (**a**) $\frac{51}{100}$ (**b**) $\frac{19}{100}$ (**c**) $\frac{17}{100}$ (**d**) $\frac{41}{100}$ (**e**) $\frac{33}{100}$ (**f**) $\frac{11}{100}$ (**g**) $\frac{37}{100}$

3 Write each decimal as a percentage and as a fraction.

   (**a**) $0 \cdot 47$ (**b**) $0 \cdot 27$ (**c**) $0 \cdot 87$ (**d**) $0 \cdot 17$ (**e**) $0 \cdot 91$ (**f**) $0 \cdot 07$ (**g**) $0 \cdot 079$

4 Copy and complete the table of equivalent percentages, fractions and decimals.

Percentage	Fraction	Decimal
23%		
59%		
	$\frac{67}{100}$	
	$\frac{13}{100}$	
		$0 \cdot 37$
		$0 \cdot 81$

11.2 Simplest form

Example

Write each percentage as a fraction in simplest form   (**a**) 64%   (**b**) 4·5%

(**a**) $64\% = \frac{64}{100}$ | Divide numerator and denominator by 4. | (**b**) $4 \cdot 5\% = \frac{4 \cdot 5}{100}$ | Multiply numerator and denominator by 10, then divide by 5. |

$\qquad = \frac{16}{25}$ $= \frac{45}{1000}$

$\qquad \qquad \qquad \qquad \qquad \qquad \qquad \qquad \qquad \qquad \qquad \qquad \qquad \quad = \frac{9}{200}$

Exercise 11.2

1 For each percentage find the equivalent fraction in simplest form.

   (**a**) 60%   (**b**) 80%   (**c**) 55%   (**d**) 62%   (**e**) 72%   (**f**) 4%   (**g**) 12%

   (**h**) 52%   (**i**) 16%   (**j**) 8%   (**k**) 3·5%   (**l**) 95%   (**m**) 15·5%   (**n**) 66%

   (**o**) $37\frac{1}{2}$%   (**p**) $62\frac{1}{2}$%   (**q**) 87·5%   (**r**) 12·5%   (**s**) 2·5%   (**t**) 0·5%   (**u**) 1·5%

2 Write each ingredient of the marinara sauce as a fraction in simplest form.

Marinara sauce
Water 28%　Tomato 56%
Oil 11%　Spices 5%

3 In a survey of tourists' holiday activities the results were:

| Sunbathing | 22% | Swimming | 14% | Shopping | 26% |
| Scuba diving | 7·5% | Sport | 22·5% | Sightseeing | 8·25% |

Change each percentage to a fraction in simplest form.

4 A bank has variable interest rates for different accounts.

Savings account 4·2%　　Current account 3·4%　　Credit card 16·5%

Change each percentage to a fraction in simplest form.

5 A garden centre has recorded its sales of seed potatoes.
Change each percentage into a fraction in simplest form.

| Golden Wonder | 12·5% | Vanessa | 3·2% |
| Desiree | 25·5% | Maris Piper | 7·25% |

11.3 Common percentages

Some percentages are used frequently.
It is useful to know these as fractions and decimals.

For example, 75% is equivalent to $\frac{3}{4}$ and 0·75

Exercise 11.3

1 Copy and complete the table of common percentages.

Percentage	Fraction	Decimal	Percentage	Fraction	Decimal
50%			40%		
25%			60%		
75%			80%		
1%			$33\frac{1}{3}$%	$\frac{1}{3}$	0·333
10%			$66\frac{2}{3}$%		
20%			5%		

$33\frac{1}{3}\% = \dfrac{33\frac{1}{3}}{100} = 0.333$, rounded to 3 decimal places.

2 Without looking at your table, write each fraction or decimal as a percentage.
　(**a**) $\frac{1}{2}$　　(**b**) 0·25　　(**c**) $\frac{3}{4}$　　(**d**) $\frac{1}{3}$　　(**e**) 0·2　　(**f**) $\frac{3}{5}$

　(**g**) 0·1　　(**h**) $\frac{2}{3}$　　(**i**) 0·333　　(**j**) 0·75　　(**k**) $\frac{4}{5}$　　(**l**) $\frac{1}{100}$

3 Write each percentage as a fraction and a decimal.
　(**a**) 10%　　(**b**) 80%　　(**c**) 50%　　(**d**) $33\frac{1}{3}$%　　(**e**) 75%　　(**f**) 40%

11.4 Percentage of a quantity without a calculator

Example 1

Calculate 25% of £480

25% of £480

$= \frac{1}{4}$ of 480

$= \frac{1}{4} \times 480 = \textbf{£120}$

Example 2

Calculate $66\frac{2}{3}$% of 960 g

Find $\frac{2}{3}$ of 960 g

$\frac{1}{3} \times 960 = 320$

So, $\frac{2}{3}$ of 960 $= 2 \times 320 = \textbf{640 g}$

> Find $\frac{1}{3}$ then multiply by 2.

Exercise 11.4

1 Without a calculator, calculate:
(**a**) 50% of £94   (**b**) 25% of £2000   (**c**) 20% of £24   (**d**) 10% of 404 g
(**e**) 1% of 6400 kg   (**f**) 10% of 52 ml   (**g**) 50% of 45·2 km   (**h**) 20% of £45.20
(**i**) $66\frac{2}{3}$% of £14.40   (**j**) $33\frac{1}{3}$% of 63 kg   (**k**) 40% of £52   (**l**) 80% of 1255 kg

2 Mel earns £64 each week at her evening job. She saves 75% of this for the summer. How much does she save each week?

3 The manufacturer receives $66\frac{2}{3}$% of the price of a chocolate bar. If a bar costs £0.81, how much does the manufacturer make?

4 Stuart and Hazel share the driving on holiday. If Stuart drives 60% of the time, how far does he drive on a 510 kilometre journey?

11.5 Using one percent

Example

Calculate how many grammes of fat there are in the lasagne.

1% of 360 g

$= \frac{1}{100} \times 360 = 3\cdot6$ g

So,   8% of 360 g $= 8 \times 3\cdot6$ g $= \textbf{28·8 g}$

> Find 1% then multiply by 8.

Lasagne 360 g
8% fat

Exercise 11.5

1 Calculate 7% of
(**a**) 200 g   (**b**) 880 km   (**c**) £720   (**d**) 8200 cm   (**e**) 409 m   (**f**) 446 kg

2 Calculate:
(**a**) 11% of 800 ml   (**b**) 6% of £480   (**c**) 7% of 1800 g   (**d**) 3% of 720 mm
(**e**) 5% of £36   (**f**) 9% of £526   (**g**) 17% of 2400 km   (**h**) 22% of 44 cm

3 The workers in a factory have won a 4% wage rise. Find the rise in each person's weekly pay.
(**a**) Sue, £235   (**b**) John, £320   (**c**) Gwen, £182   (**d**) Adam, £480

4 A diet brand of food is to have the fat content of all its products reduced by 9%. Calculate the reduction in fat content for each product:
(**a**) biscuits, 85 g   (**b**) cake, 72 g   (**c**) lasagne, 125 g   (**d**) chocolate, 222 g

11.6 Using ten percent

Example 1

Calculate the 20% commission on a £524 sale.

$$10\% \text{ of } £524$$
$$= \tfrac{1}{10} \times 524 = £52.40$$

So, 20% of £524 = 2 × £52.40 = **£104.80**

Example 2

Calculate the 35% discount on £224.

10% of £224 = $\tfrac{1}{10} \times £224$ = £22.40
30% of £224 = 3 × £22.40 = £67.20
5% of £224 = $\tfrac{1}{2} \times £22.40$ = £11.20

So, 35% of £224   = **£78.40**

Example 3

VAT is currently charged at 17·5%.
Calculate the VAT on an £80 bill.

10% of £80	=		£8
5% of £80	= $\tfrac{1}{2} \times £8$ =	£4
2·5% of £80	= $\tfrac{1}{2} \times £4$ =	£2

So, 17·5% of £80 =   **£14**

> VAT stands for value added tax.

Exercise 11.6

1 Calculate 30% of

   (**a**) £760   (**b**) 650 cm   (**c**) 1400 m   (**d**) £743   (**e**) £8240   (**f**) 945 ml.

2 Calculate:

   (**a**) 30% of £340   (**b**) 60% of 560 g   (**c**) 90% of 94 m

   (**d**) 40% of 330 km   (**e**) 55% of £45   (**f**) 85% of 580 g

   (**g**) 45% of 670 ml   (**h**) 35% of £58   (**i**) 15% of £8.60

3 A 250 gramme packet of biscuits contains 35% starch.
   How much starch is this?

4 Michael is offered 45% of £620 or 35% of £720.
   Which offer should he take?

5 120 pupils selected their favourite foods.
   Use the list to calculate how many chose each dish.

Pizza	15%
Pasta	35%
Burgers	5%
Curry	45%

6 Calculate the VAT at 17·5% on each bill.

   (**a**) Car service, £230   (**b**) Plumber, £36

   (**c**) Computer, £780   (**d**) Roof repair, £540

7 Calculate the VAT at 17·5% on each restaurant bill.

   (**a**) Subtotal £82.00   (**b**) Subtotal £66.00   (**c**) Subtotal £88.00

11.7 Percentage – increase and decrease

To find the sale price of a television costing £395:

$$10\% \text{ of } £395 = \qquad £39.50$$
$$5\% \text{ of } £395 = \tfrac{1}{2} \times £39.50 = \underline{£19.75}$$
So, 15% of £395 = £59.25

The sale price is £395 − £59.25 = £335.75

Exercise 11.7

1 Calculate the sale price of each item:

(**a**) jacket, £96   (**b**) shoes, £72   (**c**) shirt, £45   (**d**) jeans, £39

2 Calculate the sale price for each vehicle:

(**a**) estate car, £8400   (**b**) saloon car, £8340

(**c**) 4 wheel drive, £9960

3 A shoe factory has awarded a 5% wage rise to all employees.
Calculate the new wage for each grade of employee.

(**a**) technician, £320   (**b**) researcher, £540   (**c**) designer, £650

4 A confectioner plans to make its range of chocolate bars larger. The bars are advertised
as 35% bigger. Find the weight of the new, bigger bars if the original weights were:

(**a**) 60 g   (**b**) 90 g   (**c**) 120 g   (**d**) 250 g   (**e**) 75 g

5 Over a period of time the price of most things changes. Find the current price for each item.

	(**a**)	(**b**)	(**c**)	(**d**)	(**e**)
Item	Car	House	Computer	Holiday	Fridge
Old price	£9200	£84 600	£1200	£480	£395
Change in price	40% increase	$66\tfrac{2}{3}\%$ increase	5% decrease	12.5% increase	9% increase

6 The Atcins food company makes low fat foods for slimmers.
Calculate the amount of fat in each Atcins food.

Food	Normal fat content	Percentage less in Atcins
(**a**) Crisps	9 g	20%
(**b**) Pizza	15 g	25%
(**c**) Ice cream	21 g	$33\tfrac{1}{3}\%$
(**d**) Pasta sauce	3·5 g	7%

7 Add VAT at 17·5% to each bill.

(**a**) restaurant, £84   (**b**) car service, £320   (**c**) building work, £2546

8 In the Mia Roma restaurant a 10% service charge is added to each bill and then
VAT at 17·5% is added on top. What is the final bill for a meal which costs £36?

11.8 Percentages using a calculator

Example 1
Calculate 13% of £850.
0·13 × 850 = 110·5
So 13% of £850 is **£110.50**

| 13% is equivalent to 0·13 |

Example 2
Calculate 23·4% of 540 kg
0·234 × 540 = 126·36
So 23.4% of 540 kg is **126.36 kg**

| 23·4% is equivalent to 0·234 |

Exercise 11.8

1 Calculate:
   (**a**) 12% of 840 ml   (**b**) 23% of £230   (**c**) 35% of 84 ml   (**d**) 64% of £78
   (**e**) 33% of 450 m   (**f**) 85% of £85   (**g**) 19% of £2400   (**h**) 7% of 72 kg
   (**i**) 3% of £52   (**j**) 12·5% of 750 m   (**k**) 22·5% of £15   (**l**) 1·5% of £95

2 Find the weight of these ingredients in a 250 gramme packet of biscuits.

Starch 32%   Sugar 13%
Fat   15%   Fibre 7.5%

3 Calculate the volume of each ingredient in a 1·5 litre carton of fruit juice.

Water   68%   Orange juice 8%
Grape juice 6%   Apple juice   18%

11.9 Percentage – increase and decrease using a calculator

Example 1
Find the total cost, including tourist tax, of a holiday costing £855.

   15% of £855   **or**   15% added means a total of 115%
= 0·15 × £855 = £128·25   Find 115% of £855
Total cost is £855 + £128.25 = **£983.25**   Total cost = 1·15 × £855 = **£983.25**

Tourist tax 15%

Example 2
Find the sale price of a CD player which costs £620.

   35% of £620   **or**   35% off means 65% remains
= 0·35 × £620 = £217   Find 65% of £620
Sale price is £620 − £217 = **£403**   Sale price = 0·65 × £620 = **£403**

Sale 35% off

Exercise 11.9

1 For each percentage increase, write the total percentage.
   (**a**) 10%   (**b**) 20%   (**c**) 35%   (**d**) 50%   (**e**) 3%   (**f**) 22·5%   (**g**) 17·5%

2 For each percentage decrease, write the percentage remaining.
   (**a**) 25%   (**b**) 30%   (**c**) 55%   (**d**) 60%   (**e**) 28%   (**f**) 76%   (**g**) $12\frac{1}{2}$%

3 Find the sale price of each item if prices are reduced by 35%.

(**a**) Coat £116   (**b**) Dress £87   (**c**) Shoes £52.60   (**d**) Jeans £48.

4 The Oak restaurant adds a 12% service charge to every bill.
Add the service charge to each bill.

(**a**) £48   (**b**) £28.50   (**c**) £75   (**d**) £94.50   (**e**) £156.50

5 A garden centre gives a 23% discount to its staff.
Find the staff price for each item.

(**a**) Weedkiller £15   (**b**) Hedge trimmer £189

(**c**) Greenhouse £356

6 Customers in a cash and carry have different discounts.
Find the price each person will pay.

(**a**) Grace £95, 14% discount   (**b**) Lois £254, 12% discount   (**c**) Helen £440, 27·5% discount

7 Calculate each new price.

(**a**) £80, 9% increase   (**b**) £770, 23% increase   (**c**) £6540, 15·5% increase

8 In the 2001 census the percentage change in population was recorded.
Find the new population for each village.

Village	Original population	Percentage change
(**a**) Redford	12 350	8% increase
(**b**) Daltown	1675	4% increase
(**c**) Cairnston	9880	12.5% increase

9 Add VAT at 17·5% to each bill.

(**a**) Exhaust system, £102   (**b**) Curtains, £210   (**c**) Cleaning services, £84

11.10 Fractions to percentages using a calculator

Caitlin scored $\frac{57}{60}$ in her maths exam.

What is this as a percentage?

$\frac{57}{60} = 0·95 = \mathbf{95\%}$ 5 7 ÷ 6 0 = 0.95

Exercise 11.10

1 Change each fraction to a percentage.

(**a**) $\frac{9}{20}$ (**b**) $\frac{14}{40}$ (**c**) $\frac{13}{50}$ (**d**) $\frac{16}{25}$ (**e**) $\frac{13}{20}$ (**f**) $\frac{19}{76}$ (**g**) $\frac{36}{80}$

(**h**) $\frac{21}{60}$ (**i**) $\frac{34}{102}$ (**j**) $\frac{9}{15}$ (**k**) $\frac{36}{40}$ (**l**) $\frac{21}{24}$ (**m**) $\frac{36}{54}$ (**n**) $\frac{93}{150}$

2 Eve has listed her test results.

(**a**) Change each result to a percentage.

(**b**) List the subjects in order, starting with the best.

Science $\frac{84}{90}$ **French** $\frac{52}{80}$

English $\frac{48}{75}$ **Maths** $\frac{90}{150}$

11.11 Percentage of a total

A travel company has booked its clients into 5 hotels.
What percentage is staying at the Hotel Shilton?

Total number of clients = 57 + 15 + 42 + 30 + 6 = 150

Hotel Shilton: 57 out of 150 people
$$= \frac{57}{150} = 0{\cdot}38 = \textbf{38\%}$$

Hotel	Number of clients
Shilton	57
Ritz	15
Carlton	42
Balmoral	30
North	6

Exercise 11.11

1 Calculate the percentage staying in each hotel on the list above.

2 The table shows the final destinations for a plane load of passengers travelling to Italy.

(**a**) Calculate the total number of tourists.

(**b**) Calculate the percentage travelling to each resort.

Sorrento	54
Positano	63
Amalfi	18
Capri	45

3 A holiday rep has listed the activity choices for a group of tourists. Calculate the percentage choosing each activity.

Barbecue	9
Palace	20
Zoo	6
Dungeon	25

4 S2 pupils have chosen science subjects as shown.
Calculate the percentage choosing each subject.

Chemistry 45,   Biology 48,   Physics 27

5 In a traffic survey class 1B2 recorded these results.

Cars	50	Vans	13
Trucks	12	Buses	5

Calculate each kind of vehicle to the nearest percentage.

6 At the school disco, the sales of soft drinks are:

cola 75   water 180   lemonade 55   limeade 40

For each drink calculate the percentage sold, giving your answer to 1 decimal place.

7 For a dessert recipe the ingredients are:

flour 120 g,   sugar 80 g,   fat 60 g,   apples 160 g

Calculate the percentage of fat in this dessert.

Review exercise 11

1 Copy and complete the table for equivalent percentages, fractions and decimals.

Percentage	Fraction	Decimal
60%		
10%		
	$\frac{4}{5}$	
		0·333
20%		
	$\frac{1}{100}$	

2 For each percentage write the equivalent fraction in simplest form.
(**a**) 96%　　(**b**) 55%　　(**c**) 15%　　(**d**) 7·5%　　(**e**) 0·5%　　(**f**) 12·5%

3 Write each percentage as an equivalent decimal.
(**a**) 43%　　(**b**) 8%　　(**c**) $33\frac{1}{3}$%　　(**d**) 0·7%　　(**e**) 6·9%　　(**f**) $9\frac{1}{2}$%

4 Find:
(**a**) 10% of £890　　(**b**) 25% of 108 kg　　(**c**) $33\frac{1}{3}$% of 330 ml　　(**d**) 40% of 85 cm

5 Calculate:
(**a**) 8% of £280　　(**b**) 9% of 760 g　　(**c**) 11% of 96 kg

6 For each percentage increase, write the total percentage.
(**a**) 10%　　(**b**) 25%　　(**c**) 33%　　(**d**) 55%

7 For each percentage decrease, write the percentage remaining.
(**a**) 30%　　(**b**) 45%　　(**c**) 12%　　(**d**) 81%

8 In a sale all prices are reduced by 35%.
Find the sale price of a briefcase which normally costs £140.

9 A company awards a wage rise of 7·5%.
Calculate the new weekly wage for each employee.
(**a**) Denis, old wage £390　　(**b**) Doris, old wage £456

10 Add VAT at 17·5% to each hotel bill.
(**a**) Cresta, £260　　(**b**) Dorian, £546　　(**c**) Eden, £342

11 The Eldorado restaurant adds a 12·5% service charge to all bills.
Calculate the total bill for a meal which costs £86.

12 Michael listed his test results.
(**a**) What percentage did he get for each subject?
(**b**) List his subjects in order starting with the best.

English $\frac{55}{60}$　　French $\frac{72}{75}$
German $\frac{75}{80}$　　Latin $\frac{39}{40}$

13 A school surveyed the teachers on how they travel to work.
From the results, what percentage
(**a**) drive　　(**b**) walk　　(**c**) do not cycle?

| Drive | 42 | Cycle | 3 |
| Walk | 12 | Bus | 3 |

Summary

Percentages, fractions and decimals

A percentage may be written as an equivalent fraction and decimal.

91% $\dfrac{91}{100}$

0.91

48% 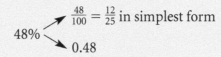 $\dfrac{48}{100} = \dfrac{12}{25}$ in simplest form

0.48

Some percentages are in common usage.

Percentage	Fraction	Decimal
1%	$\frac{1}{100}$	0.01
10%	$\frac{1}{10}$	0.1
20%	$\frac{1}{5}$	0.2
25%	$\frac{1}{4}$	0.25
50%	$\frac{1}{2}$	0.5
75%	$\frac{3}{4}$	0.75
$33\frac{1}{3}$%	$\frac{1}{3}$	0.33
$66\frac{2}{3}$%	$\frac{2}{3}$	0.67

Percentages of quantities

To calculate a percentage use $1\% = \frac{1}{100}$ or $10\% = \frac{1}{10}$

To find 7% of £165.

1% of £160 $= \frac{1}{100} \times$ £165 $=$ £1.65

So 7% of £160 $= 7 \times$ £1·65 $=$ **£11.55**

To find 17·5% of £48:

10% of £48 $= \frac{1}{10} \times$ £48 $=$ £4.80

5% of £48 $= \frac{1}{2} \times$ £4·80 $=$ £2.40

$2\cdot5\%$ of £48 $= \frac{1}{2} \times$ £2·40 $=$ £1.20

So 17·5% of £48 $=$ **£8.40**

Using a calculator   56% of 130 ml
$= 0\cdot56 \times 130$
$= 72\cdot8$ ml

Percentage increase and decrease

To add 24% to £440
Find   124% of £440
$= 1\cdot24 \times$ £440
$=$ **£545.60**

To take 11% off £320
Find   89% of £320
$= 0\cdot89 \times$ £320
$=$ **£284.80**

To change a fraction to a percentage:

$\dfrac{165}{200} = 0\cdot825$ $\boxed{1}\,\boxed{6}\,\boxed{5}\,\boxed{\div}\,\boxed{2}\,\boxed{0}\,\boxed{0}\,\boxed{=}\,\boxed{0.825}$

$= $ **82·5%**

12 2D Shape

In this chapter you will revise and extend your knowledge of triangles and quadrilaterals.

12.1 Polygons

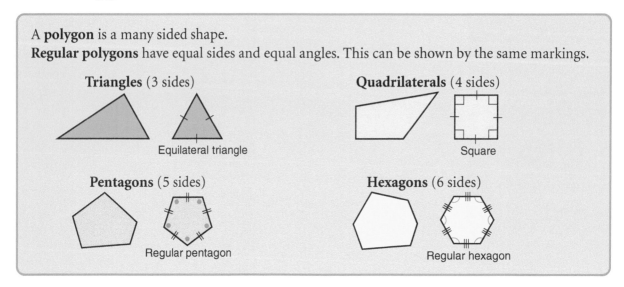

A **polygon** is a many sided shape.
Regular polygons have equal sides and equal angles. This can be shown by the same markings.

Triangles (3 sides)

Equilateral triangle

Quadrilaterals (4 sides)

Square

Pentagons (5 sides)

Regular pentagon

Hexagons (6 sides)

Regular hexagon

Exercise 12.1

1 Copy and complete the table.

Shape	Polygon name	Regular or not regular	Number of sides	Number of angles
(a)	equilateral triangle	regular	3	3
(b)				
(c)				
(d)				
(e)				
(f)				

2 Find the names of polygons which have
   (**a**) 7 sides   (**b**) 8 sides   (**c**) 9 sides   (**d**) 10 sides   (**e**) 12 sides.

12.2 Triangles

A triangle is a polygon with three sides.
Triangles can be classified by sides and classified by angles.

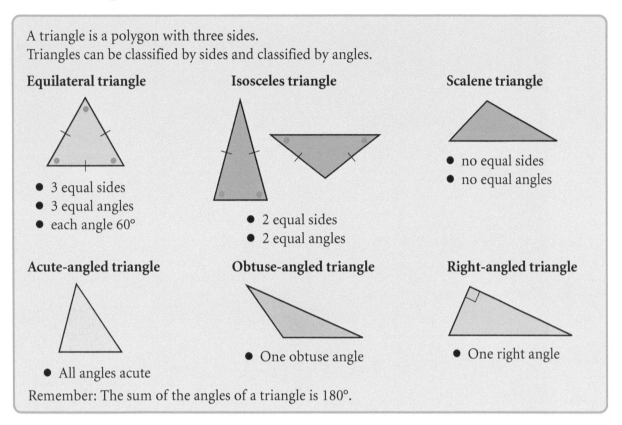

Equilateral triangle

- 3 equal sides
- 3 equal angles
- each angle 60°

Isosceles triangle

- 2 equal sides
- 2 equal angles

Scalene triangle

- no equal sides
- no equal angles

Acute-angled triangle

- All angles acute

Obtuse-angled triangle

- One obtuse angle

Right-angled triangle

- One right angle

Remember: The sum of the angles of a triangle is 180°.

Exercise 12.2

1 Write the names of the following triangles which are
(**a**) (**i**) equilateral   (**ii**) isosceles   (**iii**) scalene
(**b**) (**i**) acute-angled   (**ii**) obtuse-angled   (**iii**) right-angled
(**c**) right-angled and isosceles.

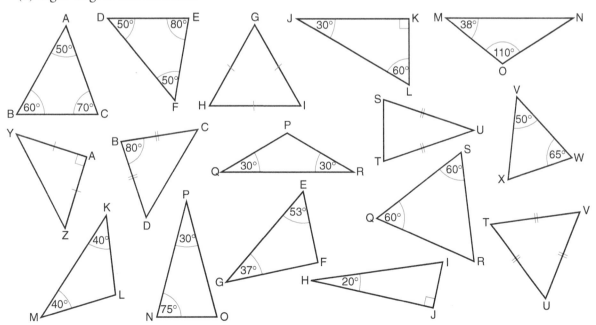

2 Trace each triangle and mark all equal sides and angles.

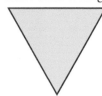 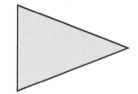 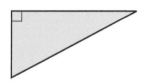

Copy and complete:

(**a**) An equilateral triangle
- has _____ axes of symmetry.
- fits its outline _____ ways, so it has rotational symmetry of order _____ .

(**b**) An isosceles triangle
- has _____ axes of symmetry.
- has rotational symmetry of order _____ .

(**c**) A right-angled triangle
- has _____ axes of symmetry.
- has rotational symmetry of order _____ .

3 Sketch each triangle. Without measuring, find the values of a, b, c, d and e.

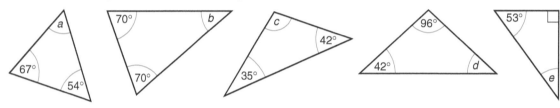

4 Sketch each isosceles triangle. Calculate all the missing angles in each triangle.

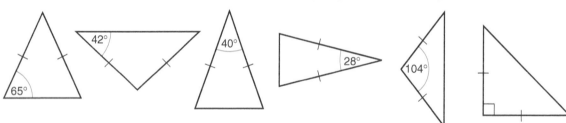

5 (**a**) Draw coordinate axes from -10 to 10.

(**b**) Plot the following triangles:

L (4, 3)   (6, 2)   (1, 1)   Q $(-3, -3)$ $(-1, -5)$ $(3, -1)$
M (1, 4)   (1, 6)   (8, 5)   R $(-1, 1)$ $(-3, 4)$ $(-8, 6)$
N (8, 6)   (5, 9)   (2, 6)   S $(-8, 0)$ $(-3, 0)$ $(-8, -5)$
P (1, 7) $(-1, 4)$ (1, 1)   T $(2, -5)$ $(5, 1)$ $(6, -5)$.

(**c**) Copy and complete the table:

	Acute angle	Obtuse angle	Right-angled
Isosceles			
Scalene		L	

6 Sketch each diagram. Calculate all the missing angles in each triangle.

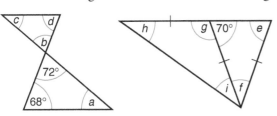 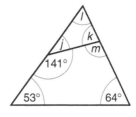 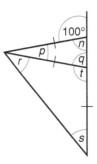

12.3 Area of a triangle

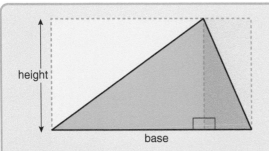

Area of triangle $= \frac{1}{2}$ of base $\times$ height

$= \frac{1}{2}bh$

In a triangle the base and height are perpendicular to each other.

  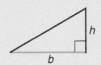 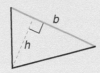 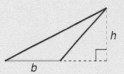

Example

Calculate the area of each triangle.

(a)

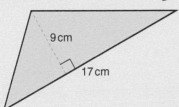

9 cm

17 cm

(b)

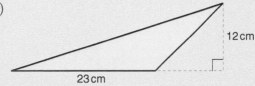

12 cm

23 cm

$A = \frac{1}{2}bh$

$= \dfrac{17 \times 9}{2}$

$= \dfrac{153}{2}$

$= 76 \cdot 5$

The area is 76·5 cm².

$A = \frac{1}{2}bh$

$= \dfrac{23 \times 12}{2}$

$= \dfrac{276}{2}$

$= 138$

The area is 138 cm².

Exercise 12.3

1 Calculate the area of each triangle.

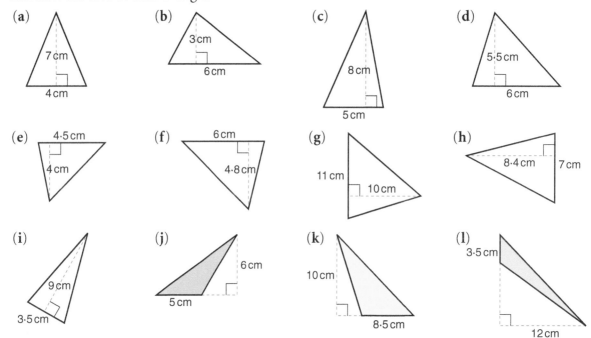

(**a**) 7 cm, 4 cm

(**b**) 3 cm, 6 cm

(**c**) 8 cm, 5 cm

(**d**) 5·5 cm, 6 cm

(**e**) 4·5 cm, 4 cm

(**f**) 6 cm, 4·8 cm

(**g**) 11 cm, 10 cm

(**h**) 8·4 cm, 7 cm

(**i**) 9 cm, 3·5 cm

(**j**) 6 cm, 5 cm

(**k**) 10 cm, 8·5 cm

(**l**) 3·5 cm, 12 cm

12.4 Quadrilaterals

Exercise 12.4

1 (**a**) You need a protractor. Measure the angles in each quadrilateral.

> A polygon with four straight sides is called a **quadrilateral**.

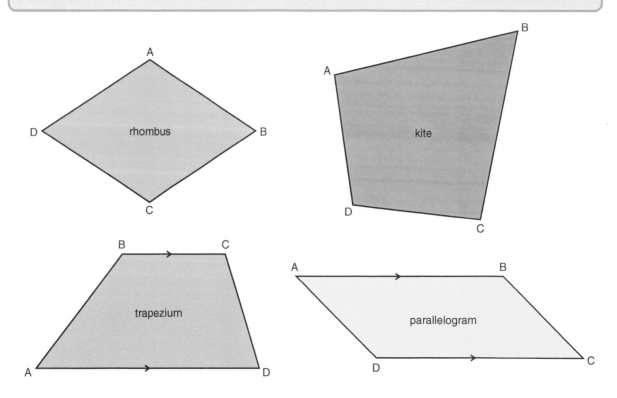

(**b**) Copy and complete the table:

	Angle A	Angle B	Angle C	Angle D	A + B + C + D
Rhombus					
Kite					
Parallelogram					
Trapezium					

2 (**a**) In any quadrilateral what do you think is the sum of the four angles?

(**b**) Draw a large quadrilateral on plain paper.
Cut out your quadrilateral.
Tear off each angle and fit them together as shown.
What is the sum of the four angles?

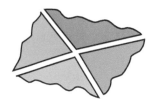

3 Copy and complete:
The sum of the angles of a quadrilateral is _____°.

4 Sketch the following quadrilaterals. Without measuring, find the values of *a* to *d*.

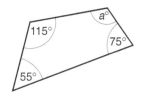 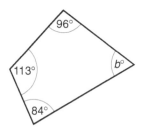 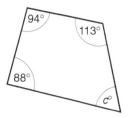 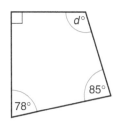

5 Quadrilateral ABCD is split into two triangles.
Copy and complete:
The sum of the angles of the yellow triangle is _____ .
The sum of the angles of the green triangle is _____ .
Hence the sum of the angles in quadrilateral ABCD is _____ .

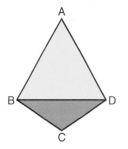

12.5 Squares

Exercise 12.5

1 You need a ruler, protractor and tracing paper.

(**a**) Draw a square with sides of length 6 centimetres and trace it.

(**b**) Using your tracing, copy and complete.
In a square:
- the length of all sides are _____ .
- all angles are _____ .
- the length of diagonals are _____ .
- the _____ bisect each other.
- the diagonals bisect each other at an angle of _____ .
- the diagonals _____ each angle of the square.
- there are _____ axes of symmetry.
- there is quarter- _____ symmetry or rotational symmetry of order _____ .

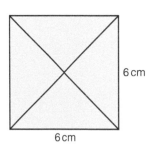

2 Sketch each square. *Without* measuring, fill in the sizes of all the missing sides and angles.

(a)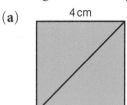
4 cm

(b)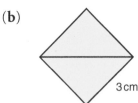
3 cm

(c)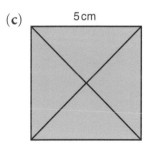
5 cm

(d)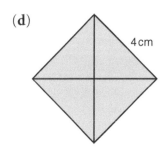
4 cm

3 Draw a square with diagonals 9 centimetres long.
Measure the lengths of each of the sides of the square.

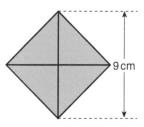
9 cm

4 Copy and complete the diagonals and draw each square.

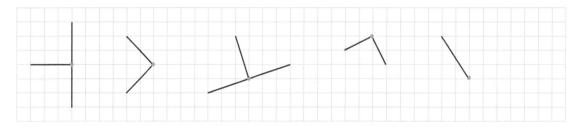

5 Draw coordinate axes from −10 to 10.

(a) A(1, 1), B(1, −3), C(5, −3) and D are the vertices of a square.
Find the coordinates of **(i)** D **(ii)** E, where the diagonals intersect.

(b) P(−2, 4), Q(8, 6), R(10, −4) and S are the vertices of a square.
Find the coordinates of **(i)** S **(ii)** T, where the diagonals intersect.

(c) JKLM is a square. J is the point (−2, 6) and L is the point (−8, 6).
Find the coordinates of **(i)** K and M **(ii)** N, where the diagonals intersect.

(d) EFGH is a square. E is the point (2, 4) and G is the point (4, 10).
Find the coordinates of **(i)** F and H **(ii)** I, where the diagonals intersect.

(e) U(10, 4), V, W and X are the vertices of a square whose diagonals intersect
at Y(7, 5). Find the coordinates of V, W and X.

12.6 Rectangles

Exercise 12.6

1 You need a ruler, protractor and tracing paper.

(**a**) Draw a rectangle 10 centimetres by 7 centimetres and trace it.

(**b**) Using your tracing, copy and complete.
In a rectangle:
  - the lengths of opposite sides are _____ .
  - all angles are _____ .
  - the lengths of the diagonals are _____ .
  - the _____ bisect each other.
  - there are _____ axes of symmetry.
  - there is _____ - _____ symmetry or rotational symmetry of order _____ .

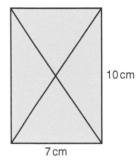

2 Sketch each rectangle and, without measuring, fill in the sizes of all the missing sides and angles.

(**a**) 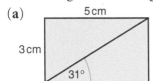　(**b**) 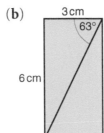　(**c**)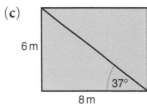

3 Use tracing paper to verify that:

(**a**) all 4 angles marked ✶ are equal

(**b**) all 4 angles marked ○ are equal

(**c**) both angles marked ✗ are equal

(**d**) both angles marked ▫ are equal.

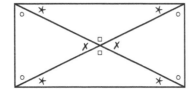

4 (**a**) What type of triangles are formed when the diagonals of a rectangle are drawn?

(**b**) Find the size of angles　(**i**) ∠DCE　(**ii**) ∠DEC.

(**c**) Sketch rectangle ABCD and fill in the sizes of all the missing sides and angles.

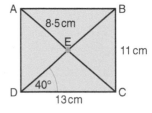

5 Sketch each rectangle and fill in the sizes of all missing sides and angles.

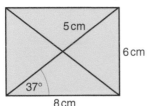　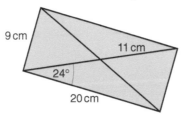　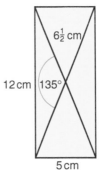

6 Copy and complete the diagonals and draw each rectangle.

7 Draw coordinate axes from −10 to 10.

(**a**) A(3, 1), B(9, 1), C(9, 3) and D are the vertices of a rectangle.
Find the coordinates of (**i**) D (**ii**) E, where the diagonals intersect.

(**b**) F(−6, 3), G(−4, 4), H(−6, 8) and I are the vertices of a rectangle.
Find the coordinates of (**i**) I (**ii**) J, where the diagonals intersect.

(**c**) K(−1, 6), L(1, 2), M and N are the vertices of a rectangle whose diagonals
intersect at P(4, 6).
Find the coordinates of M and N.

(**d**) Q(0, 1), R(2, 0), S and T are the vertices of a rectangle whose diagonals
intersect at U$(-1, -3\frac{1}{2})$.
Find the coordinates of S and T.

8 Sketch each figure and calculate the size of (**i**) ∠AFB (**ii**) ∠DBF.

(**a**) 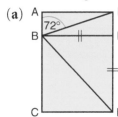 (**b**) 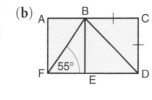 (**c**) 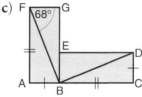 (**d**)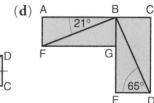

12.7 The rhombus

Exercise 12.7

1 You need a ruler, protractor and tracing paper.

(**a**) Draw a rhombus with diagonals 10 centimetres and 6 centimetres
and trace it.

(**b**) Using your tracing, copy and complete.
In a rhombus:
- _____ sides are _____ in length.
- _____ angles are equal.
- the diagonals _____ each other at an angle of _____ .
- the diagonals _____ each angle of the rhombus.
- there are _____ axes of symmetry.
- there is _____ - _____ symmetry or rotational symmetry of order _____ .

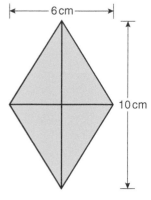

2 (**a**) Draw a rhombus with diagonals 8 centimetres and 6 centimetres.

(**b**) Measure and fill in the lengths of each of the four sides.

3 Sketch each rhombus. Without measuring, fill in all the missing lengths.

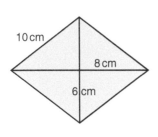 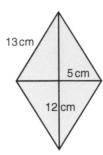 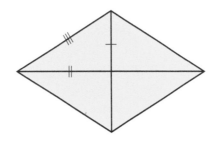

4 (**a**) Trace each rhombus.

(**b**) Measure the length of each side and the size of each angle. Write your answers on each rhombus. (Check that the angles sum to 360°.)

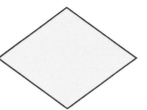 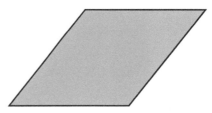

5 Sketch each rhombus. Without measuring, fill in the size of all missing angles.

(**a**) 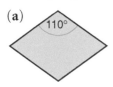   (**b**)   (**c**) 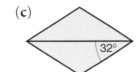   (**d**)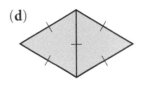

6 Use tracing paper to verify that

(**a**) all four angles marked ✶ are equal

(**b**) all four angles marked ○ are equal.

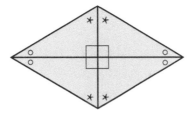

7 Sketch each rhombus. Without measuring, fill in all the missing angles.

(**a**) 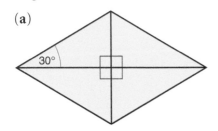   (**b**)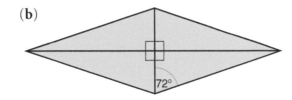

8 Copy and complete the diagonals and draw each rhombus.

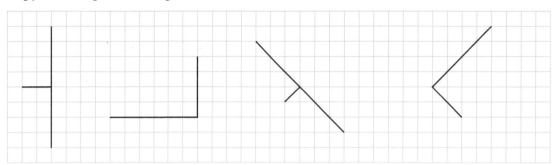

9 Draw coordinate axes from −10 to 10.

(**a**) A (8, −2),   B (6, 3),   C (8, 8) and D are the vertices of a rhombus.
   Find the coordinates of (**i**) D   (**ii**) E, where the diagonals intersect.

(**b**) F (−4, 1),   G (−10, −1),   H (−8, 5) and I are the vertices of a rhombus.
   Find the coordinates of (**i**) I   (**ii**) J, where the diagonals intersect.

(**c**) K (5, 2),   L (3, 6), M and N are the vertices of a rhombus whose diagonals
   intersect at P (2, 5).
   Find the coordinates of M and N.

(**d**) Q (−7, −6), R, S (3, −6) and T are vertices of a rhombus whose shorter
   diagonal is 6 units long.
   Find the coordinates of R and T.

10 PQRS and PQST are rhombi.
Sketch the diagram and calculate
the size of all 25 angles.

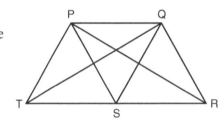

12.8 Kites

Exercise 12.8

1 You need a ruler, protractor and tracing paper.

(**a**) Draw a kite with diagonals 9 centimetres and 5 centimetres and
   trace it.

(**b**) Using tracing paper, copy and complete.
   In a kite:
   • two pairs of adjacent sides are _____ .
   • _____ pair of opposite angles is _____ .
   • one diagonal is _____ by the other.
   • the diagonals intersect each other at an angle of _____ .
   • one diagonal _____ a pair of opposite angles.
   • there is _____ axis of symmetry.
   • there is no _____-turn or _____-_____ rotational symmetry.

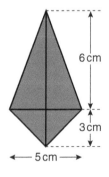

2 Draw 2 different kites with diagonals 9 centimetres and 5 centimetres.

3 Sketch each kite. Without measuring, fill in the sizes of all the missing lengths.

(**a**)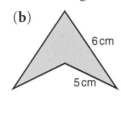
4 cm
7 cm

(**b**)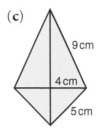
6 cm
5 cm

(**c**)
9 cm
4 cm
5 cm

(**d**)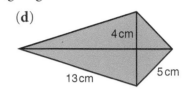
4 cm
13 cm
5 cm

4 (**a**) Trace each kite below.
　　Measure the length of each side and the size of each angle.

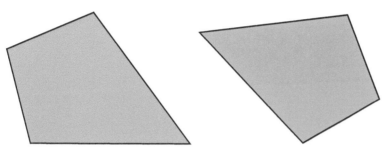

(**b**) Write your answers on each kite. (Check that the angles sum to 360°.)

5 Sketch each kite. Without measuring, fill in the sizes of all the missing angles.

(**a**)
100°
40°

(**b**)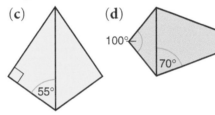
30°
200°

(**c**)
55°

(**d**)
100°
70°

(**e**)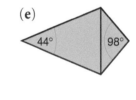
44°
98°

6 Use tracing paper to verify that:
(**a**) both angles marked ✶ are equal
(**b**) both angles marked ○ are equal
(**c**) both angles marked ✗ are equal
(**d**) both angles marked • are equal.

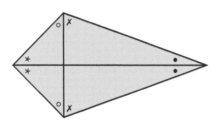

7 Sketch each kite. Without measuring, fill in the missing angles.

(**a**)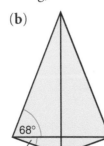
15°
30°

(**b**)
68°
19°

(**c**)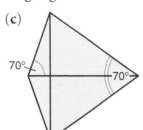
70°
70°

(**d**)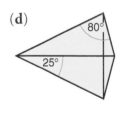
80°
25°

8 Copy and complete the diagonals and draw each kite.

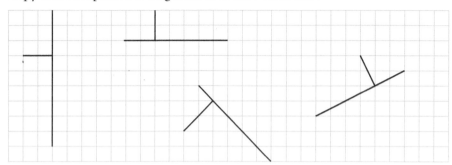

9 Draw coordinate axes from −10 to 10.

(**a**) A (−7, 8),   B (−10, 6),   C (−7, −2) and D are the vertices of a kite.
Find the coordinates of   (**i**) D   (**ii**) E, where the diagonals intersect.

(**b**) F (0, 1),   G (−3, 7),   H (0, 5) and I are the vertices of a V-kite.
Find the coordinates of I.

(**c**) J (7, −2),   K (8, −4),   L (7, −6) and M are the vertices of a kite
with axis of symmetry 7 units long. Find the coordinate of M.

(**d**) P (−1, −1),   Q (4, −2),   R (3, −5) and S are the vertices of a kite.
Find the coordinates of   (**i**) S   (**ii**) T, where the diagonals intersect.

10 A (4, 5)   B (1, 2)   C (4, −1) and D are the vertices of a kite. Find
the coordinates of D when ABCD has an axis of symmetry of length

(**a**) 8 units   (**b**) 4 units   (**c**) 2 units   (**d**) 5 units.

11 The diagrams show congruent kites.
Sketch each diagram and fill in all the missing angles.

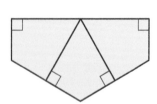 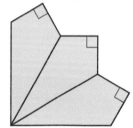 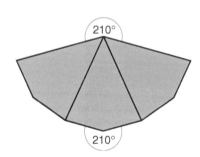

12.9 Parallelograms

Exercise 12.9

1 You need a ruler, protractor and tracing paper.

(**a**) Trace the parallelogram opposite.

(**b**) Using your tracing paper, copy and complete.
In a parallelogram:

- opposite sides are _____ in length and _____ .
- opposite angles are _____ .
- the diagonals _____ each other.
- these are _____ axes of symmetry.
- there is _____ _____ symmetry or rotational symmetry of order _____ .

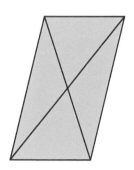

2 (**a**) Trace each parallelogram below.

(**b**) Measure the length of each side and the size of each angle.
Write your answers on each parallelogram. (Check that the angles sum to 360°.)

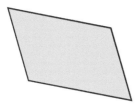 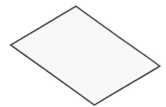

3 Sketch each parallelogram below. Without measuring fill in all
missing sides and angles.

(**a**)
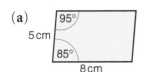

(**b**)
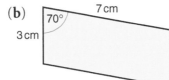

(**c**)
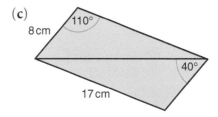

(**d**)
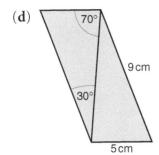

(**e**)
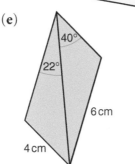

4 Trace the parallelogram opposite. Verify that:

(**a**) both angles marked ✶ are equal

(**b**) both angles marked ○ are equal

(**c**) both angles marked ✗ are equal

(**d**) both angles marked □ are equal

(**e**) both angles marked • are equal

(**f**) both angles marked ⌢ are equal.

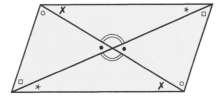

5 Sketch each parallelogram. Without measuring, fill in all the missing angles.

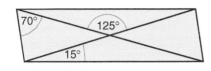 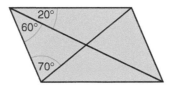

6 Measure the diagonals of this parallelogram.
Measure OA, OB, OC, and OD and write what you notice.

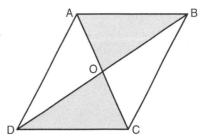

7 Draw two different parallelograms with diagonals 7 centimetres and 5 centimetres.

8 Sketch each parallelogram. Without measuring, fill in all the missing lengths.

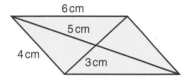
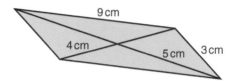

9 Copy and complete the diagonals and complete each parallelogram.

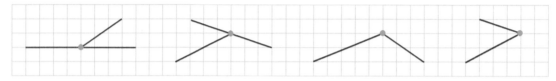

10 Draw coordinate axes from -10 to 10.
   (**a**) A $(-2, -1)$ B $(-9, -1)$ C $(-10, -5)$ and D are vertices of a parallelogram.
       Find the coordinates of (**i**) D   (**ii**) E, where the diagonals intersect.
   (**b**) F $(4, 4)$ G $(6, 5)$ H $(10, 4)$ and I are the vertices of a parallelogram.
       Find the coordinates of (**i**) I   (**ii**) J, where the diagonals intersect.
   (**c**) K $(-9, 8)$ L $(-6, 2)$, M and N are the vertices of a parallelogram whose
       diagonals intersect at P $(-6, 6)$.
       Find the coordinates of M and N.
   (**d**) Q $(1, 4)$ R $(5, 8)$, S and T are the vertices of a parallelogram whose diagonals
       intersect at U $(3, -1)$.
       Find the coordinates of S and T.

11 The diagrams below show pairs of congruent parallelograms.
   Sketch each diagram and fill in all the missing angles.
   Calculate the size of $\angle$AEC.

(**a**) 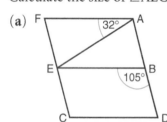   (**b**) 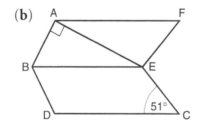   (**c**)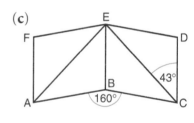

12.10 The trapezium

A **trapezium** is a quadrilateral with with one pair of parallel sides.

An **isosceles trapezium** is a trapezium with one axis of symmetry.

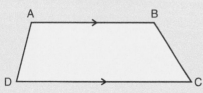
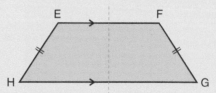

Exercise 12.10

1 (**a**) Calculate the size of the missing angles x and y.

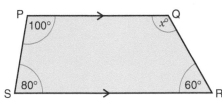 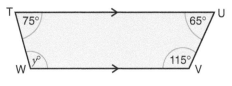

   (**b**) Find (**i**) $\angle$QPS + $\angle$PSR   (**ii**) $\angle$PQR + $\angle$QRS
          (**iii**) $\angle$TUV + $\angle$UVW (**iv**) $\angle$UTW + $\angle$TWV.

2 (**a**) Trace trapezium ABCD on the previous page.
   (**b**) Measure the size of each angle. Write your answers on the trapezium.
   (**c**) Calculate   (**i**) $\angle$ABC + $\angle$BCD   (**ii**) $\angle$BAD + $\angle$ADC.

3 (**a**) Trace trapezium EFGH on the previous page.
   (**b**) Measure the size of each angle. Write your answers on the trapezium.
   (**c**) Calculate   (**i**) $\angle$EFG + $\angle$FGH   (**ii**) $\angle$FEH + $\angle$EHG.

4 Copy and complete:
For a trapezium, two pairs of angles add up to _____°.

5 Sketch each trapezium. Without measuring, find all the angles.

(**a**) 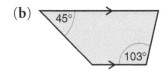   (**b**) 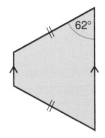   (**c**)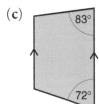

6 Sketch each isosceles trapezium. Without measuring, find all the angles.

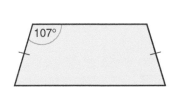 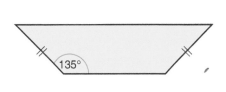

7 Sketch each trapezium. Without measuring, find all the missing angles.

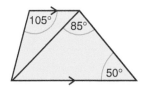 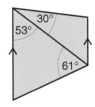 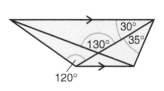 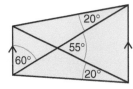

Review exercise 12

1 Name the following polygons.

(**a**) a regular 3-sided polygon   (**b**) an 8-sided polygon   (**c**) a regular quadrilateral.

2 Say whether each of the following is true or false.

(**a**) A square has 4 axes of symmetry.

(**b**) A rectangle fits its outline 4 times in one revolution.

(**c**) A rhombus has 4 equal sides.

(**d**) A kite must have diagonals the same length.

(**e**) The diagonals of a parallelogram are axes of symmetry.

(**f**) The diagonals of a square bisect each other at right angles.

(**g**) A rhombus has two pairs of equal sides.

(**h**) The diagonals of a kite bisect each other.

(**i**) For all quadrilaterals the sum of the angles is 360°.

(**j**) All the sides of a parallelogram are the same length.

3 Describe each triangle in 2 ways.

(**a**)   (**b**)   (**c**)   (**d**)

4 Calculate the missing angles in the following triangles.

  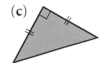

5 Sketch each quadrilateral. Without measuring, fill in all the missing sides and angles.

  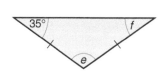

square   rectangle   rhombus

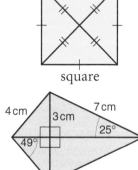 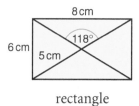 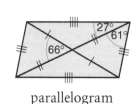 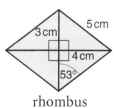

kite   parallelogram   trapezium

6 Sketch each quadrilateral in Question 5 above. Draw all axes of symmetry.

Summary

A polygon is a many sided shape.
Regular polygons have equal sides and angles.

Triangle   Square   Pentagon   Hexagon   Octagon

Triangles

Equilateral   Isosceles   Scalene

  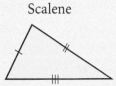

Acute-angled   Obtuse-angled   Right-angled

 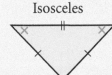 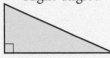

Quadrilaterals

Square

- all sides equal
- all angles equal 90°
- diagonals equal
- diagonals bisect at 90°
- diagonals bisect angles
- 4 axes of symmetry
- rotational order 4

Rectangle

- opposite sides equal
- all angles equal 90°
- diagonals equal
- diagonals bisect
- 2 axes of symmetry
- rotational order 2

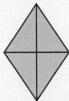

Rhombus

- all sides equal
- opposite angles equal
- diagonals bisect at 90°
- diagonals bisect angles
- 2 axes of symmetry
- rotational order 2

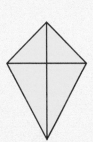

Kite

- adjacent sides equal
- 1 pair of opposite angles equal
- 1 diagonal bisected
- diagonals intersect at 90°
- 1 diagonal bisects angles
- 1 axis of symmetry
- rotational order 1

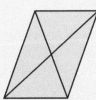

Parallelogram

- opposite sides equal
- opposite sides parallel
- opposite angles equal
- diagonals bisect
- no axes of symmetry
- rotational order 2

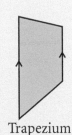

Trapezium

- 1 pair of parallel lines
- adjacent angles supplementary
- no axes of symmetry
- rotational order 1

13 Time, distance and speed

In this chapter you will revise units of time and calculate distance, speed and time from formulae.

13.1 24-hour notation

Remember: Time may be represented in 12 or 24 hour notation.

Example (a) Write 2.40 p.m. in 24 hour notation

(b) Write 7.30 a.m. in 24 hour notation

(c) Write 09 00 in 12 hour notation

(d) Write 19 53 in 12 hour notation

(a) 2.40 p.m. = **14 40**   (b) 7.30 a.m. = **07 30**

(c) 09 00 = **9.00 a.m.**   (d) 19 53 = **7.53 p.m.**

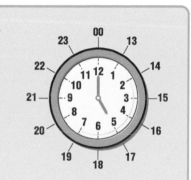

Exercise 13.1

1 Write these times in twenty four hour notation.

(**a**) 8 a.m.   (**b**) 11.20 a.m.   (**c**) 1.01 a.m.   (**d**) 12.30 a.m.

(**e**) 2 p.m.   (**f**) 6 p.m.   (**g**) 11 p.m.   (**h**) 5.05 p.m.

(**i**) 6.20 a.m.   (**j**) 6.20 p.m.   (**k**) 3.59 p.m.   (**l**) 8.20 p.m.

(**m**) 1.13 p.m.   (**n**) 11.59 a.m.   (**o**) Noon   (**p**) Midnight

2 Write these times in 12 hour notation.

(**a**) 13 00 hrs   (**b**) 07 00 hrs   (**c**) 20 00 hrs

(**d**) 14 14 hrs   (**e**) 01 01 hrs   (**f**) 12 01 hrs

(**g**) 19 20 hrs   (**h**) 22 30 hrs   (**i**) 00 10 hrs

(**j**) 03 03 hrs   (**k**) 19 45 hrs   (**l**) 15 15 hrs

(**m**) 18 15 hrs   (**n**) 11 59 hrs   (**o**) 00 01 hrs

3 Write these times in 24 hour notation.

(**a**) Five o'clock in the morning.   (**b**) Half past three in the afternoon

(**c**) Ten minutes past four in the morning.   (**d**) Twenty minutes past eight in the evening.

(**e**) Half past nine at night.   (**f**) Quarter past four in the afternoon.

(**g**) Quarter to six in the afternoon.   (**h**) Twenty to twelve in the evening.

(**i**) Twenty five past ten at night.   (**j**) Ten minutes to midnight.

(**k**) Ten minutes past noon.   (**l**) One minute after midnight.

13.2 Calculating time intervals

A time line may be used to calculate time intervals.

Example Calculate the length of time between 8.30 a.m. and 11.25 a.m.

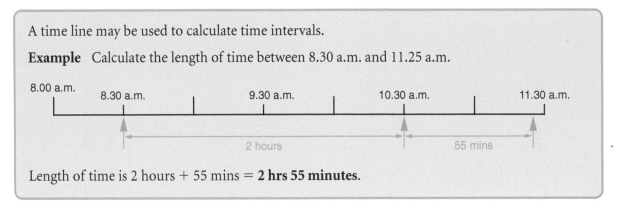

Length of time is 2 hours + 55 mins = **2 hrs 55 minutes.**

Exercise 13.2

1 Calculate the length of time between:

(**a**) 8.10 a.m. and 10.30 a.m.   (**b**) 6.20 a.m. and 10.45 p.m.

(**c**) 1.05 a.m. and 7.50 p.m.   (**d**) 2.30 p.m. and 7.05 p.m.

(**e**) 10.20 a.m. and 4.35 p.m.   (**f**) 11.55 a.m. and 8.20 p.m.

(**g**) Quarter to five in the afternoon and half past nine at night.

(**h**) Ten to twelve at night and quarter to three in the morning

(**i**) Ten to one in the morning and midnight.

2 Calculate the time intervals between:

(**a**) 08 10 and 11 40 hrs   (**b**) 16 35 and 19 45 hrs

(**c**) 18 50 and 23 15 hrs   (**d**) 23 10 and 02 45 hrs

(**e**) 14 14 and 18 18 hrs   (**f**) 20 20 and 00 05 hrs

(**g**) 07 04 and 11 27 hrs   (**h**) 09 41 and 12 27 hrs

(**i**) 10 01 and 16 59 hrs   (**j**) 18 56 and 23 03 hrs

> Some time intervals
> continue past midnight.

3 Use the timetable to answer these questions:

(**a**) How long does Bus A take from
  (**i**) Glasgow to Edinburgh
  (**ii**) Edinburgh to Stirling?

(**b**) How long does Bus A take for the complete round trip?

	Bus A	Bus B
Glasgow	1545	2205
Edinburgh	1640	
Stirling	1715	
Glasgow	1810	

(**c**) Assuming Bus B has the same journey times, write the timetable for Bus B.

(**d**) Bus C takes 18 minutes longer for each part of the journey. Write the timetable for Bus C if it arrives in Stirling at noon.

4 A school organises a cruise from Leith to Hull.
The boat leaves Leith at 10.20 p.m. and arrives in Hull the next day at 7.10 p.m.
Find the total time taken for the voyage.

Use the train timetable to answer questions 5 to 8.

Glasgow	09 00	11 30	14 16	17 53	
Garrowhill	09 09	11 39	—		—
Blairhill	09 12	11 42	—		23 03
Sunnyside	09 14	11 44	—		23 09
Airdrie	09 17	11 47	14 29		23 12

Trains do not stop at stations marked —

5 It takes Paul 15 minutes to walk from his house to the station in Blairhill.
Write the latest time he must leave home to catch the first train.

6 The last train takes 9 minutes to arrive at Blairhill. At what time did it leave Glasgow?

7 Using the same journey times as for the 09 00 leaving Glasgow, complete the timetable for the 17 53 train.

8 Mary lives next to the train station in Glasgow.
If she drives from her flat leaving at quarter past eleven she can arrive at Airdrie four minutes ahead of the 11.30 train.
How much quicker is the train journey than her car journey?

13.3 Converting units of time

Example 1
Change 2 hrs 20 mins to minutes
2 hrs 20 minutes = 120 mins + 20 mins
= **140 mins**

Example 2
Change 195 minutes to hours and minutes.
195 minutes = 180 mins + 15 mins
= **3 hrs 15 mins.**

Exercise 13.3

1 Change each of the following to minutes:
(**a**) 1 hr 30 mins (**b**) 2 hrs 10 mins (**c**) 2 hrs 40 mins
(**d**) 3 hrs 12 mins (**e**) 4 hrs 50 mins (**f**) 8 hrs 5 mins
(**g**) 3 hrs 23 mins (**h**) 2 hrs 45 mins (**i**) 5 hrs 33 mins
(**j**) 12 hrs 30 mins (**k**) one day (**l**) one week.

2 Change each of the following to hours and minutes:
(**a**) 80 mins (**b**) 200 mins (**c**) 350 mins
(**d**) 175 mins (**e**) 100 mins (**f**) 500 mins
(**g**) 280 mins (**h**) 404 mins (**i**) 750 mins
(**j**) 780 mins (**k**) 999 mins (**l**) 10 000 mins.

3 A university marathon record is 2 hours 29 minutes.
Three student times are shown for this year's run.

Jon	161 mins
Pete	146 mins
Dave	153 mins

(**a**) Change each time into hours and minutes.

(**b**) Who beat the record and by how many minutes?

4 Paula has a 4 hour video tape.

(**a**) What is the maximum number of films she can record?

(**b**) Name the films.

Mouse Race	85 mins
Menace	90 mins
Bill & Ben	73 mins
Xtence	80 mins

13.4 Converting time with fractions

Example 1

Change 4·5 hrs to hours and minutes
0·5 hrs = 0·5 × 60 mins = 30 mins
So 4·5 hrs = **4 hrs 30 mins**

Example 2

Change $2\frac{1}{3}$ hours to hours and minutes.
$\frac{1}{3}$ × 60 mins = 20 mins
So $2\frac{1}{3}$ hrs = **2 hrs 20 mins.**

Example 3

Change 3 hours and 12 minutes to hours.
12 mins = $\frac{12}{60}$ hr = $\frac{1}{5}$ hr = 0·2 hr
So 3 hrs 12 mins = **3·2 hrs.**

Exercise 13.4

1 Change each of the following to hours and minutes.

(**a**) 1·5 hrs (**b**) 2·2 hrs (**c**) 3·4 hrs (**d**) 1·6 hrs

(**e**) 4·1 hrs (**f**) 2·3 hrs (**g**) 3·7 hrs (**h**) 2·9 hrs

(**i**) 5·6 hrs (**j**) 0·8 hrs (**k**) 4·25 hrs (**l**) 3·8 hrs

(**m**) 2·25 hrs (**n**) 1·75 hrs (**o**) 4·3 hrs (**p**) 0·333 hr

2 Change each of the following to hours and minutes:

(**a**) $2\frac{1}{5}$ hrs (**b**) $1\frac{1}{4}$ hrs (**c**) $3\frac{1}{2}$ hrs (**d**) $4\frac{1}{6}$ hrs

(**e**) $3\frac{3}{10}$ hrs (**f**) $5\frac{1}{3}$ hrs (**g**) $9\frac{5}{6}$ hrs (**h**) $3\frac{2}{3}$ hrs

3 Change each of the following to hours (in decimal form):

(**a**) 1 hr 30 mins (**b**) 3 hrs 15 mins (**c**) 1 hr 18 mins

(**d**) 5 hrs 42 mins (**e**) 3 hrs 6 mins (**f**) 1 hr 45 mins

(**g**) 2 hrs 24 mins (**h**) 3 hrs 36 mins (**i**) 15 mins

(**j**) 1 hr 24 mins (**k**) 9 hrs 54 mins (**l**) 2 hrs 12 mins

(**m**) 18 hrs 18 mins (**n**) 48 mins (**o**) 1 hour 42 mins

(**p**) 200 mins (**q**) 726 mins (**r**) 45 mins

(**s**) 36 mins (**t**) 1 hr 3 mins

4 A cartoon show is exactly thirty minutes long.
Four cartoons are shown.
Bugsy is 12·5 minutes long. Tazz is 0·1 hours long.
Superspy is 5 minutes 15 seconds.
How long is the fourth cartoon?

13.5   Distance, speed and time

Example 1

What distance would a car travel in 4 hours
at a speed of 30 kilometres per hour?
The car travels 30 km in one hour.
In 4 hours it would travel $4 \times 30 = 120$ km
Distance = 120 km

Example 2

What is the speed of a boat that travels
20 kilometres in 2 hours?
20 km in 2 hours = 10 km each hour.
Speed = 10 km/h

> km/h means
> kilometres per hour

Example 3

How long would it take to jog 24 kilometres at a speed of 8 kilometres per hour?
It takes 1 hour to jog 8 kilometres per hour.
It would take 3 hours to jog 24 kilometres.
Time = 3 hours

Exercise 13.5

1 Find the average speed of
each boat in kilometres
per hour.

  (**a**) 45 kilometres in 3 hours

  (**b**) Ramsgate to Calais in
     5 hours

  (**c**) Folkestone to Calais in
     4 hours

  (**d**) Dover to Dunkirk in
     10 hours.

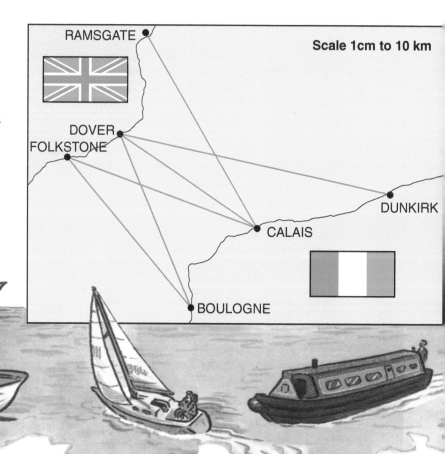

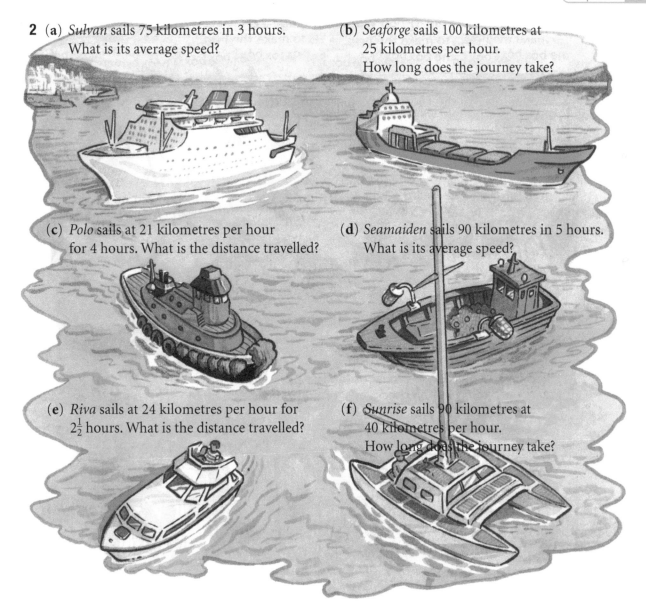

2 (**a**) *Sulvan* sails 75 kilometres in 3 hours. What is its average speed?

(**b**) *Seaforge* sails 100 kilometres at 25 kilometres per hour. How long does the journey take?

(**c**) *Polo* sails at 21 kilometres per hour for 4 hours. What is the distance travelled?

(**d**) *Seamaiden* sails 90 kilometres in 5 hours. What is its average speed?

(**e**) *Riva* sails at 24 kilometres per hour for $2\frac{1}{2}$ hours. What is the distance travelled?

(**f**) *Sunrise* sails 90 kilometres at 40 kilometres per hour. How long does the journey take?

3 The hovercraft *Cumbria* travels at an average speed of 30 kilometres per hour. Copy and complete the table.

Time	$\frac{1}{4}$ hour	$\frac{1}{2}$ hour	1 hour	2 hours	3 hours	4 hours
Distance	$7\frac{1}{2}$ km		30 km			

4 The car ferry *Cygnet* sails at an average speed of 20 kilometres per hour. Copy and complete the table:

Time	$\frac{1}{4}$ hour		1 hour				
Distance	5 km	10 km	20 km	40 km	60 km	80 km	100 km

13.6 Calculating distance using a formula

To calculate distance the speed is multiplied by the time.

Distance = Speed × Time

$$D \ = \ S \ \times \ T$$

Example

Calculate the distance travelled at 12 kilometres per hour for 3 hours 15 minutes.

$D = S \times T$

$\qquad = 12 \times 3{\cdot}25$

$\qquad = 39$

15 minutes $= \frac{1}{4}$ h $= 0.25$ h

The distance is 39 km.

Exercise 13.6

1 Use the formula $D = S \times T$ to find the distance travelled at a speed of 20 kilometres per hour for 4 hours.

2 Calculate how far you will travel in 3 hours at a speed of 60 kilometres per hour.

3 Ashanti cycles for 3 hours at a speed of 15 kilometres per hour. Calculate the distance travelled by Ashanti.

4 Calculate the distance travelled for each journey in the table:

	(a)	(b)	(c)	(d)	(e)	(f)
Speed	40 km/h	3 km/h	25 mph	7 km/h	200 km/h	14 mph
Time	3 hours	2 hours	5 hours	8 hours	3 hours	5 hours
	(g)	(h)	(i)	(j)	(k)	(l)
Speed	30 km/h	10 km/h	80 mph	120 km/h	425 km/h	56 mph
Time	1 hour 30 mins	4 hours 15 mins	half an hour	8 hours 45 mins	3 hours	$3\frac{1}{2}$ hours

5 Jason cycled at a speed of 24 kilometres per hour for 90 minutes. Carole drove for half an hour at 60 kilometres per hour. Who travelled further and by how much?

6 Alex walked at 6 kilometres per hour for two and a half hours. Bob jogged at a speed of 10 kilometres per hour for an hour and a half. Karen cycled for 45 minutes at a rate of 20 kilometres per hour. Calculate the distance travelled by each person.

7 Calculate the distance Ali the tortoise travelled if he walked at half a kilometre an hour for 30 minutes.

8 If Ali walked at half this speed, how far would he travel in 15 minutes?

13.7 Calculating average speed using a formula

To calculate speed, the distance is divided by the time.

$$\text{Speed} = \frac{\text{Distance}}{\text{Time}}$$

$$S = \frac{D}{T}$$

Example

Find the speed if 100 km was travelled in 2 hours 30 minutes.

$$S = \frac{D}{T}$$

$$= \frac{100}{2 \cdot 5}$$

$$= 40$$

Speed = 40 km/h

This is the average speed for the journey.

Exercise 13.7

1 Use the formula $S = \frac{D}{T}$ to find the speed for a 20 kilometre distance travelled in 5 hours.

2 Calculate the speed of a car which travels 180 kilometres in 3 hours.

3 Mr. Bloch jogged for 2 hours and travelled a total of 13 kilometres. Calculate his speed.

4 Calculate the speed, having travelled:

	(a)	(b)	(c)	(d)	(e)	(f)
Distance	66 km	36 km	25 miles	780 km	200 miles	55 km
Time	3 hours	2 hours	5 hours	6 hours	5 hours	2 hours
	(g)	(h)	(i)	(j)	(k)	(l)
Distance	30 km	180 km	80 miles	270 km	20 km	70 km
Time	$1\frac{1}{2}$ hours	4 hours 30 mins	half an hour	4 hours 30 mins	15 mins	1 hour 45 minutes

5 Frank travelled 120 kilometres in 3 hours.

Kevin drove for 2 hours and travelled 90 kilometres.

Calculate the difference in speed between the two drivers.

6 Alana cycled 25 kilometres in 2 hours.

Betty ran for 3 kilometres and took 20 minutes.

Caren cycled for 45 minutes and travelled 16 kilometres.

List the girls in order, from fastest to slowest.

13.8 Calculating time using a formula

To calculate time, the distance is divided by the speed.

$$\text{Time} = \frac{\text{Distance}}{\text{Speed}}$$

$$T = \frac{D}{S}$$

Example

Find the time for a journey of 28 kilometres at a speed of 5 kilometres per hour.

$$T = \frac{D}{S}$$

$$= \frac{28}{5}$$

$$= 5 \cdot 6$$

$0 \cdot 6 \times 60 = 36$

Time = 5 hours 36 mins.

Exercise 13.8

1 Use the formula $T = \frac{D}{S}$ to find the time taken to travel 80 kilometres at a speed of 20 kilometres per hour.

2 Calculate the time taken to travel 12 kilometres at a speed of 4 kilometres per hour.

3 Mrs. Black drove at a speed of 45 kilometres per hour and travelled 225 kilometres. How long did it take for her journey?

4 Calculate the time taken, having travelled:

	(a)	(b)	(c)	(d)	(e)	(f)
Distance	66 km	36 km	25 miles	180 km	21 km	50 miles
Speed	3 km/h	12 km/h	5 mph	8 km/h	5 km/h	20 mph
	(g)	(h)	(i)	(j)	(k)	(l)
Distance	3 km	2 km	45 km	460 km	550 miles	10 km
Speed	6 km/h	8 km/h	20 km/h	80 km/h	60 mph	0.5 km/h

5 A jet travels at a steady speed of 350 kilometres per hour. How long will the jet take to travel 3675 kilometres?

6 A bus travels 60 kilometres at 40 kilometres per hour then travels 30 kilometres at 60 kilometres per hour. How long did the journey take?

7 A tractor travels 4·5 kilometres at a speed of 9 kilometres per hour. A cyclist travels the same distance at twice the speed. How much less time did the cyclist take for the journey?

13.9 Calculating distance, speed and time

The three formulae may be remembered using a diagram.

Distance = S × T

Speed = $\dfrac{D}{T}$

Time = $\dfrac{D}{S}$

Exercise 13.9

1 Calculate the distance a car would have travelled at a speed of 35 kilometres per hour after 3 hours.

2 Calculate the speed of a bus that takes 4 hours to travel 96 kilometres.

3 Calculate the time taken for a man to run 28 kilometres at a steady speed of 8 kilometres per hour.

4 A car is driven on a 475 kilometre journey at 50 kilometres per hour. How long did the journey take?

5 Copy and complete the table showing all working for each missing item.

	(a)	(b)	(c)	(d)	(e)	(f)
Distance	150 km	....	20 miles	350 km	60 miles	....
Speed	25 km/h	50 km/h	....	15 km/h	....	60 km/h
Time	....	3 hours	$\frac{1}{2}$ hour	....	2 hours 30 mins	45 mins

6 (a) Calculate the time taken for each part of a delivery van's journey.

 The van stopped at Edinburgh for 45 minutes and at Stirling for $1\frac{1}{2}$ hours.

(b) Calculate the total journey time.

(c) The van left Motherwell at 21 55. What time did it arrive in:

 (i) Stirling **(ii)** Aberdeen?

(d) On the return journey the van left at 10.25 p.m., travelled at 50 kilometres per hour and did not stop. When did the van arrive in Motherwell?

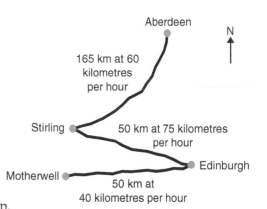

Use the distance chart shown (in kilometres), for questions 7 to 10.

7 Calculate the time taken for:

(**a**) Glasgow to Manchester at 60 kilometres per hour.

(**b**) London to Glasgow at 45 kilometres per hour.

(**c**) Carlisle to Manchester at 30 kilometres per hour.

(**d**) Carlisle to London and back at 50 kilometres per hour.

Glasgow

150	Carlisle		
360	195	Manchester	
630	500	300	London

8 Calculate the speed if:

(**a**) Glasgow to London took 9 hours

(**b**) Manchester to Glasgow took 4 hours 30 minutes

(**c**) Manchester to London took 6 hours 15 minutes.

9 Mr. Benson travelled from Glasgow to Manchester at 60 kilometres per hour.
He stayed in Manchester for 2 hours; then drove to London at
50 kilometres per hour.
If he left Glasgow at 16 45, what time did he arrive in London?

10 Rent-a-van in Carlisle had to return two vans.
One van was driven to Glasgow at 45 kilometres per hour, the other
to Manchester at 60 kilometres per hour.

(**a**) Calculate which van arrived first.

(**b**) How much faster was the first van?

11 A snail race took place over a 600 centimetre track.
Adrian Snail took 8 minutes, Bob Snail took 10 minutes and
Colin Snail took 12·5 minutes.
Calculate the speed of each snail in centimetres per second (cm/s).

Change times to seconds.

12 Light travels at 300 000 kilometres per second.

(**a**) How long would it take for light to travel from the sun to Pluto,
a distance of 3375 million kilometres?

(**b**) How far would light travel in an hour?

13 The speed of sound through water is 1460 metres per second.
Calculate the time it takes for a whale to hear a sound made
7·3 kilometres away.

14 A slug crawls 4 metres in 24 minutes.
How long at the same speed would it take to crawl 1 kilometre?

15 A car drives 200 kilometres in 3 hours and 12 minutes.
How many metres will the car travel at the same speed in 3 minutes?

Review exercise 13

1 Write these times in twenty four hour notation.
(**a**) 7 a.m.   (**b**) 4.40 p.m.   (**c**) 9.10 p.m.   (**d**) noon

2 Write these times in twelve hour notation.
(**a**) 18 00   (**b**) 04 02   (**c**) 22 13   (**d**) 00 00

3 Calculate the length of time between:
(**a**) 8.40 a.m. and 10.55 a.m.   (**b**) 16 25 and 22 55
(**c**) 9.45 p.m. and 11.20 p.m.   (**d**) 08 55 and 14 20
(**e**) 8.35 a.m. and 9.20 p.m.   (**f**) 01 42 and 17 17

4 Flight GB/1730 leaves Edinburgh at 18 40 hours and arrives in
Paris at 21 05 hrs. How long was the flight?

5 Change each of the following to minutes:
(**a**) 2 hrs 25 mins   (**b**) 4 hrs 35 mins   (**c**) 8 hrs 55 mins

6 Change each of the following to hours and minutes:
(**a**) 1·5 hrs   (**b**) 3·25 hrs   (**c**) 8·75 hrs   (**d**) 4·4 hrs
(**e**) 0·7 hrs   (**f**) 5·6 hrs   (**g**) 9·3 hrs   (**h**) 1·1 hrs

7 Change each of the following to hours:
(**a**) 2 hrs 30 minutes   (**b**) 5 hrs 45 minutes
(**c**) 2 hrs 18 minutes   (**d**) 3 hrs 48 minutes
(**e**) 24 minutes   (**f**) 27 minutes
(**g**) 3 minutes   (**h**) 90 seconds.

8 Copy and complete the table showing all working for each missing item.

	(a)	(b)	(c)	(d)	(e)	(f)
Distance	200 km	....	30 miles	54 km	95 miles	....
Speed	50 km/h	10 km/h	....	20 km/h	....	400 km/h
Time	....	2 hours	2 hours 30 mins	....	1 hour 15 mins	15 mins

9 Jennifer, Louise, Zara and Kirsten all go to the University of Glasgow.
To get there Jennifer drove at an average speed of 30 kilometres
per hour and took an hour and a half.
Louise lived 20 kilometres away and took 48 minutes.
Zara jogged 2 kilometres at an average speed of 10 kilometres
per hour.
Kirsten walked 250 metres at a speed of 5 kilometres per hour.

(**a**) How far does Jennifer live from the university?

(**b**) What was Louise's average speed?

(**c**) How long did it take Zara to jog to the university?

(**d**) How long did it take Kirsten to walk to the university?

Summary

Time notation

Time may be expressed in twelve or twenty four hour notation.
The clock shows 2.30 p.m. or 14 30 hrs.

Converting units of time

Change 3·25 hrs to hours and minutes
   0·25 hrs = 0·25 × 60 mins = 15 mins
So   3·25 hrs = **3hrs 15 mins**

Change 3 hrs and 48 mins to hours
   48 mins = $\frac{48}{60}$ hrs = 0·8 hrs
So   3 hrs 48 mins = **3·8 hrs**

Formulae for distance, speed and time

Distance = S × T

Speed = $\dfrac{D}{T}$

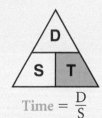

Time = $\dfrac{D}{S}$

14 Information handling

In this chapter you will extend your knowledge of ways to interpret and display information.

14.1 Interpreting tables

Information is often presented in a table.

Short break holidays in Prague

Holiday date	Number of nights	Price in £	Number of nights	Price in £	Extra night price in £
Jan-Apr	2	211	3	256	43
May-Aug	2	249	3	274	46
Sept-Dec	2	217	3	263	44

Exercise 14.1

1 From the table above find the cost of

  (**a**) 2 nights in February

  (**b**) 3 nights in November

  (**c**) 4 nights in December.

  (**d**) How much more expensive is 5 nights in October than 4 nights in August?

> For 5 nights, use the 3 night price then add 2 extra nights

2 A number of airlines fly from London to Cairo. The flight times and prices are shown in the table.

Airline/Flight number	Departs	Arrives	Cost in £
RE/1351	1210	1650	356
RE/1371	0700	1150	323
AM/231	1235	1705	370
AM/241	0915	1400	370
AM/251	1100	1545	355
GA/0035	1220	1715	328
UA/0401	1940	0040	316
UA/0501	1410	1905	345

  (**a**) Which is the cheapest flight and how long does it take?

  (**b**) How long is the Ghost Airlines (GA) flight?

  (**c**) Alex arrived in Cairo at 5.05 p.m. How much did she pay for her flight?

  (**d**) If you had to be in Cairo by 1 p.m., what is the latest flight you could take?

3 The timetable shows the train times on the Cathcrate circle line.

Newmill	08 41	—	0858
Kirkhall	08 44	—	09 01
Burnhead	08 47	—	09 04
Croftfeet	08 49	—	09 06
King's Gait	08 51	—	09 08
Neilton	—	08 41	—
Patterton	—	08 46	—
Blackcraigs	—	08 48	—
Williamhill	—	08 51	—
Muirend	—	08 53	—
Cathcrate	08 59	08 55	09 16

(**a**) At what time does the 08 58 train from Newmill arrive in Croftfeet?

(**b**) How long does it take to travel from Blackcraigs to Williamhill?

(**c**) Barry has to be in Cathcrate for 9 a.m.
  What time should he leave Burnhead?

4 The table shows mortgage rates for five building societies.

Building society	Interest rate	Monthly payment on £80 000
Alley Federal	5·65%	£376.67
Cirencester	5·75%	£383.33
National	4·64%	£309.33
SCHB	4.6%	£306.67
Southern Lock	5.79%	£386.00

(**a**) Which company has the lowest interest rate?

(**b**) How much more is the monthly payment with Cirencester than SCHB?

(**c**) What is the annual payment with Alley Federal?

(**d**) What is the annual saving for National compared to Southern Lock?

5 The table shows special offer subscription prices for a monthly magazine.

Number of months	Full price	Offer price
6	£17·40	£13.00
12	£34·80	£27.97
24	£69·60	£48.60

(**a**) How much is the saving for a six month subscription?

(**b**) What does the magazine normally cost each month?

(**c**) What is the saving **per magazine** on the 24 month offer price?

6 The table shows monthly life assurance premiums for men and women.

> Premium means payment.

	Men		Women	
	Smoker	Non-Smoker	Smoker	Non-Smoker
20 year term	£11.30	£7.20	£8.70	£6.00
25 year term	£12.50	£7.80	£9.80	£6.20

(a) What is the monthly premium for
    (i) a male smoker, 25 year term
    (ii) a female non-smoker, 20 year term
    (iii) a female smoker, 25 year term
    (iv) a male non-smoker, 20 year term?

(b) For a woman, over a 20 year term
    (i) how much more is the monthly premium for a smoker than a non-smoker?
    (ii) how much more is this per year?
    (iii) how much more is it over the full 20 years?

(c) Who pays higher premiums, men or women? Why do you think this is?

(d) Why do smokers pay higher premiums?

7 At the Hotel Friuli the room prices (€) per night are shown in the table.

(a) How much does it cost for a double room with breakfast for one night?

(b) How much cheaper is a single room than a double with single occupancy?

Room	With breakfast	Room only
Single	50	45
Double	80	70
Double (single occcupancy)	65	60
Suite for 3	110	95

(c) Three people share a suite with breakfast and half board for two nights. How much is this?

Supplement for half board per person
18

14.2 Line graphs

Information may be shown by a line graph.
The graph shows Paul's height from the age of 9 to 19.
A graph should have a title and each axis must be labelled.
Read the scale on each axis.
The **trend** of a graph is a general description of it.
For this graph the trend is increasing.

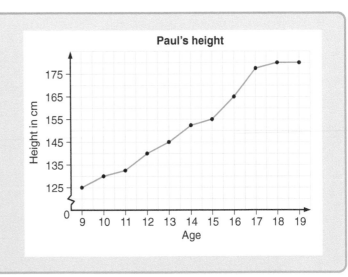

Exercise 14.2

1 From the graph in the panel on p. 154:

   (**a**) What height was Paul at age 12?

   (**b**) How old was he when he reached 152 cm?

   (**c**) Between which ages did he grow the most?

   (**d**) When did he reach his maximum height?

2 The graph shows the net migration of population from Scotland from 1962 to 1970.

   (**a**) What was the net migration in 1965?

   (**b**) Which year had the highest migration?

   (**c**) Describe the trend in migration from 1964 to 1970.

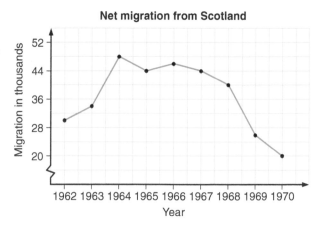

3 The table shows male and female life expectancy from 1900 to 2000.

	Year										
	1900	1910	1920	1930	1940	1950	1960	1970	1980	1990	2000
Females	50	54	59	62	65	70	73	75	78	79	80
Males	46	50	52	58	60	56	68	70	70	71	72

   (**a**) On the same diagram, draw two line graphs to show male and female life expectancy.

   (**b**) By how much did female life expectancy increase from 1950 to 2000?

   (**c**) What is the smallest difference in years between male and female life expectancy?

   (**d**) Why do you think male life expectancy dropped between 1940 and 1950?

   (**e**) Describe the overall trend of the graphs. Explain why you think the change from 1900 to 2000 is so great.

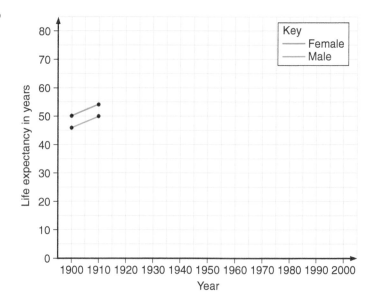

4 The table shows the monthly tuck shop sales of fruit at Alnwath Academy.

Month	Aug	Sept	Oct	Nov	Dec	Jan	Feb	Mar	Apr	May	Jun
Sales	£16	£25	£18	£28	£15	£8	£10	£18	£9	£16	£6

(a) Draw a line graph to show this information.

(b) Between which two months was there the biggest drop in sales?

(c) Which 3 consecutive months yield the highest sales figures?

5 The annual rainfall in the Borders and the Highlands is shown in the table.

	Rainfall each month in millimetres											
	Jan	Feb	Mar	Apr	May	Jun	Jul	Aug	Sep	Oct	Nov	Dec
Borders	190	125	105	95	90	85	130	145	145	160	155	170
Highlands	70	55	50	55	50	45	75	80	75	75	60	65

(a) On the same diagram, draw a line graph of each set of data.

(b) Which is the driest month in both places?

(c) Which month has the greatest total rainfall?

(d) What is the smallest difference in rainfall and when does it occur?

14.3 Conversion graphs

A line graph may provide a simple means of converting from one unit to another. This is called a **conversion graph**.

Example

Use the graph to convert the value of €25 into £. The value is £17 to the nearest £.

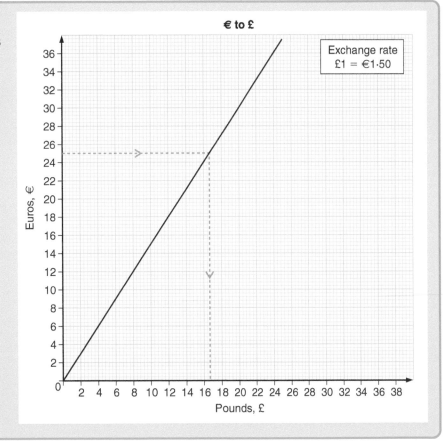

Exercise 14.3

1 Using the graph from the panel on p. 156:

(**a**) Convert to the nearest euro:
  (**i**) £12   (**ii**) £20   (**iii**) £18   (**iv**) £7

(**b**) Convert to the nearest pound:
  (**i**) €4   (**ii**) €16   (**iii**) €20   (**iv**) €31

2 The conversion graph shows the relationship between British and European women's clothes sizes.

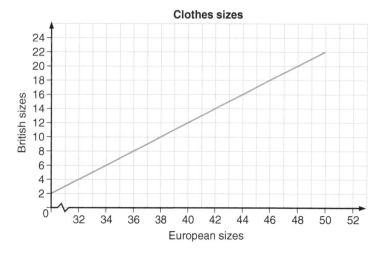

(**a**) Change to European sizes:
  (**i**) 14   (**ii**) 18   (**iii**) 10   (**iv**) 20

(**b**) Change to British sizes:
  (**i**) 44   (**ii**) 36   (**iii**) 40   (**iv**) 50

(**c**) Susan is a size 14. Her mother brings her a shirt from Italy which is a size 42. Will it fit her?

3 The graph converts marks out of 120 to percentages.

(**a**) Use the graph to convert each mark to a percentage.
  (**i**) 64   (**ii**) 80
  (**iii**) 90   (**iv**) 110

(**b**) Derek scored 65% in a test. How many marks out of 120 is this?

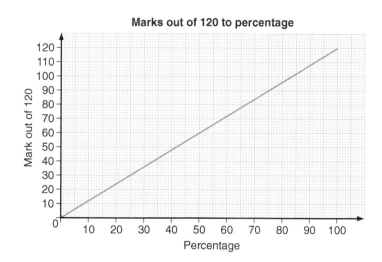

4 (**a**) Complete the table:

Marks out of 160	0	40	80	160
Percentage	0			100

(**b**) From your table draw a conversion graph.

(**c**) From your graph convert these marks to percentages:

    (**i**) 35   (**ii**) 95   (**iii**) 145

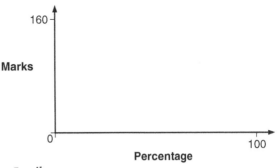

5 A distance of 8 kilometres is approximately equal to 5 miles.

(**a**) Copy and complete the table.

Miles	5	10	20	50
Kilometres	8			

(**b**) Use the table to draw a conversion graph for miles and kilometres.

(**c**) Use your graph to convert to miles:

    (**i**) 15 km   (**ii**) 20 km
   (**iii**) 48 km   (**iv**) 72 km

(**d**) Convert to kilometres:

    (**i**) 22 miles   (**ii**) 31 miles
   (**iii**) 42 miles   (**iv**) 55 miles

6 One kilogramme is approximately equal to 2·2 lbs (pounds).
Make a table and draw a conversion graph from kilogrammes to pounds.

14.4 Drawing pie charts

On a pie chart, the size of the angle in each sector is calculated as a fraction of 360°.

Example

A group of people were asked their holiday destinations.
Draw a pie chart to illustrate the information shown in the table.

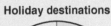

Holiday destinations

	Holiday destination				
	France	Italy	Spain	Britain	USA
Number of people	6	5	12	10	7

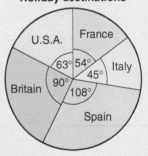

Total number of people = 40

France $\frac{6}{40} \rightarrow \frac{6}{40} \times 360 = 54°$

Italy $\frac{5}{40} \rightarrow \frac{5}{40} \times 360 = 45°$

Spain $\frac{12}{40} \rightarrow \frac{12}{40} \times 360 = 108°$

Britain $\frac{10}{40} \rightarrow \frac{10}{40} \times 360 = 90°$

USA $\frac{7}{40} \rightarrow \frac{7}{40} \times 360 = 63°$

                     Total = 360°

> Check the total is 360°

Exercise 14.4

For each question, draw a pie chart to illustrate the information given.
The radius of each circle should be at least 5 centimetres.

1 Class 1B2 methods of travel to school.

	Method of travel				
	Walk	Cycle	Car	Bus	Train
Number of pupils	14	3	8	2	3

2 Age profile of student teachers.

	Age range					
	17–20	21–24	25–28	29–32	33–36	37–40
Number of teachers	5	26	14	7	5	3

3 In a village in Switzerland, pupils identified their first language.

	Language				
	French	German	Italian	Romansch	Other
Number of pupils	21	40	15	8	6

4 School survey results on favourite TV programmes.

	Programme				
	Chart toppers	Buddy	The Smiths	Star Sport	Saprina
Percentage	20%	5%	35%	15%	25%

5 Restaurant food choices.

	Dish					
	Steak	Chicken	Pasta	Pizza	Fish	Curry
Percentage	12%	8%	20%	7%	15%	38%

14.5 Interpreting pie charts

Example

90 pupils selected their favourite subjects.
From the pie chart, calculate how many chose each subject.

Art $\frac{64}{360} \times 90 = 16$

Maths $\frac{124}{360} \times 90 = 31$

P.E. $\frac{72}{360} \times 90 = 18$

Science $\frac{100}{360} \times 90 = 25$

Total 90

Check the total is 90.

Favourite subjects

Exercise 14.5

1 The pie chart illustrates the ownership of pets by students in Alnwath Academy.
There are 840 pets in total.
Find the number of each kind of pet.

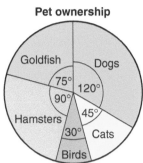

Pet ownership

2 The votes cast in an election in Wardpark constituency are shown in the pie chart. If 19 800 votes were cast, how many did each party win?

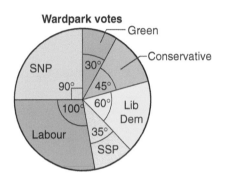

Wardpark votes

3 The owners of 120 allotments identified their most successful vegetable.
From the pie chart, list how many chose each vegetable.

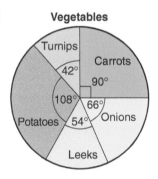

Vegetables

4 The sources of natural radiation are illustrated in the pie chart.
Using the chart, copy and complete the table.

Source	Gamma	Cosmic	Internal	Radon	Thoron
Percentage					

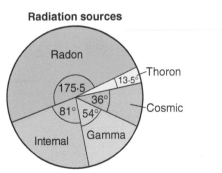

Radiation sources

14.6 Frequency tables

Data may be grouped using **class intervals** in a frequency table.

Weekly pocket money in £:

12	14	10	13	3
15	24	8	16	9
15	26	10	25	18
20	22	21	25	22

Class interval	Tally marks	Frequency
0–4			1
5–9	||	2
10–14	Ж	5
15–19	||||	4
20–24	Ж	5
25–29	|||	3

> The class interval is of size 5.

> To display on a bar graph, class intervals are usually of the same size.

> There must be no gaps between class intervals.

The information from the frequency table may be displayed on a bar graph.

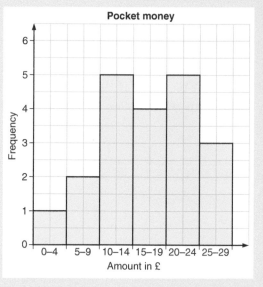

Exercise 14.6

1 From the frequency table above:
   (**a**) How many people have pocket money less than £15?
   (**b**) Which is the most common interval for pocket money?

2 (**a**) Copy and complete the frequency table using the golf scores below.

84	87	89	95	99	87	78	100	98
86	92	101	105	82	87	94	105	104
72	78	87	83	86	91	88	98	95

Class interval	Tally marks	Frequency
71–75		
76–80		
81–85		
86–90		
91–95		
96–100		
101–105		

   (**b**) Draw a bar graph to display this data.

3 (**a**) For the test marks below, draw a frequency table.

21	23	14	26	30	26	18	18	19	29	26	2
17	17	21	20	20	23	12	10	8	24	30	9
26	19	11	22	21	14	26	22	20	30	12	15

   (**b**) Draw a bar graph to display this data.
   (**c**) How many pupils scored less than 26?

4 The data below shows the amount spent, to the nearest £, by each customer at a garden centre.
Draw a frequency table using class intervals of size 20.

23	45	21	12	15	67	123	42	53
24	78	67	90	119	39	33	56	45
46	87	88	66	89	32	33	76	58

Amount spent (£)	
0–19	
20–	

5 (**a**) A magazine has conducted a survey of the age of its readers. The figures are shown below. Draw a frequency table using suitable class intervals.

19	19	15	34	23	27	28	28	34	23	21	22
23	45	31	37	26	26	31	32	28	25	28	21
21	24	24	31	32	19	27	24	23	23	36	30
24	23	26	27	28	20	32	30	26	25	22	40

(**b**) The magazine is choosing a fashion layout.
Should it aim for the teenage market, the late twenties or some other age group?
Explain your answer.

14.7 Mean and range

The **mean** of a set of data is the arithmetic average.
The **range** of a set of data = the largest figure − the smallest figure.

> The range describes the spread of the data.

Example

Calculate the mean and range of these test marks.

  6 8 10 8 5 7 7 9 4 6

$$\text{Mean} = \frac{6 + 8 + 10 + 8 + 5 + 7 + 7 + 9 + 4 + 6}{10} = \frac{70}{10} = 7 \quad \textbf{The mean is 7.}$$

Range = 10 − 4 = 6   **The range is 6.**

Exercise 14.7

For each set of data, calculate the mean and range.

1 3, 3, 6, 6, 5, 9, 9, 7

2 12, 10, 10, 8, 11, 9

3 22, 30, 34, 24, 32, 20, 13

4 1·2, 2·2, 3·2, 2·4, 2·8, 1·6, 3·2, 1·8

5 42 kg, 54 kg, 64 kg, 47 kg, 53 kg, 64 kg

6 £2, £4, £2, £3.50, £5, £4.50, £5, £6

7 12, 20, 10, 12, 12, 18, 10, 10

8 14, 14, 13, 15, 13, 12, 12, 16, 13, 11, 11, 11, 14

14.8 Mean from a frequency table

Example

From the frequency table calculate

(**a**) the mean age

(**b**) the range.

Age (yrs)	Frequency
5	3
6	3
7	6
8	2
9	1

(**a**) Add a third column to the table.

Find the total frequency and total age.

$$\text{Mean} = \frac{100}{15} = 6 \cdot 666$$

$$= 6 \cdot 67 \text{ to 2 d.p.}$$

Mean age is 6·67 yrs

Age (yrs)	Frequency	Age × Frequency
5	3	15
6	3	18
7	6	42
8	2	16
9	1	9
	15	100

> 3 people aged 5 years gives a total of 15.

(**b**) Range = 9 − 5 = 4   Range is **4**

Exercise 14.8

Calculate the mean and range for each frequency table.

1

Score	Frequency
21	2
22	1
23	3
24	4
25	2

2

Weight (kg)	Frequency
3	3
3·5	2
4	5
4·5	1
5	2
5·5	2

3

Cost (€)	Frequency
8	1
9	3
10	3
11	1
12	2
13	2

4

Height (m)	Frequency
1·5	2
2	1
2·5	2
3	2
3·5	3

5

Temperature (°C)	Frequency
0	2
1	0
2	7
3	5
4	6

6

Depth (m)	Frequency
3	1
4	3
5	0
6	8

14.9 Surveys

A survey is a method of collecting information.

Information collected may be displayed in a table, on a bar graph, line graph or pie chart.

It may be useful to calculate the mean and range of the data.

Exercise 14.9

1 Class 1W2 collected information on spending using this questionnaire.

(**a**) Use the questionnaire to collect this information for your class.

(**b**) (**i**) Copy and complete the frequency table.

Pocket money

Class interval	Tally marks	Frequency

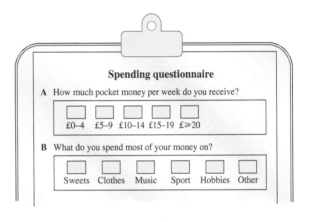

(**ii**) Draw a bar graph from your frequency table.

(**c**) Draw a pie chart to display the spending information.

2 Work with a partner for this question.

(**a**) Devise a questionnaire to collect information on family sizes and ages of family members.

(**b**) Use your questionnaire to collect the information.

(**c**) Choose a method to display each type of information.

(**d**) Compare your results with two other groups in the class.

3 Work with a partner for this question.

(**a**) Choose a topic to survey the class on.
Possible suggestions would be TV viewing habits, sports activities, heights and shoe sizes, eating habits.

(**b**) Devise a questionnaire to collect the information.

(**c**) Select appropriate ways to display the information you have collected.

Review exercise 14

1 The table shows information about six boys at a gym.

	Tom	Ian	Rob	Ali	Zac	Guy
Weight (kg)	60	56	52	70	64	62
Press ups	30	26	24	38	34	32

(**a**) How heavy is Zac?

(**b**) What is the difference in weight between the heaviest and lightest boys?

(**c**) Who completed 38 press ups?

(**d**) 'Lighter boys find press ups easier'. Do you agree? Explain your answer.

2 The graph shows average monthly temperatures in London and Naples.

(**a**) What is the temperature in London in May?

(**b**) How much warmer is Naples than London in July?

(**c**) Between which two months is there the greatest change in temperature in both cities?

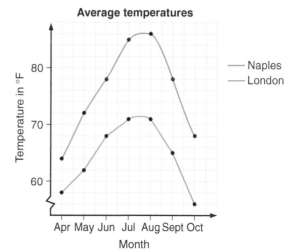

3 On a suspension bridge, the length of the support cables increases as you move out from the centre.

Distance from centre (m)	0	2	4	6	8
Length of cable (m)	5	9	21	41	69

(**a**) Use the information to draw a line graph.

(**b**) Use your graph to estimate cable lengths at a distance of
(**i**) 3 metres from the centre (**ii**) 4·5 metres from the centre

(**c**) If a support cable is 30 metres long, estimate how far from the centre it is.

4 The graph converts pounds (£) to Swiss francs (SF). Use the graph to

(**a**) Convert to Swiss francs:
(**i**) £40
(**ii**) £25
(**iii**) £35

(**b**) Convert to £:
(**i**) 100SF
(**ii**) 70SF
(**iii**) 25SF

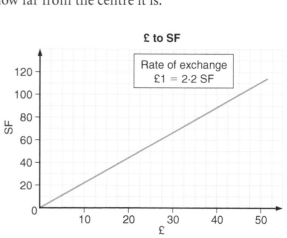

5 £5 is worth €7.

(**a**) Copy and complete the table:

Pounds	0	5	10	50
Euros		7		

(**b**) Use your table to draw a conversion graph.

6 (**a**) A local newspaper has 30 pages.
The pie chart shows the content of the paper.
List the number of pages for each topic.

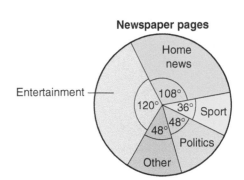

Newspaper pages

(**b**) A special edition of the paper will have 45 pages.
The table shows the number of pages for each topic.

Topic	Foreign news	Entertainment	Politics	Sport	Local news	Centenary	Other
Pages	5	3	3	5	10	9	10

Draw a pie chart to illustrate this information.

7 Calculate the mean and range for each set of data.

(**a**) 3, 6, 6, 7, 7, 7, 10, 10, 12, 12

(**b**) 14, 22, 24, 30, 30, 30

8 The data shows the scores at a basketball shoot.

5 1 3 4 5 0 3 5 4 0 2 3 4 1 4
5 1 2 1 3 4 2 4 2 5 2 3 0 4 2

(**a**) Draw a frequency table.

(**b**) Use your frequency table to draw a bar graph.

(**c**) Calculate the mean and range of the data.

9 The figures show the times (in seconds) for competitors in a race.

35 52 32 38 39 47 50 35 35 48
40 36 38 42 39 35 54 47 36 44
53 38 49 41 36 46 30 48 32 36
37 38 47 51 39 45 38 47 33 43

Time (secs)	
30–34	
35–	

(**a**) Make a frequency table using class intervals of size 5.

(**b**) Draw a bar graph to display this data.

(**c**) How many people completed the race in under
45 seconds?

Summary

Information may be displayed in several ways.

Tables

Music sales			
	Rock and pop	Classical	Jazz
Instrumental	21	10	5
Vocal	54	6	8

Line graphs

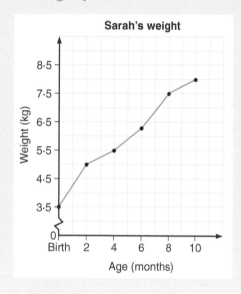

Conversion graphs

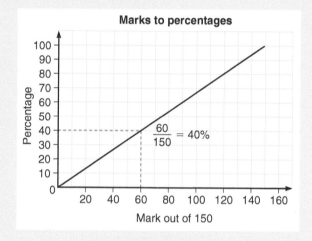

Pie charts

120 girls were surveyed on their favourite magazines.

Pink magazine $\frac{135}{360} \times 120 = 45$

45 girls chose Pink magazine.

Mean from frequency tables

Shoe sizes
5 6 6 7 4 6 7 8
4 7 9 7 5 5 6 6
7 9 4 5 5 6 6 6

Mean shoe size $= \frac{146}{24} = 6 \cdot 08$ (to 2 d.p.)

Range $= 9 - 4 = 5$

Shoe size	Tally marks	Frequency	Frequency × size
4					3	12
5	ⅢⅠ	5	25
6	ⅢⅠ |||	8	48
7	ⅢⅠ	5	35
8			1	8
9				2	18
		24	146

15 Algebra 2

In this chapter you will learn how to solve equations and inequations.

15.1 Solving equations

When two expressions are equal, this is called an **equation**.

$$x + 9 = 31$$

An equation is in balance: $\underline{x + 9}$ $\underline{31}$ △

| An equation always has an equals sign. | The value of each side is the same |

To **solve** an equation adjust each side to find the value of the variable.

$\underline{x + 9}$ $\underline{31}$ △ -9 -9 → $\underline{x}$ $\underline{22}$ △

$$x = 22$$

Example

Solve the equations

(**a**) $y + 13 = 52$

$$
\begin{aligned}
y + 13 &= 52 \\
-13 \quad &-13 \\
y &= 39
\end{aligned}
$$

(**b**) $p - 18 = 5$

$$
\begin{aligned}
p - 18 &= 5 \\
+18 \quad &+18 \\
p &= 23
\end{aligned}
$$

(**c**) $7 = 4 + x$

$$
\begin{aligned}
7 = 4 &+ x \\
-4 \quad &-4 \\
3 &= x \\
x &= 3
\end{aligned}
$$

Exercise 15.1

Solve the equation:

1 $x + 12 = 23$ **2** $y - 6 = 11$ **3** $m - 7 = 13$ **4** $21 = y + 6$

5 $15 = t - 9$ **6** $20 + y = 51$ **7** $z - 32 = 53$ **8** $r - 23 = 1$

9 $x - 1 = 7$ **10** $p + 9 = 13$ **11** $t - 15 = 6$ **12** $q - 4 = 0$

13 $24 + x = 24$ **14** $33 + y = 101$ **15** $m - 45 = 7$ **16** $x - 17 = 3$

17 $x - 4 = 2$ **18** $c - 51 = 3$ **19** $x - 11 = 2$ **20** $17 + s = 23$

21 $34 = v + 7$ **22** $13 + x = 31$ **23** $m - 3 = 19$ **24** $23 + y = 46$

15.2 Further equations

Example 1

Solve $8z = 48$

$$
\begin{aligned}
8z &= 48 \\
\div 8 \quad &\div 8 \\
z &= 6
\end{aligned}
$$

| Divide each side by 8. |

Example 2

Solve $3x - 9 = 6$

$$
\begin{aligned}
3x - 9 &= 6 \\
+9 \quad &+9 \\
3x &= 15 \\
\div 3 \quad &\div 3 \\
x &= 5
\end{aligned}
$$

Example 3

Solve $5y + 6 = 41$

$$
\begin{aligned}
5y + 6 &= 41 \\
-6 \quad &-6 \\
5y &= 35 \\
\div 5 \quad &\div 5 \\
y &= 7
\end{aligned}
$$

Exercise 15.2

Solve the equations:

1 $3y = 21$ **2** $10m = 50$ **3** $7y = 42$ **4** $2x + 3 = 9$

5 $3y - 7 = 2$ **6** $2x + 6 = 14$ **7** $5y - 2 = 13$ **8** $19 + 2z = 29$

9 $29 = 3x + 2$ **10** $7 + 4y = 11$ **11** $5m + 4 = 44$ **12** $8y = 64$

13 $7z + 3 = 38$ **14** $2 + 2c = 26$ **15** $3x - 27 = 3$ **16** $5g = 35$

17 $45 = 12 + 3x$ **18** $22 + 8x = 38$ **19** $7x + 6 = 62$ **20** $5y - 35 = 0$

21 $12x + 19 = 43$ **22** $40 = 8y$ **23** $4z - 12 = 16$ **24** $62 = 12x + 2$

25 $11c - 9 = 46$ **26** $8m - 2 = 22$ **27** $20 + 16t = 100$ **28** $60 = 3x + 24$

29 $7y - 6 = 29$ **30** $120 = 5y - 30$ **31** $10p - 21 = 39$ **32** $7s + 18 = 46$

33 $17 = 2s + 1$ **34** $5z + 3 = 48$ **35** $20x - 7 = 53$ **36** $32 + 3z = 41$

15.3 Equations: negatives and fractions

Example 1

Solve $p + 12 = 6$

$$\begin{aligned} p + 12 &= 6 \\ -12 \quad &-12 \\ p &= -6 \end{aligned}$$

Example 2

Solve $2t - 4 = 5$

$$\begin{aligned} 2t - 4 &= 5 \\ +4 \quad &+4 \\ 2t &= 9 \\ \div 2 \quad &\div 2 \\ t &= 4\tfrac{1}{2} \end{aligned}$$

Exercise 15.3

Solve the equations:

1 $x + 3 = 1$ **2** $y - 5 = -6$ **3** $12 + s = 9$ **4** $z + 6 = 5$

5 $s - 3 = -2$ **6** $21 + p = 11$ **7** $x + 10 = 2$ **8** $y + 20 = 5$

9 $6z - 9 = 33$ **10** $2y - 1 = 4$ **11** $3m + 6 = 18$ **12** $z + 15 = 9$

13 $8y + 3 = 3$ **14** $m + 24 = 4$ **15** $10p - 1 = 4$ **16** $x + 22 = 4$

17 $2r - 1 = 0$ **18** $20 = y + 30$ **19** $14 = 2z + 11$ **20** $2w + 5 = 4$

21 $x + 20 = -10$ **22** $10z = 15$ **23** $3 = 2y - 10$ **24** $13 = y + 22$

25 $3y - 1 = 2$ **26** $7y - 1 = -1$ **27** $44 = 6q + 32$ **28** $30 + 6p = 30$

29 $2z - 2 = -1$ **30** $5r = 25$ **31** $20x - 20 = 10$ **32** $9 + 2s = 18$

33 $12n + 3 = 63$ **34** $45z + 100 = 10$ **35** $2m - 4 = -1$ **36** $4z + 6 = 7$

15.4 Using equations

An equation may be used to model a problem and so find a solution.

Example 1

x is added to the number 7. The result is 11. Find x.

Express the problem as an equation. $x + 7 \ = \ 11$

Solve the equation. $-7 \quad\ \ -7$

$$x \ = \ 4 \qquad x \text{ has value of } \mathbf{4}.$$

Example 2

A class has n pupils. If 3 are absent and 23 are present, find n.

Express the problem as an equation. $n - 3 \ = \ 23$

Solve the equation. $+3 \quad\ \ +3$

$$n \ = \ 26 \qquad \text{There are } \mathbf{26} \text{ in the class.}$$

Exercise 15.4

Express each problem as an equation. Solve the equation.

1 When 5 is added to p the result is 19. Find p.

2 When 13 is subtracted from x the result is 5. Find x.

3 When 31 is subtracted from q this leaves 16. Find q.

4 The product of 8 and x is 64. What number is x?

> Multiply to find the **product**.

5 The quotient of 28 and x is 7. Find x.

> Divide to find the **quotient**.

6 The quotient of 54 and z is 9. What number is z?

7 There are n passengers on a bus. 6 get off at a bus stop.
If 25 passengers remain on the bus, what number is n?

8 When m is multiplied by itself the result is 81. Find m.

9 The sum of y and 13 is 52. What is the value of y?

10 The product of 9 and z is 63. What is the value of z?

11 The quotient of 36 and x is 2. What is the value of x?

12 A teacher gives x coloured pencils each to 8 girls.
He gives away 56 pencils in total. How many pencils did each girl receive?

13 A rectangle is 8 centimetres long and y centimetres wide. If the area
of the rectangle is 40 square centimetres, find the width.

14 The area of a square is 121 square metres. If its length is x metres, find the value of x.

15 Form an equation for each perimeter and solve it to find the missing dimension.

(a)
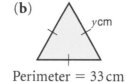
22 cm

x cm

Perimeter = 72 cm

(b)
y cm

Perimeter = 33 cm

(c)
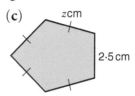
z cm

2·5 cm

Perimeter = 22·5 cm

16 Susan has 6 bags of marbles each containing y marbles.
She also has 3 loose marbles. In total she has 57 marbles.
How many are there in each bag?

17 Colin employs 8 workers each earning m pounds per week.
He has extra payroll costs of £120 per week.
If his total pay costs each week are £2120, find the value of m.

15.5 Inequations

Remember: $x > 7$ means x is greater than 7
$y \leqslant 11$ means y is less than or equal to 11

Two expressions may be unequal. This is called an **inequation**.

An inequation always has an inequality sign.

Example

Solve the inequations:
(a) $x + 3 < 5$ (b) $2y - 5 \geqslant 11$ (c) $4 < 4m - 12$

$$
\begin{array}{l}
x + 3 < 5 \\
\quad -3 \quad -3 \\
\hline
x < 2
\end{array}
$$

$$
\begin{array}{l}
2y - 5 \geqslant 11 \\
\quad +5 \quad +5 \\
\hline
2y \geqslant 16 \\
\div 2 \quad \div 2 \\
\hline
y \geqslant 8
\end{array}
$$

$$
\begin{array}{l}
4 < 4m - 12 \\
+12 \quad +12 \\
\hline
16 < 4m \\
\div 4 \quad \div 4 \\
\hline
4 < m \\
m > 4
\end{array}
$$

Exercise 15.5

Solve the inequations:

1 $x + 8 > 11$ **2** $y - 7 \leqslant 2$ **3** $z + 11 \leqslant 21$ **4** $3z + 2 > 14$

5 $4y - 5 \geqslant 19$ **6** $52 < 6z - 2$ **7** $21 < 7y + 7$ **8** $18 > 5z + 8$

9 $w + 25 \leqslant 29$ **10** $3y + 2 \geqslant 38$ **11** $5y - 1 < 54$ **12** $12 \geqslant 6m + 12$

13 $10y + 3 > 103$ **14** $x - 12 < 10$ **15** $10y + 4 \geqslant 4$ **16** $13x - 2 < 37$

17 $51 + 3y > 63$ **18** $3 + 45m > 48$ **19** $64 \leqslant 17y + 30$ **20** $9n - 17 > 64$

15.6 Inequations: negatives and fractions

Example 1

Solve $x - 5 \geqslant -11$

$$x - 5 \geqslant -11$$
$$+5 \quad +5$$
$$x \geqslant -6$$

Example 2

Solve $2z + 1 < 4$

$$2z + 1 < 4$$
$$-1 \quad -1$$
$$2z < 3$$
$$\div 2 \quad \div 2$$
$$z < 1\tfrac{1}{2}$$

Exercise 15.6

Solve the inequations:

1 $y + 4 > 2$ **2** $x - 3 < -7$ **3** $z + 2 \geqslant -6$ **4** $10x + 4 > -6$

5 $4y - 3 \leqslant 21$ **6** $2m - 11 > 3$ **7** $2y - 3 < -1$ **8** $3y - 3 < 0$

9 $8t + 2 \geqslant 74$ **10** $9y - 1 > 71$ **11** $2z + 3 > 4$ **12** $n - 5 \geqslant -23$

13 $2y + 16 < 17$ **14** $4 + m < -3$ **15** $4p \leqslant 3$ **16** $4p - 13 \geqslant 0$

15.7 Inequations on a set

Example

Solve the inequation $2x + 5 \geqslant 9$ on the set of numbers $\{0, 1, 2, 3, 4, 5, 6, 7, 8\}$.

$$2x + 5 \geqslant 9$$
$$-5 \quad -5$$
$$2x \geqslant 4$$
$$\div 2 \quad \div 2$$
$$x \geqslant 2$$

For this set, all possible solutions are $\{2, 3, 4, 5, 6, 7, 8\}$.

Exercise 15.7

1 Solve the inequations on the set of numbers $\{0, 1, 2, 3, 4, 5, 6, 7, 8, 9\}$.

     (a) $4y - 3 \leqslant 17$ **(b)** $3m + 11 > 32$ **(c)** $10z - 1 \geqslant 89$

     (d) $6m + 4 < 22$ **(e)** $56 < 5y + 16$ **(f)** $z - 7 \geqslant 0$

2 Solve the inequations on the set $\{-3, -2, -1, 0, 1, 2, 3, 4, 5\}$.

     (a) $3x + 4 > 7$ **(b)** $y - 2 \leqslant -3$ **(c)** $4x - 1 < 3$

     (d) $z + 1 > -2$ **(e)** $6m + 2 \geqslant 32$ **(f)** $2n - 2 \leqslant 0$

3 Solve the inequations on the set $\{-6, -5, -4, -3, -2, -1, 0, 1, 2\}$.

(a) $5z > 5$ 　　　　　　　(b) $x - 9 < -11$ 　　　　　(c) $y + 8 \leqslant 2$

(d) $4y + 3 \geqslant 7$ 　　　　　(e) $3n - 1 < -1$ 　　　　　(f) $4z - 1 \geqslant 7$

Review exercise 15

1 Solve each equation:

(a) $x + 9 = 21$ 　　　(b) $y - 7 = 3$ 　　　(c) $z + 2 = 23$ 　　　(d) $43 = y - 5$

(e) $21 = x + 11$ 　　(f) $5y = 35$ 　　　　(g) $63 = 9y$ 　　　　(h) $4y + 2 = 30$

2 Solve each equation:

(a) $s + 7 = -1$ 　　(b) $y - 4 = -11$ 　　(c) $6y = 3$ 　　　　(d) $4z + 1 = 13$

(e) $11 = 2y - 4$ 　　(f) $2y - 3 = 18$ 　　(g) $r - 3 = -5$ 　　(h) $x + 8 = 2$

3 For each problem, form an equation and solve it.

(a) The sum of two numbers is 53. One number is 17 and the other is x.
Find the value of x.

(b) The product of 12 and y is 72. What number is y?

(c) Clive has 8 cartons of cakes, each containing n cakes.
He also has 3 single cakes.
If Clive has a total of 59 cakes, what is the value of n?

4 Solve each inequation:

(a) $x + 5 > 5$ 　　　(b) $y - 3 \leqslant 5$ 　　　(c) $3y > 15$

(d) $2m + 1 \geqslant 11$ 　　(e) $5y - 3 > 12$ 　　(f) $6m - 3 < 15$

5 Solve each inequation:

(a) $y - 1 < -3$ 　　(b) $2x \geqslant 3$ 　　　(c) $2s + 1 \leqslant 6$

(d) $2x + 3 > 8$ 　　(e) $x + 7 \geqslant 4$ 　　(f) $11 < z + 14$

6 On the set of numbers $\{-2, -1, 0, 1, 2, 3, 4, 5\}$ find all possible
solutions to each inequation.

(a) $y - 3 \geqslant 0$ 　　　(b) $x + 4 \leqslant 5$ 　　　(c) $4 > s + 4$

(d) $3m \leqslant 3$ 　　　　(e) $2y + 1 > 9$ 　　　(f) $8y - 2 \geqslant -2$

Summary

Equations

Solve $11y - 9 = 13$

$$
\begin{aligned}
11y - 9 &= 13 \\
+9 \quad &\quad +9 \\
11y &= 22 \\
\div 11 \quad &\quad \div 11 \\
y &= 2
\end{aligned}
$$

Solve $6 = y + 15$

$$
\begin{aligned}
6 &= y + 15 \\
-15 \quad &\quad -15 \\
-9 &= y \\
y &= -9
\end{aligned}
$$

Using equations

The perimeter of this shape is 17 centimetres.
Find m.

Form an equation $3m + 2 = 17$

Solve thee equation

$$
\begin{aligned}
3m + 2 &= 17 \\
-2 \quad &\quad -2 \\
3m &= 15 \\
\div 3 \quad &\quad \div 3 \\
m &= 5
\end{aligned}
$$

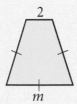

Inequations

Solve $4x - 3 \geqslant 21$

$$
\begin{aligned}
4x - 3 &\geqslant 21 \\
+3 \quad &\quad +3 \\
4x &\geqslant 24 \\
\div 4 \quad &\quad \div 4 \\
x &\geqslant 6
\end{aligned}
$$

Solve $2z + 11 < 16$

$$
\begin{aligned}
2z + 11 &< 16 \\
-11 \quad &\quad -11 \\
2z &< 5 \\
\div 2 \quad &\quad \div 2 \\
z &< 2\tfrac{1}{2}
\end{aligned}
$$

Find all possible solutions on the set $\{-2, -1, 0, 1, 2, 3, 4\}$ for the
inequation $3y - 2 \leqslant 1$

$$
\begin{aligned}
3y - 2 &\leqslant 1 \\
+2 \quad &\quad +2 \\
3y &\leqslant 3 \\
\div 3 \quad &\quad \div 3 \\
y &\leqslant 1
\end{aligned}
$$

All possible solutions are $\{-2, -1, 0, 1\}$.

16 Ratio

When quantities are mixed together it is often convenient to give the proportion or ratio of each quantity. In this chapter you will learn how to use ratios to calculate and share quantities.

16.1 Notation

To make a shade of green, mix 2 tins of yellow with 3 tins of blue.
The ratio of yellow to blue is 2 : 3.
yellow : blue = 2 : 3

> This is read as "2 to 3".

The ratio of blue to yellow is 3 : 2.
blue : yellow = 3 : 2

In this packet of sweets there are 5 blackcurrant,
6 strawberry and 8 lemon.
The ratio of blackcurrant to strawberry to lemon is 5 : 6 : 8.
blackcurrant : strawberry : lemon = 5 : 6 : 8

Exercise 16.1

1 For each of the following give the ratio of
(**i**) green tins to orange tins   (**ii**) orange tins to green tins.

(**a**)    (**b**)    (**c**)    (**d**)

2 To make orange squash drink, you mix 1 part orange juice with 6 parts water.
Write the ratio of

(**a**) orange juice to water   (**b**) water to orange juice.

3 To make a shade of purple, mix 4 tins of red with 3 tins of blue. Write the ratio of
(**a**) red paint to blue paint   (**b**) blue paint to red paint.

4 To make concrete mix 4 bags of cement with 9 bags of sand. Write the ratio of
(**a**) cement : sand   (**b**) sand : cement.

5 Write the ratio of
(**a**) circles : squares : triangles
(**b**) triangles : squares : circles
(**c**) blue shapes : red shapes : green shapes
(**d**) green shapes : red shapes : yellow shapes
(**e**) red squares : green triangles : blue squares
(**f**) blue circles : yellow triangles : green squares
(**g**) blue triangles : yellow squares : green circles.

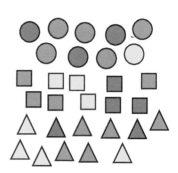

16.2 Simplifying ratios

4 tins of yellow can be mixed with 6 tins of blue to make green paint.
This can be split to make two groups of 2 tins of yellow with 3 tins
of blue.
Each group makes the same colour of green paint.

Yellow : blue = 4 : 6
          = 2 : 3

This packet of sweets contains 10 orange, 15 lemon and 25 strawberry.
Orange : lemon : strawberry = 10 : 15 : 25
                      = 2 : 3 : 5

Example

Simplify each ratio.

(**a**)   6 : 9   (**b**)   120 : 16   (**c**)   14 : 16 : 30

Answers

(**a**)   6 : 9   (**b**)   120 : 16   (**c**)   14 : 16 : 30
  = 2 : 3 (divide each   = 30 : 4 (divide each figure by 4)   = 7 : 8 : 15 (divide each
        figure by 3)   = 15 : 2 (divide each figure by 2)   figure by 2)

Exercise 16.2

1 Simplify each ratio:

(**a**) 4 : 14   (**b**) 6 : 15   (**c**) 5 : 25   (**d**) 18 : 48   (**e**) 28 : 49

(**f**) 28 : 4   (**g**) 18 : 12   (**h**) 48 : 16   (**i**) 96 : 24   (**j**) 88 : 33

(**k**) 42 : 72   (**l**) 160 : 28   (**m**)170 : 45   (**n**) 144 : 60   (**o**) 140 : 28

(**p**) 132 : 121   (**q**) 15 : 25 : 35   (**r**) 12 : 18 : 42   (**s**) 27 : 45 : 63   (**t**) 24 : 24 : 60

2 A bag of sweets contains 54 strawberry flavoured and 36 blackcurrant flavoured. Write the ratio of blackcurrant to strawberry flavoured sweets in simplest form.

3 Ailsa has shares worth £125 000 in a business. Craig has the remaining shares worth £350 000. What is the ratio of the value of Ailsa's shares to Craig's in its simplest form?

4 The total value of shares in a business is £60 000 000. Sheena has shares in the business worth £45 000 000. Greg has the remaining shares. What is the ratio of the value of Greg's shares to Sheena's in its simplest form?

5 The total value of shares in a business is £500 000 000. Mairi has shares in the business worth £150 000 000. Aimee has shares in the business worth £250 000 000. Catriona has the remaining shares. What is the ratio of the value of Mairi's to Aimee's to Catriona's shares in its simplest form?

6 The table shows the results of a survey carried out in the first year at Dun Add High School.

Calculate the following ratios in their simplest form:

(**a**) blonde haired girls to brown haired girls

(**b**) blonde haired boys to brown haired girls

(**c**) blonde haired pupils to black haired pupils

(**d**) blonde haired girls to brown haired girls to black haired girls.

(**e**) black haired pupils to brown haired pupils to blonde haired pupils

Colour of hair			
	Blonde	Brown	Black
Girls	24	36	18
Boys	18	48	31

16.3 Ratio and proportion

The Wearra Car Company makes cars, which are painted blue and red.

Example 1

The ratio of blue to red cars is 1 : 4.

If 8 cars were painted blue, how many were painted red?

Blue	Red
×8 ⟨ 1 ⟶ 8	4 ⟩ ×8 **32**

There were **32** red cars.

Example 2

The cars use either petrol or diesel.

The ratio of petrol to diesel is 7 : 3.

How many petrol cars were made when the number of diesel cars was 27?

Petrol	Diesel		Petrol	Diesel		Petrol	Diesel
7	3	→	7	3 27	→ ×9	7 ⟶ **63**	3 ⟩ ×9 27

They made **63** petrol cars.

Example 3

The company decides to include white cars in their range.
The ratio of blue to white to red cars is now 2 : 3 : 4.

If 8 cars were painted blue, how many were painted white and how many were painted red?

Blue	White	Red
×4 ⟨ 2 ⟶ 8	3 ⟩ ×4 **12**	4 ⟩ ×4 **16**

There were **12** white cars and **16** red cars.

Exercise 16.3

1 The ratio of blue cars to red cars is 1 : 4.

(**a**) How many red cars were there if the number of blue cars was

(**i**) 5   (**ii**) 8   (**iii**) 9   (**iv**) 10   (**v**) 20   (**vi**) 100?

(**b**) How many blue cars were there if the number of red cars was

(**i**) 8   (**ii**) 12   (**iii**) 28   (**iv**) 36   (**v**) 60   (**vi**) 300?

2 The ratio of petrol cars to diesel cars is 5 : 2.

   (**a**) How many diesel cars were made when the number of petrol cars was
      (**i**) 15   (**ii**) 45   (**iii**) 55   (**iv**) 50   (**v**) 125?

   (**b**) How many petrol cars were made, when the number of diesel cars was
      (**i**) 8   (**ii**) 18   (**iii**) 28   (**iv**) 42   (**v**) 100?

3 The ratio of red to blue to green cars is 5 : 3 : 2.

   (**a**) How many blue cars and how many green cars are there if the number
      of red cars is
      (**i**) 25   (**ii**) 45   (**iii**) 60   (**iv**) 100   (**v**) 400?

   (**b**) How many red cars and how many blue cars are there if the number
      of green cars is
      (**i**) 18   (**ii**) 36   (**iii**) 60   (**iv**) 120   (**v**) 480?

4 A chocolate cake recipe states that flour and sugar should be mixed in the
ratio 5 : 3. If 120 grammes of sugar are used, what weight of flour is required?

5 Green paint is made by mixing yellow paint with blue paint in the ratio
3 : 4. How many tins of yellow are needed to make this shade if 16 tins
of blue are used?

6 Sand, gravel and cement are mixed in the ratio 5 : 2 : 1 to make concrete.
How many bags of gravel and how many of cement are needed if 30 bags
of sand are used?

7 In an international football match, the
ratio of fouls committed by Scotland to
those committed by England was 4 : 10.

   (**a**) Write this ratio in simplest form.

   (**b**) The Scottish team committed 14 fouls.
      How many fouls were committed by
      the English team?

8 Rajiv and Bhavesh invested £5000 and £7500
respectively to start up a business together.

   (**a**) Write the ratio of Rajiv's investment to
      Bhavesh's in simplest form.

   (**b**) They have agreed to share any profit
      from their business in the ratio of their
      investments. What will Bhavesh receive
      if Rajiv's share is £8000?

9 Three friends, Angus, Graeme and John, started a business by investing
£2500, £2500 and £7500 respectively.

   (**a**) Write the ratio of Angus' to Graeme's to John's investments in
      simplest form.

   (**b**) They have agreed to share any profit from their business in the
      ratio of their investments. What will Angus and John receive if
      Graeme's share is £65 000?

16.4 Sharing a given quantity

Quantities often have to be shared. Sometimes the quantity is not evenly divided.

Example 1

Megan and Kathrine share the profit from their business in the ratio 4 : 3.
What will each receive if the total profit is £2100?

Step 1

Add up numbers in ratio to find the total number of parts. $4 + 3 = 7$

Step 2

Divide total by this number to find the value of 1 part. $£2100 \div 7 = £300$

Step 3

Multiply the value of 1 part by each number in the ratio.   Megan's share $= 4 \times £300 = £1200$
Kathrine's share $= 3 \times £300 = £900$

Step 4

Check that the shares add to give the total. $£1200 + £900 = £2100 =$ correct total
This can be more conveniently set out in a proportion table:

Megan	Kathrine	Total
4	3	7
		£2100

Megan	Kathrine	Total
4	3	7
1200	900	2100

×300   ×300   ×300

Megan receives **£1200** and Kathrine receives **£900**.

Exercise 16.4

1 Share each amount in the given ratio.

(**a**) 42 in the ratio 3 : 4   (**b**) 54 in the ratio 5 : 4

(**c**) 72 in the ratio 5 : 3   (**d**) 84 in the ratio 7 : 5

(**e**) £99 in the ratio 7 : 4   (**f**) £100 in the ratio 14 : 11

(**g**) 64 centimetres in the ratio 3 : 5   (**h**) 39 grammes in the ratio 6 : 7

2 Share each amount in the given ratio.

(**a**) £54 in the ratio 1 : 2 : 3   (**b**) £63 in the ratio 2 : 3 : 4

(**c**) £56 in the ratio 2 : 3 : 2   (**d**) 72 metres in the ratio 3 : 2 : 3

(**e**) 99 grammes in the ratio 2 : 4 : 5   (**f**) £90 in the ratio 4 : 3 : 3

3 Mhairi and Catriona invest in a new business. Since Mhairi invests more
than Catriona, they agree to share the profit or losses in the ratio 5 : 3.

(**a**) How much would each receive if the total profit gained is
(**i**) £80 000   (**ii**) £50 000   (**iii**) £45 000   (**iv**) £1 000 000?

(**b**) How much would it cost each person if the total losses were
(**i**) £1000   (**ii**) £3600   (**iii**) £5600   (**iv**) £20 000?

4 Sawdales High School need 330 litres of orange drink for the Fun Day. Orange concentrate and water are mixed in the ratio 2 : 9 to make the drink. How much of each will be needed?

5 Sand and cement are mixed in the ratio 3 : 5 to make a particular strength of mortar. If a builder requires 88 cubic metres of mortar, how much sand and how much cement are needed?

6 At high temperatures calcium carbonate breaks down into calcium oxide and carbon dioxide in the ratio 14 : 11. What mass of each would be produced from 100 grammes of calcium carbonate?

7 In Millarcraig Golf Club the ratio of women to men is 3 : 5. How many members are women if the total membership is 312?

8 Kirsty and Jiten invest £4000 and £3000 respectively when starting a business. They have agreed to share the profits in the same ratio.
(**a**) Write the ratio of Kirsty's to Jiten's investments in its simplest form.
(**b**) If the total profit for their business was £4200, find the amount each received.

9 The total attendance at a football match was 8100. The ratio of Dunfermline supporters to Raith Rovers supporters to neutral supporters was 3 : 4 : 2. How many of each group were there at the match?

10 In Braeriach High School football team's "Player of the Year" contest, 64 votes were cast. If the ratio of votes for Steven to Mark to Daniel was 4 : 3 : 1, how many did each receive?

11 In the year 2000 the population of Scotland was 5.1 million. This was divided into three age groups – under 16; 16 to 65; over 65 – in the ratio 20 : 65 : 15.
(**a**) Write this ratio in its simplest form.
(**b**) Calculate the number of people in each age group.

12 Edinburgh Castle, the Edinburgh Zoo and the Museum of Scotland attract visitors in the ratio of 13 : 5 : 7.

(**a**) The total number of tourists visiting these three sites in June 2003 was 200 000. How many visited each site?
(**b**) Use the table to calculate the total income for these three sites during June 2003.

Site	Entry Fee
Edinburgh Castle	£5.00
Edinburgh Zoo	£8.00
Museum of Scotland	Free

13 The diagram shows a plan of an area in a kitchen which Bob wants to tile.
(**a**) If each tile is a square of side 15 centimetres, how many tiles in total are required to cover the area shown?
(**b**) Bob wants to use blue and white tiles in the ratio 5 : 4. How many of each colour does he require?
(**c**) Boxes of blue tiles cost £5.80 and each contain 5 tiles. Boxes of white tiles cost £3.60 and each contain 10 tiles. What will it cost Bob to tile this area?

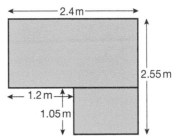

Review exercise 16

1 Simplify each ratio.
   (**a**) $12:20$ (**b**) $24:36$ (**c**) $63:35$ (**d**) $250:100$
   (**e**) $18:27:6$ (**f**) $72:56:32$ (**g**) $64:28:40$ (**h**) $350:275:125$

2 At the Tayside Derby, there were 5500 Dundee supporters and 6500 United supporters. Write the ratio of Dundee supporters to United supporters in simplest form.

3 Orange squash and water are mixed in the ratio $3:7$ to make a drink. How much water is needed if the volume of orange squash is 36 millilitres?

4 Bob makes concrete by mixing cement and sand in the ratio $2:5$. He has 35 bags of sand. How many bags of cement does he need?

5 The ratio of passes completed to incomplete passes during the Junior Cup Final was $4:5$. If 48 passes were completed, how many incomplete passes were there?

6 A chain of record shops sells folk, classical and pop CDs. Each store stocks the same proportion of each type as all other stores in the chain. In one shop there were 5000 folk, 8000 classical and 20 000 pop CDs. If the total number of folk CDs in all stores is 15 500, calculate the total number of classical and the total number of pop CDs in all stores.

7 Janine, Kathryn and Johnny invest £5000, £2500 and £4000 respectively in a business.
   (**a**) Write the ratio of Janine's to Kathryn's to Johnny's investments in simplest form.
   (**b**) They agree to share any profit or losses in the same ratio as their investments. If Kathryn's share of the profit is £500, how much will each of the others receive?

8 Share these amounts in the ratios given.
   (**a**) £484 in the ratio $5:6$ (**b**) £135 in the ratio $7:2$
   (**c**) 54 kilogrammes in the ratio $1:9$ (**d**) 72 kilogrammes in the ratio $1:2:3$
   (**e**) 120 metres in the ratio $2:7:3$ (**f**) £1250 in the ratio $6:7:12$

9 In Burnbraid Tennis Club the ratio of juniors to women to men is $2:3:4$.
   (**a**) How many members are there in each category if the total membership is 315?
   (**b**) The annual membership fees are shown in the table. How much does the club collect annually in membership fees?

Member	Fee
Junior	£25.00
Women	£50.00
Men	£65.00

10 Kayleigh, Aisha and Kerry invest £5000, £2000 and £3000 respectively when starting a business. They have agreed to share the profits in the same ratio as their investments.
   (**a**) Write the ratio of Kayleigh's to Aisha's to Kerry's investments in its simplest form.
   (**b**) If the total profit for their business was £9500, find the amount which each received.

Summary

Notation

The ratio of red counters to blue counters is 2 : 3.

Simplifying ratios

Simplify ratios by dividing each part by the same number. $14 : 16 : 30 = 7 : 8 : 15$
                                                   (divide each figure by 2)

Ratio and proportion

The ratio of petrol cars to diesel cars is 7 : 2.

How many petrol cars were made when the number of diesel cars was 27?

Petrol	Diesel
7	3

→

Petrol	Diesel
7	3
	27

→ ×9

Petrol	Diesel
7	3
63	27	×9

The ratio of blue to white to red cars is 2 : 3 : 4.

If 8 cars were painted blue, how many were painted white and how many were painted red?

Blue	White	Red
×4 2	3	4
8	**12** ×4	**16** ×4

Sharing a given quantity

Use a proportion table to split a quantity into a given ratio.
Share £2100 between Megan and Kathrine in the ratio 4 : 3.

Megan	Kathrine	Total
4	3	7
		£2100

→

Megan	Kathrine	Total
4	3	7	×300
1200	**900** ×300	2100 ×300

×300

17 3D shape

In this chapter you will review the properties of solid shapes including calculating volume.

17.1 Dimensions

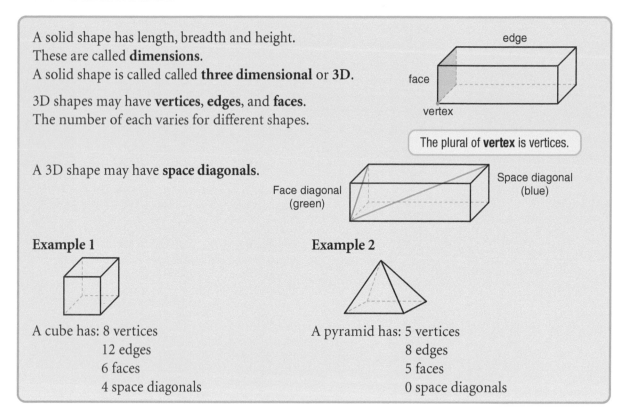

A solid shape has length, breadth and height.
These are called **dimensions**.
A solid shape is called called **three dimensional** or **3D**.

3D shapes may have **vertices**, **edges**, and **faces**.
The number of each varies for different shapes.

> The plural of **vertex** is vertices.

A 3D shape may have **space diagonals**.

Example 1

A cube has: 8 vertices
12 edges
6 faces
4 space diagonals

Example 2

A pyramid has: 5 vertices
8 edges
5 faces
0 space diagonals

Exercise 17.1

1 For each solid shape identify the blue section as a vertex, edge, face, face diagonal or space diagonal.

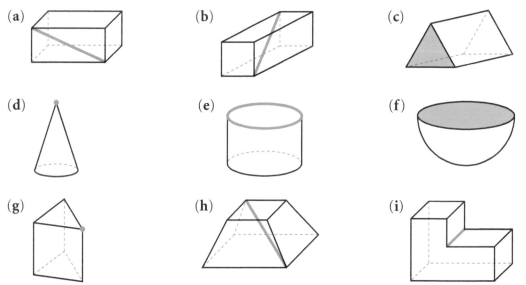

(a)   (b)   (c)

(d)   (e)   (f)

(g)   (h)   (i)

2 Name each shape in question **1(a)** to **(f)**.

3 Copy and complete the table for the shapes in question **1**.

Number of	Shape								
	(a)	(b)	(c)	(d)	(e)	(f)	(g)	(h)	(i)
vertices									
edges									
faces									
space diagonals									

17.2 Naming faces and diagonals

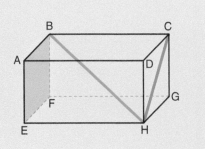

A face is identified by the letters at each vertex.
The letters are listed in order, starting at any vertex.

The blue face on this cuboid may be named
ABFE or BFEA or EFBA or …

A diagonal is named by the letters at its ends.
The green face diagonal is CH or HC.
The red space diagonal is BH or HB.

Exercise 17.2

1 There are eight ways of naming the blue face in the example above.
Find the other five ways to name it.

2 On this cuboid find two names for

  (**a**) the blue face

  (**b**) the green face

  (**c**) the yellow face.

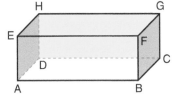

3 For each shape find two names for the blue face.

  (**a**)

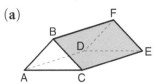

  (**b**)

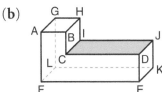

4 What colour is each face named below?

  (**a**) BCNM

  (**b**) FEDCBA.

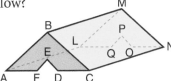

5 For this shape find two names for

  (**a**) the top   (**b**) the back

  (**c**) the front   (**d**) the right hand side.

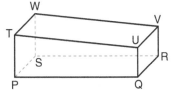

6 Sketch the cube exactly as shown.
Draw in the diagonals on the top, front and left hand side.

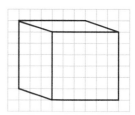

7 For this cuboid name the diagonals on
 (**a**) the front
 (**b**) the top
 (**c**) SPTW.

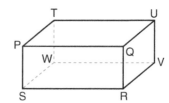

8 Sketch the cube exactly as shown.
Draw in all the space diagonals.

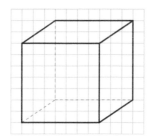

9 Sketch the cuboid exactly as shown.
Draw in all the space diagonals.

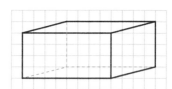

10 For each shape, name both space diagonals drawn in blue.

(**a**)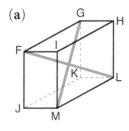

(**b**)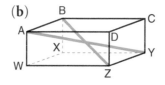

(**c**)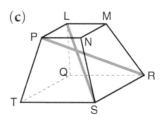

11 On the cube the space diagonal QW has been drawn.
Name the other three space diagonals.

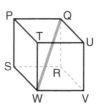

12 (**a**) How many space diagonals does this shape have?
 (**b**) Name the space diagonals.

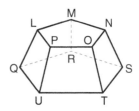

17.3 Angles

The angle shaded yellow is ∠PQW or ∠WQP.

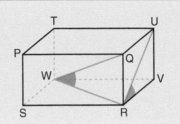

Exercise 17.3

1 On the cuboid above, name
   (**a**) the blue angle　　　　(**b**) the green angle.

2 On the cuboid name
   (**a**) the yellow angle
   (**b**) the red angle
   (**c**) the blue angle.

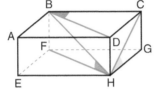

3 What colour is
   (**a**) ∠SQO
   (**b**) ∠OQM
   (**c**) ∠MRN?

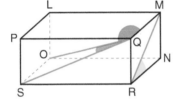

4 For each shape name the blue angle.

(**a**) 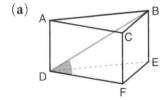　　(**b**) 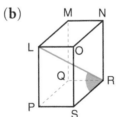　　(**c**)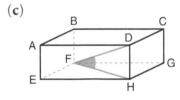

5 For each shape copy and complete the table.

(**a**)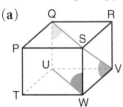

Angle	Colour
WVS	
	yellow
	red

(**b**)

Angle	Colour
	blue
	yellow
	red

(**c**)

Angle	Colour
	blue
	yellow
	red

17.4 Drawing on isometric paper

Isometric dot paper is useful for drawing 3D shapes.

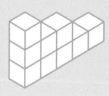 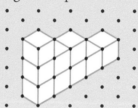

Exercise 17.4

You need isometric dot paper to complete this exercise.

Draw each 3D shape on isometric paper.

1

2
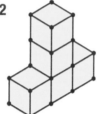

3
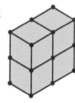

4
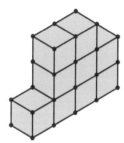

5
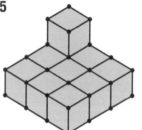

6
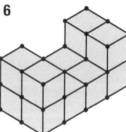

7
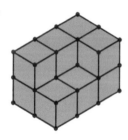

8
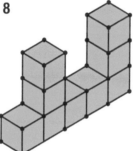

9 Draw these shapes with the red cubes removed.

(a)
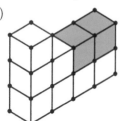

(b)
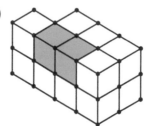

17.5 Building 3D shapes

This triangular prism has
6 edges of length 5 centimetres
3 edges of length 7 centimetres
6 vertices

A **skeleton model**, using straws and
pipe cleaners, looks like this.

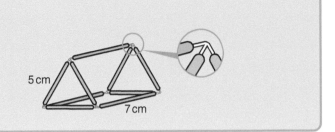

Exercise 17.5

To build the models you need straws, pipe cleaners, scissors and a ruler.
For each 3D shape:

(**a**) list the number of each edge length required

(**b**) list how many vertices are required

(**c**) build a skeleton model if you have the materials.

1
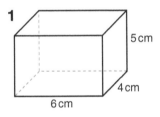

2
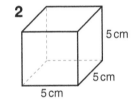

3
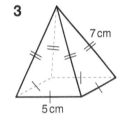

4
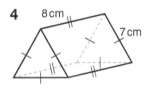

5
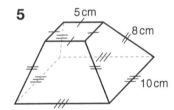

6
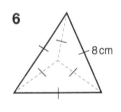

17.6 Nets

A model may be built from a **net**.

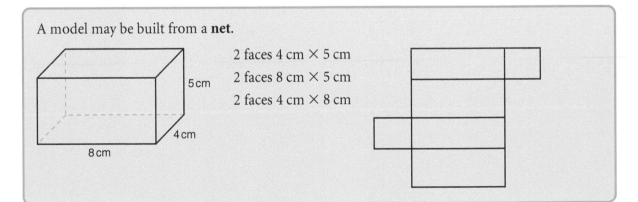

2 faces 4 cm × 5 cm

2 faces 8 cm × 5 cm

2 faces 4 cm × 8 cm

Exercise 17.6

To build the models you need 1 cm squared paper, scissors and a ruler. For each shape:

(**a**) list the number of each size of face   (**b**) draw a net   (**c**) cut out the net and build the shape.

1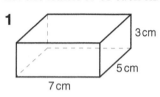

2

3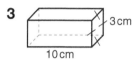

4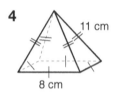

5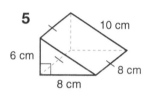

6

17.7 Volume of cube and cuboid

Remember   Volume of a cuboid = length × breadth × height

$$V = l \times b \times h$$
$$V = lbh$$

Example

Find the volume of the cuboid.

$V = lbh$
$= 7 \times 2 \times 3$
$= 42 \text{ cm}^3$ **The volume is 42 cubic centimetres.**

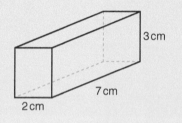

Exercise 17.7

1 Calculate the volume of each cube or cuboid:

(**a**)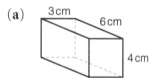

(**b**)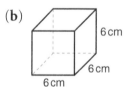

(**c**)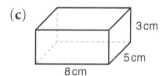

(**d**)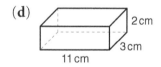

(**e**)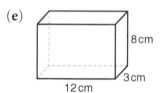

(**f**)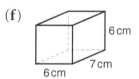

2 Des has three packing cases. Which has the greatest volume?

(**a**)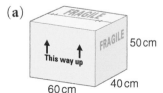

(**b**)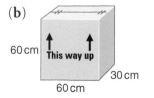

(**c**)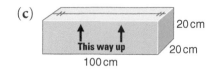

3 Calculate the volume of each cuboid.

(a)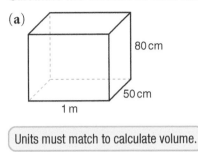
80 cm
50 cm
1 m

Units must match to calculate volume.

(b)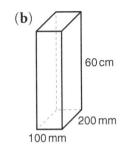
60 cm
200 mm
100 mm

(c)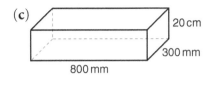
20 cm
300 mm
800 mm

4 Willie keeps tropical fish. Calculate the volume of each tank in litres.

(a)
60 cm
50 cm
80 cm

(b)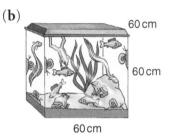
60 cm
60 cm
60 cm

(c)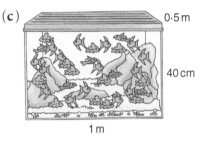
0·5 m
40 cm
1 m

5 The Technical Department makes wooden pencil cases.
Put the pencil cases in order, from smallest to largest volume.

(a)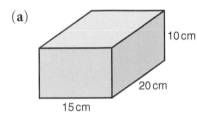
10 cm
20 cm
15 cm

(b)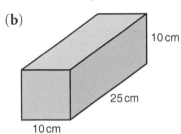
10 cm
25 cm
10 cm

(c)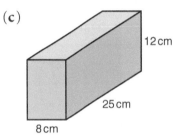
12 cm
25 cm
8 cm

6 Which microwave has the largest volume?

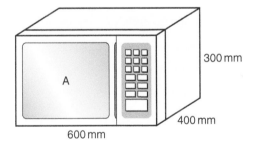
A
300 mm
400 mm
600 mm

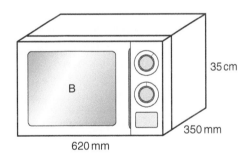
B
35 cm
350 mm
620 mm

7 The cuboids below have volume 120 cm³. Find the missing dimension in each.

(a)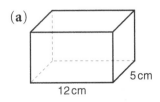
5 cm
12 cm

(b)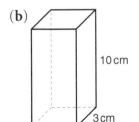
10 cm
3 cm

(c)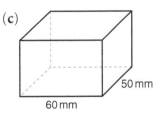
50 mm
60 mm

8 For each cuboid, find the missing dimension.

(a)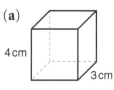

4 cm

3 cm

$V = 36\,cm^3$

(b)

$V = 64\,m^3$

(c)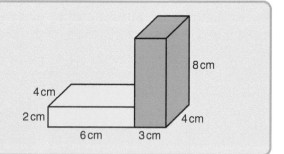

8 mm

10 mm

$V = 240\,mm^3$

9 Copy and complete the table.

Length	Breadth	Height	Volume
3 cm	4 cm	3 cm	
2 cm	5 cm	6 cm	
5 m	6 m		150 m³
4 cm	2 cm		24 cm³
	5 cm	4 cm	140 cm³

17.8 Volume of compound shapes

Example

Find the volume of this 3D shape.

Yellow cuboid: $V = 6 \times 4 \times 2 =$ 48 cm³
Blue cuboid: $V = 3 \times 4 \times 8 =$ 96 cm³

Total volume = **144 cm³**

8 cm

4 cm

2 cm

6 cm   3 cm

4 cm

Exercise 17.8

Find the volume of each compound shape.

1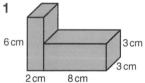

6 cm

3 cm

3 cm

2 cm   8 cm

2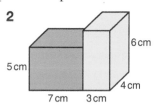

6 cm

5 cm

4 cm

7 cm   3 cm

3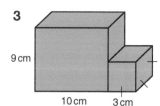

9 cm

10 cm   3 cm

4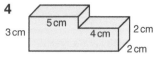

5 cm

3 cm   4 cm

2 cm

2 cm

5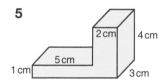

2 cm   4 cm

5 cm

1 cm   3 cm

6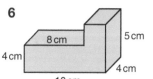

8 cm   5 cm

4 cm   4 cm

10 cm

7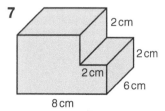

2 cm

2 cm

2 cm   6 cm

8 cm

8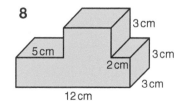

3 cm

5 cm   3 cm

2 cm   3 cm

12 cm

9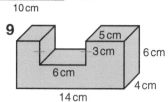

5 cm

3 cm   6 cm

6 cm

14 cm   4 cm

10 Find the volume of the removal van in   (**a**) m³   (**b**) litres.

11 How much space does the hamster have?

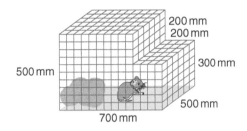

12 Colin rents out this storage facility.
What is its volume?

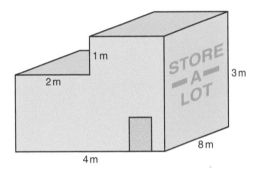

Review exercise 17

You need isometric dot paper for questions 6 and 7.

1 For each shape identify the green section as a vertex, edge, face, face diagonal or space diagonal.

(**a**) 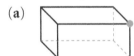   (**b**) 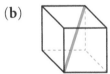   (**c**)

(**d**) 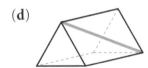   (**e**) 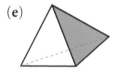   (**f**)

2 For the shapes shown in question 1, copy and complete the table.

| Shape | Number of | | | |
	Vertices	Edges	Faces	Space diagonals
(a)				
(b)				
(c)				
(d)				
(e)				
(f)				

3 For this diagram name the
   (**a**) red diagonal
   (**b**) green space diagonal
   (**c**) blue angle
   (**d**) yellow face.

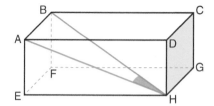

4 Sketch a cube and draw its space diagonals.

5 Name the blue angle in each diagram.

(**a**) 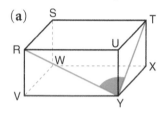   (**b**) 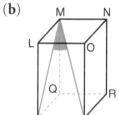   (**c**)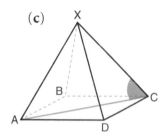

6 Draw each 3D shape on isometric dot paper.

(**a**) 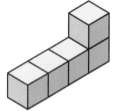   (**b**)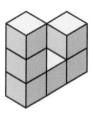

(**c**)    (**d**)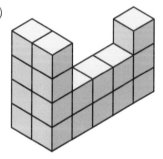

7 On isometric dot paper draw each 3D shape without the red cubes.

(**a**)   (**b**)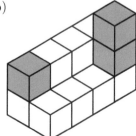

8 For each skeleton model below

  (**i**) list the number of each edge length

  (**ii**) list the number of vertices.

(**a**)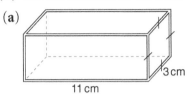

11 cm 3 cm

(**b**)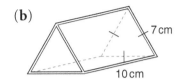

7 cm 10 cm

9 Copy and complete the table to show which net would build each shape.

3D shape	Net
A	
B	
C	

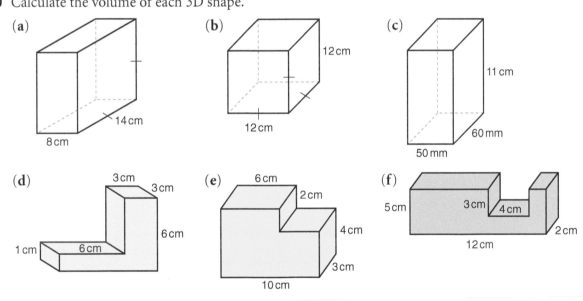

A   B   C

1   **2**   **3**

10 Calculate the volume of each 3D shape.

(**a**)

14 cm 8 cm

(**b**)

12 cm 12 cm

(**c**)

11 cm 60 mm 50 mm

(**d**)

3 cm 3 cm 6 cm 1 cm 6 cm

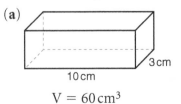

(**e**)

6 cm 2 cm 4 cm 3 cm 10 cm

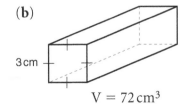

(**f**)

5 cm 3 cm 4 cm 12 cm 2 cm

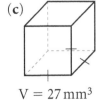

11 Find the missing dimension for each cuboid.

(**a**)

10 cm 3 cm

V = 60 cm³

(**b**)

3 cm

V = 72 cm³

(**c**)

V = 27 mm³

Summary

A solid shape has three dimensions, length, breadth and height.

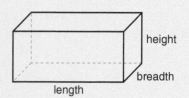

3D shapes may have vertices, edges, faces, face diagonals and space diagonals.

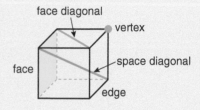

Face DCGH is blue.

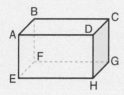

The blue angle is $\angle$XYW or $\angle$WYX.

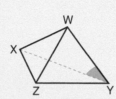

3D shapes may be drawn on isometric dot paper.

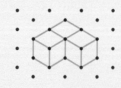

A 3D shape may be formed from its net.

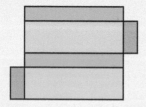
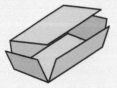

Volume = length $\times$ breadth $\times$ height
$= lbh$
$= 6 \times 4 \times 3$
$= 72 \text{ cm}^3$

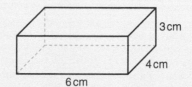

18 Formulae

In this chapter you will learn to construct and use formulae in both words and symbols.

18.1 Constructing formulae in words and symbols

The number of cars and wheels can be shown in a table.

Number of cars (c)	Number of wheels (w)
1	4
2	8
3	12
4	16

> The number of wheels increases 4 at a time.

The number of wheels is four times the number of cars.
This formula may be written using letters.
$$w = 4 \times c$$
$$w = 4c$$

For 6 cars, $c = 6$ and $w = 4 \times 6 = 24$ That is 24 wheels.

For 20 cars, $c = 20$ and $w = 4 \times 20 = 80$ That is 80 wheels.

Exercise 18.1

1

(a) Copy and complete the table.

(b) Write the increase in the number of wheels each time.

(c) Copy and complete the word formula:
The number of wheels is _____ times the number of bikes.

Number of bikes (b)	Number of wheels (w)
1	2
2	
3	
4	

(d) Copy and complete the formula: $w = $ _____ $\times b$
$$w = \text{_____} \, b$$

(e) Use your formula to find how many wheels are on
(i) 7 bikes   (ii) 50 bikes.

2

(**a**) Copy and complete the table.

Number of vans (v)	Number of wheels (w)
1	3
2	
3	
4	

(**b**) Write the increase in the number of wheels each time.

(**c**) Copy and complete the word formula:
The number of wheels is _____ times the number of vans.

(**d**) Copy and complete the formula: $w =$ _____ v

(**e**) Use your formula to find how many wheels are on
(**i**) 6 vans   (**ii**) 10 vans.

3 A truck has 6 wheels.

(**a**) Draw a table using *Number of trucks* (t) and *Number of wheels* (w)
for up to 4 trucks.

(**b**) Write the increase in the number of wheels each time.

(**c**) Copy and complete the formula: $w =$ _____

(**d**) Use your formula to find how many wheels are on
(**i**) 5 trucks   (**ii**) 12 trucks.

4 A particular class of submarine has 24 cabins.

(**a**) Draw a table using *Number of submarines* (s)
and *Number of cabins* (c).

(**b**) Write a formula for the number of cabins
when you know the number of submarines.

(**c**) Use your formula to find the number of cabins on
(**i**) 9 submarines   (**ii**) 12 submarines.

5 A passenger aircraft requires a crew of nine.

(**a**) Draw a table using *Number of aircraft* (a) and *Number of crew* (c).

(**b**) Copy and complete the formula: $c =$ _____

(**c**) Use your formula to find the number of crew needed for
(**i**) 7 aircraft   (**ii**) 25 aircraft.

(**d**) How many aircraft could be in service if 72 crew were available?

18.2 Formulae from graphs

Information from a graph can be used to make a table and then the formula may be constructed as before.

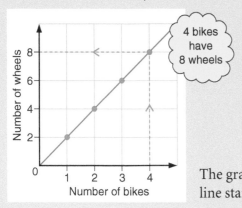

4 bikes have 8 wheels

Number of bikes (b)	Number of wheels (w)
1	2
2	4
3	6
4	8

The number of wheels increases 2 at a time.

The graph is a straight line starting at zero.

Formula: $w = 2b$
For 24 bikes, $b = 24$ and
$w = 2 \times 24 = 48$ wheels.

Exercise 18.2

1 (**a**) Using the graph, copy and complete the table.

Number of chairs (c)	Number of legs (l)
1	
2	
3	
4	

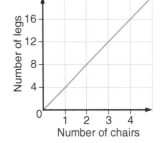

(**b**) Write the increase in the number of legs each time.

(**c**) Write a formula for the number of legs when you know the number of chairs.

(**d**) Use the formula to find the number of legs on (**i**) 5 chairs (**ii**) 12 chairs.

2 (**a**) Using the graph, make a table to show *Number of goldfish* (g) and *Number of fins* (f) and write a formula for the number of fins when you know the number of goldfish.

(**b**) How many fins are on (**i**) 7 goldfish (**ii**) 15 goldfish?

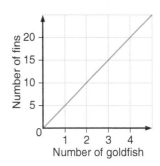

3 (**a**) Using the graph, make a table to show *Number of pounds* (p) and *Number of euros* (e) and write a formula for the number of euros when you know the number of pounds.

(**b**) How many euros would you receive for (**i**) £100 (**ii**) £550?

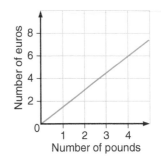

18.3 More formulae in words and symbols

In a motorcade each limousine has two motorcycle outriders on either side. There is also an outrider at both the front and back of the motorcade.

1 limo   2 limos   3 limos   4 limos

This can be shown in a table.

Number of limos (l)	Number of outriders (r)
1	6
2	10
3	14
4	18

> The number of outriders increases by 4 at a time.

The number of outriders is 4 times the number of limos **plus 2**.
The formula may be written using letters. $r = 4 \times l + 2$
$$r = 4l + 2$$

For 12 limos, $l = 12$ and $r = 4 \times 12 + 2$
$$r = 48 + 2$$
$$= 50$$

There are **50** outriders.

Exercise 18.3

1 In a restaurant, tables can be placed together as shown.

    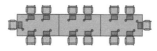

1 table   2 tables   3 tables

(**a**) Draw the next pattern in the sequence.

(**b**) Copy and complete the table.

(**c**) Write the increase in the number of chairs each time.

(**d**) Copy and complete the word formula:

Number of tables (t)	Number of chairs (c)
1	
2	
3	
4	

The number of chairs is _____ times the number of tables plus _____ .

(**e**) Write the formula using letters.

(**f**) Use your formula to find how many chairs are needed for
   (**i**) 6 tables   (**ii**) 9 tables.

2 In a park, triangular paving slabs are edged with metre-long stones.

  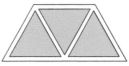

1 slab   2 slabs   3 slabs

(**a**) Draw the next pattern in the sequence.

(**b**) Copy and complete the table.

(**c**) What is the increase in the number of edging stones each time?

(**d**) Write the formula.

Paving slabs (p)	Number of stones (s)
1	3
2	
3	
4	

(**e**) Use the formula to find the number of edging stones required for the following number of slabs.
   (**i**) 7   (**ii**) 15

3 Fencing is constructed using vertical posts (v) and planks (p) as shown

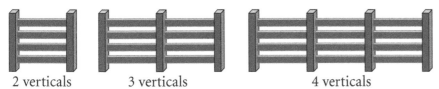

2 verticals   3 verticals   4 verticals

(**a**) Draw the next pattern in the sequence.

(**b**) Copy and complete the table.

(**c**) Write a formula for the number of planks when you know the number of verticals.

Verticals (v)	Planks (p)
2	
3	
4	

(**d**) Use the formula to find the number of planks needed for
   (**i**) 9 vertical posts   (**ii**) 12 vertical posts.

4 At the garden festival, triangular flower beds (b) are bordered by small shrubs (s).

 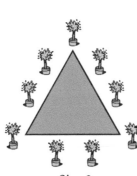 

Size 1   Size 2   Size 3

(**a**) Write a formula, using letters, for the number of shrubs.

(**b**) Use the formula to find the number of shrubs for flower bed size
   (**i**) 6   (**ii**) 15.

(**c**) What flower bed size would have 36 shrubs?

18.4 Solving problems using formulae

At a breakdown, if a car has to be towed back to the garage, the costs are as follows:

Charge per mile of towing **£5**
Call-out fee **£30**

For a distance of 3 miles, total cost = 5 × 3 + 30
$$= 15 + 30 = £45$$

For a distance of 4 miles, total cost = 5 × 4 + 30
$$= 20 + 30 = £50$$

The increase in the cost for each mile is 5.

The formula is $c = 5m + 30$

For a distance of 11 miles, $m = 11$ $c = 5 × 11 + 30$
$$= 55 + 30$$
$$= 85$$ The total cost is **£85**.

Exercise 18.4

1 A plumber charges £25 per hour and a call-out fee of £15.

  (**a**) How much does it cost for a job which lasts
    (**i**) 2 hours   (**ii**) 3 hours?

  (**b**) Write the increase in the cost each time.

  (**c**) Copy and complete the formula for the total cost.
    $c = $ ____ $h + $ ____

  (**d**) Calculate the cost of a job which takes
    (**i**) 9 hours (**ii**) 13 hours.

2 A piano teacher charges £18 per lesson plus a fixed amount of £5 for music books.

  (**a**) How much does she charge for three lessons?

  (**b**) Write the formula for the cost of lessons: $c = $ ____ $l + $ ____

  (**c**) What would she charge for
    (**i**) 10 lessons (**ii**) 20 lessons?

3 The charge for mixing cement on a building site is £135 per day plus a fixed charge of £50.

  (**a**) Calculate the cost of hiring a cement mixer for 2 days.

  (**b**) Find a formula for the total cost (c) when you know the number of days (d) hired.

  (**c**) How much does it cost to hire a cement mixer
    (**i**) for a week (**ii**) for 12 days?

4 (**a**) Find a formula for the cost (c) of hiring a barge when you know the number of days (d).

  (**b**) How much does it cost for
    (**i**) a 10-day holiday   (**ii**) a 3-week holiday?

Barge hire
£100 plus £ 5 per day

5 At an apple orchard, pickers are paid £6 for every crate of apples picked. They are also charged £5 per day for food and transport.

Number of crates (c)	Earnings in £'s (e)
1	1
2	

(**a**) Copy and complete the daily earnings table for up to 4 crates picked.

(**b**) Write the increase in earnings for each crate picked.

(**c**) Find a formula for earnings (e) when you know the number of crates (c) picked.

(**d**) What would Jim earn in a day when he picked
    (**i**) 7 crates   (**ii**) 12 crates?

6 A small factory produces circuit boards. Each board is sold for £750. The factory has weekly costs of £680 for salaries and materials.

(**a**) Find a formula for the profit (p) each week when you know the number of boards (b) sold.

(**b**) Find the weekly profit if
    (**i**) 6 boards are sold   (**ii**) 11 boards are sold.

7 Triangular metal plates are fitted together to form barriers of different lengths. The 3-metre barrier is shown.

(**a**) Make a table to show *Barrier length* (l) and *Number of plates* (p).

(**b**) Write a formula for number of plates when you know the barrier length.

(**c**) How many plates are needed for
    (**i**) a 7-metre length   (**ii**) a 15-metre length?

(**d**) What length of barrier has 45 plates?

3 metres

Review exercise 18

1 A Baker's Dozen catering pack of morning rolls contains 13 rolls.
(**a**) Draw a table using *Number of packs* (p) and *Number of rolls* (r).
(**b**) Write a formula for *Number of rolls* when you know the *Number of packs*.
(**c**) Use your formula to find the number of rolls in
    (**i**) 6 packs   (**ii**) 12 packs.

2 The graph shows the distance run by athletes on a running track.
(**a**) Using the graph make a table to show *Number of laps* (l) and *Distance in metres* (d).
(**b**) Write a formula for the distance run when you know the number of laps.
(**c**) Use the formula to find the distance run in
    (**i**) 5 laps   (**ii**) 25 laps.

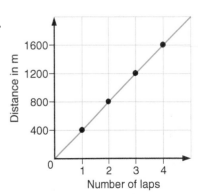

3 Rectangular mirrors are surrounded by small decorative ceramic squares.

(**a**) Draw the next pattern in the sequence.

(**b**) Make a table to show *Mirror size (m)* and *Number of squares (s)*.

(**c**) Write a formula, using letters, for the number of squares when you know the mirror size.

  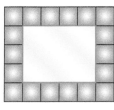

Size 1   Size 2   Size 3

(**d**) Use the formula to find the number of squares for
   (**i**) mirror size 6   (**ii**) mirror size 10.

4 This pattern of shapes has been made from matchsticks.

Shape 1   Shape 2   Shape 3

(**a**) Draw the next pattern in the sequence.

(**b**) Make a table to show *Shape number (s)* and *Number of matches (m)*.

(**c**) Write a formula for the number of matches when you know the shape number.

(**d**) Use the formula to find the number of matches in the seventh shape.

5 A cycling holiday costs £55 per day plus a fixed charge of £30 for bike and helmet hire.

(**a**) Make a table to show *Number of days (d)* and *Total cost (c)* for up to 4 days.

(**b**) Find a formula for the total cost of a cycling holiday when you know the number of days.

(**c**) Use the formula to find the total cost of
   (**i**) a one week holiday   (**ii**) a ten day holiday.

6 A ferryman can only row one person at a time across the river.

One person requires   Two people require   Three people require
1 crossing   3 crossings   5 crossings

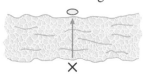 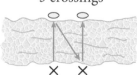 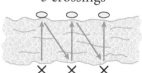

(**a**) Make a table to show *Number in group (g)* and *Number of crossings (c)*.

(**b**) Find a formula for the number of crossings when you know the number in the group.

(**c**) Use the formula to find the number of crossings for a group of
   (**i**) 6 people   (**ii**) 15 people.

Summary

To construct a formula

Identify the pattern by
- drawing the next picture
- studying the graph
- understanding the word explanation.

Seats and tables

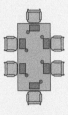 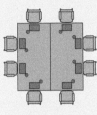 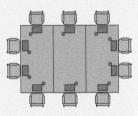

Table 1   Table 2   Table 3

Draw a table to show the pattern of numbers.

Number of tables (t)	Number of seats (s)
1	6
2	8
3	10
4	12

Find the **increase number** from the right-hand column of the table.

The number of seats increases by 2 each time.

Write the formula
- in words using the headings from the table or with symbols
- use the increase number to multiply
- check to see if a number has to be added or subtracted.

Number of seats is 2 times number of tables, plus 4.

$$s = 2t + 4$$

Use the formula

For 8 tables the number of seats is given by

$s = 2t + 4$

$s = 2 \times 8 + 4$

$s = 16 + 4$

$s = 20$

The number of seats is 20.

19 Problem solving

1 The four numbers at the ends of this cross add up to the number in the middle.

(a) Find the numbers to complete the crosses.

(i) 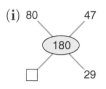 (ii) 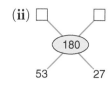 (iii) 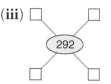 (iv) 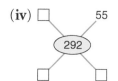 (v)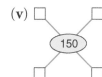

                                   Make all four   Make the other   Use four
                                   numbers the   three numbers   consecutive.
                                   same.   the same.   numbers.

(b) Use these numbers to complete both crosses.   (i) 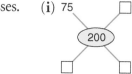   (ii)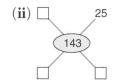

     30   38   39   42   45   49

(c) (i) Use four of these numbers.

18   25   38   42   52   62

(ii) Use four of these numbers to make a total between 150 and 160.

8   17   35   42   51   68

(iii) Two of these numbers are consecutive. The other two are double the first two.

2 Finding solutions to **several** simpler cases often helps to solve a difficult problem. By listing the results systematically you may see a pattern which leads you to the answer.

(a) Each student in a class of 20 gives a Christmas card to every other student. How many cards are given?
First find the answers for 1, 2, 3, 4 and 5 students in the class.
List the results in a table like this:

Number of students	1	2	3	4	5		20
Number of cards	0						

(b) There are 27 girls in Eileen's guide company. They all have lots of comics and decide to exchange them with one another. Each girl gives all the other girls a comic. How many comics are exchanged?

3 A group of **ten** friends all wanted to play on the see-saw in the park. They decided that, to be fair, each of them would partner each of the others for one turn. How many different pairs were there?
First try working out the number of pairs for smaller groups.

4 Chris employs 3 carpet fitters, Andrew, Craig and Michael.
They each work from 9 a.m. to 5 p.m. with 1 hour off for lunch.
They have to do these jobs on Wednesday.

Chris makes up daily work schedules for his fitters.
He started Wednesday's schedule by giving job 2 to Andrew.

(**a**) Copy and complete Wednesday's schedule.

Wednesday Schedule									
	9 am	10 am	11 am	noon	1 pm	2 pm	3 pm	4 pm	5 pm
Andrew									
Craig									
Michael									

(**b**) Here is Thursday's work.

Copy and complete the schedule for Thursday.

Thursday Schedule									
	9 am	10 am	11 am	noon	1 pm	2 pm	3 pm	4 pm	5 pm
Andrew									
Craig									
Michael									

5 Mr Timmons sells potatoes in 3 kg and 25 kg bags. He has 202 kg of potatoes in his van. How many bags of each weight could he have? Make tables like these to help you.

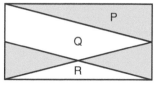

3 kg bags	
Number	Weight
1	3 kg
2	6 kg
3	9 kg

25 kg bags	
Number	Weight
1	25 kg
2	50 kg
3	

6 Ronnie uses rectangles to design coloured panels. He has divided this rectangle into regions. He has coloured it using these rules:

- regions sharing a boundary, like P and Q, **must** have different colours.
- regions which meet only at a point, like Q and R, **may** have the same colour.

(**a**) Copy these rectangles and use Ronnie's rules to colour the regions using as **few** colours as possible. Write the number of colours **needed** for each rectangle.

(**i**) 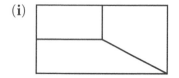   (**ii**) 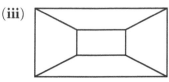   (**iii**)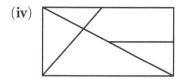

(**iv**)    (**v**) 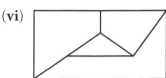   (**vi**)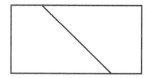

(**b**) (**i**) Using Ronnie's rules, design and colour some rectangles of your own.
   (**ii**) How many different colours are **needed** to colour a rectangle of any design?

(**c**) Ronnie's new range uses rectangles divided into regions by drawing straight lines from **edge to edge**.

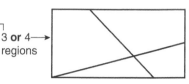

1 line makes 2 regions.   2 lines make a **maximum** of 4 regions.

Find the maximum number of regions Ronnie can make by drawing
   (**i**) 3 lines   (**ii**) 4 lines?

(**d**) (**i**) Copy and complete the table.
   (**ii**) Describe the pattern in your table.
   (**iii**) What do you **think** the maximum number of regions is for 5 lines?
   (**iv**) Check your answer to part (**iii**) by drawing. Were you correct?
   (**v**) Discuss how to draw the lines to give the maximum number of regions.

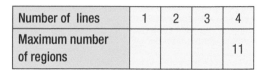

Number of lines	1	2	3	4
Maximum number of regions				11

(**e**) Colour each of your rectangles in the same way as those above. What do you notice?

7 Tom, Ally, Sue and Rehana are looking at a **mystic cube**.
Here is the cube split into layers.

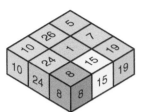
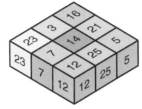
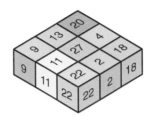

(**a**) This is the face that Tom sees.

10	24	8
23	7	12
9	11	22

Draw the faces that Ally, Sue and Rehana see.

(**b**) (**i**) For each face, add up each row and each column.
What do you notice?
(**ii**) Find the sum of the diagonals. What do you notice?

(**c**) Here are the layers of another mystic cube.
Draw all six faces of the cube and find the missing numbers.

Top layer   Middle layer   Bottom layer

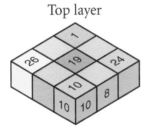
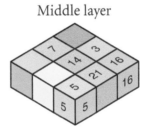
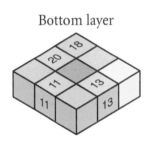

(**d**) (**i**) Here is the net of a mystic cube.
Copy it on 1 cm squared paper, fill in the missing numbers and then construct the cube.
(**ii**) Draw the three **layers** of this mystic cube.

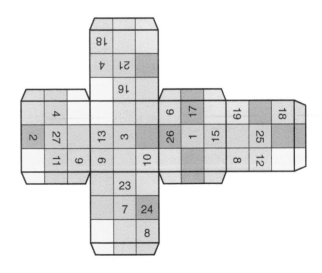

8 Secret Agent Kooper is gathering information about an enemy agent. Solve the problems below to help her.

(**a**) Use the clues in the notebook below, together with her list to find the country in which the agent is hiding.

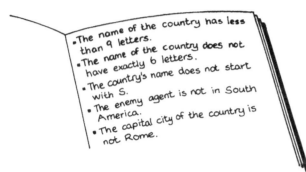

(**b**) Use the clues in the telegram, together with this list to find the town in which the agent was last spotted.

Aspatria	Biddulph	Bude	Caistor
Chard	Eye	Hibaldstow	Holt
Kilve	Milton	Tenterden	Wem
	Wetwang	Zelah	

```
NAME OF TOWN HAS MORE THAN 4 LETTERS STOP
HAS AN EVEN NUMBER OF LETTERS STOP DOES
NOT CONTAIN 3 LETTER 'A's STOP DOES NOT
START OR END WITH AN 'H' STOP
```

(**c**) Kooper knows that the agent's hideout is between 30 and 60 miles from London. Use the clues to pinpoint the distance.

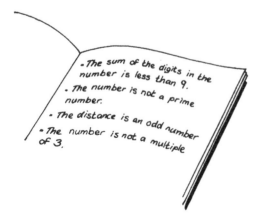

(**d**) Use the clues in this secret
file to find the agent's age
in years.

TOP SECRET

AGENT NAME : UNKNOWN

AGENT AGE : ■ AN EVEN NUMBER BETWEEN 21 AND 51
■ THE SUM OF THE DIGITS IS BETWEEN 7 AND 10
■ THE NUMBER IS NOT A MULTIPLE OF 4

(**e**) Kooper has entered some information
in the table about the agent's hideout.
Using the clues copy and complete the
table to find the address.
The crosses for the first clue have been
entered for you.

• Tay Road has houses numbered up to 10.
• The two words in the address are of different lengths.
• The house number is a square number.
• The house number is not a multiple of 5.

	House number						
Street name	2	7	14	16	22	24	25
Topper Square							
Tay Road			✗	✗	✗	✗	✗
Abbey Street							
Sand Park							

(**f**) Kooper discovers that the agent's first name is either Amanda,
Henrietta, John, Maria or Tom. The agent's second name is either
Adams, Bond, Stanhope or Trapper. Using these clues copy and
complete the table to find the agent's full name.

	First name				
Second name					

• The second name has less than 7 letters.
• The second name has 2 letters more than the first.

(**g**) The enemy agent has four assistants called Abel, Bluff, Conman and Dunn.
Study the drawings and use the clues to match the correct name to each one.

 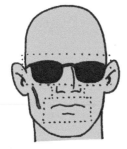  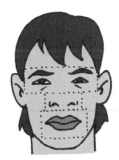

- Abel does not have a scar.
- Bluff has never had a beard.
- Dunn is not bald.
- Conman is clean-shaven and always wears glasses.

Answers

Chapter 1

Exercise 1.1

		(i)	(ii)	(iii)
1	(a)	6170	6200	6000
	(b)	18 780	18 800	19 000
	(c)	5220	5200	5000
	(d)	126 250	126 300	126 000
	(e)	5210	5200	5000
	(f)	37 510	37 500	38 000
	(g)	8400	8400	8000
	(h)	7260	7300	7000
	(i)	129 790	129 800	130 000
	(j)	1000	1000	1000

		(i)	(ii)	
2	(a) Aberdeen	180	200	
	Argyll	7020	7000	
	Dundee	60	100	
	Edinburgh	260	300	
	Fife	1340	1300	
	Glasgow	180	200	
	Highland	25 730	25 700	
	Midlothian	350	300	
	Moray	2240	2200	
	Perth	5490	5400	

		(i)	(ii)	(iii)
	(b) Aberdeen	212 100	212 000	210 000
	Argyll	91 300	91 000	90 000
	Dundee	145 700	146 000	150 000
	Edinburgh	451 700	452 000	450 000
	Fife	349 400	349 000	350 000
	Glasgow	611 400	611 000	610 000
	Highland	208 600	209 000	210 000
	Midlothian	80 900	81 000	80 000
	Moray	2200	2000	0
	Perth	134 900	135 000	130 000

		(a)	(b)	(c)
3				
	(b) Japan	8 120 000	8 100 000	8 000 000
	Germany	5 300 000	5 300 000	5 000 000
	USA	4 880 000	4 900 000	5 000 000
	Spain	2 210 000	2 200 000	2 000 000
	UK	1 490 000	1 500 000	1 000 000
	Brazil	1 480 000	1 500 000	1 000 000

Exercise 1.2

		(i)	(ii)	(iii)
1	(a)	65	65·4	65·37
	(b)	19	18·7	18·73
	(c)	21	20·7	20·75
	(d)	140	139·7	139·69
	(e)	18	18·1	18·05
	(f)	235	234·9	234·92
	(g)	675	674·6	674·60
	(h)	240	239·5	239·50
	(i)	12	12·2	12·16
	(j)	19	19·0	19·00
	(k)	36	36·2	36·21
	(l)	19	18·9	18·93

2	USA	215		3	3S1	53p
	Bahrain	128			3S2	49p
	Luxemburg	120			4S1	56p
	UK	85			4S2	31p
					5S	41p

		(a)	(b)
4	Italy	239·1	239·10
	Germany	235·4	235·35
	Belgium	221·1	221·05
	Austria	210·0	209·98
	San Marino	202·1	202·06

5 (a) 17·538   (b) 12·8997   (c) 467·281
(d) 9·112   (e) 5·003   (f) 23·2030

Exercise 1.3

1 £5887   2 786   3 £1773   4 No, 8 kg too heavy   5 256
6 (a) £456   (b) 1368
7 (a) 45 049   (b) 14 703

Exercise 1.4

1 (a) 82 300   (b) 45 000   (c) 2600
(d) 17·5   (e) 205   (f) 21 034·1
2 (a) 420   (b) 2160   (c) 72 800   (d) 43·4
(e) 1560   (f) 910   (g) 3000   (h) 43 500
(i) 122 304   (j) 70 200   (k) 630 000   (l) 186·3
(m) 30 171   (n) 140 000   (o) 8 024 400
3 £1855   4 £7.20
5 (a) €6.67   (b) €26.68   (c) €66.70   (d) €333.50
6 (a) £14.98   (b) £22.47   (c) £37.45
7 (a) 23 kg   (b) 690 kg   (c) 3450 kg
8 £7850
9 No (Cost = £7200)

Exercise 1.5

1 (a) 4   (b) 0·16   (c) 1·084   (d) 20·8   (e) 0·176
(f) 0·07
2 (a) 23   (b) 32   (c) 8   (d) 23   (e) 17
(f) 1·2   (g) 0·012   (h) 82   (i) 15   (j) 0·00002
(k) 4·8   (l) 0·06   (m) 3·2   (n) 0·0114
3 £17.18 (total)   4 £4.18
5 (a) £191.14   (b) £10 122
6 150 days   7 20 months   8 22·5 l

Exercise 1.6

1 690 km   2 10 672 miles   3 £8

4	(a)	(b)
Unleaded	£5.10	£16.77
Diesel	£4.61	£15.16
Lead	£5.45	£17.92

5 147 m
6 (a) £654.57   (b) £628.73
7 £20   8 £196.70   9 14 400
10 (a) 73 × 81   (b) 1 × 3 × 7 × 8
11 18, 19, 20   12 one

Exercise 1.7

1 3p   2 £2.65
3 (a) €9.56   (b) €22.30   (c) €48.41   (d) €34.72
4 67
5 (a) 500 g   750 g   1000 g
   0·196p/g   0·166p/g   0·158p/g
(b) 1000 g cheapest
6 (a) 4 rolls   9 rolls   12 rolls
   £0.43/roll   £0.41/roll   £0.4073/roll
(b) 12 rolls
7 (a) £15.59   (b) Smith   Reeves
         32·51 l   39·74 l
8 Chicken   5
   Fish   8

Exercise 1.8

1 (a) 1   (b) 12   (c) 93   (d) 27   (e) 430   (f) 11
2 (a) 6   (b) 126   (c) 14   (d) 16   (e) 5   (f) 28
(g) 624   (h) 15   (i) 6
3 (a) 20   (b) 33   (c) 3   (d) 11   (e) 25   (f) 19
4 (a) 340   (b) 1600   (c) 4   (d) 5
5 (a) 5 + (4 × 8)   (b) (5 + 4) × 8
(c) 6 + (15 ÷ 3)   (d) (6 + 15) ÷ 3
(e) 5 + (4 + 3) × 7   (f) 16 + 3 × (2 + 5)
(g) 24 ÷ (4 + 2) × 7   (h) 240 ÷ (5 + 7) − (4 × 3)
6 1, 3, 5

Exercise 1.9

1 (a) £27.98   (b) £55.92   (c) £89.91   (d) £65.95
(e) £66.93
2 (a) 42   (b) 96   (c) 100   (d) 8
(e) 21   (f) 69   (g) 30   (h) 14
(i) 39
3 (a) 300   (b) 600   (c) 180   (d) 90
(e) 140   (f) 600   (g) 420   (h) 180
(i) 160   (j) 360   (k) 1200   (l) 300
4 (a) 42   (b) 7050   (c) 0   (d) 115
(e) 100   (f) 53   (g) 6900   (h) 16
(i) 240   (j) 40   (k) 2500   (l) 28

Review exercise 1

		(i)	(ii)	(iii)
1	(a)	2 472 700	2 473 000	2 470 000
	(b)	8 774 200	8 774 000	8 770 000
	(c)	3 999 300	3 999 000	4 000 000
	(d)	4 798 300	4 798 000	4 800 000
		(i)	(ii)	(iii)
2	(a)	1	1·5	1·49
	(b)	5	4·7	4·75
	(c)	10	10·1	10·07
	(d)	0	0·0	0·05
	(e)	60	60·1	60·10
	(f)	100	100	100

3 21·6 m
4 £634.69
5 (a) 47·84, 47·96, 48·06
   48·09, 48·5 48·77
  (b) 0.93 secs
6 Flour   0·55 kg
  Sugar   0·42 kg
  Eggs   2
  Butter   0·56 kg
7 £48
8 £23.17
9 (a) 7400 (b) 1120 (c) 81 (d) 600 (e) 4640 (f) 7320
10 (a) 0·09 (b) 0·34 (c) 1·8 (d) 0·008 (e) 1·07 (f) 0·029
11 (a) 396 (b) 147 (c) 7 (d) 168 (e) 144 (f) 7
12 Yes, 448 kg less than 1000
13 £19.68
14 2130
15 (a) 250 g   500 g   1000 g
     0·392p/g 0·25p/g 0·158p/g
   (b) 1000 g cheapest.

Chapter 2

Exercise 2.1

1 (a) 6 (b) 12 (c) 18
2 (a) 16, 19, 22 (b) 33, 40, 47 (c) 22, 18, 14
  (d) 37, 25, 13 (e) 81, 243, 729 (f) 4, 2, 1
3 (a) add 3 (b) add 7 (c) subtract 4
  (d) subtract 12 (e) multiply by 3 (f) divide by 2
4 (a) 3, 8, 13, 18, 23, 28 (b) 8, 17, 26, 35, 44, 53
  (c) 50, 44, 38, 32, 26, 20 (d) 92, 81, 70, 59, 48, 37
  (e) 2, 4, 8, 16, 32, 64 (f) 729, 243, 81, 27, 9, 3
  (g) 1, 10, 100, 1000, 10 000, 100 000 (h) 42, 37, 32, 27, 22, 17
  (i) 0, 10, 20, 30, 40, 50 (j) 0·1, 0·6, 1·1, 1·6, 2·1, 2·6
  (k) 99, 90, 81, 72, 63, 54 (l) 7000, 6500, 6000, 5500, 5000, 4500
  (m) 5, 5, 5, 5, 5, 5 (n) 208, 104, 52, 26, 13, 6·5
  (o) 96, 48, 24, 12, 6, 3 (p) $0, \frac{1}{4}, \frac{1}{2}, \frac{3}{4}, 1, 1\frac{1}{4}$

		(i)	(ii)	(iii)
5	(a)	5	35	41
	(b)	56	31	26
	(c)	3	96	192
	(d)	10 000	0·1	0·01
	(e)	1	21	28
	(f)	2	33	65

6 (a) 15, 21, 28 (b) 20, 30, 42 (c) 16, 25, 36
7 (a) (i) 34, 55 (ii) 45, 73 (iii) 90, 146 (iv) 106, 170
  (b) add previous 2 terms
8
```
      1       5    10     10     5     1
   1     6    15     20    15     6     1
1     7    21     35    35    21     7    1
```
9 £8

Exercise 2.2

1 32, 36, 40, 44, 48, 52, 56, 60, 64, 68
2 56, 63, 70, 77, 84, 91, 98
3 (a) 18, 48, 108 (b) 81, 36, 54, 117, 162
4 (a) 36 (b) 10, 20, 30 (c) 56 (d) 15
  (e) 72 (f) 28 (g) none
5 (a) 10 (b) 36 (c) 6 (d) 30 (e) 168
6 2020 7 11·30 a.m. 8 210 m
9 (a) 15, 60, 3, 1 (b) 15, 3, 1, 9 (c) 1, 3, 15
10 (a) 1, 2, 3, 4, 6, 12 (b) 1, 2, 3, 4, 6, 8, 12, 16, 24, 48
   (c) 1, 2, 4, 5, 10, 20, 25, 50, 100 (d) 1, 5
   (e) 1, 3, 9, 27 (f) 1, 2, 4, 7, 8, 14, 28, 56

		(a)	(b)
11	(i)	1, 2, 4	4
	(ii)	1, 3, 9	9
	(iii)	1, 2, 3, 6	6
	(iv)	1, 3, 5, 15	15

12 (a) 7 (b) 8 (c) 12 (d) 8
13 24
14 (a) 4 (b) 9, 16, 25 (c) square numbers
15 (a) 9 (b) 24
16

(a)	(b)	(c)
1 × 120	1 × 400	1 × 620
2 × 60	2 × 200	2 × 310
3 × 40	4 × 100	4 × 155
4 × 30	5 × 80	5 × 124
5 × 24	8 × 50	10 × 62
6 × 20	10 × 40	20 × 31
8 × 15	16 × 25	
10 × 12	20 × 20	

Exercise 2.3

2 2, 3, 5, 7, 11, 13, 17, 19, 23, 29, 31, 37, 41, 43, 47, 53, 59, 61, 67, 71, 73, 79, 83, 89, 97

Exercise 2.4

1 (a) all 2 × 2 × 3 × 5 (b) 2, 3, and 5
2 (a) 3, 5 (b) 2, 3 (c) 3
  (d) 2, 3, 7 (e) 2, 3, 13 (f) 2
  (g) 5 (h) 2, 3, 7 (i) 2, 3, 5, 7
  (j) 2, 5, 23 (k) 3, 7, 13 (l) 2, 3, 5

Exercise 2.5

1 (a) 25 (b) 64 (c) 36 (d) 1 (e) 49
  (f) 144 (g) 0 (h) 121 (i) 10 000 (j) 225
2 $169 = 13^2$ $196 = 14^2$ $25 = 5^2$
  $81 = 9^2$ $400 = 20^2$ $10 000 = 100^2$
3 144, 121, 225, 10 000
4 256, 625
5 400, 441, 484
6 $3^3 = 27$ $4^3 = 64$ $5^3 = 125$ $6^3 = 216$
  $7^3 = 343$ $8^3 = 512$ $9^3 = 729$ $10^3 = 1000$
7 $125 = 5^3$ $8000 = 20^3$ $1 = 1^3$
  $64 = 4^3$ $1000 = 10^3$ $27 = 3^3$
8 (a) 4 (b) 36 (c) 169 (d) 216 (e) 1
  (f) 8 (g) 1000 (h) 900 (i) 360 000 (j) 64
9 (a)

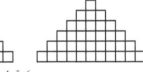

  (b) Shape no 1 2 3 4 5 6
      Tiles   1 4 9 16 25 36
  (c) (i) 25 (ii) 81 (iii) 225
  (d) Square the number.
10 (a) Students' own drawing
   (b)

Shape no	1	2	3	4
Tiles	1	8	27	64

   (c) (i) 125 (ii) 343 (iii) 1000
   (d) Cube the number.

Exercise 2.6

1 (a)
```
    37
  ×  7
   259
```
(b)
```
   344
 +  25
   369
```
(c)
```
   353
  ×  7
  2471
```
(d)
```
  5586
 −1909
  3677
```
2 (a) 816
     357
     492
  (b) 71 211
     14 106
     9813
  (c) 172 221
     242 016
     191 823
3 420
4 1p, 2p, 4p, 5p, 7p, 10p, 13p, 17p, 19p, 22p,
5 (a)
```
       7
     8   9
   6  10  5
```
(b)
```
       9
     3   0
   1      4
     5   2
       7
```
(c)
```
  15  11  20
  12      17
  19  18   9
```
6

6	13	8
11	9	7
10	5	12

7 (a) 64   (b) 2   (c) 121   (d) 225
8 31, 32, 33, 34

Review exercise 2

1   (i)   (ii)
  (a) 31, 38   add 7
  (b) 56, 45   subtract 11
  (c) 256, 1024   multiply by 4
  (d) 9, 3   divide by 3
2 (a) 17, 26, 35, 44, 53, 62   (b) 99, 90, 81, 72, 63, 54
  (c) 23, 23, 23, 23, 23, 23   (d) 3125, 625, 125, 25, 5, 1
3 (a) 8, 32, 128   (b) 9, 25, 49
4 (2) (4) (11) (13) (16) (19) (29)
5 (a) (i) 4, 8, 12, 16, 24, 32, 48   (ii) 9, 27, 45, 63
  (b) (i) 2, 4, 8, 16, 32   (ii) 2, 4, 8, 12, 16, 24, 48
6 (a) 18   (b) 20   (c) 70
7 (a) 6   (b) 9   (c) 12
8 (a) 14   (b) 117   (c) 30
9 (a) 35   (b) 24   (c) 12   (d) 40
10 (a) 25   (b) 64   (c) 100   (d) 121
  (e) 225   (f) 27   (g) 1   (h) 8
  (i) 1000   (j) 2500

Chapter 3

Exercise 3.1

2 (a) 2   (b) 1   (c) 0   (d) 2   (e) 6   (f) 4
3 a, c, d, g
4 (a) 0   (b) 0   (c) 1   (d) 1   (e) 1
  (f) 3   (g) 5   (h) 6   (i) 1   (j) 8
5 (a) 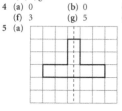   (b)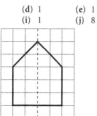

(c)   (d) none

(e)    (f) none

(g)   (h)

(i)   (j)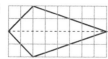

(k) none   (l)

Exercise 3.2

1 (a)   (b)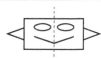

(c)   (d)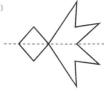

2 (a)   (b)

(c)

3 (a)   (b)   (c)

(d)   (e)   (f)

(g)   (h)   (i)

(j)   (k)   (l)

Exercise 3.3

1   **2**

3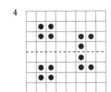

4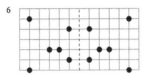

(c)

(d)

5

6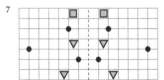

(e)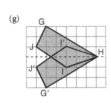

(f)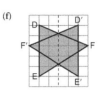

7

8

(g)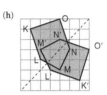

(h)

Exercise 3.5

1 a b d f g h i j k n o
2 (a) 2   (b) 4   (c) 3   (d) 6
  (e) 5   (f) 4   (g) 2   (h) 2
  (i) 4   (j) 4   (k) 2   (l) 1
  (m) 5   (n) 4   (o) 8
3   H   I   N   O   S   X   Z
    2   2   2   ∞   2   4   2
4 (a) Fits 4 ways when rotated.

9

10

Exercise 3.6

1

2

3

11

12

4

5

6

13

14

7

8

9

Exercise 3.4

1 (a)

(b)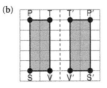

10

11

12

(c)

(d)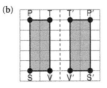

13 (a)

(b)

2 (a)

(b)

(c)

(d)

Review exercise 3

1 a d
2 (a) 4　　　　　(b) 4　　　　　(c) 0　　　　　(d) 6
3 (a)

(b)

(c)

(d)

4 (a)

(b)

(c)

5 (a) 4　　　　　(b) 2　　　　　(c) 7　　　　　(d) 6
3 (a)
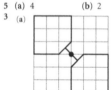
(b)
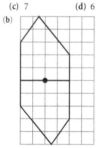

(c)

(d)

Chapter 4

Exercise 4.1

1 (a) $\times 3$　　　　　(b) $\times 5$　　　　　(c) $\times 10$
　　(d) $\times 6$　　　　　(e) $\times 9$　　　　　(f) $\times 6$
2 (a) $\frac{10}{16}$　　(b) $\frac{9}{30}$　　(c) $\frac{36}{40}$　　(d) $\frac{7}{28}$
　　(e) $\frac{5}{9}$　　(f) $\frac{30}{55}$　　(g) $\frac{30}{45}$　　(h) $\frac{12}{16} = \frac{24}{32}$
3 $\frac{1}{6} = \frac{2}{12}, \frac{3}{7} = \frac{12}{28}, \frac{5}{9} = \frac{20}{36}, \frac{7}{8} = \frac{14}{16}, \frac{12}{18} = \frac{2}{3}, \frac{45}{50} = \frac{9}{10}, \frac{6}{15} = \frac{2}{5}, \frac{15}{20} = \frac{3}{4}$
4 (a) $\frac{5}{12}, \frac{8}{12}, \frac{9}{12}, \frac{10}{12}$　　(b) $\frac{3}{4}$　　(c) $\frac{7}{24}$

Exercise 4.2

1 (a) $\frac{1}{2}$　(b) $\frac{1}{2}$　(c) $\frac{1}{3}$　(d) $\frac{5}{18}$　(e) $\frac{1}{3}$
　　(f) $\frac{1}{10}$　(g) $\frac{1}{5}$　(h) $\frac{1}{7}$　(i) $\frac{3}{4}$　(j) $\frac{3}{4}$
　　(k) $\frac{2}{7}$　(l) $\frac{1}{13}$　(m) $\frac{9}{56}$　(n) $\frac{1}{3}$
2 (a) $\frac{2}{9}$　(b) $\frac{1}{3}$　(c) $\frac{7}{12}$　(d) $\frac{3}{10}$　(e) $\frac{5}{6}$　(f) $\frac{4}{7}$
　　(g) $\frac{12}{29}$　(h) $\frac{2}{9}$　(i) $\frac{2}{7}$　(j) $\frac{5}{8}$　(k) $\frac{3}{8}$　(l) $\frac{31}{72}$
　　(m) $\frac{7}{8}$　(n) $\frac{1}{4}$　(o) $\frac{2}{3}$　(p) $\frac{1}{2}$　(q) $\frac{2}{7}$　(r) $\frac{1}{3}$
　　(s) $\frac{3}{8}$　(t) $\frac{3}{5}$　(u) $\frac{1}{25}$　(v) $\frac{47}{81}$　(w) $\frac{6}{7}$　(x) $\frac{9}{10}$
3 $\frac{1}{4}$　　4 (a) $\frac{3}{5}$　(b) $\frac{2}{5}$　　5 (a) $\frac{1}{6}$　(b) $\frac{5}{6}$

Exercise 4.3

1 (a) $\frac{1}{2}$　(b) $\frac{1}{4}$　(c) $\frac{3}{4}$　(d) $\frac{1}{2}$　(e) $\frac{1}{2}$　(f) $\frac{3}{4}$
　　(g) 1　(h) $\frac{1}{4}$　(i) $1\frac{1}{2}$　(j) $\frac{3}{4}$　(k) $\frac{3}{4}$　(l) $1\frac{1}{4}$
　　(m) $\frac{4}{5}$　(n) $\frac{2}{7}$　(o) 1　(p) $\frac{2}{9}$　(q) $1\frac{2}{3}$　(r) $2\frac{1}{4}$
2 (a) $\frac{1}{4}$ kg　(b) $1\frac{1}{5}$ kg　(c) $4\frac{2}{3}$ l　(d) $1\frac{6}{7}$ m　(e) $\frac{1}{2}$　(f) 1 m
　　(g) $5\frac{8}{9}$ miles

Exercise 4.4

1 (a) $\frac{5}{8}$　(b) $\frac{3}{8}$　(c) $\frac{7}{8}$　(d) $\frac{3}{8}$　(e) $1\frac{1}{8}$　(f) $1\frac{1}{8}$
　　(g) $\frac{1}{6}$　(h) $\frac{5}{9}$　(i) $\frac{1}{2}$　(j) $1\frac{1}{12}$　(k) $1\frac{5}{9}$　(l) $\frac{2}{15}$
　　(m) $\frac{7}{10}$　(n) $\frac{1}{5}$　(o) $1\frac{1}{10}$　(p) 0　(q) $1\frac{7}{10}$　(r) $\frac{1}{5}$
　　(s) $\frac{5}{6}$　(t) $\frac{7}{12}$　(u) $\frac{1}{12}$　(v) $\frac{1}{6}$　(w) $\frac{9}{16}$　(x) $\frac{5}{18}$
2 $\frac{9}{16}$　　3 $\frac{1}{3}$　　4 $2\frac{1}{2}$ miles

Exercise 4.5

1 (a) $1\frac{1}{6}$　(b) $\frac{1}{12}$　(c) $\frac{1}{12}$　(d) $\frac{17}{24}$　(e) $\frac{19}{24}$　(f) $\frac{7}{24}$
　　(g) $\frac{1}{10}$　(h) $\frac{9}{20}$　(i) $\frac{3}{20}$　(j) $1\frac{2}{15}$　(k) $1\frac{1}{15}$　(l) $\frac{3}{14}$
　　(m) $\frac{10}{21}$　(n) $\frac{17}{40}$　(o) $\frac{17}{30}$　(p) $\frac{23}{42}$　(q) $\frac{37}{56}$　(r) $\frac{2}{35}$
　　(s) $1\frac{1}{12}$　(t) $\frac{7}{12}$　(u) $\frac{2}{48} = \frac{1}{24}$　(v) $\frac{34}{40} = \frac{17}{20}$　(w) $\frac{2}{15}$　(x) $\frac{31}{40}$
2 (a) $1\frac{1}{12}$　(b) $\frac{2}{5}$　(c) $1\frac{7}{12}$　(d) $\frac{7}{12}$　(e) $\frac{1}{4}$　(f) $1\frac{7}{30}$
　　(g) $1\frac{5}{8}$　(h) $\frac{1}{24}$　(i) $\frac{1}{9}$　(j) $1\frac{9}{20}$　(k) $\frac{1}{7}$　(l) $\frac{59}{70}$
3 $\frac{1}{6}$　　4 No. It took $1\frac{5}{24}$ hrs.　　5 $2\frac{1}{4}$ km　　6 No. Total $1\frac{1}{12}$ l.　　7 $\frac{13}{60}$

Exercise 4.6

1 (a) 14 g　(b) 12 m　(c) 16 tonnes (d) 12 ℓ　(e) 7 p
　　(f) 78 km　(g) 14 ℓ　(h) 36 g　(i) 209 g
2 (a) 125 m　　　　　(b) £30　　　　　(c) 57 km
　　(d) 48 g　　　　　(e) 81 mm　　　　(f) £88
　　(g) 168 cm　　　　(h) £126　　　　 (i) 240 kg
　　(j) 630 g　　　　　(k) 600 m　　　　(l) 2250 g
　　(m) 800 ml　　　　(n) 800 m　　　　(o) 4500 kg
　　(p) 150 m　　　　　(q) 72 mins　　　(r) 30 days
　　(s) 40 hrs　　　　　(t) 61 days　　　 (u) £2.70
3 (a) 360　(b) 240　(c) 180　(d) 144　(e) 90　(f) 72
4 (a) £1 050 (b) £840　(c) £600　(d) £525　(e) £420　(f) £210
5 (a) 480　(b) 540　(c) 600　(d) 288　(e) 450　(f) 648
6 (a) 360　(b) 160　(c) 288
7 (a) 216°　(b) 300°　(c) 225°　(d) 160°　(e) 252°　(f) 330°

Exercise 4.7

1 (a) $\frac{5}{6}$　　　(b) 1　　　(c) $\frac{5}{8}$　　　(d) 1
　　(e) $\frac{2}{5}$　　　(f) 5　　　(g) $1\frac{3}{5}$　　(h) $2\frac{3}{4}$
　　(i) 2 kg　　(j) 6 km　　(k) $\frac{9}{10}$ cm　(l) $1\frac{1}{9}$ ℓ
　　(m) $2\frac{6}{7}$ m　(n) $2\frac{5}{8}$ miles　(o) $5\frac{5}{6}$ kg　(p) $3\frac{7}{8}$ m
2 (a) 3 kg　(b) $2\frac{3}{4}$ kg　(c) $2\frac{2}{3}$ kg　(d) $2\frac{4}{5}$ kg　(e) $3\frac{1}{3}$ kg　(f) $1\frac{9}{10}$ kg
3 (a) $10\frac{2}{3}$ ℓ　(b) $10\frac{4}{5}$ ℓ　(c) $10\frac{1}{2}$ ℓ　(d) $13\frac{1}{3}$
4 (a) $5\frac{3}{5}$ ℓ　(b) $5\frac{3}{5}$ kg　(c) $2\frac{4}{7}$ ℓ　(d) $5\frac{1}{4}$ m　(e) $5\frac{1}{4}$ hrs
5 (a) 40　　(b) 18　　(c) 40　　(d) 36　　(e) 100
　　(f) 236　(g) 35　　(h) 40　　(i) 27　　(j) 35
　　(k) 70　　(l) 91　　(m) $12\frac{1}{2}$　(n) $22\frac{1}{2}$　(o) $25\frac{2}{3}$
　　(p) $9\frac{3}{5}$　(q) $20\frac{2}{3}$　(r) $16\frac{2}{3}$　(s) $24\frac{3}{4}$　(t) $11\frac{1}{3}$

Exercise 4.8

1 (a) $\frac{1}{15}$　(b) $\frac{1}{42}$　(c) $\frac{1}{6}$　(d) $\frac{7}{16}$
　　(e) $\frac{15}{32}$　(f) $\frac{2}{7}$　(g) $\frac{1}{16}$　(h) $\frac{7}{15}$
　　(i) $\frac{21}{100}$　(j) $\frac{2}{9}$　(k) $\frac{3}{7}$　(l) $\frac{5}{36}$
　　(m) $\frac{9}{16}$　(n) $\frac{1}{2}$　(o) $\frac{2}{3}$　(p) $\frac{2}{21}$
　　(q) $\frac{49}{64}$　(r) $\frac{20}{27}$　(s) $\frac{1}{8}$　(t) $\frac{1}{3}$

2 (a) $\frac{1}{4}$　　　(b) $\frac{7}{64}$　　　(c) $\frac{1}{7}$　　　(d) $\frac{1}{18}$
　(e) $\frac{3}{7}$　　　(f) $\frac{5}{27}$　　　(g) $\frac{1}{5}$　　　(h) $\frac{1}{5}$
3 (a) $\frac{1}{15}$　　　(b) $\frac{1}{12}$　　　(c) $\frac{1}{10}$　　　(d) $\frac{1}{8}$

Exercise 4.9

1 (a) 2　　　(b) 4　　　(c) 6　　　(d) 10　　　(e) 3
2 (a) 3　　　(b) 6　　　(c) 9　　　(d) 4　　　(e) 17
3 (a) 6　　　(b) 15　　　(c) 40　　　(d) 5　　　(e) 23
　(f) 17
4 (a) 6　　　(b) 14　　　(c) 39
5 (a) 12　　　(b) 9
6 (a) $\frac{1}{4}$　　　(b) 24　　　(c) $\frac{1}{24}$

Exercise 4.10

1 (a) 27　　　(b) 60　　　(c) 120　　　(d) 78
　(e) 510　　　(f) 81　　　(g) 80　　　(h) 3
　(i) 16　　　(j) 20　　　(k) 35　　　(l) 42
　(m) 81　　　(n) 75　　　(o) 300　　　(p) 40
　(q) 49　　　(r) 70　　　(s) 63　　　(t) 144
2 (a) 40　　　(b) 16　　　(c) 24　　　(d) 125
　(e) 40　　　(f) 54　　　(g) 75

Review exercise 4

1 (a) $\frac{14}{16}$　　　(b) $\frac{64}{72}$　　　(c) $\frac{21}{36}$　　　(d) $\frac{12}{100}$
　(e) $\frac{6}{10} = \frac{9}{15}$　　(f) $\frac{6}{21} = \frac{10}{35}$　　(g) $\frac{10}{18} = \frac{25}{45}$
2 $\frac{6}{24}, \frac{9}{24}, \frac{4}{24}, \frac{10}{24}, \frac{12}{24}, \frac{7}{24};$　　　$\frac{1}{6}, \frac{1}{4}, \frac{7}{24}, \frac{3}{8}, \frac{5}{12}, \frac{1}{2}$
3 (a) $\frac{1}{3}$　　　(b) $\frac{2}{9}$　　　(c) $\frac{1}{19}$　　　(d) $\frac{3}{5}$　　　(e) $\frac{3}{4}$
4 (a) $1\frac{1}{2}$　　　(b) $\frac{3}{4}$　　　(c) $1\frac{1}{8}$　　　(d) $\frac{5}{6}$　　　(e) $\frac{8}{15}$
5 1 m　　　6 $1\frac{1}{8}$ hrs
7 (a) $\frac{11}{20}$　　　(b) $\frac{7}{30}$　　　(c) $\frac{1}{24}$　　　(d) $\frac{1}{6}$
8 $1\frac{1}{3}\,\ell$
9 (a) 52 km　　(b) 63 g　　(c) 1350 m　　(d) 150°
10 (a) $\frac{7}{18}$　　　(b) 280
11 (a) 35　　　(b) 49　　　(c) 88　　　(d) $13\frac{1}{2}$　　　(e) 14
12 25 hrs
13 (a) $\frac{5}{16}$　　　(b) $\frac{28}{81}$　　　(c) $\frac{2}{35}$　　　(d) $\frac{81}{880}$
14 $\frac{1}{5}$　　　15 43
16 (a) 56　　　(b) 36　　　(c) 810
17 48

Chapter 5

Exercise 5.1

1 (a) ∠EFH (obtuse), ∠HFG (acute), ∠EFG (straight)
　(b) ∠RTU (obtuse), ∠UTV (acute), ∠STV (obtuse)
　　　∠RTS (acute), ∠RTU ∠STU (straight)
　(c) ∠PQR ∠SPQ (obtuse), ∠QRS ∠RSP (acute)
2 (a) 3　　　(b) ∠FBC, ∠FBA, ∠ABC
3 (a) acute　　(b) acute　　(c) straight　　(d) obtuse

Exercise 5.2

2 (b) (i) 94°　　　(ii) 83°　　　(iii) 35°

Exercise 5.3

1 (a) 48°　　(b) 17°　　(c) 57°　　(d) 143°　　(e) 59°
　(f) 74°　　(g) 71°　　(h) 127°　　(i) 54°
2 (a) 90°　(b) 180°　(c) 360°　(d) 30°　(e) 6°　(f) 252°
3 (a) 3 o'clock, 9 o'clock.
　(b) No. Small hand midway between 9 and 10.
　(c) 6 o'clock.
　(d) No. Small hand midway between 12 and 1.
4 (a) (i) 55°　　(ii) 22°　　(iii) 73°
　(b) decreases by 15°
　(c) increases by 20°
　(d) $(90 - x)°$
5 (a) (i) 38°　　(ii) 53°　　(iii) 73°
　(b) decreases by 15°
　(c) increases by 20°
　(d) $(180 - x)°$

Exercise 5.4

1 (a) 70°　(b) 50°　(c) 1°　(d) 19°　(e) 72°　(f) 87°
2 (a) 60°　(b) 35°　(c) 1°　(d) 107°　(e) 168°　(f) 171°
3 (a) (i) ∠QPR　(ii) 34°
　(b) (i) ∠KMO　(ii) 69°
　(c) (i) ∠XUW　(ii) 41°
4 (a) (i) ∠EFH　(ii) 127°
　(b) (i) ∠KNL　(ii) 62°
　(c) (i) ∠RQP　(ii) 61°
　　　∠SQT　　　54°
5 (a) 52°　　(b) 33°　　(c) 60°　　(d) 72°　　(e) 60°
　(f) 45°　　(g) 45°　　(h) 30°　　(i) 21°
6 (a) ∠PQS, ∠TQR
　(b) 113°
　(c) 67°
　(d) (i) $180 - x$　(ii) $x°$
　(e) ∠PQT = ∠RQS
　　　∠PQS = ∠TQR

Exercise 5.5

2 (a) 47°　　(b) 124°　　(c) 56°　　(d) 123°　　(e) 57°
　(f) 123°　　(g) 108°　　(h) 72°　　(i) 72°　　(j) 78°
　(k) 25°　　(l) 77°　　(m) 97°　　(n) 45°　　(p) 38°
　(q) 45°　　(r) 126°　　(s) 54°　　(t) 63°　　(u) 54°
3 (a) 65°　　(b) 50°　　(c) 80°　　(d) 32°　　(e) 104°
　(f) 40°　　(g) 78°　　(h) 22°　　(i) 44°
4 (b) 4
　(c) ABC　　30, 120, 30　　180
　　　ACD　　30, 90, 60　　180
　　　ADF　　30, 90, 60　　180
　　　FED　　30, 120, 30　　180
　(d) All 180°

Exercise 5.6

1 (a) 55°　(b) 80°　(c) 100°　(d) 31°　(e) 73°
　(f) 92°　(g) 28°　(h) 69°　(i) 93°　(j) 69°
2 (a) 55°　(b) 36°　(c) 61°　(d) 70°　(e) 60°
　(f) 40°　(g) 30°
3 (a)

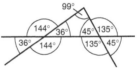

　(b)

　(c)

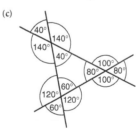

　(d)

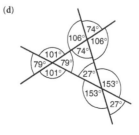

(e)

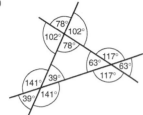

(f)

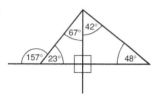

(g)

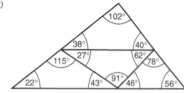

4 (a) $x = 72°$ $z = 108°$
   (b) $x = 60°$ $y = 60°$ $z = 120°$
   (c) $x = 45°$ $y = 67·5°$ $z = 135°$
   (d) $x = 36°$ $y = 72°$ $z = 144°$
   (e) $x = 30°$ $y = 75°$ $z = 150°$

Exercise 5.7

1 (d) $a = e$, $b = f$, $c = g$, $d = h$, $f = j$, $n = l$, $g = k$
2 (a) 137°   (b) 64°   (c) 55°   (d) 72°
   (e) 50°   (f) 130°   (g) 60°   (h) 120°
   (i) 100°   (j) 100°   (k) 105°   (l) 75°
   (m) 75°   (n) 105°
3

4

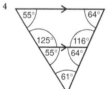

5 (a)

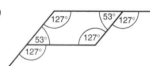

(b) same

6 113°, 67°, 113°, 67°
7 (a) $x = 60°$

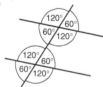

(b) $x = 45°$

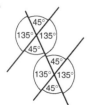

(c) $x = 45°$

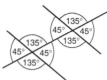

(d) $x = 20°$

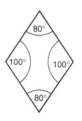

(e) $x = 30°$

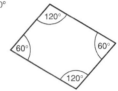

(f) $x = 18°$

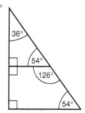

8 (a) ∠EGF = 88° meets regulations.   (b) 155°

Exercise 5.8

1 (d) $f = i$, $a = g$, $e = j$, $i = f$
2 $m = 59°$ $n = 48°$ $o = 48°$ $p = 115°$ $q = 65°$
   $r = 50°$ $s = 50°$ $t = 85°$ $u = 95°$ $v = 25°$
   $w = 49°$ $x = 65°$ $y = 60°$ $z = 55°$
3

4

5

Exercise 5.9

1 $x = 60°$ $y = 60°$ $z = 120°$
2 (a) Interior   135°   Exterior   45°
   (b) Interior   144°   Exterior   36°
   (c) Interior   150°   Exterior   30°
3 (a)

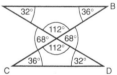

	square	pentagon	hexagon	octagon	dodecagon
No. sides	4	5	6	8	12
Angle centre	90°	72°	60°	45°	30°
Interior angle	90°	108°	120°	135°	150°
Exterior angle	90°	72°	60°	45°	30°

(b) same   (c) 40°   (d) Add to 180°   (e) 140°
(f) Interior 170°. Exterior 10°   (g) (180 − Angles at centre)

Review exercise 5

1 (a) 102°   (b) 21°
2 (a) ∠QPR, ∠RPS (complementary) ∠QPR is 43°
   (b) ∠SUT, ∠TUV and ∠SYX, ∠VUX (supplementary)
     ∠SUT = 111°, ∠VUX = 90°
3 (a) 55°   (b) 57°   (c) 120°   (d) 135°
   (e) 55°   (f) 45°   (g) 57°   (h) 68°
   (i) 62°   (j) 54°   (k) 37°   (l) 26°
4 (a) 39°   (b) 45°   (c) 46°   (d) 60°   (e) 36°
5 (a) $x = 60°$

   (b) $x = 22.5°$

7 Interior 144°   Exterior 36°

Chapter 6

Exercise 6.1

1 (a) 12°C   (b) −3°C   (c) 27°C   (d) −7°C   (e) 3°C
2 (a) −2°C   (b) −2°C   (c) −3°C   (d) 6°C   (e) 7°C
   (f) −7°C   (g) −7°C   (h) −14°C
3 (a) 14°C   (b) 8°C   (c) 17°C   (d) 7°C
4 −3°C   5 33°C
6 (a) 7°C   (b) 24°C   (c) 7°C   (d) 25°C

Exercise 6.2

1 (a) 9   (b) −5   (c) 3   (d) 2   (e) 5
   (f) 9   (g) 10   (h) −3   (i) −17   (j) 77
2 (a) 2   (b) −16   (c) −3   (d) −8   (e) −7
   (f) −9   (g) −10   (h) −17   (i) −47   (j) −77
3 (a) 7   (b) −1   (c) −8   (d) −3   (e) 7
   (f) −15   (g) −18   (h) 24   (i) −13   (j) 39

Exercise 6.3

1 (a) 22 A.D.   (b) 90 B.C.   (c) 1300 B.C.   (d) 430 B.C.
2 2402   3 £85
4 Loss £3000   5 −2: 30: 00
6 (a) −10, −9, −6, 0, 1, 5, 7, 13
   (b) −10, −6, −5, −2, 12, 13, 15
   (c) −12, −8, −6, −2, −0.5, 0, 1, 6, 7
   (d) −1, −0.9, −0.7, −0.5, −0.3, −0.1, 0.2, 0.6, 0.7, 0.8,
   (e) −2.1, −2, −1.3, −0.6, −0.4, 0.1, 0.3, 1.5, 1.8
7 (a) Ulan Bator, Moscow, Montreal, Stockholm, Budapest, Edinburgh,
     London, Casablanca, Los Angeles, Madras, Brisbane, Singapore
   (b) Singapore, Ulan Bator
   (c) 45.6°

Exercise 6.4

1 (a) 7 − 6 = 1   (b) 7   (c) −5   (d) −13
2 (a) 4   (b) −7   (c) −6   (d) −5
   (e) −18   (f) 0   (g) −9   (h) −16
   (i) −26   (j) −36   (k) −38   (l) −38
3 (a) −12   (b) 2   (c) 7   (d) −38
   (e) 33   (f) −45   (g) −15   (h) −23
   (i) −19   (j) 24   (k) −9   (l) −41
4   Tom + Val   5
   Mandy + Alan   2
   Ron + Eileen   4
   Fred + Ginger   −5
5 (a)

	−4	−2	0	2
−5	−9	−7	−5	−3
−3	−7	−5	−3	−1
−1	−5	−3	−1	1
1	−3	−1	1	3

(b)

	−10	−6	−5	21
−23	−33	−29	−28	−2
−18	−28	−24	−23	3
−7	−17	−15	−12	14
4	−6	−2	−1	25

6 (a) 1   (b) 10   (c) −5
7 (a) 7   (b) 11   (c) −23   (d) −27
   (e) −2   (f) −101   (g) −73   (h) 19
   (i) 30   (j) 0   (k) 18   (l) 85
8 (a) −2   (b) −4   (c) −11   (d) 7
   (e) −15   (f) 64
9 200
10 (a)

11 2°C

Exercise 6.5

1 (a) 6   (b) 8   (c) 12   (d) 3
   (e) 17   (f) 4   (g) 15   (h) 6
2 (a) 8   (b) 7   (c) −4   (d) 7
3 (a) 6   (b) 9   (c) 3   (d) −2
   (e) 1   (f) −4   (g) 8   (h) −6
   (i) 13   (j) 8   (k) −5   (l) 5
   (m) 0   (n) 6   (o) 10   (p) 17
4 (a) 6   (b) 11   (c) 8   (d) −2
   (e) 6   (f) −7   (g) 6   (h) −10
   (i) 16   (j) −10   (k) −16   (l) 1
   (m) −6   (n) 6   (o) −4   (p) 0
5 (a) 1   (b) 6   (c) 0
6 (a) 2   (b) −10   (c) −3   (d) 12
   (e) −6   (f) 1   (g) −2   (h) 3
   (i) 0   (j) 4   (k) 13   (l) 1
   (m) 8   (n) 0   (o) −2
7 (a) −8   (b) −7   (c) 2
8 (a) −14, −18   (b) −6, 2
   (c) −172, −165   (d) −6, −20
9 Game 1 = Meena 3, Callum 10, Callum wins
   Game 2 = Meena 8, Callum 2, Meena wins
10 (a) −3   (b) −16   (c) −25   (d) −15
   (e) −6   (f) −18
11 Multiplication

Exercise 6.6

1 (a) T   (b) T   (c) F   (d) T
   (e) F   (f) T   (g) F   (h) T
   (i) F   (j) F
2 (a) <   (b) <   (c) <   (d) <
   (e) <   (f) <   (g) >   (h) >
3 (a) <   (b) >   (c) >   (d) >
   (e) <   (f) >   (g) >   (h) <

Review exercise 6

1 (a) 252 B.C.   (b) 1930 B.C.
2 −1.5, −1, −0.9, −0.8, −0.7, −0.1, 0.4, 0.7, 1.1, 1.8
3 (a) −8   (b) −6   (c) 5   (d) −33
   (e) −157   (f) −42   (g) −68   (h) −96
4 69°
5 (a) −2°C   (b) 0°C   (c) 7°C   (d) −11°C
6 6
7 (a) −10   (b) −3   (c) 7   (d) 8
   (e) −119   (f) 696   (g) 22   (h) 457
   (i) −29   (j) −33   (k) −72   (l) −174
8 (a) T   (b) T   (c) T   (d) T
9 (a) <   (b) <   (c) >   (d) <

Chapter 7

Exercise 7.1

1 (a) A(2, 1) B(4, 3) C(3, 9) D(9, 9) E(9, 4) F(0, 2) G(7, 6) H(11, 0)
   (b) (i) 9   (ii) 7   (iii) 0   (iv) 11   (v) 3
   (c) (i) 1   (ii) 0   (iii) 6   (iv) 2   (v) 9
   (d) E and D   (e) C and D   (f) D   (g) (7, 9)
2 (a) A(1, 4) B(5, 4) C(5, 1)   (b) D(1, 1)   (c) E(5, 2½)
3 (1, 5) and (5, 1)

Exercise 7.2

1
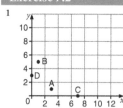

2
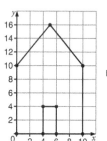

3 (a)
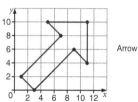
House

(b)
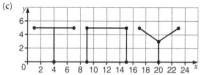
Arrow

(c)
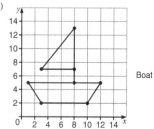
Toy

(d)
Boat

(e)
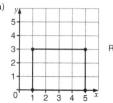
Tree

4 (a)
Rectangle

(b)
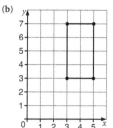
Rectangle

5
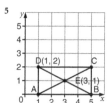

6
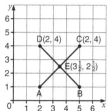

7
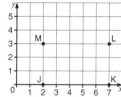

8
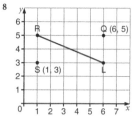

9
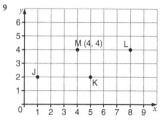

Exercise 7.3

1 A(3, 5) B(4, −2) C(−2, 1) D(−4, −2) E(0, −3)
2 F(−1, 4) G(−5, 1) H(−3, 0) I(−1, −4) J(5, −4)
3 K(5, 0) L(−5, 3) M(−3, −3) N(0, −1) P(1, −5)
4 (a) C and G. H and K. D and B. E and M. I and J.
   (b) J and K. E, F and N. H and M. L and G.
   (c) M

5 (a) Suntown   (2, 1)
   Sunrock   (4, 5)
   Sun Point   (−5, 4)
   Sunport   (1, −1)
   Suntrap   (2, −3)
   Sun Beach   (3, −4)
   Sun City   (−5, −2)
   Lighthouse   (−4, −5)
  (b) (i) Lighthouse (ii) Suntrap (iii) Sun Beach
  (c) Sunport   (d) Sun Beach

Exercise 7.4

1
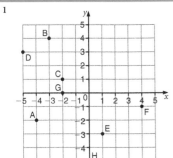

2 (a) (b)
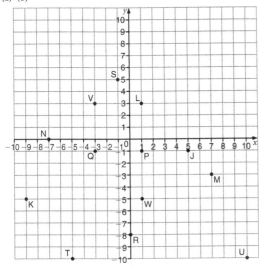

  (c) LVQP   (d) LQWJ

3 (a)
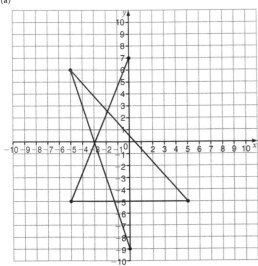

(b)
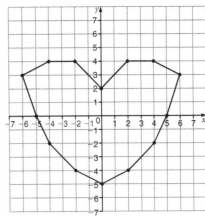

(c)
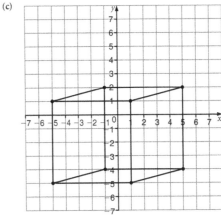

4 (a) D(−3, 2)
  (b) (0, 3) and (4, 3) or (0, −5) and (4, −5)
  (c) I(−3, 1), L(1, 4) or I(3, −7), L(7, −4)
  (d) (1, −4) (−3, 0)
  (e) (2, −3), (−2, 3)
5 (a) M(−1, 0)
  (b) M(2, 1), M(2, −3)
  (c) M($\frac{1}{2}$, $\frac{1}{2}$) or M($3\frac{1}{2}$, $-3\frac{1}{2}$)
  (d) M(−1, −2)
  (e) M(0, 0)
6 (a) M(−1, 8)
  (b) N(−1, 2)
7 (a) T(−1, −8)
  (b) U(−1, −4)
8 (1, −2), (5, −8)
9 (a) R(−1, −5), S(5, −3)
  (b) (1, −1)

Exercise 7.5

1 (a) A′(1, −2) B′(5, −4) C′(−3, −1) D′(−5, −3) E′(0, −4) F′(−5, 0)
  (b) Same x-coordinate.
  (c) Same point.
2 (a) A′(−1, 2) B′(−5, 4) C′(3, 1) D′(5, 3) E′(0, 4) F′(5, 0)
  (b) Same y-coordinate.
3 (a) P′(5, −1) Q′(3, −3) R′(−2, −3) S′(1, 4) T′(−3, 0) U′(−5, 4)
4
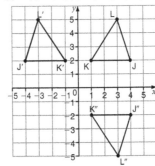

5

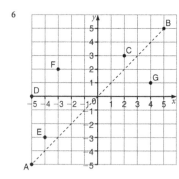

6

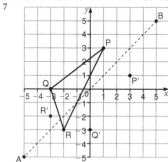

C'(3, 2) D'(0, −5) E'(−3, −4) F'(2, −3) G'(1, 4)

7

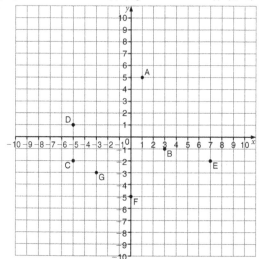

P'(3, 1) Q'(0, −3) R'(−3, −2)

Review exercise 7

1 P(3, −4) Q(3, 3) R(−3, −4) S(−3, −4) T(−3, 0) U(−5, −3)
(b) Q and P. R, S and T.
(c) R and Q. S and P.
(D) PQRS   **(e)** (0, ½)   **(f)** (0, −4)
2

(c) H(0, 1)   (d) J(0, −2)
3 (2, −5), (−3, −4), (−2, 1)
4 (a) J'(2, 3) K'(3, −4) L'(5, 0) M'(6, −6) N'(−57, 29)
   (b) J'(−2, −3) K'(−3, 4) L'(−5, 0) M'(−6, 6) N'(57, −29)
5

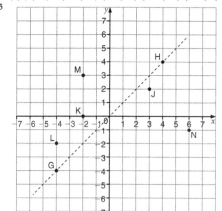

(c) J'(2, 3) K'(0, −2) L'(−2, −4) M'(3, −2) N'(−1, 6)
6

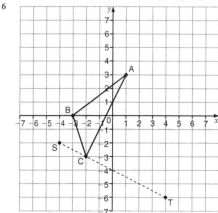

A'(−5, −9) B'(−5, −4) C'(−2, −3)

Chapter 8

Exercise 8.1

1 19·5 cm, 195 mm, 19 cm 5 mm
2 (a) 4·2 cm   (b) 18·9 cm   (c) 0·6 cm   (d) 8·5 cm
   (e) 15·9 cm   (f) 500 cm   (g) 845 cm   (h) 4750 cm
   (i) 87·5 cm   (j) 565·9 cm
3 (a) 58 mm   (b) 873 mm   (c) 7 mm   (d) 43 mm
   (e) 8 000 000 mm (f) 5000 mm   (g) 8450 mm   (h) 47 500 mm
   (i) 47 000 000 mm (j) 4070 mm
4 (a) 4·19 m   (b) 90·45 m   (c) 8·04 m   (d) 10·899 m
   (e) 8·043 m   (f) 4·002 m   (g) 5·658 m   (h) 0·525 m
   (i) 0·23 m   (j) 0·05 m   (k) 0·5126 m   (l) 0·999 m
   (m) 0·057 m   (n) 0·001 m   (o) 0·005 m
7 (a) 8 km   (b) 0·625 km   (c) 0·086 km   (d) 0·004 km
   (e) 58·971 km
8 (a) 9 cm   (b) 4 cm   (c) 602 cm   (d) 801 cm
   (e) 2 cm   (f) 9 cm   (g) 0 cm   (h) 87 cm
9 (a) 4 m   (b) 97 m   (c) 5527 m   (d) 9 m
   (e) 7 m   (f) 99 001 m   (g) 90 m   (h) 6986 m
10 25·3 cm, 2 m 53 mm 2503 mm 251·3 cm, 2·53 m

Exercise 8.2

1 (a) 212·5 mm   (b) 30 350 mm   (c) 420 mm
2 (a) 36·2 m   (b) 46 m   (c) 35·24 m
3 2 × (length + breadth)
4 (a) 22 m   (b) 40·02 m   (c) 58·4 m
5 (a) 2·07 m   (b) 16 mm   (c) 1·18 m   (d) 11·3 cm
6 (a) 77   (b) £211.75
7 (a) 38   (b) £87.92
8 899

Exercise 8.3

2 (a) tonnes   (b) grammes   (c) mg
  (d) mg   (e) kg   (f) kg
3 (a) 8·5 g   (b) 6·042 g   (c) 0·587 g
  (d) 0·001 g   (e) 34 002 g   (f) 6 800 000 g
4 (a) 3200 mg   (b) 6794 mg   (c) 42 640 mg
  (d) 320 mg   (e) 1 000 000 mg   (f) 1 000 000 000 mg
5 (a) 8·625 kg   (b) 14·025 kg   (c) 8·25 kg
  (d) 0·54 kg   (e) 0·000 025 kg   (f) 3100 kg
6 (a) 8·625 t   (b) 0·000 000 5 t   (c) 0·000 025 t
  (d) 0·001 t   (e) 0·000 005 25 t   (f) 0·09 t

Exercise 8.4

1 286·8 kg
2 340·3 kg
3 2450 kg
4 76·4 kg
5 No, 5 tonnes overweight.
6 (a) 9750 kg   (b) 195   (c) £1330
7 No, 895 kg too heavy.

Exercise 8.5

1 (a) 6·5 ℓ   (b) 5·042 ℓ   (c) 0·655 ℓ
  (d) 3·657 ℓ   (e) 12·689 ℓ   (f) 5200 ℓ
2 (a) 5·785 m³   (b) 0·0253 m³   (c) 0·00505 m³
  (d) 120·673 m³   (e) 0·00001 m³   (f) 0·25 m³
3 (a) 5600 mℓ   (b) 8165 mℓ   (c) 235 mℓ
  (d) 65 500 mℓ   (e) 8 025 000 mℓ   (f) 6125 mℓ
4 (a) 4500 cm³   (b) 7325 cm³   (c) 125 cm³
  (d) 5005 cm³   (e) 25 cm³   (f) 0·5 cm³
5 (a) 100   (b) 1 000 000   (c) 1 000 000 ÷ 1000
6 (a) 4·5 ℓ   (b) 3   (c) £5.25
7 (a) 60   (b) 19·8 ℓ   (c) No, needs 21 ℓ
8 (a) 625 mins   (b) 1 200 m³
9 (a) 20 000 ℓ   (b) £12 460   (c) 1·5 ℓ (more per penny)
10 (a) 41 950 mℓ   (b) 45

Review exercise 8

1 (a) 12·4 cm   (b) 12·474 km   (c) 125 mm
2 462 m
3 (a) 9   (b) 15 cm
4 0·0689 kg
5 (a) 534   (b) Safe. (Only has 12 015 t on bridge)
6 (a) 75   (b) 21·75 ℓ   (c) 5437·5 kg
7 (a) (i) 500 m³ (ii) 500 000 ℓ   (b) 500 tonnes
8 (a) 955   (b) ·£350

Chapter 9

Exercise 9.1

1 (a) 20 cm   (b) 24 cm   (c) 21 cm
2 (a) 200 cm   (b) 360 cm   (c) 100 cm   (d) 125 cm
3 (a) 300 × 200 cm   (b) 750 × 525 cm
4 HQ to :   A   15 m   B   6·6 m
            C   6 m   D   6·4 m
            E   4·8 m   F   2·8 m
            G   7·6 m
5 6 m
6 Yes. Car 2·4 m × 1·35 m. Garage 3·6 m × 2·4 m

Exercise 9.2

1 (a) 49·85 m   (b) 1·93 m   (c) 200 m   (d) 45 000 m
  (e) 32 m   (f) 190 050 m   (g) 36 800 m   (h) 9 073 900 m
2 (a) 4·5· km   (b) 9·7 km   (c) 3·45 km   (d) 0·05 km
  (e) 820 km   (f) 456 km
3 (a) 700 000 cm   (b) 7 km
4 (a) 1 km   (b) 6 km   (c) 2 km   (d) 3·75 km
5 (a) 2 km   (b) 2·5 km   (c) 1·5 km   (d) 2·75 km
6 A → B   400 m
   B → C   550 m
   C → D   320 m
   D → E   550 m
   E → F   250 m
7 (a) 104 cm   (b) No, only 2·7 m²
8 (a) 9 km   (b) 2 hrs 15 mins
9 332·5 km
10 360 cm   11 675 cm

Exercise 9.3

1 (a) 2·3 cm   (b) No. 92 cm long
2 Yes
3 (a)

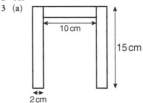

4 (a) (i)

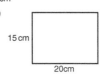

  (ii)

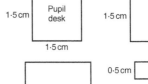

5 (a) 10 cm by 8 cm   (b) 25 cm by 20 cm
  (c) 0·5 cm by 0·4 cm
6 (a) (i) 60 cm × 35 cm   (ii) 24 cm × 14 cm   (iii) 1·2 cm × 0·7 cm
  (b) 1 : 25
7 1 : 50 (b)
8 (a) 4·1 km   (b) Alliston
  (c) Alliston and Macklestone   (d) South and North farm

Exercise 9.4

1 (a) 1 : 7 (35 cm)   (b) 1 : 25 (100 cm)
2 (a) 1 : 14   (b) 112 cm
3 1 : 600
4 (a) 128 cm   (b) 80 cm
5 (a) 1 : 150   (b) 9 m
6 1 : 50
7 Yes   Height scale   1 : 2500
  (same scale)   Width scale   1 : 2500

Exercise 9.5

4 (a)   (b)   (c)

  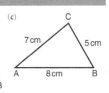

Exercise 9.5

6

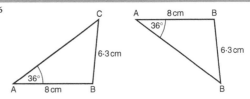

Exercise 9.6

1 (a) 46·2 m   (b) 369·2 m   (c) 190·5 m
2 32 m
3 (a) 60°   (b) 139 m
4 (a)   (b) 25 m

5 150 m
6 137·8 m

Exercise 9.7

1 (a) 135°   (b) 90°
2 (a) NW   (b) NE   (c) SE
3 (a)   (b) 233°

4 (a)   (b) 325°

5 (a)   (b) 040°

6 (a)   (b) 125°

7 Start → 1   117°
     1 → 2   084°
     2 → 3   018°
     3 → 4   307°
     4 → 5   205°
     5 → Start 258°

Exercise 9.8

1 050° 1·9 km
2 Modan   100°   400 m
  Heatherly 072°   450 m
3 A → B   700 m   020°
  B → C   260 m   072°
  C → D   500 m   090°
  D → E   270 m   109°
  E → F   770 m   258°
  F → G   700 m   215°
4 (a) 054°   4·9 km
  (b) 125°   4·4 km
  (c) 071°   6 km
5 (a) 040°   (b) 077°   (c) 130°
  (d) 257°   (e) 220°   (f) 310°

Exercise 9.9

1

2 (a)   (b) 10·8 cm (10·8 km)

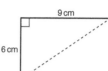

3 (a)   (b) 5·8 cm

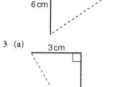

4 (a) 7·8 cm   (b) 5·5 km
5 (a)   (b) 6·6 km

Review exercise 9

1 (a) 225 cm   (b) 110 cm
2 5·75 km   3 30 cm   4 $\frac{1}{50}$
5 54·6 cm   7 29·4 m·
8 A → B   3 km   070°
  B → C   3·25 km 095°
  C → D   2·5 km   230°
  D → E   2·75 km 205°
  E → F   3·5 km   310°

Chapter 10

Exercise 10.1

1 (a) $2x$ (b) $3m$ (c) $3a$ (d) $4t$
  (e) $6b$ (f) $7g$ (g) $5k$ (h) $8h$
2 (a) $6a$ (b) $9b$ (c) $24c$ (d) $12m$
  (e) $12e$ (f) $40f$ (g) $5t$ (h) $7e$
  (i) $15a$ (j) $27v$ (k) $33b$ (l) $39f$
  (m) $23p$ (n) $29r$ (o) $17x$ (p) $31h$
  (q) $159k$ (r) $70u$ (s) $66k$ (t) $24p$
3 (a) $11b$ (b) $2t$ (c) $2h$ (d) $2k$
  (e) $17g$ (f) $2p$ (g) $9d$ (h) w
  (i) $37x$

Exercise 10.2

1 (a) $5e + y$ (b) $8a + 2b$ (c) $6t + 6y$ (d) $10g + 4f$
  (e) $11n + 6v$ (f) $7b + 12g$ (g) $5y + 12w$ (h) $20k + 6s$
2 (a) $4b + 4a$ (b) $5a + b$ (c) $9p - 2a$ (d) $10e - 8f$
  (e) $5y + 3$ (f) $14x + 2a$ (g) $74w + 10$ (h) $52z + 67a$
  (i) $a + 6b$ (j) $6e - 5f$ (k) $2f + 7$ (l) $9 + a$
  (m) $5w + 21$ (n) $61k + 39t$ (o) $52u - 51p$
3 (a) $7a + 4b + 7$ (b) $10r + 6s + 5u$
  (c) $11p + 11r + 8q$ (d) $8e + 10i + 7$
  (e) $8u + 8d + 6e$ (f) $9v + 5a + 8$
  (g) $6a + 5b + 6c$ (h) $10t + 4s + 6$
  (i) $10p + 5q + 5r$ (j) $3a + 11e + 14i$
  (k) $10k + 11t + 10y$ (l) $13p + 11i + 12g$
  (m) $22f + 12b + 7v$ (n) $27p + 18u + 70$
4 (a) $f + 3v$ (b) $2d + 3$ (c) $4e + 6g$ (d) $4p + 22k$
  (e) $9z + 15h$ (f) $7t + 7$ (g) $3a + 2b$ (h) $2f + 3$
  (i) $2y + h$ (j) $5t$ (k) $5r + 11s$ (l) a
  (m) $3y + 3$ (n) 0

Exercise 10.3

1 (a) $a + b + c$ (b) $3a + 6b - c$ (c) $5b - 3c + a$
$= 3 + 2 + 1$ $= 9 + 12 - 1$ $= 10 - 3 + 3$
$= 6$ $= 20$ $= 10$
2 (a) 10 (b) 19 (c) 8 (d) 0
(e) 2 (f) 30 (g) 38 (h) 0
(i) 5 (j) 59 (k) 13 (l) 1
3 (a) 32 (b) 16 (c) 20 (d) 26
(e) 4 (f) 44 (g) 40 (h) 2
(i) 17 (j) 0 (k) 35 (l) 5
4 (a) 80 (b) 0 (c) 100 (d) 4
(e) 7 (f) 15 (g) 3·5 (h) 1
(i) 0
5 (a) 126 (b) 54 (c) 30 (d) 180
(e) 360 (f) 60 (g) 3750 (h) 12 350
(i) various

Exercise 10.4

1 (a) $A = 35$ (b) $V = 36$ (c) $P = 0.55$
(d) $S = 4$ (e) $P = 16$ (f) $K = 3.5$
(g) $D = 30$ (h) $V = 60$ (i) $F = 77$
(j) $A = 48$ (k) $P = 120$ (l) $V = \frac{4}{3}$
2 (a) $F = 6000$ (b) $P = 18$ (c) $V = 70$
(d) (i) $K = 32$ (ii) $K = 104$ (iii) 209.6
(e) $T = 90$ (f) $P = 17\,000$

Review exercise 10

1 (a) $3a$ (b) $4g$ (c) $7z$
(d) $5y$ (e) $9k$ (f) $12b$
(g) $12t$ (h) $7d$ (i) $15e$
2 (a) $7a + 2b$ (b) $8w + 2x$ (c) $7p + 2m$
(d) $4x + 10q$ (e) $4w + 3z$ (f) $7a + 8k$
(g) $2h$ (h) $12j$ (i) 0
(j) $2b + 3a$ (k) $y + 2x$ (l) $2r$
(m) $2e + 2t$ (n) $w + 2z$ (o) a
3 (a) 7 (b) 7 (c) 0
(d) 15 (e) 20 (f) 10
(g) 15 (h) 24 (i) 0
4 (a) 6 (b) 4 (c) 9 (d) 4
5 (a) 24 (b) 59

Chapter 11

Exercise 11.1

1 (a) $\frac{53}{100}$ 0·53 (b) $\frac{81}{100}$ 0·81 (c) $\frac{17}{100}$ 0·17 (d) $\frac{21}{100}$ 0·21
(e) $\frac{87}{100}$ 0·87 (f) $\frac{57}{100}$ 0·57 (g) $\frac{3}{100}$ 0·03
2 (a) 51% 0·51 (b) 19% 0·19 (c) 17% 0·17 (d) 41% 0·41
(e) 33% 0·33 (f) 11% 0·11 (g) 37% 0·37
3 (a) 47% $\frac{47}{100}$ (b) 27% $\frac{27}{100}$ (c) 87% $\frac{87}{100}$ (d) 17% $\frac{17}{100}$
(e) 91% $\frac{91}{100}$ (f) 7% $\frac{7}{100}$ (g) 7·9% $\frac{79}{1000}$

4

Percentage	Fraction	Decimal
23%	$\frac{23}{100}$	0·23
59%	$\frac{59}{100}$	0·59
67%	$\frac{67}{100}$	0·67
13%	$\frac{13}{100}$	0·13
37%	$\frac{37}{100}$	0·37
81%	$\frac{81}{100}$	0·81

Exercise 11.2

1 (a) $\frac{3}{5}$ (b) $\frac{4}{5}$ (c) $\frac{11}{20}$
(d) $\frac{31}{50}$ (e) $\frac{18}{25}$ (f) $\frac{1}{25}$
(g) $\frac{3}{25}$ (h) $\frac{13}{25}$ (i) $\frac{4}{25}$
(j) $\frac{2}{25}$ (k) $\frac{7}{200}$ (l) $\frac{19}{20}$
(m) $\frac{31}{200}$ (n) $\frac{33}{50}$ (o) $\frac{3}{8}$
(p) $\frac{5}{8}$ (q) $\frac{7}{8}$ (r) $\frac{1}{8}$
(s) $\frac{1}{40}$ (t) $\frac{1}{200}$ (u) $\frac{3}{200}$
2 water $\frac{7}{25}$ tomato $\frac{14}{25}$ oil $\frac{11}{100}$ spices $\frac{1}{20}$
3 sunbathing $\frac{11}{50}$ swimming $\frac{7}{50}$ shopping $\frac{13}{50}$ scuba diving $\frac{3}{40}$ sport $\frac{9}{40}$
sightseeing $\frac{33}{400}$
4 savings $\frac{21}{500}$ current account $\frac{17}{500}$ credit card $\frac{33}{200}$
5 Golden Wonder $\frac{1}{8}$ Vanessa $\frac{4}{125}$ Desiree $\frac{51}{200}$ Maris Piper $\frac{29}{400}$

Exercise 11.3

1

Percentage	Fraction	Decimal
50%	$\frac{1}{2}$	0·5
25%	$\frac{1}{4}$	0·25
75%	$\frac{3}{4}$	0·75
1%	$\frac{1}{100}$	0·01
10%	$\frac{1}{10}$	0·1
20%	$\frac{1}{5}$	0·2
40%	$\frac{2}{5}$	0·4
60%	$\frac{3}{5}$	0·6
80%	$\frac{4}{5}$	0·8
$33\frac{1}{3}$%	$\frac{1}{3}$	0·333
$66\frac{2}{3}$%	$\frac{2}{3}$	0·667
5%	$\frac{1}{20}$	0·05

2 (a) 50% (b) 25% (c) 75%
(d) $33\frac{1}{3}$% (e) 20% (f) 60%
(g) 10% (h) $66\frac{2}{3}$% (i) 33·3%
(j) 75% (k) 80% (l) 1%
2 (a) $\frac{1}{10}$ 0·1 (b) $\frac{4}{5}$ 0·8 (c) $\frac{1}{2}$ 0·5
(d) $\frac{1}{3}$ 0·333 (e) $\frac{3}{4}$ 0·75 (f) $\frac{2}{5}$ 0·4

Exercise 11.4

1 (a) £47 (b) £500 (c) £4.80
(d) 40·4 g (e) 64 kg (f) 5·2 ml
(g) 22·6 km (h) £9.04 (i) £9.60
(j) 21 kg (k) £20.80 (l) 1004 kg
2 £48
3 £0.54
4 306 km

Exercise 11.5

1 (a) 14 g (b) 61·6 km (c) £50.40
(d) 574 cm (e) 28·63 m (f) 31·22 kg
2 (a) 88 mℓ (b) £28.80 (c) 126 g (d) 21·6 mm
(e) £1.80 (f) £47.34 (g) 408 km (h) 9·68 cm
3 (a) £9.40 (b) £12.80 (c) £7.28 (d) £19.20
2 (a) 7·65 g (b) 6·48 g (c) 11·25 g (d) 19·98 g

Exercise 11.6

1 (a) £228 (b) 195 cm (c) 420 cm
(d) £222.90 (e) £2472 (f) 283·5 ℓ
2 (a) £102 (b) 336 g (c) 84·6 m
(d) 132 km (e) £24.75 (f) 493 g
(g) 301·5 mℓ (h) £20.30 (i) £1.29
3 87·5 g
4 45% of 620
5 pizza 18 pasta 42 burger 6 curry 54
6 (a) £40.25 (b) £6.30 (c) £136.50 (d) £94.50
7 (a) £14.35 (b) £18.55 (c) £15.40

Exercise 11.7

1 (a) £81.60 (b) £61.20 (c) £38.25 (d) £33.15
2 (a) £5600 (b) £5560 (c) £6640
3 (a) £336 (b) £567 (c) £682.50
4 (a) 81 g (b) 121·5 g (c) 162 g (d) 337·5 g (e) 101·25 g
5 (a) £5520 (b) £141 000 (c) £1140 (d) £540 (e) £430.55
6 (a) 7·2 g (b) 11·25 g (c) 14 g (d) 3·255 g
7 (a) £98.70 (b) £376 (c) £2991.55
8 £46.53

Exercise 11.8

1 (a) 100·8 ml (b) £52.90 (c) 29·4 ml (d) £49.92
(e) 148·5 m (f) £72.25 (g) £456 (h) 5·04 kg
(i) £1.56 (j) 93·75 m (k) £3.38 (l) £1.43
2 starch 80 g sugar 32·5 g fat 37·5 g fibre 18·75 g
3 water 1·02 ℓ orange juice 0·12 ℓ grape juice 0·09 ℓ
apple juice 0·27 ℓ

Exercise 11.9

1 (a) 110%   (b) 120%   (c) 135%   (d) 150%
   (e) 103%   (f) 122·5%   (g) 117·5%
2 (a) 75%   (b) 70%   (c) 45%   (d) 40%
   (e) 72%   (f) 24%   (g) 87½%
3 (a) £75.40   (b) £56.55   (c) £34.19   (d) £31.20
4 (a) £53.76   (b) £31.92   (c) £84   (d) £105.84
   (e) £175.28
5 (a) £11.55   (b) £145.53 (c) £274.12
6 (a) £81.70   (b) £223.52 (c) £319
7 (a) £87.20   (b) £947.10 (c) £7553.70
8 (a) 13 338   (b) 1742   (c) 11 115
9 (a) £119.85 (b) £246.75 (c) £98.70

Exercise 11.10

1 (a) 45%   (b) 35%   (c) 26%   (d) 64%
   (e) 65%   (f) 25%   (g) 45%   (h) 35%
   (i) 33⅓%   (j) 60%   (k) 90%   (l) 87·5%
   (m) 66⅔%   (n) 62%
2 (a) Science 93⅓%   French 65%   English 64%   Maths 60%
   (b) Maths French English Science

Exercise 11.11

1 Ritz 10%   Carlton 28%   Balmoral 20%   North 4%
2 (a) 180
   (b) Sorrento 30%   Positano 35%   Amalfi 10%   Capri 25%
3 Barbecue 15%   Palace 33⅓%   Zoo 10%   Dungeon 41⅔%
4 Chemistry 37½%   Biology 40%   Physics 22½%
5 Cars 63%   Vans 16%   Trucks 15%   Buses 6%
6 Cola 21·4%   Water 51·4%   Lemonade 15·7%   Limeade 11·4%
7 14·3%

Review exercise 11

1

Percentage	Fraction	Decimal
60%	$\frac{3}{5}$	0·6
10%	$\frac{1}{10}$	0·1
80%	$\frac{4}{5}$	0·8
33⅓%	$\frac{1}{3}$	0·333
20%	$\frac{1}{5}$	0·2
1%	$\frac{1}{100}$	0·01

2 (a) $\frac{24}{25}$ (b) $\frac{11}{20}$ (c) $\frac{3}{20}$ (d) $\frac{3}{40}$ (e) $\frac{1}{200}$ (f) $\frac{1}{8}$
3 (a) 0·43   (b) 0·08   (c) 0·333   (d) 0·007   (e) 0·069   (f) 0·095
4 (a) £89   (b) 27 kg   (c) 110 ml   (d) 34 cm
5 (a) £22.40 (b) 684 g   (c) 10·56 kg
6 (a) 110%   (b) 125%   (c) 133%   (d) 155%
7 (a) 70%   (b) 55%   (c) 88%   (d) 19%
8 £91
9 (a) £419.25 (b) £490.20
10 (a) £305.50 (b) £641.55 (c) £401.85
11 £96.75
12 (a) English 91⅔%   French 96%   German 93¾%   Latin 97½%
   (b) Latin French German English
13 (a) 70%   (b) 20%   (c) 95%

Chapter 12

Exercise 12.1

1

equilateral triangle	regular	3	3
quadrilateral	not regular	4	4
hexagon	regular	6	6
square	regular	4	4
pentagon	not regular	5	5
pentagon	regular	5	5

2 (a) heptagon   (b) octagon   (c) nonagon   (d) decagon
   (e) dodecagon

Exercise 12.2

1 (a) (i) GHI, QSR, TUV
       (ii) YAZ, DBC, KLM, DEF, PQR, SUT, XVW, PNO
       (iii) ABC, JKL, MNO, GEF, HIJ
   (b) (i) ABC, DEF, GHI, XVW, BCD, SUT, PNO, QSR, TUV
       (ii) MNO, PQR, MKL
       (iii) JKL, YAZ, GEF, HIJ
   (c) YAZ

2

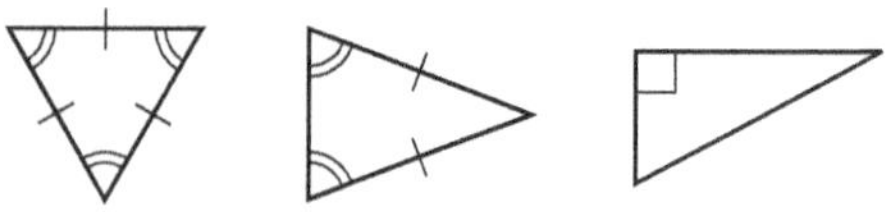

   (a) an equilateral triangle
       • has 3 axes of symmetry
       • fits its outline 3 ways, so it has rotational symmetry of order 3
   (b) an isosceles triangle
       • has 1 axis of symmetry
       • has rotational symmetry of order 1
   (c) a right angled triangle
       • has 0 axes of symmetry
       • has rotational symmetry of order 1

3 $a = 59°$ $b = 40°$ $c = 103°$ $d = 42°$ $e = 37°$
4 65°, 50°   42°, 96°   70°, 70°   76°, 76°   38°, 38°   45°, 45°
5

	Acute angle	Obtuse angle	Right angle
Isosceles	M	P	SN
Scalene	T	LR	Q

6 $a = 40°$ $b = 72°$ $c = 40°$
   $d = 68°$ $e = 70°$ $f = 40°$
   $g = 110°$ $h = 35°$ $i = 35°$
   $j = 39°$ $k = 78°$ $l = 63°$
   $m = 82°$ $n = 80°$ $p = 100°$
   $q = 20°$ $r = 40°$ $s = 40°$

Exercise 12.3

1 (a) 14 cm²   (b) 9 cm²   (c) 20 cm²
   (d) 16·5 cm²   (e) 9 cm²   (f) 14·4 cm²
   (g) 55 cm²   (h) 29·4 cm²   (i) 15·75 cm²
   (j) 15 cm²   (k) 42·5 cm²   (l) 21 cm²

Exercise 12.4

1

	Angle A	Angle B	Angle C	Angle D	A + B + C + D
Rhombus	115°	65°	115°	65°	360°
Kite	95°	65°	95°	105°	360°
Parallelogram	35°	145°	35°	145°	360°
Trapezium	52°	128°	107°	73°	360°

2 (a) 360°   (b) 360°
3 The sum of the angles of a quadrilateral is 360°.
4 $a = 115°$ $b = 67°$ $c = 65°$ $d = 107°$
5 The sum of the angles of the yellow triangle is 180°.
   The sum of the angles of the green triangle is 180°.
   Hence the sum of the angles in a quadrilateral ABCD is 360°.

Exercise 12.5

1 (b) • equal   • equal   • equal   • diagonals   • 90°
       • bisect   • 4   • turn, 4
2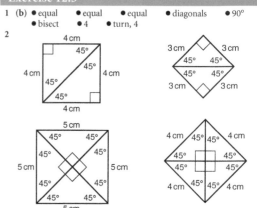

3

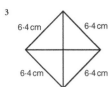

6·4 cm   6·4 cm

6·4 cm   6·4 cm

4

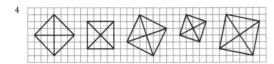

5 (a)

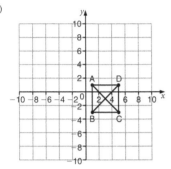

(i) O = (5, 1)
(ii) C = (3, −1)

(b)

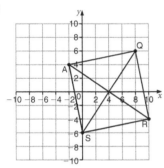

(i) S = (0, −6)
(ii) T = (4, 0)

(c)

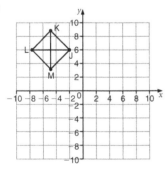

(i) K = (−5, 9)
    M = (−5, 3)
(ii) N = (−5, 6)

(d)

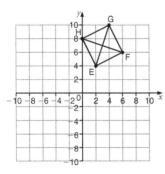

(i) F = (6, 6)
    H = (0, 8)
(ii) I = (3, 7)

(e)

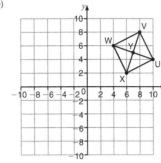

V = (8, 8)
W = (4, 6)
X = (6, 2)

Exercise 12.6

1 (b) ● equal   ● equal   ● equal   ● diagonals   ● two
● one half   ● two

2

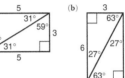

(a)   5
31°
59°
3   59°   3
31°
5

(b)   3
63°
6   27°   6
27°
63°
3

(c)   8
37°
6   53°   53°   6
37°
8

4 (a) isosceles triangles   **(b) (i)** DĈE = 40°   **(ii)** DÊC = 100°

(c)

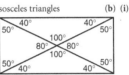

40°   40°
50°   50°
100°
80°   80°
100°
50°   50°
40°   40°

5

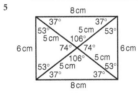 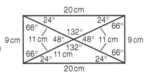

8 cm
37°   37°
53°   5 cm   53°
5 cm   106°
6 cm   74°   74°   6 cm
106°   5 cm
53°   5 cm   53°
37°   37°
8 cm

20 cm
24°   24°
66°   132°   66°
9 cm   11 cm   48°   48°   11 cm   9 cm
132°
66°   11 cm   66°
24°   24°
20 cm

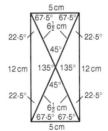

5 cm
67·5°   67·5°
6½ cm
22·5°   22·5°
45°
12 cm   135°   135°   12 cm
45°
22·5°   22·5°
6½ cm
67·5°   67·5°
5 cm

6

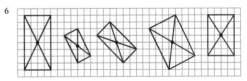

7 (a)

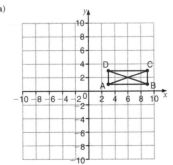

(i) D = (3, 3)
(ii) E = (6, 2)

(b)

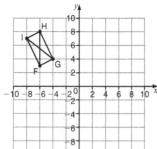

(i) I = (−8, 7)
(ii) J = (−6, 5½)

(c)

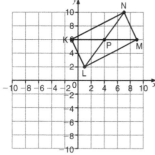

M = (9, 6)
N = (7, 10)

(d)

S = (−2, −8)
I = (−4, −7)

8 (a) (i) 18° (ii) 63° (b) (i) 35° (ii) 80°
(c) (i) 22° (ii) 90° (d) (i) 69° (ii) 94°

Exercise 12.7

1 (b) ● all, equal ● opposite ● bisect, 90°
● bisect ● 2 ● half turn, 2

2 (a)

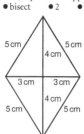

3

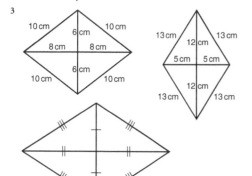

4

5 (a) (b) (c)

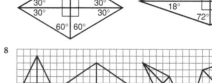

(d)

7 (a) (b)

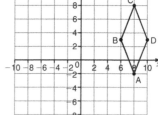

8

9 (a)

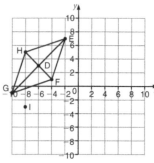

(i) D = (10, 3)
(ii) E = (8, 3)

(b)

(i) I = (−2, 7)
(ii) J = (−6, 3)

(c)

M = (−1, 8)
N = (1, 4)

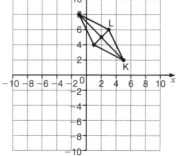

(d)

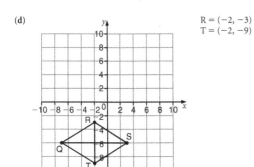

R = (−2, −3)
T = (−2, −9)

10

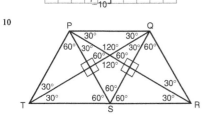

1 (b) ● equal   ● one, equal   ● bisected   ● 90°   ● bisects
● one   ● half , quarter-turn

3

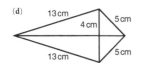

4

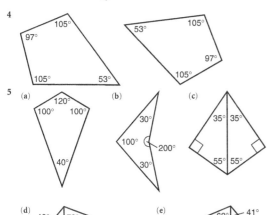

5

7

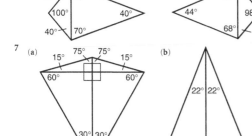

(c)

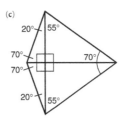

(d)

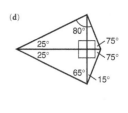

8

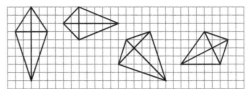

9 (a)

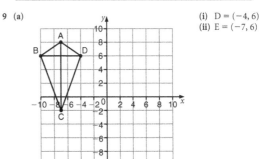

(i) D = (−4, 6)
(ii) E = (−7, 6)

(b)

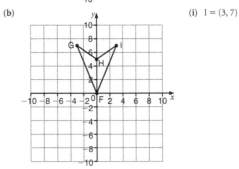

(i) I = (3, 7)

(c)

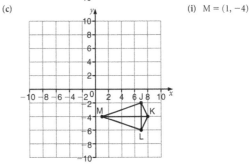

(i) M = (1, −4)

(d)

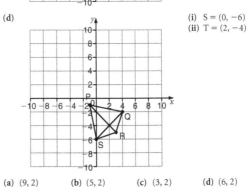

(i) S = (0, −6)
(ii) T = (2, −4)

10 (a) (9, 2)   **(b)** (5, 2)   **(c)** (3, 2)   **(d)** (6, 2)

11

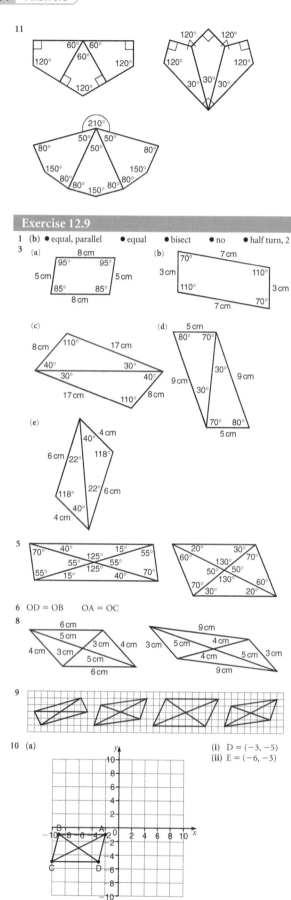

Exercise 12.9

1 (b) ● equal, parallel   ● equal   ● bisect   ● no   ● half turn, 2

3 (a) ... (b) ... (c) ... (d) ... (e) ...

5 ...

6 OD = OB   OA = OC

8 ...

9 ...

10 (a)

(i) D = (−3, −5)
(ii) E = (−6, −3)

(b)

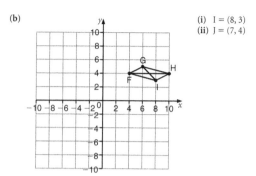

(i) I = (8, 3)
(ii) J = (7, 4)

(c)

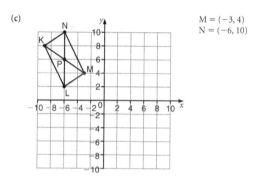

M = (−3, 4)
N = (−6, 10)

(d)

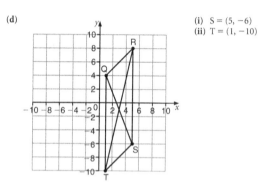

(i) S = (5, −6)
(ii) T = (1, −10)

11 (a) ...   (b) ...   (c) ...

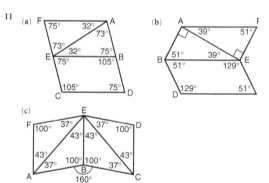

Exercise 12.10

1 (a) x = 120°   y = 105°
  (b) (i) 180°   (ii) 180°   (iii) 180°   (iv) 180°

2

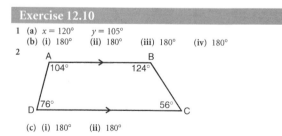

(c) (i) 180°   (ii) 180°

3

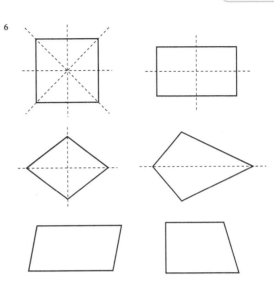

(c) (i) 180°   (ii) 180°

4 For a trapezium, two pairs of angles add up to 180°

5 (a), (b), (c)

6

7

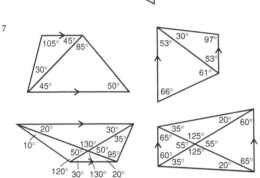

Review exercise 12

1 (a) equilateral triangle   (b) octagon   (c) square
2 (a) true   (b) false   (c) true
   (d) false   (e) false   (f) true
   (g) false   (h) false   (i) true
   (j) false
3 (a) acute angled – equilateral
   (b) obtuse angled – scalene
   (c) right angled – isosceles
   (d) acute angled – isosceles
4 $a = 45°$ $b = 45°$ $c = 65°$
   $d = 65°$ $e = 110°$ $f = 35°$
   $g = 60°$ $h = 60°$ $i = 60°$
5

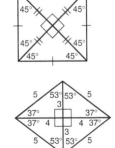 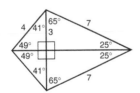  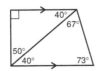

Chapter 13

Exercise 13.1

1 (a) 0800   (b) 1120   (c) 0101   (d) 0030
   (e) 1400   (f) 1800   (g) 2300   (h) 1705
   (i) 0620   (j) 1820   (k) 1559   (l) 2020
   (m) 1313   (n) 1159   (o) 1200   (p) 0000
2 (a) 1 pm   (b) 7 am   (c) 8 pm   (d) 2.14 pm
   (e) 1.01 am   (f) 12.01 pm   (g) 7.20 pm   (h) 10.30 pm
   (i) 12.10 am   (j) 3.03 am   (k) 7.45 pm   (l) 3.15 pm
   (m) 6.15 pm   (n) 11.59 am   (o) 12.01 am
3 (a) 0500   (b) 1530   (c) 0410   (d) 2020
   (e) 2130   (f) 1615   (g) 1745   (h) 2340
   (i) 2225   (j) 2350   (k) 1210   (l) 0001

Exercise 13.2

1 (a) 2 hrs 20 mins   (b) 16 hrs 25 mins   (c) 18 hrs 45 mins
   (d) 4 hrs 35 mins   (e) 6 hrs 15 mins   (f) 8 hrs 25 mins
   (g) 4 hrs 45 mins   (h) 2 hrs 55 mins   (i) 23 hrs 10 mins
2 (a) 3 hrs 30 mins   (b) 3 hrs 10 mins   (c) 4 hrs 25 mins
   (d) 3 hrs 35 mins   (e) 4 hrs 4 mins   (f) 3 hrs 45 mins
   (g) 4 hrs 23 mins   (h) 2 hrs 46 mins   (i) 6 hrs 58 mins
   (j) 4 hrs 7 mins
3 (a) (i) 55 mins   (ii) 35 mins   (b) 2 hrs 25 mins
   (c) Edinburgh   2300   (d) Glasgow   0954
      Stirling   2335   Edinburgh   1107
      Glasgow   0030   Stirling   1200
                          Glasgow   1313

4 20 hr 50 mins   **5** 0857   **6** 2254
7 Glasgow   1753
   Garrowhill   1802
   Blairhill   1805
   Sunnyside   1807
   Airdrie   1810
8 11 minutes

Exercise 13.3

1 (a) 90 mins   (b) 130   (c) 160   (d) 192
   (e) 290   (f) 485   (g) 203   (h) 165
   (i) 333   (j) 750   (k) 1440   (l) 10 080
2 (a) 1 hr 20 mins   (b) 3 hrs 20 mins   (c) 5 hrs 50 mins
   (d) 2 hrs 55 mins   (e) 1 hr 40 mins   (f) 8 hrs 20 mins
   (g) 4 hrs 40 mins   (h) 6 hrs 44 mins   (i) 12 hrs 30 mins
   (j) 13 hrs   (k) 16 hrs 39 mins   (l) 166 hrs 40 mins
3 (a) Jon 2 hrs 41 mins   Pete 2 hrs 26 mins   Dave 2 hrs 33 mins
   (b) Pete 3 minutes
4 (a) 3   (b) Mouse Race, Bill & Ben, Xtence.

Exercise 13.4

1 (a) 1 hr 30 mins   (b) 2 hrs 12 mins   (c) 3 hrs 24 mins
   (d) 1 hr 36 mins   (e) 4 hrs 6 mins   (f) 2 hrs 18 mins
   (g) 3 hrs 42 mins   (h) 2 hrs 54 mins   (i) 5 hrs 36 mins
   (j) 48 mins   (k) 4 hrs 15 mins   (l) 3 hrs 48 mins
   (m) 2 hrs 15 mins   (n) 1 hr 45 mins   (o) 4 hrs 18 mins
   (p) 20 mins

2 (a) 2 hrs 12 mins **(b)** 1 hr 15 mins **(c)** 3 hrs 30 mins
(d) 4 hrs 10 mins **(e)** 3 hrs 18 mins **(f)** 5 hrs 20 mins
(g) 9 hrs 50 mins **(h)** 3 hrs 40 mins
3 (a) 1·5 hrs **(b)** 3·25 hrs **(c)** 1·3 hrs **(d)** 5·7 hrs
(e) 3·1 hrs **(f)** 1·75 hrs **(g)** 2·4 hrs **(h)** 3·6 hrs
(i) 0·25 hrs **(j)** 1·4 hrs **(k)** 9·9 hrs **(l)** 2·2 hrs
(m) 18·3 hrs **(n)** 0·8 hrs **(o)** 1·7 hrs **(p)** 3·333 hrs
(q) 12·1 hrs **(r)** 0·75 hrs **(s)** 0·6 hrs **(t)** 1·05 hrs
4 6 mins 15 seconds

Exercise 13.5

1 (a) 15 km/h **(b)** 12 km/h **(c)** 13·75 km/h **(d)** 7·5 km/h
2 (a) 25 km/h **(b)** 4 hours **(c)** 84 km **(d)** 18 km/h
(e) 60 km **(f)** 2 hrs 15 mins

3

Time	$\frac{1}{4}$ hr	$\frac{1}{2}$ hr	1 hr	2 hrs	3 hrs	4 hrs
Distance	$7\frac{1}{2}$ km	15 km	30 km	60 km	90 km	120 km

4

Distance	5 km	10 km	20 km	40 km	60 km	80 km	100 km
Time	$\frac{1}{4}$ hr	$\frac{1}{2}$ hr	1 hr	2 hrs	3 hrs	4 hrs	5 hrs

Exercise 13.6

1 80 km **2** 180 km **3** 45 km
4 (a) 120 km **(b)** 6 km **(c)** 125 km **(d)** 56 km
(e) 600 km **(f)** 70 miles **(g)** 45 km **(h)** 42·5 km
(i) 40 miles **(j)** 1050 km **(k)** 1275 km **(l)** 196 miles
5 Jason 6 km
6 Alex 15 km Bob 15 km Karen 15 km
7 0·25 km **8** 0·0625 km

Exercise 13.7

1 4 km/h **2** 60 km/h **3** 6·5 km/h
4 (a) 22 km/h **(b)** 18 km/h **(c)** 5 miles/h **(d)** 130 km/h
(e) 40 miles/h **(f)** 27·5 km/h **(g)** 20 km/h **(h)** 40 km/h
(i) 160 miles/h **(j)** 60 km/h **(k)** 80 km/h **(l)** 40 km/h
5 5 km/h
6 Caren $21\frac{1}{3}$ km/h Alana $12\frac{1}{2}$ km/h Betty 9 km/h

Exercise 13.8

1 4 hrs **2** 3 hrs **3** 5 hrs
4 (a) 22 hrs **(b)** 3 hrs **(c)** 5 hrs
(d) 22 hrs 30 mins **(e)** 4 hrs 12 mins **(f)** 2 hrs 30 mins
(g) 30 mins **(h)** 15 mins **(i)** 2 hrs 15 mins
(j) 5 hrs 45 mins **(k)** 9 hrs 10 mins **(l)** 20 hrs
5 10 hrs 30 mins **6** 2 hrs **7** 15 mins·

Exercise 13.9

1 105 km **2** 24 km/h **3** 3 hrs 30 min
4 9 hrs 30 min
5 (a) 6 h **(b)** 150 km **(c)** 40 mph **(d)** 23 h 20 min
(e) 24 **(f)** 45 km
6 (a) Motherwell–Edinburgh 1 h 15 min
Edinburgh–Stirling 40 min
Stirling–Aberdeen 2 h 45 min
(b) 6 hrs 55 mins
(c) (i) 0035 **(ii)** 0450 **(d)** 3.43 am
7 (a) 6 hrs **(b)** 14 hrs **(c)** 6 hrs 30 mins **(d)** 20 hrs
8 (a) 70 km/h **(b)** 80 km/h **(c)** 48 km/h
9 6.45 am
10 (a) Manchester – van **(b)** 5 mins
11 Adrian 1·25 cm/s Bob 1 cm/s Colin 0·8 cm/s
12 (a) 11 250 seconds **(b)** 1 080 000 000 km
13 5 seconds **14** 100 hours **15** 3·125 m

Review exercise 13

1 (a) 0700 **(b)** 1640 **(c)** 2110 **(d)** 1200
2 (a) 6 pm **(b)** 4·02 am **(c)** 10·13 pm **(d)** midnight
3 (a) 2 hrs 15 mins **(b)** 6 hrs 30 mins **(c)** 1 hr 35 mins
(d) 5 hrs 25 mins **(e)** 12 hrs 45 mins **(f)** 15 hrs 35 mins
4 2 hrs 25 mins
5 (a) 145 mins **(b)** 275 mins **(c)** 535 mins
6 (a) 1 hr 30 mins **(b)** 3 hrs 15 mins **(c)** 8 hrs 45 mins
(d) 4 hrs 24 mins **(e)** 42 mins **(f)** 5 hrs 36 mins
(g) 9 hrs 18 mins **(h)** 1 hr 6 mins
7 (a) 2·5 h **(b)** 5·75 h **(c)** 2·3 h **(d)** 3·8 h
(e) 0·4 h **(f)** 0·45 h **(g)** 0·05 h **(h)** 0·025 h

8

Distance	200 km	20 km	30 miles	54 km	95 miles	100 km
Speed	50 km/h	10 km/h	12 mph	20 km/h	76 mph	400 km/h
Time	4 hrs	2 hrs	2 hrs 30 min	2 hrs 42 min	1hr 15 min	15 mins

9 (a) 45 km **(b)** 25 km/h **(c)** 12 min **(d)** 3 min

Chapter 14

Exercise 14.1

1 (a) £211 **(b)** £263 **(c)** £307 **(d)** £31
2 (a) UA/0401 5 hrs **(b)** 4 hrs 55 mins **(c)** £370 **(d)** 0700
3 (a) 0906 **(b)** 3 minutes **(c)** 0847
4 (a) SCHB **(b)** £76.66 **(c)** £4520.04 **(d)** £920.04
5 (a) £4.40 **(b)** £2.90 **(c)** £0.875
6 (a) (i) £12.50 **(ii)** £6.00 **(iii)** £9.80 **(iv)** £7.20
(b) (i) £2.70 **(ii)** £32.40 **(iii)** £648
(c) men – shorter life expectancy
(d) more at risk – shorter life expectancy
7 (a) €80 **(b)** €15 **(c)** £328

Exercise 14.2

1 (a) 140 **(b)** 14 **(c)** 16 and 17 **(d)** 18
2 (a) 44 000 **(b)** 1964 **(c)** Decreased
3 (a)

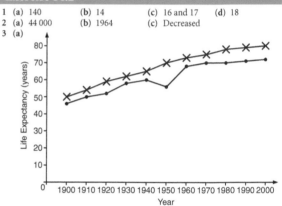

(b) 10 years **(c)** 4 years **(d)** World war II
(e) Better living conditions, food, health and hygiene.
4 (a)

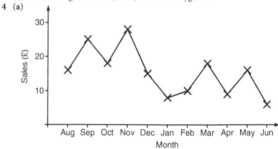

(b) Nov–Dec **(d)** Sept, Oct, Nov.
5 (a)

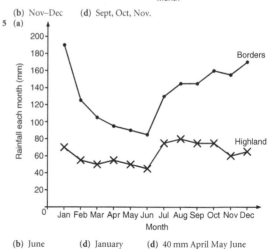

(b) June **(d)** January **(d)** 40 mm April May June

Exercise 14.3

1 (a) (i) 18€   (ii) 30€   (iii) 27€   (iv) 10€
   (b) (i) £3   (ii) £11   (iii) £13   (iv) £21
2 (a) (i) 42   (ii) 46   (iii) 38   (iv) 48
   (b) (i) 16   (ii) 8   (iii) 12   (iv) 22
   (c) Yes.
3 (a) (i) 53%   (ii) 67%   (iii) 75%   (iv) 92%
   (b) 78 marks
   (c) men – shorter life expectancy

4 (a)

Marks out of 160	0	40	80	160
Percentage	0	25	50	100

(b)

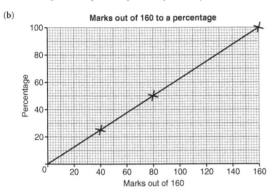

Marks out of 160 to a percentage

(c) (i) 22   (ii) 59   (iii) 91

5 (a)

Miles	5	10	20	50
Kilometres	8	16	32	80

(b)

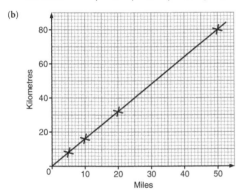

(c) (i) 9 miles   (ii) 12·5   (iii) 30   (iv) 45
(d) (i) 35   (ii) 50   (iii) 67   (iv) 88

6

Kilograms	1	2	3	4
Pounds	2·2	4·4	6·6	8·8

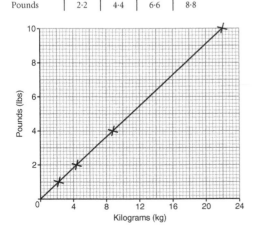

Exercise 14.4

1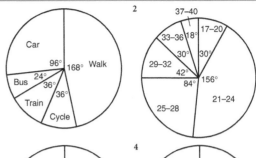

2

3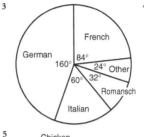

4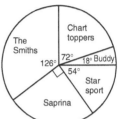

5

Exercise 14.5

1 Goldfish 175   Dogs 280   Hamsters 210   Birds 70   Cats 105
2 SNP 4950   Green 1650   Conservatives 2475   Lib Dem 3300
   SSP 1925   Labour 5500
3 Turnips 14   Carrots 30   Onions 22   Leeks 18   Potatoes 36
4

Source	Gamma	Cosmic	Internal	Radon	Thoron
Percentage	15	10	22·5	48·75	3·75

Exercise 14.6

1 (a) 8   (b) 10–14 and 20–24
2 (a)

Class interval	Tally marks	Frequency
71–75	|	1
76–80	||	2
81–85	|||	3
86–90	||||| |||	8
91–95	|||||	5
96–100	||||	4
101–105	||	4

(b)

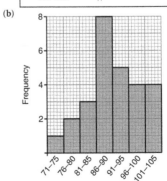

3 (a)

Class interval	Tally marks	Frequency
1–5	|	1
6–10	|||	3
11–15	⊬|| |	6
16–20	⊬|| ||||	9
21–25	⊬|| |||	8
26–30	⊬|| ||||	9

(b)   **(c)** 27

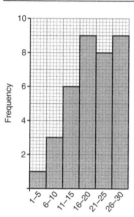

4

Class interval	Tally marks	Frequency
0–19	||	2
20–39	⊬|| ||	7
40–59	⊬|| ||	7
60–79	⊬||	5
80–99	||||	4
100–119	|	1
120–139	|	1

5 (a)

Class interval	Tally marks	Frequency
15–19	||||	4
20–24	⊬|| ⊬|| ⊬|| |	16
25–29	⊬|| ⊬|| ||||	14
30–34	⊬|| ⊬||	10
35–39	||	2
40–44	|	1
45–49	|	1

(b) It should aim for the early twenties.

Exercise 14.7

1 6, 6	**2** 10, 4	**3** 25, 21
4 2·3, 2·0	**5** 54 kg, 22	**6** £4, 4
7 13, 10	**8** 13, 5	

Exercise 14.8

1 23·25, 4	**2** 4·1, 2·5	**3** 10·5, 5
4 2·65, 2	**5** 2·65, 4	**6** 5·25, 3

Review exercise 14

1 (a) 64 kg
  (b) 18 kg
  (c) Ali
  (d) No. Heavier boys do more press ups.
2 (a) 62°F   **(b)** 14°F   **(c)** Sept–Oct

3

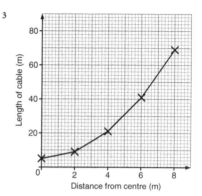

(b) (i) 15 m   **(ii)** 25 m   **(c)** 5 m
4 (a) (i) 88 SF   **(ii)** 55 SF   **(iii)** 77 s.f.
  (b) (i) £45   **(ii)** £32   **(iii)** £11
5 (a)

Pounds	0	5	10	50
Euros	0	7	14	70

(b)

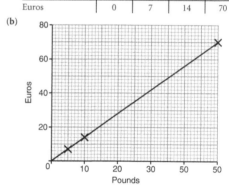

6 (a) Entertainment 10   Home news 9   Sport 3   Politics 4   Other 4
  (d)

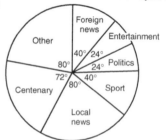

7 (a) 8, 9   **(b)** 25, 16
8 (a)

Score	Tally	Frequency
0	|||	3
1	||||	4
2	⊬|| |	6
3	⊬||	5
4	⊬|| ||	7
5	⊬||	5

Mean = 2·8   Range = 5

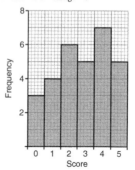

9 (a)

Class intervals	Tally	Frequency
30–34	||||	4
35–39	⊥⊥⊥⊥ ⊥⊥⊥⊥ ⊥⊥⊥⊥ ||	17
40–44	⊥⊥⊥⊥	5
45–49	⊥⊥⊥⊥ ||||	9
50–54	⊥⊥⊥⊥	5

(b)

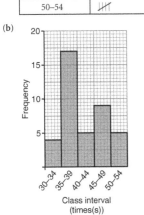

(c) 26

Chapter 15

Exercise 15.1

1 $x = 11$	2 $y = 17$	3 $m = 20$	4 $y = 15$
5 $t = 24$	6 $y = 31$	7 $z = 85$	8 $r = 24$
9 $x = 8$	10 $p = 4$	11 $t = 21$	12 $q = 4$
13 $x = 0$	14 $y = 68$	15 $m = 52$	16 $x = 20$
17 $x = 6$	18 $c = 54$	19 $x = 13$	20 $s = 6$
21 $v = 27$	22 $x = 18$	23 $m = 22$	24 $y = 23$

Exercise 15.2

1 $y = 7$	2 $m = 5$	3 $y = 6$	4 $x = 3$
5 $y = 3$	6 $x = 4$	7 $y = 3$	8 $z = 5$
9 $x = 9$	10 $y = 1$	11 $m = 8$	12 $y = 8$
13 $z = 5$	14 $c = 12$	15 $x = 10$	16 $g = 7$
17 $x = 11$	18 $x = 2$	19 $x = 8$	20 $y = 7$
21 $x = 2$	22 $y = 5$	23 $z = 7$	24 $x = 5$
25 $c = 5$	26 $m = 3$	27 $t = 5$	28 $x = 12$
29 $y = 5$	30 $y = 30$	31 $p = 6$	32 $s = 4$
33 $s = 8$	34 $z = 9$	35 $x = 3$	36 $z = 3$

Exercise 15.3

1 $x = -2$	2 $y = -1$	3 $s = -3$	4 $z = -1$
5 $s = 1$	6 $p = -10$	7 $x = -8$	8 $y = -15$
9 $z = 7$	10 $y = 2\frac{1}{2}$	11 $m = 4$	12 $z = -6$
13 $y = 0$	14 $m = -20$	15 $p = \frac{1}{2}$	16 $x = -18$
17 $r = \frac{1}{2}$	18 $y = -10$	19 $z = 1\frac{1}{2}$	20 $w = -\frac{1}{2}$
21 $x = -30$	22 $z = 1\frac{1}{2}$	23 $y = 6\frac{1}{2}$	24 $y = -9$
25 $y = 1$	26 $y = 0$	27 $q = 2$	28 $p = 0$
29 $z = \frac{1}{2}$	30 $r = 5$	31 $x = 1\frac{1}{2}$	32 $s = 4\frac{1}{2}$
33 $n = 5$	34 $z = -2$	35 $m = 1\frac{1}{2}$	36 $z = \frac{1}{4}$

Exercise 15.4

1 $p + 5 = 19 : p = 14$
2 $x - 13 = 5 : x = 18$
3 $q = 16 = 13 : q = 47$
4 $8x = 64 : x = 8$
5 $\frac{28}{x} = 7 : x = 4$
6 $\frac{54}{z} = 9 : z = 6$
7 $n - 6 = 25 : n = 31$
8 $m^2 = 81 : m = 9$
9 $13 + y = 52 : y = 39$
10 $9z = 63 : z = 7$
11 $\frac{36}{x} = 2 : x = 18$
12 $8x = 56 : x = 7$
13 $8y = 40 : y = 5$
14 $x^2 = 121 : x = 11$
15 (a) $72 = 44 + 2x : x = 14$
   (b) $33 = 3y : y = 11$
   (c) $2.5 + 4z = 22.5 : z = 5$
17 $6y + 3 = 57 : y = 9$
18 $8m + 120 = 2120 : m = 250$

Exercise 15.5

1 $x > 3$	2 $y \leqslant 9$	3 $z \leqslant 10$	4 $z > 4$
5 $y \geqslant 6$	6 $z > 9$	7 $y > 2$	8 $z < 2$
9 $w \leqslant 4$	10 $y \geqslant 12$	11 $y < 11$	12 $m \leqslant 0$
13 $y > 10$	14 $x < 22$	15 $y \geqslant 0$	16 $x < 3$
17 $y > 4$	18 $m > 1$	19 $y \geqslant 2$	20 $n > 9$

Exercise 15.6

1 $y > -2$	2 $x < -4$	3 $z \geqslant -8$	4 $x > -1$
5 $y \leqslant 6$	6 $m > 7$	7 $y < 1$	8 $y < 1$
9 $t \geqslant 9$	10 $y > 8$	11 $z > \frac{1}{2}$	12 $n \geqslant -18$
13 $y < \frac{1}{2}$	14 $m < -7$	15 $p \leqslant \frac{3}{4}$	16 $p \geqslant 3\frac{1}{4}$

Exercise 15.7

1 (a) $y < 5$ $\{0, 1, 2, 3, 4, 5\}$ (b) $m > 7$ $\{8, 9\}$
  (c) $z \geqslant 9$ $\{9\}$ (d) $m < 3$ $\{0, 1, 2\}$
  (e) $y > 8$ $\{9\}$ (f) $z \geqslant 7$ $\{7, 8, 9\}$
2 (a) $x > 1$ $\{2, 3, 4, 5\}$ (b) $y \leqslant -1$ $\{-3, -2, -1\}$
  (c) $x < 1$ $\{-3, -2, -1, 0\}$ (d) $z > -3$ $\{-2, -1, 0, 1, 2, 3, 4, 5\}$
  (e) $m \geqslant 5$ $\{5\}$ (f) $n \leqslant 1$ $\{-3, -2, -1, 0, 1\}$
3 (a) $z > 1$ $\{2\}$ (b) $x < -2$ $\{-6, -5, -4, -3\}$
  (c) $y \leqslant -6$ $\{-6\}$ (d) $y > 1$ $\{1, 2\}$
  (e) $n < 0$ $\{-6, -5, -4, -3, -2, -1\}$
  (f) $z \geqslant 2$ $\{2\}$

Review exercise 15

1 (a) $x = 12$ (b) $y = 10$ (c) $z = 21$ (d) $y = 48$
  (e) $x = 10$ (f) $y = 7$ (g) $y = 7$ (h) $y = 7$
2 (a) $s = -8$ (b) $y = -7$ (c) $y = \frac{1}{2}$ (d) $z = 3$
  (e) $y = 7\frac{1}{2}$ (f) $y = 10\frac{1}{2}$ (g) $r = -2$ (h) $x = -6$
3 (a) $17 + x = 53 : x = 36$
  (b) $12y = 72 : y = 6$
  (c) $8n + 3 = 59 : n = 7$
4 (a) $x > 0$ (b) $y \leqslant 8$ (c) $y > 5$
  (d) $m \geqslant 5$ (e) $y > 3$ (f) $m < 3$
5 (a) $y < -2$ (b) $x \geqslant 1\frac{1}{2}$ (c) $s \leqslant 2\frac{1}{2}$
  (d) $x > 2\frac{1}{2}$ (e) $x \geqslant -3$ (f) $z > -3$
6 (a) $y \geqslant 3 : \{3, 4, 5\}$ (b) $x \leqslant 1 : \{-2, -1, 0, 1\}$
  (c) $s < 0 : \{-2, -1\}$ (d) $m \leqslant 1 : \{-2, -1, 0, 1\}$
  (e) $y > 4 : \{5\}$ (f) $y \geqslant 0 : \{0, 1, 2, 3, 4, 5\}$

Chapter 16

Exercise 16.1

1 (a) (i) $2 : 3$ (ii) $3 : 2$ (b) (i) $3 : 1$ (ii) $1 : 3$
  (c) (i) $3 : 2$ (ii) $2 : 3$ (d) (i) $1 : 3$ (ii) $3 : 1$
2 (a) $1 : 6$ (b) $6 : 1$
3 (a) $4 : 3$ (b) $3 : 4$
4 (a) $4 : 9$ (b) $9 : 4$
5 (a) $9 : 10 : 11$ (b) $11 : 10 : 9$ (c) $8 : 7 : 7$ (d) $7 : 7 : 8$
  (e) $2 : 3 : 3$ (f) $3 : 4 : 2$ (g) $2 : 3 : 2$

Exercise 16.2

1 (a) $2 : 7$ (b) $2 : 5$ (c) $1 : 5$ (d) $3 : 8$
  (e) $4 : 7$ (f) $7 : 1$ (g) $3 : 2$ (h) $3 : 1$
  (i) $4 : 1$ (j) $8 : 3$ (k) $7 : 12$ (l) $40 : 7$
  (m) $34 : 9$ (n) $12 : 5$ (o) $5 : 1$ (p) $12 : 11$
  (q) $3 : 5 : 7$ (r) $2 : 3 : 7$ (s) $3 : 5 : 7$ (t) $2 : 2 : 5$
2 $2 : 3$ 3 $5 : 14$ 4 $1 : 3$ 5 $3 : 5 : 2$
6 (a) $2 : 3$ (b) $1 : 2$ (c) $6 : 7$ (d) $4 : 6 : 3$ (e) $7 : 12 : 6$

Exercise 16.3

1 (a) (i) 20 (ii) 32 (iii) 36 (iv) 40 (v) 80 (vi) 400
  (b) (i) 2 (ii) 3 (iii) 7 (iv) 9 (v) 15 (vi) 75
2 (a) (i) 6 (ii) 18 (iii) 22 (iv) 20 (v) 50
  (b) (i) 20 (ii) 45 (iii) 70 (iv) 105 (v) 250
3 (a) (i) 15, 10 (ii) 27, 18 (iii) 36, 24 (iv) 60, 40 (v) 240, 160
  (b) (i) 45, 27 (ii) 90, 54 (iii) 150, 90 (iv) 300, 180 (v) 1200, 720
4 200 g   5 12 tins   6 12 gravel 6 cement
7 (a) $2 : 5$ (b) 35   8 (a) $2 : 3$ (b) £12 000
9 (a) $1 : 1 : 3$ (b) Angus £65 000
  John £195 000

Exercise 16.4

1 (a) 18, 24   (b) 30, 24   (c) 45, 27   (d) 49, 35
  (e) 63, 36   (f) 56, 44   (g) 24, 40   (h) 18, 21
2 (a) 9, 18, 27   (b) 14, 21, 28   (c) 16, 24, 16   (d) 27, 18, 27
  (e) 18, 36, 45   (f) 36, 27, 27
3 (a) (i) £50 000, £30 000   (ii) £31 250, £18 750
    (iii) £27 500, £16 500   (iv) £675 000, £375 000
  (b) (i) £625, £375   (ii) £2250, £1350
    (iii) £3500, £2100   (iv) £12 500, £7500
4 60, 270   5 33, 55   6 56, 44   7 117
8 (a) 4 : 3   (b) 2400, 1800
9 2700, 3600, 1800   10 32, 24, 8
11 (a) 4 : 13 : 3   (b) 1 020 000, 3 315 000, 765 000
12 (a) 104 000, 40 000, 56 000 (b) £840 000
13 (a) 216   (b) blue 120 white 96   (c) £175.20

Review exercise 16

1 (a) 3 : 5   (b) 2 : 3   (c) 9 : 5   (d) 5 : 2
  (e) 6 : 9 : 2   (f) 9 : 7 : 4   (g) 16 : 7 : 10   (h) 14 : 11 : 5
2 11 : 13   3 84 ml   4 14 bags   5 60   6 24 800 62 000
7 (a) 10 : 5 : 8   (b) 1000, 800
8 (a) £220, £264   (b) £105, £30
  (c) 5·4 kg, 48·6 kg   (d) 12 kg, 24 kg, 36 kg
  (e) 20 m, 70 m, 30 m   (f) £300, £350, £600
9 (a) 70, 105, 140   (b) £16 100
10 (a) 5 : 2 : 3   (b) £4750, £1900, £2850

Chapter 17

Exercise 17.1

1 (a) face diagonal   (b) space diagonal   (c) face
  (d) vertex   (e) edge   (f) face
  (g) vertex   (h) space diagonal   (i) edge
2 (a) cuboid   (b) cuboid   (c) triangular prism
  (d) cone   (e) cylinder   (f) hemisphere
3

Number of	a	b	c	d	e	f	g	h	i
vertices	8	8	6	1	0	0	6	8	12
faces	6	6	5	2	3	2	5	6	8
edges	12	12	9	1	2	1	9	12	16
space diagonals	4	4	0	0	0	0	0	0	4

Exercise 17.2

1 FEAB EABF FBAE BAEF AEFB
2 (a) FGCB, CBFG...   (b) EHDA, EADH...   (c) CDHG, CGHD...
3 (a) BFEC, CBFE...   (b) CIJD, DCIJ...
4 (a) yellow   (b) green
5 (a) WVUT, UVWT   (b) WSRV, RVWS
  (c) TPQU, UQPT   (d) UVRQ, QUVR
6

7 (a) PR, QS   (b) TQ, PU   (c) TS, PW
8

9

10 (a) FL, GM   (b) AY, BZ   (c) LS, PR
11 PV, TR, US
12 (a) 10   (b) PR, PS, LS, LT, MU, MT, NQ, NU, OR, OQ

Exercise 17.3

1 (a) ∠URV   (b) ∠QWR
2 (a) ∠CHG   (b) ∠OBC   (c) ∠BHF
3 (a) blue   (b) green   (c) yellow
4 (a) ∠BDF   (b) ∠LRS   (c) ∠DFH
5 (a) Angle colour   (b) Angle colour   (c) Angle colour
    WVS   blue   DBC   blue   RVP   blue
    UQS   yellow   HCG   yellow   PVT   yellow
    UWS   red   AHC   red   RPV   red

Exercise 17.4

Students' own answers

Exercise 17.5

1 (a) 4 × 6 cm, 4 × 4 cm, 4 × 5 cm   (b) 8
2 (a) 12 × 5 cm   (b) 8
3 (a) 4 × 7 cm, 4 × 5 cm   (b) 5
4 (a) 3 × 8 cm, 6 × 7 cm   (b) 6
5 (a) 4 × 10 cm, 4 × 5 cm, 4 × 8 cm   (b) 8
6 (a) 6 × 8 cm   (b) 4

Exercise 17.6

1 (a) 7 cm × 3 cm: 2; 5 cm × 3 cm: 2; 5 cm × 7 cm: 2
  (b)

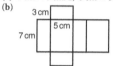

2 (a) 5 cm × 5 cm: 6
  (b)

3 (a) 3 cm × 3 cm: 2; 3 cm × 10 cm: 4
  (b)

4 (a) 8 cm × 8 cm: 1; 4 triangular
  (b)

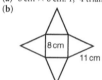

5 (a) 8 cm × 8 cm: 1; 6 cm × 8 cm: 1; triangular: 2;
    10 cm × 8 cm: 1
  (b)

6 (a) triangular: 3
  (b)

Exercise 17.7

1 (a) 72 cm³   (b) 216 cm³   (c) 120 cm³
  (d) 66 cm³   (e) 288 cm³   (f) 252 cm³
2 A : yellow case
3 (a) 400 000 cm³   (b) 1 200 000 mm³
  (c) 4 800 000 mm³
4 (a) 240 l   (b) 216 l   (c) 200 l
5 green (2400 cm³), red (3000 cm³), blue (2500 mm³),   6 B
7 (a) 2 cm   (b) 4 cm   (c) 4 cm
8 (a) 3 cm   (b) 4 cm   (c) 3 mm
9

length	breadth	height	volume
3 cm	4 cm	3 cm	36 cm³
2 cm	5 cm	6 cm	60 cm³
5 m	6 m	5 m	150 m³
4 cm	2 cm	3 cm	24 cm³
7 cm	5 cm	4 cm	140 cm³

Exercise 17.8

1 108 cm³   **2** 212 cm³   **3** 297 cm³   **4** 46 cm³   **5** 39 cm³
6 168 cm³   **7** 168 cm³   **8** 153 cm³   **9** 264 cm³
10 (a) 24 m³   (b) 24 000 litres
11 155 000 000 mm³
12 80 m³

Review exercise 17

1 (a) vertex   (b) space diagonal   (c) edge
   (d) face diagonal   (e) face   (f) face
2

shape	vertices	edges	faces	space diagonals
a	8	12	6	4
b	8	12	6	4
c	0	2	3	0
d	6	9	5	0
e	4	6	4	0
f	0	1	2	0

3 (a) AH   (b) BH   (c) ∠AHB   (d) CDHG
4

5 (a) ∠RYT   (b) ∠SMP   (c) ∠XCA
6 Pupils on drawings.
7 (a)   (b)

8 (a) (i) 4 × 11 cm, 8 × 3 cm, (ii) 8   (b) (i) 6 × 7 cm, 3 × 10 cm (ii) 6
9

3D shape	Net
A	1
B	3
C	2

10 (a) 1568 cm³   (b) 1728 cm³   (c) 330 cm³   (d) 72 cm³
    (e) 156 cm³   (f) 96 cm³
11 (a) 2 cm   (b) 8 cm   (c) 3 mm

Chapter 18

Exercise 18.1

1 (a)

Number of bikes (b)	Number of wheels (w)
1	2
2	4
3	6
4	8

   (b) 2
   (c) The number of wheels is 2 times the number of bikes.
   (d) $w = 2 \times b$, $w = 2b$
   (e) (i) 14   (ii) 100
2 (a)

Number of vans (v)	Number of wheels (w)
1	3
2	6
3	9
4	12

   (b) 3
   (c) The number of wheels is 3 times the number of vans.
   (d) $w = 3v$
   (e) (i) 18   (ii) 30

3 (a)

Number of trucks (t)	Number of wheels (w)
1	6
2	12
3	18
4	24

   (b) 6
   (c) $w = 6t$
   (d) (i) 30   (ii) 72
4 (a)

Number of submarines (s)	Number of cabins (c)
1	24
2	48
3	72
4	96

   (b) $c = 24s$
   (c) (i) 216   (ii) 288
5 (a)

Number of aircraft (a)	Number of crew (c)
1	9
2	18
3	27
4	36

   (b) $c = 9a$
   (c) (i) 63   (ii) 225
   (d) 8

Exercise 18.2

1 (a)

Number of chairs (c)	Number of legs (l)
1	4
2	8
3	12
4	16

   (b) 4
   (c) $l = 4c$
   (c) (i) 20   (ii) 48
2 (a)

Number of goldfish (g)	Number of fins (f)
1	5
2	10
3	15
4	20

$f = 5g$

   (b) (i) 35   (ii) 75
3 (a)

Number of pounds (p)	Number of euros (e)
1	1·5
2	3
3	4·5
4	6

$e = 1·5p$

   (b) (i) 150 euros   (ii) 825 euros

Exercise 18.3

1 (a)

   (b)

Number of tables (t)	Number of chairs (c)
1	6
2	10
3	14
4	18

   (c) 4
   (d) The number of chairs is 4 times the number of tables plus 2.
   (e) $c = 4t + 2$ (f) (i) 26   (ii) 38

2 (a)

(b)

Paving slabs (p)	Number of stones (s)
1	3
2	5
3	7
4	9

(c) 2
(d) $s = 2p + 1$
(e) (i) 15 (ii) 31

3 (a)

(b)

Verticals (v)	Planks (p)
2	4
3	8
4	12
5	16

(c) $p = 4v - 4$ (d) (i) 32 (ii) 44

4 (a) $s = 3b + 3$ (b) (i) 21 (ii) 48 (c) 11

Exercise 18.4

1 (a) (i) £65 (ii) £90 (b) £25
(c) $c = 25h + 15$ (d) (i) £240 (ii) £340

2 (a) £59 (b) $c = 18l + 5$ (c) (i) £185 (ii) £365

3 (a) £320 (b) $c = £135d + 50$ (c) (i) £995 (ii) £1670

4 (a) $c = 45d + 100$ (b) (i) £550 (ii) £1045

5 (a)

Number of crates (c)	Earnings in £'s (e)
1	1
2	7
3	13
4	19

(b) 6
(c) $e = 6c - 5$
(d) (i) 37 (ii) 67

6 (a) $p = 750b - 680$ (b) (i) £3820 (ii) £7570

7 (a)

Barrier length (l)	Number of plates (p)
1	1
2	3
3	5
4	7

(b) $p = 2\ell - 1$ (c) (i) 13 (ii) 29 (d) 23

Review exercise 18

1 (a)

Number of packs (p)	Number of rolls (r)
1	13
2	26
3	39
4	52

(b) $r = 13p$ (c) (i) 78 (ii) 156

2 (a)

Number of laps (l)	Distance in metres (d)
1	400
2	800
3	1200
4	1600

(b) $d = 400l$ (c) (i) 2000 m (ii) 10 000

3 (a)

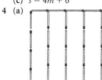

(b)

Mirror size (m)	Number of squares (s)
1	10
2	14
3	18
4	22

(c) $s = 4m + 6$ (d) (i) 30 (ii) 46

4 (a)

(b)

Shape number (s)	Number of matches (m)
1	8
2	13
3	18
4	23

(c) $m = 5s + 3$ (d) 38

5 (a)

Number of days (n)	Total cost (c)
1	85
2	140
3	195
4	250

(b) $c = 55d + 30$ (c) (i) £415 (ii) £585

6 (a)

Number in group (g)	Number of crossings (c)
1	1
2	3
3	5
4	7

(b) $c = 2g - 1$ (c) (i) 11 (ii) 29

Chapter 19

1 (a) (i) 80 47 180 24 29 (ii) 50 50 180 58 27 or others (iii) 73 73 292 73 73

(iv) 79 55 292 79 79 (v) 36 37 150 38 39

(b) (i) 75 42 200 45 38 (ii) 30 25 143 39 49

(c) (i) 18 42 174 52 62 (ii) 68 42 153 35 8 (iii) 20 21 123 40 42

2 (a)

Number of students	1	2	3	4	5	20
Number of cards	0	2	6	12	20	380

(b) 702

3 45

4

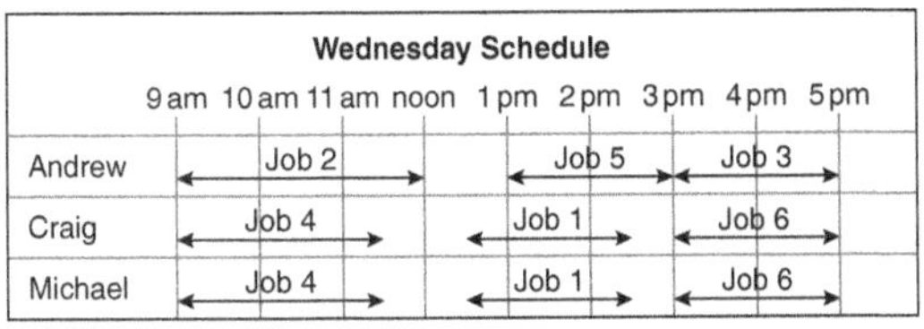

Wednesday Schedule

9 am 10 am 11 am noon 1 pm 2 pm 3 pm 4 pm 5 pm

Andrew	Job 2 → Job 5 → Job 3 →
Craig	Job 4 → Job 1 → Job 6 →
Michael	Job 4 → Job 1 → Job 6 →

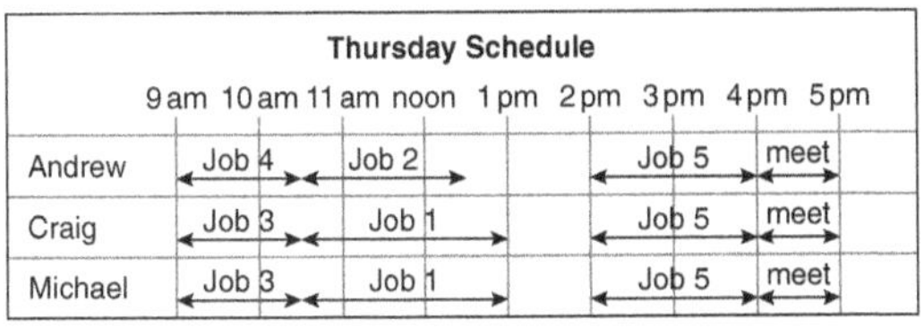

Thursday Schedule

9 am 10 am 11 am noon 1 pm 2 pm 3 pm 4 pm 5 pm

Andrew	Job 4 → Job 2 → Job 5 → meet
Craig	Job 3 → Job 1 → Job 5 → meet
Michael	Job 3 → Job 1 → Job 5 → meet

5 1×25 kg $+ 59 \times 3$ kg
   4×25 kg $+ 34 \times 3$ kg
   7×25 kg $+ 9 \times 3$ kg

6 (a) (i) 3   (ii) 3   (iii) 3   (iv) 3   (v) 2   (vi) 4
   (b) (i) pupil diagram   (ii) 4
   (c) (i) 7   (ii) 11
   (d) (i)

Number of lines	1	2	3	4
Maximum number of regions	2	4	7	11

   (ii) Add on the next number of lines to the number of regions.
   (iii) 16
   (e) They need 4 colours or less.

7

Ally

8	15	19
12	25	5
22	2	18

Sue

19	17	6
5	21	16
18	4	20

Rehana

6	26	10
16	3	23
20	13	9

(b) Add up to 42.   (c) Divisible by 3

Top

26	15	1
6	19	17
10	8	24

Bottom

4	20	18
11	9	22
27	13	2

10	8	24
5	21	16
27	13	2

26	6	10
12	25	5
4	11	27

1	15	26
23	7	12
18	20	4

26	17	1
16	3	23
2	22	18

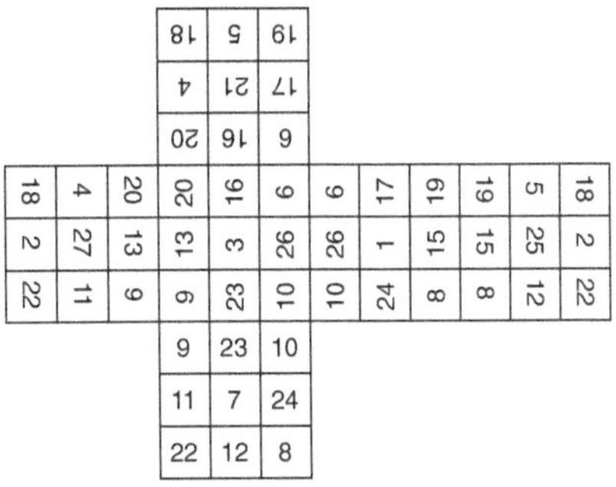

(cross-shaped arrangement of grids)

Top (shown upside down):

18	5	19
17	21	4
20	16	9

Horizontal arms:

18	4	20	20	16	9	9	17	19	19	5	18
2	27	13	31	3	26	26	1	15	15	25	2
22	11	9	6	23	10	10	24	8	8	12	22

Bottom:

9	23	10
11	7	24
22	12	8

7 (d) (ii)

Top

9	13	20
23	3	16
10	26	6

Middle

11	27	4
7	14	21
24	1	17

Bottom

22	2	18
12	25	5
8	15	19

8 (a) England   (b) Milton   (c) 35   (d) 26
   (e) 16 Abbey Street   (f) Tom Adams
   (g) 1 Dunn   2 Conman   3 Abel   4 Bluff

Index